THE COMPLETE BOOK OF
RAW
FOOD

HEALTHY, DELICIOUS VEGETARIAN CUISINE MADE WITH LIVING FOODS
INCLUDES OVER 375 RECIPES FROM THE WORLD'S TOP RAW FOOD CHEFS

JULIE RODWELL & JUNE EDING, EDITORS

HATHERLEIGH PRESS

NEW YORK · LONDON

hatherleigh

5-22 46th Avenue, Suite 200
Long Island City, NY 11101
www.hatherleighpress.com

Hatherleigh Press is committed to preserving and protecting the natural resources of the Earth. Environmentally responsible and sustainable practices are embraced within the company's mission statement.

Hatherleigh Press is a member of the Publishers Earth Alliance, committed to preserving and protecting the natural resources of the planet while developing a sustainable business model for the book publishing industry.

PEA Member   Sustainable Forestry   Cause Supporting

Unfortunately, due to low availability of materials, this particular printing does not contain recycled content.

Sustainable Forestry: The paper used in the manufacturing of this book comes from trees harvested from sustainable forestry programs.

Cause-Supporting: A portion of the proceeds from the sale of this book supports initiatives in organic farming.

Library of Congress Cataloging-in-Publication Data is available.

ISBN 978-1-57826-278-6

The Complete Book of Raw Food is available for bulk purchase, special promotions, and premiums. For more information, please contact the manager of our Special Sales Department at 1-800-528-2550.

PROJECT CREDITS

Hatherleigh Press Staff
President and CEO: **Andrew Flach**

Editor: **June Eding**
Editorial Assistants: **Linda Chen, Anna Krusinski**
Cover and Interior Designer: **Barbara Balch**
Photographer: **Peter Field Peck**
Food Stylist: **Tracey Medeiros**

10 9 8 7 6 5 4 3 2

Contents

PART III: APPENDIX & RESOURCES

Acknowledgements

Many people helped to create both first and second editions of *The Complete Book of Raw Food*. First and foremost are the chefs and product manufacturers who contributed their recipes and expertise.

Julian Huerta, a new contributing chef in the second edition, also served as an assistant editor and played a major role in bringing the second edition to fruition.

Special thanks go to raw chefs Eddie D. Robinson and Lillian Butler, who gave their time so generously and prepared recipes for the initial photo shoot.

Special thanks also to Dr. Ellen Cutler for contributing the Foreword.

For updates on individual chefs' programs and publications, contact each of the featured chefs (see Biography section starting on page 409).

Preface

Dr. Ellen W. Cutler is the nation's leading authority on enzyme therapy and the founder of BioSET, an innovative healing system that combines the use of enzyme supplements with other complementary medicine disciplines to treat a variety of chronic illnesses and achieve optimum health. Author of *The Food Allergy Cure* and *MicroMiracles: Discover the Healing Power of Enzymes,* among other books, Dr. Cutler resides in Marin County, California.

As a doctor who has worked closely with patients and their eating habits for over 20 years, and as someone who has been eating a raw food diet for seven years, I am excited to introduce the revised, second edition of this important book, *The Complete Book of Raw Food.* My research has shown that it is the enzymes in food that hold the key to health and weight loss. And an easily accessible, ready source of enzymes is available in a raw food diet (enzymes are basically raw food ingredients).

Why are enzymes so important? Well, we've all heard the saying, "You are what you eat." But the real bottom line is: *"You are what your body is able to digest."* Good digestion is the key to getting the full nutritional value from your meals, staying healthy, and keeping off unwanted pounds. The truth is, no matter how closely you watch what you eat and limit your calorie consumption, you cannot maintain a healthy weight if your digestive system isn't functioning properly.

Digestive stress from allergies and food sensitivities not only leads to weight gain, but contributes to numerous chronic medical conditions, including cardiovascular problems, cancer, type 2 (adult onset) diabetes, osteoarthritis, and sleep disorders. And an inefficient digestive system is more common than you may realize—today, 20 million Americans are dealing with some kind of digestive problem.

Let's take a look at the main causes of digestive stress and how the enzymes in a raw food diet can improve digestion and help you shed excess pounds and maintain a healthy weight . . . for a lifetime.

WEIGHT-LOSS STRATEGIES THAT HAVE LED US ASTRAY

These days, everyone seems to be climbing on the nutrition bandwagon. Books and articles offering dietary advice abound, and health food stores are thriving. The trouble is, much of the available information is contradictory and inaccurate at best—and potentially harmful at worst.

Working with thousands of patients over the years, I've seen almost every weight-loss strategy known to humankind—low-fat diets, high protein diets, low-carb diets, diet pills, semi-starvation diets, liposuction, and all kinds of exercise programs for fat loss. While all of these methods can enable you to lose pounds in the short run, none of them really addresses the underlying causes of excessive weight gain: a poor digestive system.

When the digestive system can't properly break down foods due to an insufficient supply of enzymes, our bodies run low on key nutrients. In response, we begin to crave the foods that supply the missing nutrients. We eat more but are still undernourished and keep gaining weight. Because poor digestion is at the root of our weight woes, no diet will be truly effective unless it involves enzymes available in raw food meals. We may drop some pounds, but the loss won't last.

Let's take a look at some of the specific benefits of raw food eating and how it can lead to a better digestive system.

EAT RAW . . . YOU WILL CONSUME LESS SUGAR

Bottom line: there is far too much refined sugar in our diet. The average American eats 156 pounds of sugar per year. In fact, table sugar and soft drinks are two of the top four sources of carbohydrate intake in the U.S.

Excessive sugar is not only a big factor in our national weight crisis but also contributes to many side effects and diseases such as hyperactivity, highs and lows in blood sugar, depression, and restless sleep. This is as true for children as it is for adults.

Sugar is addictive, both physically and emotionally, making it the number-one ingredient in "comfort foods" such as cookies, candies, and ice cream. Food manufacturers capitalize on this by pouring sugar into their products, including foodstuffs that we would never expect to contain sugar. Even if we manage to avoid the biggest offenders, we are still getting sugar from less obvious sources such as ketchup, salad dressings, and even potato chips!

From a purely nutritional perspective, sugar contains no fiber, no nutrients, and no enzymes. Basically, it's nothing more than empty calories. Eating sugar instead of wholesome, nutritious raw foods fills you up without providing any food value, thereby taking the place of necessary nutrients needed to repair and maintain the body. (This is especially true for children, who have such small stomachs.) And because sugar interferes with the absorption of the nutrients you do take in, it contributes to both malnutrition and weight gain.

For our bodies to function optimally, they require very little sugar. It's best to get your sugar from organic fruits and certain organic raw vegetables such as carrots and sugar beets, which have healthy amounts of fiber, anti-oxidants, vitamins, and other nutrients mixed in with their sugar content.

EAT RAW . . . YOU WILL CUT DOWN ON GRAINS AND CARBS

Most people have trouble digesting carbs, and its quite possible that you are one of them—without even knowing it! Although the types of foods that challenge the digestive system vary considerably from one person to the next, in my experience, carbohydrate intolerance is a much more likely contributor to weight gain and obesity than protein/fat intolerance.

Another culprit is grains. In my practice, I have found that the majority of people have great difficulty digesting grains. In spite of this, we continue to view grains as dietary staples, even though research has shown that they may be behind many incurable chronic illnesses. I know from my own research and clinical experience that most people with chronic illnesses do much better once they eliminate grains from their diets.

Personally, I haven't eaten grains for more than 25 years—and I am not deprived of any key nutrients. In fact, people routinely comment on how healthy and energetic I am, and how I seem to thrive on less food and less sleep than most.

Eliminating most grains from your diet can do wonders for your waistline, promoting rapid, significant weight loss.

THE BOTTOM LINE

A raw food diet (combined with a carbohydrate digestive enzyme) will gradually minimize your cravings for grains, as well as other sugars and starches. You won't even feel as though you're missing anything from your diet! Once my patients adopt a mostly raw food diet and enzyme therapy, they usually tell me, "I can't believe it—this is the first time in my life that I don't crave foods!" And they usually notice that difference *within 48 hours*.

As enzyme therapy and a raw food diet coax your body toward a naturally healthy weight, you will find that those pounds that seemed to be a permanent addition to your midsection will melt away permanently. As a bonus, you'll feel more vital and energetic than before because you are finally getting adequate nourishment—all because your body is breaking down food and assimilating those essential nutrients abundant in raw foods. The answer to permanent weight loss is that simple.

When you eat an assortment of raw food items such as what is emphasized in *The Complete Book of Raw Food* you will notice energy and vitality unlike you had ever imagined, as well as better sleeping habits and mood and a permanent svelte torso. So what are you waiting for? Jump right in!

Why Raw?

Raw food: Maybe you've heard about this type of vegetarian cuisine on television or read about it in newspapers or magazines. Raw food restaurants and cafés are springing up all across the country and it seems that raw food is the next big cuisine.

But what exactly do people on a raw food diet eat? How is it prepared? Why would anyone want to eat that way? And—most important—How does it taste?

You'll find answers to all of those questions in this book. *The Complete Book of Raw Food* is filled with the collective wisdom and experience of the world's leading raw food chefs. They offer their advice about everything that concerns a raw food diet, from what ingredients to buy, to how you can prepare delicious meals full of nutritional benefits. Not only will you find what may be the largest collection of raw food recipes in print—more than 400 in all—you'll also learn about the tools you need to prepare them, and how to make your raw meals taste and look delicious.

If you're worried that 400 raw food recipes means 400 recipes for salad and carrot sticks, you'll be delighted to find recipes for savory dishes such as Savory Neatballs with Tomato Sauce by Mary Rydman, Layered Portobello with Thick Pine Nut and Sesame Cream by Julian Huerta, Full Monty Raw Soup by Maya Adjani, Avocado Burritos by David Wolfe, Super Broccoli Quiche by Shazzie and desserts including Chocolate Chia Cookie by Peggy Kenney, Mud Pie by Rose Lee Calabro and Creamed Strawberry Pie by Karie Clingo.

But before we head into the kitchen, let's start with some raw food basics. Raw food—sometimes called living food—is plant or animal food that has not been heated above (about) 115°F. Raw foodists believe that when heated above this temperature, the enzymes in the food are destroyed or denatured, and cannot provide the same nutritive value. A new section in the dehydration discussion of Chapter 2, based on research by Mary Rydman, explains the heat/not-to-heat issue in more depth.

Many people who follow a raw food diet are also vegetarian or vegan. Vegetarians eat no flesh foods (meat, fish, poultry). Vegans choose to avoid all animal products and byproducts, such as eggs, dairy or honey. Many, but not all, raw fooders are also technically raw vegans.

WHY WOULD I WANT TO EAT THAT WAY?

Everyone knows that fresh fruits and vegetables are nutritious. But raw fooders have additional reasons for "going raw." Following are some of them.

• The food is in its natural state, allowing the body to derive more nutritional benefit from it. Live enzymes and vitamins offer best nutrition.

• Eating an organic raw food diet allows the body to release toxins. Many raw fooders believe that the diet can lead to better health and even eliminate disease.

• Eating a raw food diet will almost always lead to weight loss for those who need to lose weight—without the feelings of hunger and fatigue that accompany most diets.

• People who eat a raw food diet experience improvement in their skin. They also have more energy and often start to look younger.

In *The Complete Book of Raw Food*, we've intentionally avoided endorsing any health claims about a raw food diet, beyond the benefits associated with eating a diet high in fruits, vegetables, nuts, and seeds. Our primary intention is to introduce readers to the wonderful flavors of the cuisine.

However, the chefs who contributed to this book believe strongly in the health benefits of a raw food lifestyle. To learn more about their beliefs, read their personal stories in the bio section that starts on page 409 and check out the suggested reading that begins on page 397.

Do you have to be a vegan to eat raw food? Of course not! You don't even have to be a vegetarian. In fact, there are very few people who eat a 100-percent raw food diet. Many people who consider themselves "raw fooders" eat a diet composed of 50 to 100 percent raw food.

The Complete Book of Raw Food is for anyone who wants to eat more fruits, nuts, and vegetables and prepare them in exciting new ways.

HOW TO USE THIS BOOK

If you want hundreds of delicious vegetarian recipes, dig right into Part II (page 55), where you'll find recipes for every course, from Salads & Dressings to Snacks and Entrées to Desserts including Pies & Cakes, even Ice Cream.

If you want to learn more about the raw food lifestyle, turn to Part I (page 5). There you'll learn how to stock a raw kitchen, how to use some of the common tools raw fooders rely on, and how to make every raw dish look and taste like a gourmet creation.

Part III is full of useful information, including biographies of our raw food chefs, a suggested reading list, and a resources section that lists Web sites and companies that sell ingredients and equipment.

To gather recipes for *The Complete Book of Raw Food*, we initially approached 15 raw food chefs and asked each to contribute up to 10 recipes. By the time the second edition was ready, our pool of chefs had grown to over 50 and our recipe collection swelled to double our initial estimates—thanks to the overwhelming generosity of our chefs.

Rather than cut recipes to make sure that each chef was represented by an equal number of recipes, we decided to keep as many recipes as space would allow. That means there are more recipes by some chefs than by others, and some are variations of the same basic concept.

PART I

THE RAW KITCHEN

1 The Right Ingredients

CHEF'S TIPS

To ensure your spices are truly raw, buy them whole and grind them yourself using either a Vita-Mix blender or a coffee grinder.

—Rhio

* * *

Keep your herbs and salad greens fresh by first removing any rubber bands and storing the greens in an air filled plastic bag in the refrigerator. You can also keep herbs fresh by placing the stems in a glass of water in the refrigerator.

—Matt Amsden

So what exactly do raw fooders eat? As you can imagine, lots and lots of fresh and dried fruits and vegetables, herbs and spices, nuts and seeds.

There are many familiar foods in the raw kitchen: Apples, bananas, and lemons; carrots, cucumbers, and peppers. But you'll also find many foods with unfamiliar names such as nama shoyu, Celtic sea salt, flaxseed, and Bragg Liquid Aminos®. Here's a basic introduction to some of the foods you find in the raw kitchen—along with some helpful advice from our chefs about how to use and store them.

IN THE PANTRY

The raw pantry is full of staples, including dried fruit, grains and legumes, seaweed, oils, and herbs and spices. All of these foods need to be kept in airtight containers and stored out of direct sunlight (for more, see Food Storage on page 12).

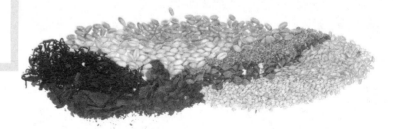

The Raw Kitchen

DRIED FRUITS

apricots
dates
figs
mangoes
pineapple
raisins

GRAINS

buckwheat
kamut
oat groats
quinoa

LEGUMES

black beans
chickpeas
lentils
mung beans
soy beans

SEEDS

flax
pumpkin
sesame (unhulled)
sunflower

DRIED SEAWEEDS

aramé
dulse
hiziki
kelp
nori
wakamé

OILS

coconut oil
cacao butter
cold-pressed virgin
   olive oil
flaxseed oil

grapeseed oil
hemp oil

SEASONINGS

nama shoyu
Bragg Liquid Aminos
Celtic sea salt

NUTS

Brazil nuts
cashews (not always
   raw)
filberts
peanuts
pine nuts
walnuts
almonds
cacao beans

Herbs and Spices

If you really love fresh herbs, you may want to grow an herb garden or window box, depending on your inclinations as a gardener, your space, and the local climate.

To dry herbs at home, buy them fresh in season and then hang them to dry in your kitchen. Homemade dried herbs are more flavorful than store-bought. In addition to those fresh and dried herbs, fresh and powdered garlic, and dried hot peppers such as habanera, jalapeño or Thai dragon are handy to have.

IN THE FRIDGE

Perishables are stored in the refrigerator. In addition to fresh herbs and greens, nuts should also be kept in the fridge. Unless they are eaten quickly, nuts can soon go rancid. Place them in a sealed plastic or glass container in your refrigerator to prevent this. (Nuts in the shell will keep for a very long time without refrigeration).

IN THE RAW

Many raw foodists use green powders as dietary supplements. The powder contains concentrated amounts of vitamins, minerals, and enzymes found in fresh fruits and vegetables. Green powder is "an acquired taste," but many of our chefs swear by it. Some popular brands include Vitamineral Green, Perfect Food, ProGreens, Green Vibrance, and Green Magma. You can purchase green powders in many health food stores or from on-line vendors.

Fresh Fruits and Vegetables

Fresh greens (chard and kale, for example) are plentiful in the raw food kitchen, as are ready-grown sprouts of different varieties and other vegetables to grate and slice for salads and other dishes. Fresh lemons are a must-have for many recipes, as are many other fresh fruits. If you own a dehydrator, you can experiment with drying fruit slices to eat when your favorites are out of season.

STOCKING UP

When it comes to shopping for raw food ingredients, you sometimes have to go beyond the local grocery store. Raw chefs Jinjee and Storm Talifero have lots of experience food shopping. "We shop at several specialty stores, such as the Asian market, farms, and farmers' markets, sometimes visiting four different locations in a day and even driving two hours each way to connect with farm produce." Here's their advice about how and where to find the right ingredients.

Farmers' Markets. These are ideal places to connect with farmers and their fresh organic produce. A farmers' market is like an old-fashioned street market, which you can still find permanently set up in Europe. Here in the United States, farmers' markets are usually weekly affairs. Farmers set up their stalls for three or four hours in the nearest town in a large parking lot and sell their freshly harvested produce directly to consumers. Sometimes, toward the

REJUVELAC

One basic in the raw food kitchen is rejuvelac, a fermented wheat beverage that raw foodists believe imparts great health benefits. It has a tart, lemony flavor; and because it is fermented, it's slightly carbonated, too. Here's how to make it.

WHAT YOU'LL NEED

1/2- to 1-gallon jar, with a wide mouth
spring wheat berries (usually sold in bulk
   at better health food stores)

filtered water
cheesecloth
rubber bands

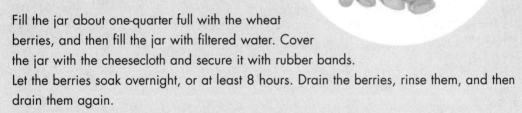

Fill the jar about one-quarter full with the wheat berries, and then fill the jar with filtered water. Cover the jar with the cheesecloth and secure it with rubber bands. Let the berries soak overnight, or at least 8 hours. Drain the berries, rinse them, and then drain them again.

Place the jar upside down but at a slight angle so that water can drain and air can circulate.

Rinse the wheat berries twice a day. After about two days, they will begin to sprout. When that happens, rinse and drain the sprouts well. Fill the jar once more to the top with water and let the sprouts soak for about two days. During that time, the liquid will ferment and become rejuvelac. Transfer the rejuvelac to a jar or pitcher and refrigerate.

You can get two more batches of rejuvelac out of the same sprouts, but let the sprouts soak for only 24 hours for each successive batch.

end of the day, you can get free "leftovers" or "seconds" (produce that will be too ripe to sell the next day, for instance).

Jinjee recommends buying Certified Organic food. Keep in mind that many farmers who do sell organic produce can't afford to be certified, so simply ask whether they're organic. You can judge for yourself whether they are truthful.

SWEETENERS

Sweeteners, at least in small amounts, are essential for preparing flavorful raw food. Sugar is not raw. To some chefs, the sweetener comprises such a small portion of most recipes that whether or not the sweetener is raw is of no importance. But chefs who want to be 100 percent raw use only raw sweeteners.

Here are just a few of the sweeteners used by raw chefs.

Date sugar. This product is made by pulverizing dried dates. It contains all the nutrients and minerals of dates in addition to fiber.

Dried fruits. These include apricots, dates, pineapple, prunes, and raisins. All provide lots of natural sweetness and can be chopped or blended or food processed along with other ingredients.

Raw honey. Bees make honey from the nectar of flowering plants. To be considered raw, the honey must not have been heated during the extraction process. The flavor of honey depends on the plant from which the nectar was derived. Raw honey reportedly has medicinal benefits, too, and contains enzymes and small amounts of minerals and B-complex vitamins.

True vegans do not use honey—it's an animal byproduct—but it is a staple in the kitchen of most raw food chefs. Our chefs recommend shopping for organic, non-pasteurized honey. The beehives are in an area free of spraying, which means pesticide residue will be absent. (Note: It is unsafe for babies younger than 18 months to eat honey, which can contain spores that cause botulism.)

Sucanat® and Sucanat® with Honey. This is the brand name of a certified organic, unrefined whole cane sugar. It is produced from concentrated, dried cane juice that is granulated. Only water is removed, which means Sucanat retains the mineral salts, trace elements, and part of the vitamins and vegetable fibers found naturally in the sugar cane plant.

Turbinado sugar. This is a partially refined raw sugar from which about two-thirds of the molasses has been removed.

Stevia. This powerful natural sweetener is an easy to use powder; not everyone likes its slight aftertaste.

Agave. Agave isn't just for tequila any more! Raw, organic agave syrup is an excellent, inexpensive sweetener with a low glycemic index.

To find out where and when the farmers' markets in your area take place, search the Internet or check your local health food store, library, phone book, or Yellow Pages.

Health Food Stores. Many health food stores sell only supplements. But some also offer produce, and bulk foods such as nuts, seeds, grains, and occasionally dried fruit. There are some stellar health food stores out there, as well as some really good chain stores. Whole Foods, Mother's, and Lassens are some of the chain stores Jinjee recommends. These chains are just starting to sprout up, so they are often just in one or two states at this point. Prices tend to be high, but it's worth supporting these outfits and the organic farmers that they in turn support.

Get involved in your health food store. Put on events and lectures there. Post flyers there. Have conversations with the staff, management, and customers. Make shopping a social event. Help to make it a fun community place for like-minded people to gather.

Asian Markets. These markets are a great source for tropical exotic fruits such as durians, tamarinds, guavas, lychees, mangostines, and young coconuts. And if the market doesn't carry a fruit you want, you can usually order it. You'll find listings for Asian markets in the phone book and Yellow Pages.

Supermarkets. Become friendly with your local supermarket produce person and the owner/manager. You can influence them to start an organic section if the store doesn't yet have one. You can also ask them to special order organic produce for you. It may end up being less expensive than other options. Encourage them to keep a cover on salad mixes, for a longer-lasting product that's not soaked hourly by their spray system.

Farms. What could be better than connecting with the farms and farmers where food is grown? You can find farms listed on-line, in the yellow pages, or simply by driving through the countryside.

Farm Stores. Some farms run stands or even stores in the countryside or in small towns. A single farm, or several farms may run these stores together. To find one, look up "farm stores," in your phone book. The produce may or may not be organic.

Buying Clubs. Some natural foods wholesalers sell foods to "buying groups" which are usually made up of a few families who get together and place a big order once a month. Through these groups you can save money on expensive bulk items such as nuts, honey, Celtic sea salt, oils, and sometimes produce, too. To find a buying club, search on-line using the keywords food, buying, clubs, and co-op. You may also find them listed in your local Yellow Pages.

Food Co-ops. These are special health food stores where you can become a member and can get better prices than at health food stores.

CSA Programs. Community Supported Agriculture, or CSA, is becoming more popular. A farm (or group of farms) puts together boxes of fresh produce every week. Each member of the CSA gets a weekly box (sometimes called a "share") for a very reasonable price. You don't often know in advance what will be in a particular week's share, so it's a bit like Christmas. It's also an inspiration to create new recipes that are healthfully ideal because they are organic, fresh, locally grown, and in-season.

On-line Ordering. There are many on-line sources of great food. Many of them are listed in Part III.

> ## CHEF'S TIP
>
> Remove the stickers from fruit and tomatoes as soon as you get the fruit home. That way, you won't accidentally blend or chop the sticker into a recipe later.
>
> —Matt Amsden

FOOD STORAGE

Raw food ingredients are just that: Raw. Unless you've been eating canned and frozen foods exclusively, you know that fresh food can attract pests or contain eggs of pests. The good news is that keeping them away from your raw ingredients is as simple as choosing the right storage containers. Anything that isn't refrigerated should be stored in plastic or glass containers with tight-fitting lids.

ORGANIC DEFINED

Fifteen years ago, few people knew what the word "organic" meant as it related to the foods they ate. Today all that has changed and there is ever increasing demand for organically grown produce.

But what exactly does organic mean? Before October 2002, the use of the term "organic" was unregulated by the United States Department of Agriculture (USDA), though several independent certifying organizations did exist. On October 21, 2002, the USDA put into place a set of national standards that food labeled "organic" must meet, whether grown in the United States or imported from other countries. Here is the definition of organic, as set forth by the USDA:

Organic food is produced by farmers who emphasize the use of renewable resources and the conservation of soil and water to enhance environmental quality for future generations. Organic meat, poultry, eggs, and dairy products come from animals that are given no antibiotics or growth hormones. Organic food is produced without: conventional pesticides, fertilizers made with synthetic ingredients or sewage sludge; organic products are processed without bioengineering or ionizing radiation. Before a product can be labeled "organic," a Government-approved certifier inspects the farm where the food is grown to make sure the farmer is following all the rules necessary to meet USDA organic standards. Companies that handle or process organic food before it gets to your local supermarket or restaurant must be certified, too.

Keep in mind that foods labeled Organic aren't necessary 100 percent organic. Here's how it breaks down:

- One hundred percent certified-organic products can be labeled as 100 percent Organic.
- Products with 95 percent or more organic ingredients can be called organic on the primary package label.
- Products with 75 percent to 95 percent organic ingredients can be described as made with organic ingredients, and up to three organic ingredients can be listed.
- Products with less than 70 percent organic ingredients may use the term organic only on the ingredient information panel.

Organic foods are still harder to find and tend to cost more than non-organic; however, even Wal-Mart stores today are stocking organic produce. Is it important? Recent research has investigated the amount of pesticide residue on specific non-organic foods and dubbed those with the highest amount the "dirty dozen;" for these items, consumers may want to commit to organic. They are: meat, milk, coffee, peaches, apples, sweet bell peppers, celery, strawberries, lettuces, grapes, potatoes and tomatoes.

2 Essential Tools

A raw dinner menu is not composed solely of cold, hard, crunchy foods. On the contrary: raw chefs can prepare sweet potato pie with a filling as smooth and dense as a baked version and creamy puréed soups that are as velvety as any you've had. Chefs achieve those results with some common kitchen tools and a few pieces of specialized equipment.

Gearing up to prepare raw food can get expensive. If you're the type of person who loves to have the latest kitchen gadgets, you can easily spend $1,000 or more on equipment. On the other hand, you can achieve fantastic results with tools you may already own. "When I first began a 100 percent raw diet my only equipment was an old blender, a hand grater, a good knife, and a cutting board," says raw chef Nomi Shannon. "I was 100 percent raw for six months using only that equipment before I purchased any other machines."

Here's an overview of the tools you'll find in a raw food kitchen, from the most basic to the most elaborate.

BASIC TOOLS

You may already own some of the kitchen tools that are useful for raw food preparation. Those listed below are used for everything from chopping and slicing to preparing and presenting food. Those that you don't yet own are often fairly inexpensive and available at kitchen supply shops.

The Raw Tool Kit: Basics

blender
cake decorating kit
cake pans
citrus juicer
cutting boards (wash-
    able)
electric and hand
    beaters
food processor
funnels (various sizes)
    and spout widths

garlic press
grater
honey dipper
kitchen knives
knife sharpener
ladles
mesh bags
palette knife
potato masher
    (for making gua-
    camole)

rolling pin
strainers (various
    sizes)
spatulas (various sizes)
stirring and serving
    spoons (large and
    small)
wire beater (coiled)
mango cutter'
    citrus zester

NOT-SO-COMMON TOOLS

The following tools are ones you may not be as familiar with. However, if you progress in the living foods lifestyle, you may come to consider them to be indispensable. These items require a larger investment, so shop around for the best deals. We've listed the item along with the names of some of the more popular brands.

Spiral slicer (Saladacco®). This ingenious tool can turn vegetables such as onions, zucchini, sweet potatoes, and winter squash into fine, spaghetti-like strands (for raw pasta) or long, thin ribbons. The spiral slicer can also create thin slices and julienne strips.

Champion®, or other "masticating" juicer. The Champion juicer is very strong and powerful and handles any kind of hard or soft fruit, nut, or vegetable. The juicing plate separates the food into juice and pulp (When juicing, re-process the pulp until it is woody and dry). See chapter 3 for more about juicers and juicing.

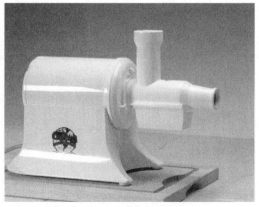

Champion juicers are powerful enough to easily juice hard fruits and vegetables.

Heavy-duty blender (Vita-Mix®). Any standard household blender can make a smoothie, but turning raw sweet potatoes into an airy mousse requires something a bit more powerful. The Vita-Mix heavy-duty blender boasts a two-plus horsepower motor (that's about the size of a small boat motor). A good blender can tackle some of the same jobs that a heavy-duty model can, but serious raw fooders invest in a high-powered blender. Manufacturers are creating less expensive blenders with plenty of horse power; for example, an Osterizer® ten speed blender retails for about $40—that's one tenth the cost of a Vita-Mix®.

Dehydrator (Excalibur®). A dehydrator adds significantly to your ability to create a large repertoire of raw food recipes. With a dehydrator you can warm foods on a cold day, make your own raw cookies, crackers, and burgers, prepare seasoned nuts

A heavy-duty blender, such as the Vita-Mix®, is required to turn hard vegetables such as beets and potatoes into smooth soups.

CHEF'S TIP

Buy a less expensive blender or use the one you have, and put $1 in a jar every time you operate it. By the time you burn out the motor, you should be well on your way to having saved enough for a Vita-Mix®!

—Julie Rodwell

With a dehydrator you can warm food on a cold day, prepare your own dried fruit, or make your own seasoned nuts and seeds.

and seeds for snacks, and make dried fruit slices and fruit leathers. For raw food-ers, a model with a thermostat is best, as it allows the user to control the temper-ature. For more about using dehydrators, see Chapter 5.

Coffee grinder. No, coffee is not raw, but a coffee mill or grinder comes in handy for grinding dried herbs and dry nuts and seeds such as flax. It can also grind hot dried pep-pers, but remember to clean the machine afterward by grinding some flax seed. We don't recommend using the same grinder to process coffee and other foods, as the flavors will intermingle. However, coffee grinders are fairly inexpensive, so it may be worth buying an additional machine.

Stovetop board. While a stovetop board is far from essential, it can be handy if you reach the point at which your range top is no longer used for cooking. A board gives you more counter space for food preparation and covers the burner pans, which pre-vents food from falling into them. Larger home improvement stores sell pine boards that they'll cut to size for you or you can buy a cutting board of the right size.

Food processor (Cuisinart®). Food processors are handy for preparing all sorts of raw recipes. Most models have an "S" blade that lies low in the drum and is sharp enough to grind nuts, carrots, and many other foods.

Most food processors have an "S"-shaped blade that can chop or grind food.

3 Juicers & Juicing

Raw food preparation requires that you learn some simple techniques. Read over the recipes in Part II of this book and you'll notice that some terms appear again and again: juicing, sprouting, soaking, dehydrating, and so on. In the next three chapters, you'll learn these easy steps, and gain the skills you need to create fabulous, mouthwatering raw meals from scratch.

For raw fooders, and many other healthy-minded individuals, juice is a delicious treat, and juicing is an essential part of their daily routine. Why? Juices—vegetable and fruit—taste good. And drinking juice is an easy way to absorb lots of nutrients quickly and easily (would you rather eat 6 large carrots or drink 8 ounces of carrot juice?).

Beyond Juicing. A new trend initiated by raw chef Victoria Boutenko is green smoothies. While juicing gives you all the minerals, enzymes and vitamins of raw fruits and vegetables, it does not give you the fiber. A high-powered blender such as the Vita-Mix®, started out with a little water, can process almost any types of greens. Look for new green smoothie ideas in the recipe section starting on page [tk].

CHOOSING A JUICER

On the face of it, juicing seems pretty self-explanatory—produce goes in, juice comes out—right? Although *juicing* is easy, shopping for a juicer can be a little more tricky. Most people don't initially realize how many *types* of juicers are available, and can become overwhelmed by the number of choices.

The kind of juicer you should choose depends on what you'll be juicing. To help you decide which type is best for you, here's an overview of the features of a few different types of juicers, courtesy of John Kohler of The Living and Raw Foods Marketplace (www.living-foods.com):

Centrifugal Juicers are among the oldest design types. The produce goes into the top of the machine, and is pressed through a chute, where it hits a spinning shredder disc. The shredded produce goes into the strainer basket, where the force from its high speed spinning pushes out the juice, similar to how the spin cycle in a washing machine removes excess water from clothes. Because the pulp stays in the machine, however, this type of juicer can make only one or two quarts of juice at a time before it needs to be stopped and cleaned. *Example:* Acme Juicer.

Centrifugal Ejection Juicers operate in much the same way as the centrifugal juicer detailed above, with one important difference: the sides of the centrifugal ejection juicer strainer basket are slanted, allowing it to be "self cleaning." Simply put, this type of juicer expels pulp as it juices, usually into a collection bin or basket that can be lined with a plastic bag for easy cleanup. Both types of centrifugal juicers are good for juicing most fruits and vegetables, and the small size and ease of operation of many centrifugal ejection juicers make them ideal for older individuals or those with limited physical capabilities. *Example:* L'Equip Juicer.

Masticating Juicers combine three operations into one. They first grate the produce, then masticate or "chew" the pulp to further break it down, and then mechanically press or squeeze the pulp to extract the juice. Masticating juicers do more than just juice: by using a blank plate to block the juice spout, you can use the juicer's homogenizing function to make, among other items, tomato sauces, raw applesauce, and nut butters. If you assemble your juicer without a blank or a juicer screen, you can use it to grate or to make shaved ice. This type of juicer juices most types of vegetables well, with the exception of leafy greens. Because it

> **C**hampion juicers don't juice leafy materials such as celery leaves, cilantro, and wheat grass well—but you can sneak some in if you intersperse the leaves between hard crunchy items such as apple and carrot pieces. A hard chunky item will also generally relieve the clog if your Champion gets blocked.
>
> —Julie Rodwell

Using a juicer is rather simple; fruits or vegetables go in one end and the juice comes out another. Pulp is forced out a separate nozzle.

Not all juicers can handle greens, such as wheat grass, well. Twin-gear press juicers such as the Green Star shown on this page are best for the job.

takes a little strength to feed the machine, this type of juicer is not recommended for people with physical limitations. *Example:* Champion Juicer.

Manual press juicers use pressure to squeeze juice from fruits and vegetables. This is a two-step process: First the produce must be shredded, and then it is juiced. Some more expensive juicers perform both steps, but if you want to save money, you can shred or grate the produce in a Champion juicer, then put it through a manual press. Pressing causes the least oxidation of the juice methods, and, because the liquid is strained through cotton or linen bags that can be washed and reused, it produces pulp-free juice. This type of juicer juices fruits (especially soft ones) better than the other juicer types. *Example:* Norwalk.

Single Auger juicers crush the produce into the walls or screen of the juicer, extracting the juice. Because this type runs at a low RPM, there is little oxidation. Though single auger machines juice vegetables about as well as twin-gear juicers (see below), they are not as effective at juicing carrots. Additionally, it is not the best machine for juicing fruits, and the juices produced tend to be quite pulpy (a condition quickly remedied by pouring the juice through a juice bag). *Example:* Samson.

Twin-Gear Press juicers have two gears that work together to press out the juice from produce. The gears first shred the produce, then squeeze out the juice. The twin-gear press juicer is best for juicing vegetables because it relies on the fibrous material of their cell walls to push the pulp out of the machine. Twin-gear press juicers tend to be more expensive than other types, but they have one bonus: they can juice wheatgrass, and save you the trouble of having to buy a separate wheatgrass juicer. Also, like masticating juicers, you can use a blank plate to block the juice spout to produce raw condiments such as applesauce and nut butters. This feature is not available with the Green Star juicer. *Examples:* Green Star, Green Life (an older model).

In recent years, numerous food safety scares have put people on edge. Because a raw food diet doesn't involve meat, the chances of your food making you sick are greatly reduced. However, it is important to note that, because raw food preparation does not involve the heating that one would otherwise count on to kill harmful bacteria, extra precautions must be taken to ensure the safety of your food. We suggest that you buy organic produce whenever possible, and carefully wash all fruits and vegetables before consuming them (scrubbing vegetables with a vegetable brush is a good way to make sure you get them extra clean). Always wash your hands before preparing food. Most importantly, make sure to clean your equipment (juicers, blenders, etc.) after each use.

Now that you know all about juicers, which type should you choose? Though the main consideration should be what type of produce you plan to juice most, there are also special considerations to keep in mind when buying a juicer for a raw food diet. Because many recipes require you to run ingredients through a juicer with a homogenizing function, we suggest you buy either a masticating or twin gear press juicer.

Any juicer you buy will come with extensive instructions, but to help you get acquainted with the ins and outs of juicing, we're including instructions on how to use, clean, and assemble a Champion juicer. This is the most popular of the masticating juicers—so popular that many of our chefs mention it by name in their recipes.

USING YOUR JUICER

The following are some rules and tips to help you get started, courtesy of Champion Juicers and the Living and Raw Foods Marketplace:

For best results, use fresh, crisp, pre-cooled vegetables. If you find yourself with too much fresh produce to use at once, cut it into pieces small enough to fit in your juicer's chute, then freeze it for later use. Keep in mind that freezing only slows the aging process. For best flavor, use frozen produce within two to three months.

Clean the vegetables before you start juicing. Even organic produce should be washed thoroughly. Root vegetables, such as carrots, should be scrubbed carefully to remove any dirt (plastic mesh pot scrubbers are especially good for cleaning carrots).

Apple seeds contain some cyanide, so be sure to core apples and remove seeds before juicing.

Do not juice carrot greens, rhubarb greens, or the skins of oranges or grapefruits, because they contain toxic substances. However, the white pithy part of citrus just underneath the skin is very nutritious. To benefit from this pith, grate the skin off oranges and grapefruits instead of peeling.

The leaves of celery are often bitter, so you may wish to remove them before juicing.

The skins of fruits such as kiwi and papaya should also be removed prior to juicing, but the skins of lemons and limes may be left on.

All pits, such as plum pits and peach pits, should be removed before juicing. However, the seeds of lemons, limes, grapes, and melons may be put through your juicer.

Form leafy vegetables into compact balls or rolls before inserting them into the juicer's feed chute.

Juicing avocados or bananas produces a purée rather than a juice. We recommend blending them instead, or bananas can be frozen.

The softer the texture of a fruit or vegetable, the thicker the juice produced. Apricots, peaches, pears, melons, and strawberries are soft-textured fruits. The juice that is extracted from these fruits is very thick and is known as nectar. It is best to combine these juices with thinner juices, such as carrot or apple.

Beet greens, parsley, spinach, and watercress yield very rich and thick juices. They are very strong-flavored and taste best when combined with other fruits and vegetables. For example, green vegetable juice mixed with carrot juice provides a sweeter vegetable flavor.

Pulp from the first two or three fruits or vegetables fed into the juicer may contain more moisture than normal. Refeed wet pulp to obtain the maximum amount of juice.

The flavor, color, and consistency of fresh juice will be different from that of canned juices.

If you desire a clear juice, filter your juice through layers of cheesecloth or a nut milk bag. This will also remove any foam that forms during juicing. You may also strain the juice through a fine mesh strainer (often included when you buy your juicer) to further reduce pulp and foam.

Serve juices immediately, as the flavor and nutrient content decreases rapidly when juices are stored. If it is necessary to juice fruits and vegetables some time before using them, store the juice in an airtight container with no

> ## CHEF'S TIP
>
> When you make green juice, the machine may make a lot of foam. Place the foam in your blender on high for two seconds only, and it becomes liquid.
>
> —Robert Angell

extra airspace (you can add filtered water to take up the extra airspace) or, better yet, use a food saver to remove all air. Do not store homemade juice for more than 24 hours.

To keep juices from discoloring during storage, add a few teaspoons of lemon juice before storing them.

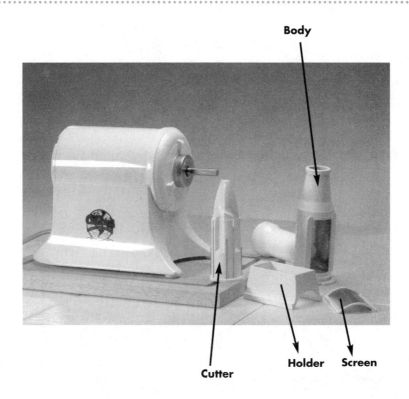

The juicer is one of the most useful pieces of equipment in the raw food kitchen. Here, courtesy of Champion Juicer, is an overview of how to assemble and disassemble its juicer.

Assembling Your Juicer

Make sure the juicer is unplugged before you begin.

Make sure the shaft is greased with olive oil or coconut oil. Do not use other liquid oils, butter, or petroleum jelly. Slide the cutter into the shaft. About 1/4 inch into the shaft, the cutter may stop; turn and jiggle the cutter slightly in either direction so that the flat edge of the shaft will match the flat edge of the cutter hole. It will then slide on easily.

Slide the body over the cutter, holding it in a horizontal position, with the feeder throat down.

Place the juicer screen into the recessed grooves and hold it in position with one hand. Now slide the juicer screen holder over the screen. Hold the edge of the screen down for an easier start. (Note: the screen holder will slide over the screen only one way. The raised lip indicates the front and the flat portion is the starting end.) The screen holder should be level for easier starting. The nylon blank is inserted in the same manner. Once the screen holder is over the screen, slide the holder completely forward until the raised lip makes contact with the body.

Pull the body forward slightly, so it is completely clear of the prongs in the hub. Turn the body one notch to the left, counter clock-wise, and match the openings in the back of the body with the prongs on the hub. Slide the body all the way back and turn it to the left until it stops. It is now locked in position for use.

The juicer is now in the proper position to juice. To homogenize, replace the screen with the blank.

Add the funnel when feeding small materials such as berries and nuts. Never use the funnel when juicing.

Disassembling Your Juicer

Before disassembling the juicer, turn it and disconnect the electric cord. Turn the body one notch to the right, clock-wise. Jiggle the body slightly and remove.

The screen, blank, and cutter will slide off easily. However, if the cutter becomes vacuum locked, place a small screwdriver at the back of the cutter and push it forward slowly.

4 Sprouting and Greening

Sprouts are a staple food to raw fooders, who extol their nutritional virtues as concentrated natural sources of vitamins, minerals, enzymes, trace elements, amino acids, and proteins. Not only that, but sprouts are crunchy and flavorful, too. You can buy sprouts at many grocery stores and markets. But it's easy to grow your own at home. One benefit of sprouting at home is that you can prepare just as much as you need, and that means less waste. On the following pages, our raw food pros offer all the know-how you'll need to grow plenty of healthy, delicious sprouts—in almost no time at all.

SPROUTING AT HOME

Growing your own sprouts at home is an easy, three step process:

1. Clean and soak the seeds.

2. Rinse and thoroughly drain the seeds for the suggested time.

3. Harvest and store sprouts.

GETTING STARTED

When you think of sprouts, what comes to mind? For most people, it's the thin alfalfa sprouts you've probably eaten in sandwiches. For others, it's the thicker, white mung bean sprouts found in many salad bars and in Asian cuisine. Though these two are the most popular varieties of sprouts, many home sprouters like to branch out and experiment with other types, such as broccoli, clover, onion, and radish. These seed varieties are available at health food stores and many on-line seed companies (see page 400 for listings). Many sprout seed suppliers also sell seed mixes made up of combinations whose flavors complement each other.

Which should you choose? It's all up to you. The following is an overview of some popular sprouts and their flavors, courtesy of Ken Kimes of the New Natives sprout farm:

Alfalfa is native to western Asia and the eastern Mediterranean region, but is a familiar feature on supermarket shelves here as well. It has a sweet, clean, and refreshing taste and is great on sandwiches and in salads.

Arugula ("rocket" in UK and elsewhere) has long been popular in Italian cuisine. Though relatively new to the sprouting scene it has become popular for its spicy flavor and nutritional value. Arugula sprouts have been shown to be a very rich source of iron as well as vitamin A and C.

Broccoli grows quickly and produces a sprout with a mildly spicy flavor and a fresh crisp texture. It is a member of the brassica family, which also includes brussels sprouts, cabbage, cauliflower, kale, mustard, rutabaga, and spinach, all of which can be sprouted. These have similar flavors, with a spicy mustard tone.

Fennel sprouts provide the wonderful licorice flavor in mixes and have recently grown in popularity.

Fenugreek is familiar in Middle Eastern cuisine. As a sprout, it adds significant nutrition as well as a pungent flavor.

Lentils have an excellent flavor, and are fast and easy to sprout.

Mustard sprouts have a spicy flavor and therefore have some warming qualities. Older roots will have a slightly blue hue; this is mustard, not mold.

Radish sprouts are good and spicy, and are similar to mustard in their warming qualities.

Red clover is native to Asia, Europe, and North America. Subtle differences distinguish clover from alfalfa. Red clover is not as sweet as alfalfa and grows in a lighter shade of green.

CHEF'S TIP

Nuts and seeds are easier for your body to digest and assimilate after they are soaked and sprouted. The oil (fat) content is reduced, as some of the oil is released into the soak water, and some more is used up in the process of sprouting.

—Rhio

Choosing a Method

There are several ways to sprout seeds and each method uses a different tool. The most common tools are bags, jars, trays, and tubes. Here's a brief description of each method.

Bags. Sprouting bags are made from hemp or nylon mesh. The fine weave of the fabric means that you can use the bag to sprout seeds of any size; the bag's porous nature makes drainage easy as well—in fact, all you have to do is hang the bag over the sink after rinsing, and the fabric does the rest. However, since the fabric dries out easily, you may find that you have to rinse more often. Sprouting bags fold up easily and are great for travel, and you can also use them to grow micro-greens and make seed and nut cheeses, making this one of the most versatile pieces of sprouting equipment available.

Jars. If you want to sprout seeds without buying a lot of equipment up front, we suggest you use the jar method. When we say jar, we mean just that—any glass Mason or Ball jar you have around the house. To keep the seeds in the jar as you

rinse and drain, secure a fine mesh screen (nylon screen works best and is easiest to clean, but cheesecloth works well, too) over the opening, either with the screw-on ring that comes with most jars or with a thick rubber band. Some sprout seed purveyors also sell ready-made mesh lids that screw on to the large glass jars. Old pantyhose serve well, too!

Jar Lids. Canning jars usually come with flat metal lids and screw rings. Ball, a common manufacturer of canning supplies, also makes 2 sizes of white plastic lids which are easier to use and won't rust. One or other size fits virtually all makes of canning jars.

Trays. Tray sprouters are made of plastic, with plastic mesh bottoms and covers. All that mesh makes draining with a tray sprouter fairly easy, although not as low maintenance as a sprouting bag. Because tray sprouters are stackable, they are great if you want to grow a lot of sprouts, or a few different crops at once. You can also use this type of sprouter to experiment with growing greens and grasses without soil.

Tubes. The tube method allows for air circulation and easy draining because there is a screened lid on either end. Most tube sets come in kits with a clear plastic tube and screw-on lids with mesh in three different sizes. These allow you to choose the largest mesh possible without letting your seeds slip out.

We recommend the jar method if you're just starting out, because it is the simplest. We provide directions for that method below; however, the rinsing and draining cycle is the same for all types of sprouters.

SEED PREPARATION

No matter what type of seed you decide to sprout, it's a good idea to rinse them before soaking. Because we recommend purchasing organic seeds, rinsing simply washes off any dust that may have collected on them.

Next, cull your seeds before continuing with the sprouting process. Culling seeds is easy: Sort through them to remove foreign objects such as pebbles, plant parts, or weed seeds. If you spread your seeds out on your table or countertop, it is quick and easy to see what doesn't belong.

Soaking

Dry seeds are dormant, so you must soak them to "wake them up." You can never use too much water for soaking, but different varieties of seeds do absorb different amounts of water. As a rule, we suggest using 2 to 3 parts water to one part seeds. And keep in mind that raw fooders suggest using filtered or spring water. Make sure to mix your seeds around every once in a while, so that they all get enough water.

Though you can never use too much water when soaking your seeds, it is possible to soak them for too long. That's why it's important to follow the supplier's instructions. Most seeds should be soaked for an average of 8 to 12 hours; some require more, others less. After your seeds have soaked, run your fingertips over any seeds floating on the surface to see if they will sink. If they don't, skim them off and throw them away. Drain off the water. The rest of your crop is now ready for sprouting; just pour the seeds into your sprouting jar and cover it with the straining mesh.

CHOOSING A SPROUTING LOCATION

Because growing sprouts is so easy, your sprouting jar will spend a lot of time just sitting around. Where should you put it? The most important factor to consider when choosing a sprouting location is air circulation. Sprouts need air circulation to grow. We suggest you keep your sprouter near the sink to facilitate draining.

A common misconception is that sprouts need to be kept out of light. In fact, incandescent light or diffuse sunlight will not hurt them. However, because sprouts do not have leaves, they do not undergo photosynthesis. So it is important not to put them in direct sunlight—sprouts generate heat as they grow, and the extra heat from the sun could contribute to spoiling. Light helps prevent mold as long as it is not direct light. The warmer your sprouts are kept, the faster they will grow—but must be rinsed more often to prevent spoilage.

RINSING AND DRAINING

Like any plant, sprouts need to be watered. Because they do not grow in soil, watering once a day isn't enough—there's nothing to hold the water in. So your sprouts need to be rinsed two or three times a day. This gives them the water they need to grow. Tap water if fine for this

Here are some suggestions for rinsing:

- Use cool water (60°F to 70°F).
- Use high pressure water whenever possible; this keeps the sprouts from clumping together and ensures that they all get a drink.
- Use a *lot* of water. Less water might make for easier draining, but it will result in a less healthy crop.

When using a sprouting jar, fill it with water, then turn it over and drain. That's all you have to do. Easy as it is, however, you must be careful to drain off as much water as possible. This extra effort is important—if your sprouts sit in water, they could spoil. So, make sure to spend a little extra time shaking the water out of the jar and, between rinsings, store it at a 45-degree angle, screen side down. This will help any excess water drain out of the jar.

SOAKING/SPROUTING CHART

Seeds	Quantity	Soaking Time	Sprouting Time	Yield
Alfalfa	3 tablespoons	4 to 6 hours	5 days	3 cups
Amaranth	3 tablespoons	4 to 6 hours	24 hours	3/4 cup
Anise	3 tablespoons	4 to 6 hours	2 days	1 cup
Barley	1/2 cup	8 to 10 hours	2 to 3 days	1 cup
Buckwheat	1 cup	4 to 6 hours	24 hours	2 to 3 cups
Cabbage	1 tablespoon	4 to 6 hours	4 to 5 days	1 1/2 cups
Chia	1 tablespoon	4 to 6 hours	3 to 5 days	1 1/2 cups
Chickpeas (garbanzos)	1 cup	10 to 12 hours	2 to 4 days	3 cups
Clover	1 tablespoon	4 to 6 hours	4 to 6 days	2 1/2 cups
Corn	1 cup	8 to 10 hours	2 to 3 days	2 cups
Fenugreek	4 tablespoons	4 to 6 hours	3 to 5 days	1 cup
Flax	1 tablespoon	5 to 7 hours	2 days	1 cup
Green Peas	1 cup	10 to 12 hours	2 to 3 days	2 cups
Lentils	1 cup	6 to 8 hours	2 to 3 days	2 cups
Millet	1 cup	6 to 8 hours	1 to 2 days	1 1/2 cups
Most Beans	1 cup	8 to 10 hours	3 to 4 days	3 to 4 cups
Most Nuts	1 cup	8 to 12 hours	do not sprout	1 1/2 cups
Mung Beans	1 cup	8 to 10 hours	4 days	3 to 4 cups
Mustard	1 tablespoon	4 to 6 hours	3 to 5 days	1 cup
Oats	1 cup	8 to 10 hours	1 to 2 days	2 cups
Onion	1 tablespoon	4 to 6 hours	4 to 5 days	1 cup
Pumpkin Seeds	1 cup	6 to 8 hours	1 to 2 days	1 1/2 cups
Quinoa	1 cup	4 to 6 hours	2 to 3 days	2 1/2 cups
Radish	1 tablespoon	4 to 6 hours	3 to 5 days	1 cup
Rye	1 cup	8 to 10 hours	2 to 3 days	2 1/2 cups
Sesame Seeds	1 cup	4 to 6 hours	1 to 2 days	1 1/2 cups
Soy Beans	1 cup	10 to 12 hours	4 to 5 days	2 1/2 cups
Sunflower Seeds	1 cup	6 to 8 hours	5 to 8 days	1 1/2 cups
Watercress	1 tablespoon	4 to 6 hours	4 to 5 days	1 1/2 cups
Wheat	1 cup	10 to 12 hours	2 to 3 days	1 1/2 cups
Wild Rice	1 cup	8 to 10 hours	4 days	1 1/2 cups

HARVESTING

As your sprouts grow, they will begin to fill the jar and grow "tails." How do you know when your sprouts are ready to harvest? The best advice is to follow the seed supplier's instructions. Different types of sprouts take different amounts of time to grow, but if you have been following the instructions that came with your seeds, you can be confident that you're harvesting them at the right time.

When harvesting your sprouts, you need to decide whether you want to de-hull them. Hulls (seed casings) are edible and are actually a good source of fiber, but some people choose to get rid of them for aesthetic or textural reasons. The only sprouts that it is essential to de-hull are those of brassicas, such as broccoli and radish, because they shed thick hulls that retain moisture, and moisture causes stored sprouts to spoil more quickly.

To de-hull your sprouts, pour them into a bowl of cool water and swirl them around with your fingers, breaking up any clumps. The hulls will begin to float to the surface. Keep moving them around for a minute or so, or until your sprouts are hull-free enough for you. Then simply reach into the bowl and pull out the sprouts, a handful at a time, leaving the hulls floating in the bowl (some people like to skim the hulls off the top of the water first, and you should try that if you like). Give the sprouts one last rinse and drain, and let them dry for 8 to 12 hours or run them through a salad spinner before storing.

STORAGE

Sprouts should be stored in the refrigerator. Airtight containers such as plastic bags or glass and plastic containers are ideal. It's unnecessary to let your sprouts "breathe" at this point, as the air circulation will dry them out. However, if you are storing them slightly wet, poke some holes in the bag to let them dry a bit, then switch them to an airtight container later. Remember that you should let your sprouts dry as much as possible before storing. Sprouts stored wet will spoil more quickly. If properly stored, your sprouts should stay crisp and delicious for 7 to 10 days, depending on the type of sprouts you have.

SPROUTER CARE

No matter what kind of sprouter you use, it's important to keep it clean by washing and disinfecting it regularly. To clean your sprouter, disassemble and wash it thoroughly with soap and water or in the top rack of the dishwasher after each use. You might find that a few sprouts have become stuck in the mesh; simply use a paper clip or toothpick to dislodge them. After every few uses, disinfect your sprouter by soaking it for 10 to 20 minutes in a weak bleach and water solution (1 tablespoon bleach per pint of water), then scrubbing it thoroughly. Make sure to rinse it very well—you don't want the bleach on your sprouts.

GREENING

Sprouts, if grown long enough and in the right conditions, will start to grow into plants with leaves. The major difference between sprouts and greens is that

Buckwheat seeds are among the most popular for greening.

sprouts are eaten roots and all, whereas we generally discard the roots of greens and harvest and eat only the leaves. Also, greens are generally grown in soil. Popular greens include sunflower, buckwheat, and pea—and with the right mix of seeds, you can even grow your own mesclun salad greens.

Two types of seeds are appropriate for growing greens. The first, called *micro-greens*, come from tiny seeds such as arugula, alfalfa, broccoli, and clover. Many micro-green seeds are mucilaginous, meaning they hold water within the seed casing. This saves you the step of having to soak or pre-sprout them before planting. The second type, *traditional greens*, generally need to be soaked and pre-sprouted, using the method above.

The following is an easy method for growing greens and micro-greens. As with sprouts, different types of greens may require different steps, so be sure to follow the instructions that come with your seeds.

Choosing a Medium

First, you must decide on a growing medium. Most greens are grown in trays with soil, but micro-greens may be grown on the surface of a dampened sprouting bag, kitchen towel or paper napkin—unbleached if possible. When using a tray, make sure that there are holes in the bottom to facilitate drainage—otherwise, you'll drown the seeds. On-line seed purveyors, such as the Sproutpeople (www.sproutpeople.com), sell suitable trays, and you can also find them at your local garden center. When setting up your growing area, be sure to put a drip tray (or, in the case of micro-greens grown on a sprouting bag, a plate) under your tray to avoid making a mess.

Pre-Sprouting

Pre-sprout the seeds, if necessary (information about whether or not the seeds you've chosen need to be pre-sprouted will be included in any instructions packed with the seeds). Most seeds need to be soaked and pre-sprouted until they grow a root of about 1/8- to 1/4-inch long. To do this, follow the instructions for sprouting on page 25. Once the seeds are pre-sprouted, spread them evenly over the moistened planting medium and cover the tray. For a cover, you could use an inverted tray of the same type as your planting tray, or any cover with holes that will allow for proper air circulation.

Store your covered tray in low light at room temperature. Water lightly every day or two until the greens are 2 to 3 inches long (for traditional greens) or just until the greens grow leaves (for micro-greens).

Once the greens reach the appropriate length, you'll probably notice that they're yellow—not green. That means it's time to expose them to sun: Uncover the tray and move it to a well-lit location. Direct sunlight is not necessary, but if you do use it, remember to give your greens enough water to compensate. In a few days, your greens will be green, grown, and ready to eat. To harvest, use scissors to cut them off above soil level. Store them in the refrigerator in a plastic bag or airtight container.

GRASSES

Like greens, grasses have a high nutritional value, and many can be juiced and consumed along with your favorite vegetable and fruit juices.

The grasses used for juicing are similar to the ones that grow in your backyard. You may have seen trays full of wheat grass, looking like miniature lawns, at health food stores and juice bars. Although wheat grass is the most popular grass for juicing, there are other grasses that are powerfully nutritious in juice form as well. The best part is, they are all equally easy to grow; once you know how to grow one, you can branch out and try whichever you like. To help you decide which to try, the following is a description of the different types of cereal grasses, courtesy of Gil Frishman of the Sproutpeople:

Wheat Grass. The most popular of the cereal grasses. When juiced, it has a slightly sweet yet intense flavor, which may take some getting used to, but stick

with it. You might want to mix wheat grass juice (or any other grass juice) with other juices such as apple or carrot to make a tastier juice with all the same nutritional benefits. *Note:* Even those with wheat sensitivities can usually tolerate wheat in its grass stage.

Barley Grass. A broad blade grass with a lighter green color than wheat, barley grass is consumed by many people in capsule form. The juice is more potent than the powder, which is true of all fresh foods. The juice has a very intense flavor, so we advise mixing it with other grasses, such as wheat grass, to come up with your tastiest juice.

Rye Grass. Rye produces a red tinged blade of grass. It has much the same flavor as wheat grass, and is just as nutritious, but you might want to try rye instead if you feel like growing something festive.

Spelt Grass. Spelt also has flavor and nutritional benefits similar to those of wheat grass, and is recommended for those with wheat allergies who want to enjoy the benefits of grass juices.

The method for growing all of these grasses is the same, and it is quite similar to the method for growing greens. Fill a tray, with perforations for water drainage, with soil, moisten the soil, and spread the seeds over the soil. There is no need to pre-sprout grass seeds. Cover the tray with another perforated tray that allows for air circulation, and water often enough to keep the soil moist (about every 1 to 2 days). Once the grass is about 1 or 2 inches high, uncover it to allow the blades to get green. You may use direct or indirect sunlight, but remember to water more often if using direct sunlight. After about 9 or 10 days, the grass can be harvested.

Cut the grass just above soil level, using scissors or a knife. The blades of grass will keep for up to a week in the refrigerator; however, to obtain maximum nutritional benefits, it is generally recommended to juice and consume grasses immediately after harvesting.

5 Dehydrating

Drying food to use later is as old as humanity. If food is dried at low temperatures—118°F or lower and preferably not above 105°F—the living enzymes are not denatured and the food remains raw.

There are three ways to dehydrate food. You can:

- Hang it to dry in your kitchen—this works for herbs and leaves such as bay leaves;
- Place it in the hot sun outside—this works fine as long as you can keep bugs and critters off; or you can
- Use an electric dehydrator.

USING AN ELECTRIC DEHYDRATOR.

The first two options for drying your food—hanging it in your kitchen or placing it in the sun—have limited capabilities. You cannot hang some foods to dry in your home, as they will often simply fall apart—at best—or start a giant infestation of bugs and other pests. And drying your food in the sun works well indeed, when there *is* sun. Outside factors such as the weather can be a real obstacle, and since many raw recipes require you to dry the food that you eat, you may want to think about investing in a dehydrator.

Dehydrators

There are many types of dehydrators, and most provide not just heat but a fan to facilitate more even drying. A popular brand among rawfooders is Excalibur,® whose 3926 model is large, with nine trays, enough for a family-size batch of food.

There are four basic components to a dehydrator—the oven itself, the plastic rigid trays, the flexible polyscreen tray inserts, and the Teflex™ tray insert liners or sheets. The shelves and polyscreen inserts can be removed to facilitate cleaning and to dry larger foods—such as cakes and pies—that require more clearance and space. Dehydrators are incredibly simple to use, and every Excalibur comes with a free how-to booklet, offering tips on its assembly and use.

Using Your Dehydrator

Unlike ovens, dehydrators use very low heat, and it can take hours—and sometimes days—to dry your food to a point where it can be eaten, or safely stored away. It is a good idea to check your food periodically, especially in the beginning as you're learning to use your machine.

In general, most foods are best when flipped at some point during the drying process. Some, such as fruit, can be turned by hand, but crackers and other products that start with wet batter or dough need more care. A quick way to do this is to place another polyscreen tray insert on top of the food, then another rack, and then turn over this "sandwich" carefully using both hands. Remove the rack that's now on top, then the polyscreen tray insert, then gently peel the Teflex sheet off of the semi-dry batter. Score the dough into the shapes you desire with a spatula or knife, and dry it for another 12 to 24 hours until it becomes crisp or chewy, according to your preference.

Dehydrator Heat Settings. While raw fooders agree in principle that the goal is to not heat food beyond where enzymes will be denatured, in practice the opinions about correct heat settings for your dehydrator (or for any heating system you use) are as varied as the chefs in this book. The usual point of view is that anything above 115° Fahrenheit is too warm for the enzymes. However, a large, thick tray of raw dough, for example, will take a long time to heat through when the temperature is less than 115°, and, in the meantime, mold or bacteria can develop in its center because of the warm, wet material. New contributing chef Mary Rydman, the author of *Raw and Radiant: Simple Raw Recipes for the Busy Lifestyle*, investigated this issue in depth with the Excalibur®. She says:

The temperature debate—Low temperature dehydrating warms and dries food without destroying all enzymes, although some are still destroyed. Common knowledge is that enzymes are destroyed at temperatures above 118 degrees. That is coming into question, however, as the research that temperature was based on is an outside **water** temperature of 118, not the surrounding air temperature. What matters is what temperature the food reaches, not what the air temperature is. The main problem is there has been no real research done on this subject and no one really knows at what outside air temperature the food enzymes will be destroyed. Recent research by the Excalibur Dehydrator Company found that a higher than usual temperature to start will speed drying time and lessen the chance of mold and bacterial growth (the longer a food is exposed to warmth, the more potential for bacteria to grow), with no threat to enzyme health. The high water content of the food will keep it from actually reaching the initial drying temperature, so enzymes are not in danger, as long as you remember to turn it down after the designated time. For a more complete explanation see Gabriel Cousen's book *The Secrets of Rainbow Green Live-Food Cuisine*. The Excalibur company recommends using a starting temperature of 145 degrees for 2 hours, depending on the water content of the food (very low water content foods, such as bananas, perhaps should stay at that temperature less time), then lowering to desired temperature for the duration of drying time. **This is only recommended for the Excalibur dehydrators** and not other brands, because of the Excalibur fan system and precise temperature control.

Mary offers some other tips about dehydrating:

Flavors get more concentrated in the drying process, so be careful when adding salt or other flavors—you may end up with a too salty or strong tasting finished product. It takes a bit of experimenting to find out what works for you to get the best end result. The wet mixture should taste not quite salty and spicy enough to you.

Turning over—Crackers, cookies, etc. started out on the Teflex sheets should be turned over and placed on the screens when they are dry enough to hold together. This will speed drying and make the drying more even.

Water content—The less water you process your crackers and cookies with the less time it will take to dehydrate them. That means more energy saved and less time for mold and bacteria to grow in the warm air. That will mean more stopping the food processor to scrape down the sides, but it will be worth the extra effort.

Dehydrating Dos and Don'ts

As with any piece of kitchen equipment, there are some important considerations to keep in mind to ensure that your dehydrator is used correctly. A full list of these is available from the manufacturer, and will likely be found in the instruction manual that comes with your machine. We have compiled our own list of dehydrating dos and don'ts, based on our chefs' experiences with drying raw foods.

DO

- Use your dehydrator for warming soups and stuffed vegetables; for making crackers, sprouted breads, trail mixes, fruit leathers, sliced dried fruit, scones, and raw "cookies."
- Make your batter wet but not runny, and cover it with a Teflex sheet, using a rolling pin to spread it out evenly.
- Remember that seasonings will be twice as strong after drying.
- Remember that the thickness of crackers and other dough-based foods will be about half after drying—if you make them too thin, your crackers will be lacy and brittle. Make them too thick and you'll break a tooth biting into them.
- Dry products thoroughly, allowing them to cool at room temperature and storing them in an airtight container such as a glass jar with a screw-on lid. If your fruits are soft and moist or your crackers not quite crunchy, they will quickly develop mold.
- Rotate the trays from top to bottom when you flip your crackers or check the oven—the top DOES get the most heat despite the fan.
- Store the spare trays and polyscreen tray inserts in the oven while in use—they are not harmed.
- Clean your machine with warm water from time to time, especially the bottom where crumbs may gather and attract pests. Grain moths love to lay eggs in the dehydrator if it's not kept clean.
- Remember that your lead time for dehydrated food may be as much as five days—three for sprouting the ingredients, and two for preparing, flipping and drying your food.

DON'T

- Be afraid to experiment.
- Inhale when checking a batch of drying jalapeños or habaneras.
- Store unused trays on top, where they can accidentally get bumped and re-set the thermostat.

The dehydrator is a great piece of equipment to own, any raw chef will tell you. Start simply as you learn to use your new machine, with some seasoned snacks or fruit. Pretty soon you'll be dehydrating whole cakes, and scrumptious raw "cookies" to share with all your friends. To get you started, here are some more tips about dehydrating food from our experienced raw chefs.

- To dry Teflex sheets, plastic trays, and milk bags, purchase one of the little circular folding drying racks made for camping. They have a coat-hanger type hook and eight folding arms with tiny clothes pegs on the end. They can be hung over the sink to let things drip overnight. At a class on sustainability, one of our chefs met someone who is still using a 10-year old baggie, so now she washes her Ziplocs and hangs them up there, too.

- Finding space for raw tools can be a problem in a tiny kitchen. We discovered that our Excalibur dehydrator fits perfectly inside the oven cavity of our range. The range door and oven racks have been consigned to storage and the dehydrator is super convenient.

- At first, we couldn't figure out where to store the dehydrator racks and plastic trays. Inside the dehydrator works fine (duh!) because even if some shelves are in use, the heat is too low to harm the empty racks, unlike a conventional oven.

- Never leave your dehydrator teflex sheets stacked wet. An easy drying method is to put them back in the empty dehydrator and turn it on high for 15 minutes to get perfectly dried sheets. If the dehydrator is full, then dry each sheet with a towel.

- What do you do with pulp after you've strained juice or soup? I like to make pulp into little burger shapes, dehydrate them out in the sun for a day or two and eat them with the next day's soup! If you don't have the sunshine, you can always use a dehydrator, an airing cupboard, the top of a radiator, or an oven on its lowest setting with the door open. Also, try adding soaked minced nuts, and making loaves out of them, dehydrating in the same way, but only until still moist inside.

6

Advice
From the Pros

Once you have the right tools and ingredients, you're well on your way toward preparing appealing and delicious raw food dishes. The missing elements are know-how and imagination.

In this chapter, our chefs offer their expert advice on raw food preparation, and share some simple techniques that will spark your creativity. To get you started, here is some advice from Victoria Boutenko about how to create tasty raw meals that will make your mouth water and satisfy your palate.

THE BALANCE OF FIVE TASTES

(adapted from *12 Steps to Raw Food* by Victoria Boutenko)

Can raw food be as tasty as cooked food? Absolutely! We have learned how to prepare delicious raw food, and our family has been successfully teaching secrets of raw gourmet dishes to hundreds of men and women of different ages. During the last few years, we have simply stopped telling people that our food is raw unless they ask.

There is one principal difference between cooking a meal and preparing live food. In the cooked dishes, sugar is always sugar, flour is always flour, and salt is always salt. In the raw world, no two lemons are alike. One is bigger and has more juice; another has thick skin and is more sour. You could prepare the same recipe, measure carefully, follow every step, and still it would turn out different each time because of the variables inherent in live food. Cooked corn, cooked zucchini, cooked peas, and other cooked vegetables taste almost the same and

INVENTING NEW RECIPES

Inventing New Recipes

Being creative is so important when you prepare meals, and it is also lots of fun! After you learn the basics by following the recipes in this book, it will be time to invent some of your own. Just take the plunge and experiment!

Here are some tips to get you started:

- Use the freshest, ripest organic produce available.
- Try to use raw foods to mock/imitate your favorite cooked food recipes.
- Try foods you haven't used before.
- Experiment with equipment, such as a food processor, blender, and juicer. A coffee grinder can also do interesting things to nuts and seeds, like making a fine flour out of them.
- Experiment with using all the food left in your house before heading to the store. Setting this restriction often encourages you to be more creative with the foods that you have, and it will also save you money.
- Go inward and meditate upon what your body wants to eat. Feel the flavors, the texture, the scents, and the energy, and you will create in your mind new kinds of feasts! This works especially well when you are very hungry or fasting.
- Look at the recipes others have created (www.rawfoods.com, for instance, which offers thousands of raw recipes) and adapt them to your own taste. Give them a twist of your own style.
—Jinjee and Storm Talifero

require added oil and salt at the least. Raw corn, zucchini, peas, and other raw vegetables all have their own unique flavors that are impossible to confuse.

When we prepare a raw dish, we use recipes only as ideas, as general guidelines, or just for the ingredients. Then we adjust the final flavor using a method of five tastes. There are thousands of different tastes in natural food, but when we balance the five major ones, the food is so delicious that everyone says, "Wow!" These five tastes are: sweet, sour, salty, spicy, and bitter. When you learn to balance the five tastes, you will make delicious food. When all five groups of taste buds on your tongue are excited, you too will say, "Wow!"

When you attempt to un-cook a delicious meal, make sure that all five tastes are present in the final flavor and that not one is missing. Each of the five tastes doesn't have to be strong, but just enough for a particular dish. For example, the strongest tastes in a garden burger should be sweet, spicy, and salty with only a touch of sour and bitter, but all five need to be present. Otherwise, the garden burger will taste bland.

After several months of eating raw food, you will start to notice that more and more often you prefer to eat whole food rather than prepared. In fact, all whole foods, if they are ripe, already naturally have the most balanced bouquet of flavors. However, the taste of natural food is so delicate that unfortunately, after many years of consuming cooked food packed with chemicals, our taste buds can no longer enjoy natural flavors. That is why we need a transition time.

The following is a list of suggested ingredients for the five taste groups. This is only a fraction of what is available on planet Earth. Many plants possess different flavors but have one or two that are more dominant. You have to apply common sense and not add vanilla to the soup or garlic to the candy. Please be creative: these are just ideas for you.

FOR SOUR TASTE ADD:

apple cider vinegar
cranberries
lemon grass
lemons
nut or seed yogurt
rejuvelac
rhubarb
sorrel
sour grass

FOR SWEET TASTE, ADD:

apple juice
dry fruit such as figs,
    dates, prunes,
    raisins
fresh fruits such as
    ripe banana,
    mango, peach,
    pear
fresh stevia leaves

orange juice
raw honey

FOR SPICY TASTE, ADD:

cayenne pepper
garlic leaves or cloves
ginger
herbs, fresh or dry,
    such as basil, dill,
    cilantro, rosemary,
    or peppermint
spices such as cinna-
    mon, nutmeg, or
    vanilla
horseradish
mustard greens or
    seeds
onion leaves or bulbs
radish
seaweed
wasabi

FOR SALTY TASTE ADD:

celery
cilantro, dill, parsley
sea vegetables such
    as dulse, kelp, nori,
    aramé, or Celtic
    sea salt

FOR BITTER TASTE, ADD:

celery tops
dandelion leaves
endive
garlic
onion
parsley
poultry seasoning
sage

Tips on Presentation

Your raw dishes should not only taste, but *look* delicious. As always, presentation is important because it makes delicious food even more appealing. Here are some of chef Jinjee Talifero's favorite ways to garnish food.

- Place fruit and/or vegetable slices around the edges of the plate in a circle.

- Create an artistic flourish or arrangement of garnishing using colors and shapes.

- Place the food on a bed of red or green leaf lettuce.

- Cut garnishes into pretty or interesting shapes.

- Banana slices, kiwi slices, strawberries, strawberry slices, dried coconut sprinkles, and almonds make the prettiest garnishes for fruit dishes.

- Red onion rings, lettuce, carrot slices, thin curly carrot strips, different colored bell peppers, cucumber slices, different colored cabbage cut in curly strips, jicama wedges, and asparagus tops make nice garnishing for vegetable dishes.

- As a general rule, review your array of ingredients before you decide which to reserve for garnish. For instance, if a recipe calls for walnut halves, set aside the nicest looking 7 or 8 for decoration.

Above all, be creative! Have fun and experiment with new ways to present the foods you love to eat.

TIPS ON INGREDIENTS

The ingredients you will use in your delicious raw recipes range from the ordinary to the exotic. As you learn to experiment with their natural flavors, some questions are bound to arise. What is the best way to open a Thai coconut? How can you keep your guacamole fresh? To answer these and other questions, read on. Our experienced chefs offer you their insider tips here on how to make the most of nature's ingredients.

Avocados

When cutting an avocado, first remove the hard stem. Otherwise, it may end up in your recipe.
—*Matt Amsden*

If you're making guacamole a few hours in advance, add the juice of a lemon to the ingredients before blending and place the avocado pits in the middle of the guacamole. Though it may just be an old wives' tale, some say the added pits will keep it fresher.
—*Shazzie*

To make the most of your avocados when making guacamole, purée 2 stalks of celery with 2 tablespoons of olive oil in a food processor for *every* avocado you will be using. Mix it all together with seasonings. It will be so green and creamy, no one will suspect that it's not all avocado. It's also a great way to get kids to eat celery.
—*Elaina Love*

Celery

Cut celery into 1-inch pieces so that you don't end up with long strings that will get stuck in your teeth.
—*Rhio*

Use a celery stalk as your spatula to keep things moving in the blender.
—*Elaina Love*

Buy some business card stock and make yourself some of these cards for eating out:

I EAT ONLY RAW, UNCOOKED FOODS.

I would like a salad or vegetable plate with only fresh uncooked items such as arugula • avocado • beets • bell peppers • bok choy • broccoli • cabbage • carrots • cauliflower • celery • chard • cilantro • cucumber • kale • lettuce • mushrooms • onion • parsley • radish • scallions • spinach • sprouts • tomato • zucchini

THANK YOU FOR YOUR CREATIVE EFFORTS!

—Jonathan Weber

About Salt

Salt is vital to the body's functioning, and needs to be replaced every day through foods or condiments. Some chefs and nutritionists, raw and otherwise, believe that a healthy human diet requires no *added* salt. They point to high blood pressure and other ailments being triggered by too much salt. But as anyone who has climbed a mountain on a hot day knows, it's possible to experience very unpleasant side effects from too little salt—leg cramps, hyperventilation and exhaustion. So where's the happy medium? Celery, cilantro, dill, and sea vegetables provide natural sources of salt. If you do add salt, make sure it's pure and clean, not chemically processed. That's why you'll see references to Celtic sea salt in so many recipes. Nama shoyu or raw tamari are also good sources of salty flavor. So, like you always should, taste before you shake, and remember not to over-salt food that's to be dehydrated. If, in your opinion, a recipe seems to call for too much salt, add gradually and taste as you go. If in doubt, leave it out.

Celtic Sea Salt

Raw food chefs use Celtic sea salt because dissolves in water. It can break down and dissolve in your system, unlike normal table salt, which should be avoided at all costs! Like honey, Celtic sea salt is very healthful, as long as it is used in moderation. Otherwise, it can be damaging.
—Jinjee Talifero

A note about over-sprouting:

For sunflower pâtés, after soaking, allow the sunflower seeds to sit out on the counter for 2 to 4 hours, but no longer. If the seeds sprout for more than 4 hours, the result will be a bitter tasting pâté. You will not see a "tail" at this stage.

After sprouting, rinse thoroughly, removing as many as possible of the fine inner husks that float to the surface. Drain well. The sunflower seeds are now ready to use in the recipe. If you are not able to make the recipe at this time, refrigerate the seeds until you are ready.

Garlic

If you are blending garlic in a Vita-Mix blender, it is not necessary to completely remove it from its papery husk. This husk is safe to eat and this powerful machine will blend the husk completely.
—Matt Amsden

To peel a clove of garlic, place it under the flat side of a knife blade and strike it carefully with the side of your hand.
—Matt Amsden

When blending fresh ginger, peeling it first will decrease its bitterness.
—Matt Amsden

Lettuce

Wilted lettuce? Revive it by wrapping it in a wet towel and placing it in the refrigerator.
—*Matt Amsden*

Limes

Placing limes on a sunny windowsill for a few months will dry them. Once ground, these sun-dried limes make an excellent spice for Thai and other ethnic dishes.
—*Matt Amsden*

Nut Meal

To make nut meal, blend nuts in food processor or blender or coffee grinder until they turn to powder.
—*Jinjee Talifero*

Cleaning the Coffee Grinder

1. Reserve one grinder just for coffee, if you drink it.
2. Buy another grinder for your raw kitchen and clean it between products by grinding 1/2 tablespoon flax seeds. Toss when done.

Mushrooms

Keep mushrooms fresh by storing them in a paper bag in the refrigerator.
—*Matt Amsden*

Okra

When buying okra, pick the smallest ones. They are less gelatinous.
—*Matt Amsden*

Thai Coconuts

To open a young Thai coconut, hold it upright and insert a sharp knife at a 45-degree angle about two inches from the top. Work the knife carefully all the way around the coconut and then pop off the "lid," keeping the coconut upright to avoid spilling the water. To remove the water first, punch out three holes near the top where you can feel three indentations. Pour out the water or drink it with a straw. Yum!
—*Vern Curtis*

When scraping the flesh from a Thai coconut, turn the spoon upside down so that the convex side is up. This makes it easier to remove the flesh from the shell in one piece.
—*Matt Amsden*

Vanilla

Vanilla powder is simply ground vanilla bean: cut 3 dried vanilla beans into small pieces and grind them as fine as possible in a nut or coffee grinder. Store in a small glass jar in the refrigerator. The vanilla powder keeps for months. If it develops an off smell, throw it away; but I've never seen this happen. The alternative to making vanilla powder would be to just cut a small piece of vanilla from the pod and blend into the recipe. Depending on the quality of your equipment, it may or may not break down completely. If your vanilla bean is too moist and doesn't powder up in the nut mill, then leave the vanilla bean out at room temperature for a couple of days so that it dries a bit. Do not put the vanilla bean in a food dehydrator, because it will lose all its flavor. You can grind a moist vanilla bean, but it will come out the texture of ground tobacco, instead of as a powder. This has just as much flavor and works just as well in the recipes. Store it in the refrigerator.
—*Rhio*

Commercial vanilla extract usually contains alcohol and may be extracted with solvents. Solvents have no place in a healthy diet.
—*Rhio*

TIPS ON SOAKING

Apart from the soaking that's done to kick off a sprouting process (discussed in Chapter 4), you may often use soaking as a means of improving foods. Soaking nuts and seeds for a few hours releases the enzyme (growth) inhibitors and makes them "live" even if you don't go on to sprouting them. But not all soak water should be retained. Here's a quick list:

Almonds—soak for a few hours to release the tannin; drain and toss the soak water.

Cashews—soaking for as little as 20 minutes makes them soft and ready to spin with honey and lemon for a wonderful frosting. Here you want to keep the soak water.

Dried or sundried tomatoes—the soak water used for reconstituting them can either have a wonderful taste that adds to a recipe's flavor, or it can be overly salty—so be sure to taste before deciding!

Flax seed—soaking for a few hours or overnight creates a gluey mixture that would be almost impossible to rinse off, and it's high in protein so you want to incorporate this into your recipe.

Nut cheeses (made by draining off the nutmilk)—both the liquid and the solid should be kept, but likely for use in different recipes.

Prunes—soak water becomes a thin prune juice; definitely worth using.

To the extent possible, our recipes specify whether to incorporate or toss the soak water.

TIPS ON FLAVORING DISHES

The seasonings and herbs you include in your recipes can make even the blandest ingredients come to life. To help you add spice to your raw food dishes, here's some advice from our creative raw chefs.

I use numerous herbal seasonings to add accents to my recipes, including rosemary, thyme, basil, tarragon, oregano, summer savory, cayenne, paprika, cumin, curry, turmeric, sage, vanilla bean, etc. If you can get these herbs fresh, or grow them in your kitchen or garden, all the better. Otherwise, organic dried versions are acceptable.
—*Jinjee and Storm Talifero*

To sweeten foods we use honey. You can replace this with medjool dates or raw agave (cactus) nectar. Some people believe honey is not vegan because bees make it. However, we distinguish between insects and other animals and therefore don't see honey as animal product. We have done extensive research on honey and are convinced it is extremely healthful, as long as it is used in moderation.
—*Jinjee and Storm Talifero*

Add more seasoning than you think you will need!
—*Karie Clingo*

USING AND CARING FOR YOUR TOOLS

The tools you use to prepare your raw dishes should be clean and well-maintained. To help you use them and keep them running, here are some suggestions from our chefs.

The Champion juicer quickly gets stained by beet, carrot, tomato, and other juices. The same problem exists for green juicing machines; you can wash them, but the plastic absorbs stains and after the first use, your gadget will no longer look white. A lost cause? Not at all.

I tried Regent's Kleenite® Denture Cleanser on a used Champion whose parts were not only stained but also coated with a sticky goo. After three days of soaking the parts in a hot strong mix of the denture cleanser, and some scrubbing with an old toothbrush, they look like new.

—Julie Rodwell

I use ceramic, not metal, knives in the kitchen. Ceramic knives stay sharper much longer than metal ones and they don't cause oxidation as metal knives do.

—Stephen Arlin

When using your Champion to make ice-cream, chill the rotor blade and blank plate in the freezer, then install them.

—David Klein

Above all, don't be afraid to experiment with herbs and spices. Use common sense, and taste your food as you go along. Remember which flavors work best with which dishes, and write these down in a notebook for later use. The more you learn, the more fun you'll have—and the better your food will taste.

TIPS ON TECHNIQUES

The techniques you use to prepare your food can affect how a dish looks and tastes. To help you avoid waste and become more efficient in the kitchen, our chefs offer their advice on the best ways to prepare your favorite raw recipes.

Pay special attention to your seasonings:

- Buy pure extracts not made with alcohol

- Substitute raw carob powder for cocoa

- Stock up on raw organic honey and other sweeteners of your choice.

* * *

Here's a way to keep all your favorite recipes protected and in one place. Purchasing a ring binder and some clear plastic sheets with holes punched down the left hand side. Photocopy pages from your favorite recipe books and slip them in the plastic wallets. You can also use the folder to keep handy phone numbers for food suppliers, mail-order catalogs, even food prep hints and tips. And because the wallets are clear plastic you can protect everything from water, spills, and staining.

—**Karen Knowler**

When a recipe calls for raspberries to be blended, use a food processor rather than a blender. When done in a blender, the raspberry seeds become like sand.
—*Emily Lee Angell*

When a blended recipe calls for fresh parsley, dill, or cilantro, blend only the stems and save the leaves for garnish or another recipe.
—*Matt Amsden*

TIPS ON GENERAL FOOD PREPARATION

When making pâtés and burgers/nutmeats, chop a portion of the ingredients by hand very finely for a coarser and more interesting texture and mix them into the main pâté or burger mix.
—*Shazzie*

When weighing down a batch of kim chee or sauerkraut, cover it first with plastic wrap, then put a weight on top. I use unopened bags of lentils, as they form well to the shape of the bowl.
—*Shazzie*

Un-Cooking

Now that you've learned how to create fantastic raw meals, it is time to take this raw knowledge to the kitchen. The recipes in the section that follows should serve to guide you as you learn to prepare these delicious live foods. Remember that no recipe is ever written in stone—you should not be afraid to experiment and add your own ingredients and spices.

As you get more comfortable with your tools and techniques, you may even decide to close this book and invent some recipes all on your own. That's fine! Keep *The Complete Book of Raw Food* handy to turn to as new questions arise.

FOOD CRAVINGS

When you start a raw diet, you may experience cravings for the foods you used to eat. We've listed some of these cravings below and suggested raw replacements. They can all be found in the next section on recipes.

When You Crave This:	Eat or Drink This:
Apple Pie	Raw Apple Pie
Burritos	Sunflower Herb Pâté
Candy Bar	Almond Butter Candy
Candy	Nut Candy
Cheese	Tahini Cheese
Chip Dip	Sprouted Hummus
Chocolate	Raw Carob Treat
Dessert	Sensuous Fruit Salad
Drugs and Alcohol	Green Juice
Ice Cream	Nutmilk Smoothie with Almond Butter, chilled
Ice Cream, Milk Shakes, Candy	Fruit Smoothies
Liverwurst, Meat, Beans & Rice	Seed Pâté
Meat, Meat Loaf	Nut Loaf
Meat, Sushi	Nut Sushi
Milk	Cantaloupe Milk
Milk	Nutmilk
Milkshake	Nutmilk Smoothie
Pastry, Breakfast Cereal, Pies	Oatmeal Treat
Pizza	Nut Pizza
Protein Shake	Tahini Milk
Purée, Pudding, Jello	Watermelon Juice
Ratatouille, Italian Sauce Dishes	Raw Ratatouille, Raw Tomato Sauce
Salad Dressings	Raw Salad Dressings
Sushi	Veggie Sushi Rolls
Thai Food	Raw Thai Lemon Coconut Soup

Some other basic cooking replacements Jinjee and Storm Talifero suggest we use are flax oil in place of butter, nut meal in place of meat, and marinated vegetables in place of cooked vegetables.

A Word on Preparation Times

Unlike most conventional food preparation, raw food preparation can sometimes require several days of lead time. Needless to say, it's disappointing to pick out an enticing recipe for supper and then realize it will require several days of soaking and sprouting beforehand—and perhaps several days of dehydrating afterwards—before that enticing meal will make it to your dinner table. Therefore, at the start of each recipe in this Second Edition, we have specified both the **advanced preparation time ("Advanced prep")** along with the specific activities that need to be done far in advance, and the **immediate preparation time ("Immediate prep")**, meaning the chopping, blending and mixing that is similar to what's required for cooked recipes. Of course, there are also many recipes that are extremely quick to create, and you'll notice that these don't require any "Advanced prep" time.

Mediterranean Black Olive and Walnut Tapenade By Cherie Soria

Borscht By Victoria Boutenko

PART II | RECIPES

7

Salads & Dressings

Applenut Salad

BY STEPHEN ARLIN

ADVANCED PREP: 5 to 8 days for sunflower sprouts   **IMMEDIATE PREP:** 10 min
YIELDS 4 to 5 cups   **SPECIAL EQUIPMENT** None

INGREDIENTS

1 head red leaf lettuce
1 cup sunflower sprouts

1 apple, diced
1 cup grapes
1/2 cup chopped walnuts

DIRECTIONS

Make a bed of lettuce and sprouts. Add the apple and grapes, and sprinkle with chopped walnuts.

Arugula-Orange Salad with Cranberry Vinaigrette Dressing

BY JULIE RODWELL

ADVANCED PREP: None   **IMMEDIATE PREP:** 15 min
SPECIAL EQUIPMENT Blender   **SERVES** 2

INGREDIENTS

Salad:
1/2 bag of arugula
1/2 cup crushed walnuts
2 large oranges, chopped into bite size pieces
Dressing:
1/2 bag frozen cranberries or fresh

3 cloves garlic
1/4 cup olive oil
1/2 tsp sea salt
1.5 in full apple cider vinegar
6 medium dates
1–1.5 cups water

DIRECTIONS

Toss all salad ingredients. Blend all dressing ingredients in Vita-Mix

Asparagus Avocado Salad

By Rita Romano

Advanced prep: 3 to 5 days for radish sprouts   **Immediate prep:** 20 min

Serves 4   **Special Equipment** None

INGREDIENTS

- 2 small avocados, peeled and chopped
- 1/2 pound asparagus tips
- 1 small jicama, peeled and chopped
- 1 pink grapefruit, peeled, seeded, chopped
- 2 limes, juiced
- 2 tablespoons mint, chopped

- 4 tablespoons green onion, chopped
- 2 tablespoons red onion, minced
- Bragg Liquid Aminos® or sea salt to taste
- 2 tablespoons chopped lemon balm herb, (optional)
- 1 cup radish sprouts (or other sprouts of your choice)
- lettuce for garnish

DIRECTIONS

Combine the avocado, asparagus, jicama, grapefruit, lime juice, mint, green onion, red onion, Bragg Liquid Aminos or sea salt, and lemon balm, if using. Serve on a bed of lettuce topped with a few sprouts.

Hint: Remove the white pith from the grapefruit for a sweeter dish.

Broccoli & Carrot "Noodle" Salad

By Elaina Love

Advanced prep: 5 to 8 days for sunflower sprouts   **Immediate prep:** 10 min

Serves 2 to 3   **Special Equipment** Spiral slicer

INGREDIENTS

- 1 head broccoli, stalks peeled and florets removed
- 1 carrot
- 1 English cucumber
- 1 cup sunflower sprouts

DIRECTIONS

Using a spiral slicer, cut the broccoli, carrot, and cucumber into veggie noodles. Chop or cut the noodles so they won't be excessively long. Mix in the sunflower sprouts and serve with your choice of dressing on the side.

Contributor's note: This salad is a light and flavorful accompaniment to nori rolls or an Asian wild rice dish. Raw broccoli contains almost as much calcium as whole milk, is an antioxidant, and protects against cancer. Sunflower greens are high in protein and loaded with enzymes and chlorophyll.

Cabbage Salad

By Eddie D. Robinson
Advanced prep: 2 to 3 days   **Immediate prep:** 30 min
Serves 8 to 10   **Special Equipment** Blender or food processor

INGREDIENTS

For the salad:
1 head green cabbage
1 head red cabbage
7 carrots, shredded
1 red onion, chopped
3 red bell peppers, chopped
1/2 cup fresh cilantro, chopped

For the dressing:
1 1/2 cups sesame oil
1/4 cup nama shoyu
1/4 cup lime juice
1 tablespoon *each* oregano, basil, tarragon
1/4 cup fresh squeezed orange juice

DIRECTIONS

Peel the outer leaves off the cabbages and set them aside. Chop the rest of the cabbage, and place it in a large bowl along with the carrots, onion, bell peppers and cilantro.

To make the salad dressing, pulse all the dressing ingredients in a blender or food processor for 3 seconds.

Pour the dressing over the salad and mix well. Cover the bowl with the cabbage leaves. Place a plate and a weight on top, and let the bowl sit at room temperature for 2 to 3 days (or until it suits your taste). Store in the refrigerator for up to 3 weeks.

Note: Fermentation time varies according to room temperature and humidity.

Caesar Salad

By Jalissa Letendre
Advanced prep: None **Immediate prep:** 20 min
Serves 5 **Special Equipment** None

INGREDIENTS

For the salad:
1 head romaine lettuce
1 cucumber, chopped
1 red pepper, chopped
1/2 cup chopped red onion
1 large carrot, shredded
1/2 cup dried coconut, grated

For the dressing:
2 tablespoons olive oil
1 lemon, juiced
1 tablespoon honey
1/2 teaspoon cumin powder
1 large garlic clove, pressed
1/2 teaspoon Herbamare® or sea salt
1/4 cup pumpkin seeds, ground

DIRECTIONS

Combine the lettuce with the cucumber, red pepper, onion, carrot, and coconut in a large bowl.

Mix all the dressing ingredients together in a measuring cup.

Pour over the vegetables and toss well before serving.

Chakra Salad

By Shazzie
Advanced prep: 10–20 min for High Vibe Dressing **Immediate prep:** 20 min
Serves Depends on quantities used **Special Equipment** Food Processor

INGREDIENTS

zucchini
yellow pepper
pumpkin or other squash
carrot

broccoli
tomatoes
red cabbage
beets

DIRECTIONS

Using the "S" blade of a food processor, process each item separately, until coarsely chopped. To preserve the colors of the vegetables, process them in the order listed above, zucchini first, beets last. For added variety, use your spiral slicer to slice the zucchini, carrot, and pumpkin, and use a mandolin to slice the beets and red cabbage. Serve the shredded vegetables in a heaping mound, with High Vibe Dressing (page 90) in a small bowl at the center of the plate.

Contributor's note: Chakra salad is great for parties; serve it on an attractive dish and watch everyone dip in! Or make up a great big batch all for yourself; that way there's always something ready-made in the fridge for healthy snacking.

Citrus, Avocado and Mango Salad

By Rhio

Advanced prep: None   **Immediate prep:** 25 min
Serves 2 to 4   **Special Equipment** None

INGREDIENTS

1/2 pound mesclun salad mix

1 large avocado, diced

1 large mango, diced

1 to 2 oranges, segmented, seeded, and chopped

1 grapefruit, segmented, seeded, and chopped

3/4 pint cherry tomatoes

1/2 medium onion, sliced or diced

handful chopped walnuts

handful pine nuts

paprika powder for garnish

For the dressing:
1/4 cup extra-virgin olive oil

1/2 lemon, juiced

1/2 teaspoon prepared Dijon mustard

dash dried or fresh thyme

dash Celtic sea salt

DIRECTIONS

In a large bowl combine the mesclun salad mix, avocado, mango, oranges, grapefruit, tomatoes and onion. Toss to mix and set aside.

To make the dressing, mix the olive oil, lemon juice, mustard, thyme, and sea salt in a small bowl.

Pour the dressing over the salad and toss well.

Top with walnuts and pine nuts. Garnish the edge of the plate with paprika powder and serve.

Cocochina Salad

BY ROBERT YAROSH AND LISA SOTO

ADVANCED PREP: None **IMMEDIATE PREP:** 20 min

SERVES 2 **SPECIAL EQUIPMENT** None

INGREDIENTS

1 Roma tomato, sliced

meat of 1 large young coconut, sliced into 2-inch circles

5 to 7 fresh basil leaves, chopped or whole

1 tablespoon olive oil

pinch Celtic sea salt

pinch dried oregano

DIRECTIONS

Arrange the ingredients on a plate and serve.

Cucumber Crunch

BY SHAZZIE
ADVANCED PREP: 15 min for Macadamia Cream   **IMMEDIATE PREP:** 15 min
SERVES 2   **SPECIAL EQUIPMENT** None

INGREDIENTS

1 cucumber, peeled and finely diced
4 sprigs fresh mint, finely chopped
1/2 teaspoon dill seeds
2 teaspoons Macadamia Cream (page 189)
1/2 white onion, finely diced

DIRECTIONS

Mix all of the ingredients together in a large bowl and serve.

Dulse Sprout Salad

BY RITA ROMANO
ADVANCED PREP: 4 days for Mung Beans   **IMMEDIATE PREP:** 25 min
SERVES 6   **SPECIAL EQUIPMENT** None

INGREDIENTS

3 cups mung bean sprouts
1 carrot, shredded
1 yellow bell pepper, cut in thin strips
3 jalapeño peppers, minced
1/2 bunch scallions, minced (green part only)
2 limes, juiced

3 tablespoons extra virgin olive oil
1/2 cup fresh cilantro, minced
2 tablespoons chopped fresh basil
1/4 cup sesame seeds, soaked 8 hours and dehydrated 8 hours
1/2 cup dulse, dehydrated 4 hours and crumbled (or store-bought)
Bragg Liquid Aminos® or sea salt to taste (optional)

DIRECTIONS

Combine all the ingredients in a large bowl for an exciting salad treat. Dehydration gives the seeds a toasty flavor, though this step can be skipped if you are pressed for time.

Fast Avocado Salad

By Stephen Arlin

Advanced prep: None **Immediate prep:** 10 min
Yields 2 to 3 cups **Special Equipment** None

INGREDIENTS

3 to 4 handfuls wild or organic greens and/or herbs

2 large avocados, pitted, peeled, and diced

30 to 40 Raw Power! olives

1 tablespoon extra virgin cold-pressed olive oil

1 medium orange, peeled and juiced

DIRECTIONS

Make a bed of wild or organic greens and/or herbs. Add the avocado, olives, olive oil, and orange juice to taste.

Note: Raw Power! olives are free-grown Kalamata-style olives packed in pure water, a dash of fresh oregano, 1 ripe cayenne pepper, and a dash of Celtic sea salt. Call (800) 205-2350 to order by phone or visit www.sunfood.com for more details.

Kale Medicine Salad

BY MAYA ADJANI

ADVANCED PREP: None   **IMMEDIATE PREP:** 15–20 min

SPECIAL EQUIPMENT None   **SERVES** 2

INGREDIENTS

For the salad:
1 bunch Lacinato kale
1–2 ripe avocados
1 zucchini
1/2 1 large beet,
1 bunch basil
2" ginger root
2" turmeric root

For the dressing:
1 clove garlic, pressed
1/4 cup olive oil
Celtic sea salt to taste
Green powder to taste (see below)
Lemon juice
Agave Nectar (to taste)

DIRECTIONS

Mix dressing ingredients in a small bowl with a fork until smooth. Place finely chopped kale in a large bowl, pour on dressing and massage with love and gratitude. The massaging softens the kale. De-pit avocados and slice into cubes, chop or shred the beet, zucchini, turmeric and ginger root and add to bowl. Add the basil leaves, whole or chopped.

Contributor's note: This yummy, highly potent and deeply nourishing meal is rich in chlorophyll, essential amino acids (protein) and minerals. Eaten regularly the body will begin to ask for it. Vitamineral Green powder by Healthforce Nutritionals is highly recommended, or Spirulina is also excellent and readily available.

Kale Mixed Green Salad

BY ABEBA WRIGHT

ADVANCED PREP: None **IMMEDIATE PREP:** 25 min

SERVES 15 **SPECIAL EQUIPMENT** None

INGREDIENTS

For the salad:
1 to 2 bunches dinosaur kale
1 red bell pepper, chopped
1/4 red onion, chopped
1/2 cup green onion, chopped
1/4 cup fresh dill, chopped
3 cloves garlic, crushed in garlic press
1/2 cup dried cranberries (optional)
2 tomatoes, chopped (optional)
1/2 to 1 pound mixed salad greens

For the dressing:
nama shoyu to taste
lemon juice or apple cider vinegar to taste
olive oil to taste
honey to taste

DIRECTIONS

Tear the kale into bite-size pieces. To tenderize it, massage by squeezing until the fibers are broken down.

Gradually work the ingredients of the dressing into the kale as you massage it. Start by sprinkling the nama shoyu on the kale. Massage, then add the lemon juice or apple cider vinegar. Massage again. Add the olive oil, and continue to massage. Add the honey, and massage until the kale feels limp.

There should be extra dressing in the bottom of the bowl. Adjust to taste and add the pepper, onions, dill, garlic, cranberries (if using), tomatoes (if using), and mixed greens. Gently toss the salad and serve.

Karyn's Tomato and Pea Salad

By Karyn Calabrese

Advanced prep: 1 to 2 hours to marinate   **Immediate prep:** 20 min

Serves 4   **Special Equipment** Blender

INGREDIENTS

For the dressing:

1/4 cup lemon juice

1 tablespoon honey

1 tablespoon tahini

1/4 cup Bragg Liquid Aminos

1/4 cup cold-pressed oil, sesame oil preferred

For the salad:

3 or 4 tomatoes, chopped

1/4 cup fresh or frozen peas or trimmed beans cut into 1/2-inch pieces

1 green onion, white and part of green, chopped

DIRECTIONS

In the jar of a blender, combine lemon juice, honey, tahini and Bragg Liquid Aminos. Blend, then slowly add the sesame oil to make a thick mixture. Set aside.

In a bowl, combine the chopped tomatoes, peas and green onion. Mix with the dressing and toss. Cover and marinate in the refrigerator or at room temperature for 1 to 2 hours. Stir and serve.

Lentil Salad

BY RITA ROMANO
ADVANCED PREP: 2 to 3 days for lentils   **IMMEDIATE PREP:** 25 min
SERVES 6   **SPECIAL EQUIPMENT** Blender

INGREDIENTS

3 cups lentils, sprouted
1/2 red onion, minced
1 young parsnip, shredded
1/2 yellow pepper, minced
1 tablespoon orange peel, grated
1/4 cup tahini
1 or more lemons, juiced
pinch cayenne
Bragg Liquid Aminos or soy sauce to taste
1/2 bunch parsley, cleaned, stemmed, minced
1/2 teaspoon dried thyme

DIRECTIONS

Combine the lentil sprouts, onion, parsnip, yellow pepper, and orange peel and set aside.

Blend the tahini, lemon juice, cayenne, and Bragg Liquid Aminos or soy sauce with enough water to make a thin dressing.

Transfer to a bowl and mix in the parsley and thyme. Pour the dressing over the lentil salad and enjoy.

Marinated Baby Bok Choy Salad

By Matt Samuelson

ADVANCED PREP: None   **IMMEDIATE PREP:** 20 min

SERVES 4   **SPECIAL EQUIPMENT** Blender

INGREDIENTS

For the salad:

4 heads baby bok choy or 1 large bok choy, leaves chopped into 1/2-inch strips and stems sliced thinly

1 large carrot, shaved into strips with a vegetable peeler

For the marinade:

1 small lemon, juiced

1 lime, juiced

4 to 5 large dates

2-inch piece or 3 tablespoons ginger, thinly sliced

1/2 cup olive oil

3 tablespoons nama shoyu

DIRECTIONS

Blend all the marinade ingredients together well. Combine half the marinade with bok choy and carrots and mix well. Add more marinade as desired.

Marinated Collard Ribbons

By Rhio

ADVANCED PREP: 6–9 hours or overnight to marinade   **IMMEDIATE PREP:** 10 min

SERVES 2   **SPECIAL EQUIPMENT** None

INGREDIENTS

1 bunch collard greens, stems removed (save for juicing)

For the marinade:
1 to 1 1/2 tablespoons olive oil and flaxseed oil mixed
1/2 to 1 lemon or lime, juiced
1 tablespoon nama shoyu or a sprinkle of Celtic sea salt

DIRECTIONS

Place the collard leaves one on top of the other and then fold them in half. Roll the whole bunch into a tight roll. Starting at one end of the roll, cut the collard greens into very thin slivers and transfer to a large bowl.

Mix together the oil, lemon juice, and nama shoyu for the marinade.

Pour the marinade over the greens and toss well until all the ribbons are well coated. Cover the greens and marinate in the refrigerator overnight. This dish will keep for 2 to 3 days in the refrigerator.

Hint: Weigh down the greens by placing some heavy plates on top. The weight helps the marinade penetrate into the leaves to soften them up.

Variation 1: Add sprouted, blanched, and dehydrated almonds; thinly sliced red bell pepper; diced onions, and shallots or scallions.

Variation 2: Add mellow white miso mixed with a little water and pressed garlic.

Variation 3: Add Spicy Party Mix (page 115).

Variation 4: This recipe also works well with red and green chard leaves, kale and beet tops.

Variation 5: Wild leafy plants, such as amaranth and lamb's-quarter can be chopped and mixed with the marinade for a delicious alternative to cultivated herbs.

Nature's First Slaw

By Jackie Ayala and David Steinberg

Advanced prep: None   **Immediate prep:** 30 min

Yields 5 to 6 cups   **Special Equipment** Cuisinart, Vita-Mix

INGREDIENTS

For the slaw:
1 cup green cabbage
1 cup Savoy cabbage
1/2 cup chopped black kale
1/2 cup chopped carrot
1/2 cup chopped broccoli
3 tablespoons chopped red onion
1 tablespoon diced garlic
1/2 cup chopped celery (soft inner heart including leaves)
1 tablespoon diced fresh herbs, such as parsley, dill, basil, and mint

For the dressing:
1 young coconut, water and meat
1/4 cup lemon juice
2 cloves garlic, with skin
1 tablespoon dill, chopped
1 tablespoon Celtic sea salt
2 honey dates, pitted
1/2 cup stone crushed olive oil

DIRECTIONS

Place both the green and Savoy cabbage in your food processor. (If Savoy cabbage is unavailable use 2 cups of the green cabbage.) Process until fine.

Scrape the sides of the machine, and process again. Transfer the cabbage to a large bowl.

Place all the remaining ingredients reserved for the slaw in your food processor and process until fine. Scrape the sides, and process again. Add this to the cabbage and mix together thoroughly.

Blend the coconut water and meat with the lemon juice, garlic, dill, sea salt, and dates until smooth. Add the olive oil and blend until creamy. Pour the sauce over the slaw, mix thoroughly, and enjoy!

"No" Egg Salad Spread

BY SHARON ELAM
ADVANCED PREP: None   IMMEDIATE PREP: 10 min
SERVES 4   SPECIAL EQUIPMENT None

INGREDIENTS

1 pound Almond Cheese (page 207)
3 to 4 stalks celery
1 small onion
1 teaspoon fresh ground mustard
1/2 to 1 teaspoon fresh ground pepper

pinch Celtic salt
1 1/2 teaspoons apple cider vinegar
1 to 2 teaspoons turmeric (for color)

DIRECTIONS

Mix all ingredients. Adjust spices to taste. Allow the spread sit for at least one hour to allow all the flavors to blend before serving.

Orange Spinach Salad

BY RHONDA MALKMUS
ADVANCED PREP: None   IMMEDIATE PREP: 20 min
YIELDS 4 to 5 cups   SPECIAL EQUIPMENT None

INGREDIENTS

For the salad:
1 cup small orange slices, such as mandarin, cut in half
handful romaine lettuce leaves, torn into bite-size pieces
handful spinach leaves, torn into bite size pieces
1/2 cup green grapes, cut in half
1/2 cup green onions, chopped
1 cup almonds, chopped

For the dressing:
2/3 cup extra virgin olive oil
1/3 cup fresh orange juice
1/8 to 1/4 cup honey
1 teaspoon celery seed
3 tablespoons fresh lemon juice
1 teaspoon dry mustard (optional)

DIRECTIONS

Combine orange, lettuce, spinach, grapes, onions, and almonds. Mix well.
In a jar, combine the olive oil, orange juice, honey, celery seed, lemon juice, and
dry mustard (if using). Shake well.
Pour the dressing over the salad and enjoy!

Quinoa Tabouli

By Elaina Love

Advanced prep: 2 to 3 days   **Immediate prep:** 20 min

Serves 6   **Special Equipment** None

INGREDIENTS

4 cups sprouted quinoa (about 2 cups
  before sprouting)

4 green onions, thinly sliced

20 mint leaves, minced

1 large tomato, seeded and finely diced

3/4 cucumber, peeled in strips, seeded and finely diced (if using an
  English cucumber, don't seed it)

1/4 cup parsley, minced

4 to 6 tablespoons extra virgin olive oil

3 to 5 tablespoons lemon or lime juice

1 to 2 tablespoons tamari or Bragg
  Liquid Aminos or 1 to 2 teaspoons
  Celtic sea salt to taste

1/2 teaspoon fennel seed, soaked 1
  hour if desired

DIRECTIONS

Mix everything together in a large bowl. Let sit 1 hour to allow the flavors to
meld before serving.

Hint: To sprout the quinoa, soak for 4 to 8 hours, drain water and rinse. Sprout
in a jar or in The Amazing Nut Milk, Juice and Sprout Bag for another 18 hours
or more, rinsing the quinoa every 8 hours. To test whether the sprouts are ready,
chew one. It should be firm, yet soft—and not too crunchy.

Rainbow Veggie Slaw

BY JOHN LARSEN

ADVANCED PREP: None   **IMMEDIATE PREP:** 20 min

SERVES 6 to 8   **SPECIAL EQUIPMENT** Food processor, coffee grinder

INGREDIENTS

For the salad:
1/2 medium head purple cabbage
1 yellow onion
1 large head broccoli
1 head cauliflower
2 red bell peppers
2 yellow bell peppers
3 carrots

For the dressing:
1/2 cup olive oil
sea salt to taste
2 teaspoons white pepper
1 cup macadamia nuts
1 to 1 1/2 lemons, juiced

DIRECTIONS

Roughly chop the cabbage, onion, broccoli, cauliflower, bell peppers, and carrots and process together in a food processor until mixture is granulated.

Transfer the shredded vegetables to a large bowl. Grind the macadamia nuts in a coffee grinder or a small blender.

Mix the lemon juice, olive oil, sea salt, and white pepper together and combine with the ground macadamia nuts. Slowly pour over veggies while mixing. Add extra salt to taste.

Red-Hot-Pepper-Powerman's Tasmanian Tandoori Cucumber Salad

By Jackie Ayala and David Steinberg

Advanced prep: 5 to 8 days for sprouting; 30 min for soaking

Immediate prep: 20 min

Yields 10 cups   **Special Equipment** Blender

INGREDIENTS

3 medium pickled cucumbers, cut on bias (see Hint)

3 small yellow squash, cut on bias (see Hint)

1 medium red onion, sliced into thin half moons

meat from 2 young Thai coconuts

1 cup romaine lettuce, chopped small

1 cup broccoli, finely diced, including stems

1 cup arugula, chopped

1 bunch celery "hearts," diced

2 cups sunflower greens

1 cup cashews, soaked for 30 minutes

DIRECTIONS

Mix all the ingredients together in a large wood or glass bowl.

Hint: To cut on a "bias" (a fancy diagonal cut), simply cut the cucumbers in half lengthwise, place them cut side down, and cut 2 times lengthwise (horizontally). Chop from the top of the cucumber to the bottom diagonally, and presto!

Simple & Saucy Cucumber-Coconut Salad

BY ELAINA LOVE

ADVANCED PREP: 20 min for marinating **IMMEDIATE PREP:** 15 min

SERVES 4 **SPECIAL EQUIPMENT** None

INGREDIENTS

Meat of 2 young coconuts or 3/4 cup dried, shredded coconut

1 large cucumber, peeled, halved and thinly sliced

1/4 large red onion peeled, halved and thinly sliced

1 nori sheet, torn into small squares or 2 tablespoons dulse flakes or 1 small handful of dulse torn into pieces

1/2 teaspoon garlic powder

3/4 teaspoon Celtic sea salt

2 teaspoons liquefied coconut oil or olive oil

DIRECTIONS

Mix everything together in a bowl and let marinate for at least 20 minutes before serving. This salad will keep in the refrigerator for at least 2 days.

Spinach Hiziki Salad

BY RITA ROMANO

ADVANCED PREP: 6 to 9 hours for marinating; 5 to 8 days for sprouting

IMMEDIATE PREP: 25 min **SERVES** 4 **SPECIAL EQUIPMENT** Food processor

INGREDIENTS

1 pound baby spinach

1/2 cup hiziki, soaked and drained

2 tablespoons chives, minced

1 carrot, shredded

1 or more limes, juiced

2 tablespoons extra virgin olive oil

garlic-flavored Bragg Liquid Aminos, to taste (see Hint)

cumin to taste (about 1/2 teaspoon)

2 tablespoons parsley, chopped

1 clove garlic, pressed

radicchio leaves and sunflower sprouts

DIRECTIONS

Chop the spinach for a few seconds in the food processor using the "S" blade. Combine the spinach, hiziki, chives, carrot, lime juice, olive oil, Bragg Liquid Aminos, cumin, parsley, and 1 clove garlic in a large bowl. Mix well and serve over a bed of radicchio and sprouts.

Hint: To make garlic flavored Bragg Liquid Aminos, marinate one or more garlic cloves in two cups of Bragg overnight or longer. It will keep well in the refrigerator.

Summer Salad

BY ROSE LEE CALABRO

ADVANCED PREP: 5 to 8 days for sprouting   **IMMEDIATE PREP:** 20 min

SERVES 2 to 3   **SPECIAL EQUIPMENT** None

INGREDIENTS

For the salad:
4 cups mixed greens
1 tomato, finely chopped
1/2 cup red cabbage, finely shredded
1/2 cup sunflower sprouts, chopped
1 avocado, diced
1 carrot, shredded
1/4 cup finely chopped red onion
10 sun-dried black olives
1 tablespoon hemp seeds
dash Celtic sea salt

For the dressing:
2 tablespoons cold-pressed extra virgin olive oil
1 tablespoon raw apple cider vinegar

DIRECTIONS

Combine all of the ingredients in a large mixing bowl and toss gently.

Sunflower Salad

BY VERN CURTIS

ADVANCED PREP: None   **IMMEDIATE PREP:** 15 min
SPECIAL EQUIPMENT Blender   **SERVES** 2–3

INGREDIENTS

Salad:
- 3 cobs corn, cut off (or out of season, I bag frozen corn, thawed)
- 1/3 medium red onion, chopped
- 2 large tomatoes (1 pound), chopped
- 5 cups sunflower sprouts

Dressing:
- 2/3 red onion
- 1/2 cup olive oil
- 5 garlic cloves
- 1/2 cup parsley
- 1/2 cup apple cider vinegar
- 5 dried apricots
- 1/4 cup pine nuts
- 1 cup water

DIRECTIONS

Blend salad by hand in bowl

Blend dressing ingredients at high speed

Superfood Tabouli

By KAREN PARKER

ADVANCED PREP: None   **IMMEDIATE PREP:** 20 min
SERVES 2 to 4   **SPECIAL EQUIPMENT** None

INGREDIENTS

- 1 cup seeded and diced cucumbers
- 2 cups finely chopped tomatoes
- 3/4 cup minced parsley
- 1 tablespoon minced fresh mint
- 2 teaspoons minced fresh garlic
- 1/2 cup hemp seeds
- 1/3 cup olive oil
- 1/3 cup lemon juice
- 2 tablespoons Celtic sea salt
- 1/2 cup Jerusalem artichokes, minced
- dash cayenne pepper

DIRECTIONS

Mix all the ingredients together by hand in a large bowl and serve.

Thai Salad

BY SHAZZIE

ADVANCED PREP: 24 hrs for marinating **IMMEDIATE PREP:** 35 min

SERVES 4 **SPECIAL EQUIPMENT** Juicer, Vita-Mix

INGREDIENTS

For the salad:

1/2 cup fresh cilantro, finely chopped

1 tablespoon minced fresh ginger

1 small hot chili, seeded and finely chopped

1 clove garlic, minced

2 tablespoons olive oil

2 tablespoons sesame oil

1 lemon, juiced

1 cup diced red and orange bell peppers

4 green onions, finely chopped

1 cup raw peanuts, roughly chopped

4 cups portobello mushrooms, stalks and gills removed, cubed

For the dressing:

1 stick of lemongrass, juiced

1 inch piece galangal root, juiced

1 lime, juiced

1 cup fresh coconut meat with its water

Chinese cabbage leaves

small handful dried sea lettuce, soaked 2 to 24 hours

DIRECTIONS

Mix the cilantro, ginger, chili, garlic, olive oil, sesame oil and lemon juice in a bowl. Add the diced peppers, green onions, chopped peanuts, and mushrooms to the bowl and mix thoroughly. Cover and let marinate for 24 hours.

Juice the lemongrass, galangal and the lime. Blend this juice with the coconut meat and enough coconut water to make a sauce. It may need to be processed in a food processor first, and then blended in a coffee mill, unless you have a high-powered blender.

Drain the salad and spoon it on Chinese Napa cabbage leaves. Chop the sea lettuce into fine ribbons and spread them over the salad. Pour the dressing over the top. Zest some of the lime and lemon and sprinkle it over the top.

Contributor's note: This is a filling and hearty meal.

Trio of Shaved Cabbages with Sweet Sesame Vinaigrette

BY CHAD SARNO

ADVANCED PREP: 4 days for sprouts **IMMEDIATE PREP:** 25 min

SERVES 6 **SPECIAL EQUIPMENT** None

INGREDIENTS

For the salad:

1 cup Napa cabbage, finely shredded

1 cup green cabbage, finely shredded

1 cup red cabbage, finely shredded

1/2 cup red and yellow bell pepper, cut into thin strips

1 cup Asian bean sprouts

For the dressing:

1/4 cup olive oil

3 tablespoons nama shoyu

3 tablespoons honey or date paste

1 tablespoon minced garlic

1 tablespoon minced ginger

1/2 tablespoon toasted sesame oil (optional)

1/2 tablespoon hot pepper, minced

1/2 teaspoon Celtic sea salt

DIRECTIONS

Separate the 3 cabbages into 3 small bowls. Add an even amount of the bell pepper and Asian bean sprouts to each bowl. Set aside.

In a small bowl whisk together the olive oil, nama shoyu, honey, garlic, ginger, sesame oil, hot pepper and sea salt.

Before serving, toss each bowl with an equal amount of dressing. To serve, place a small mound of each cabbage on the plate, and garnish with seasoned nuts.

Wakamé Escarole Salad

BY RITA ROMANO

ADVANCED PREP: None   **IMMEDIATE PREP:** 25 min

SERVES 4   **SPECIAL EQUIPMENT** Mortar and pestle

INGREDIENTS

1 head escarole, washed and chopped fine

1 small red onion, minced

1/4 cup wakamé, soaked and drained

2 tablespoons flaxseed oil or extra virgin olive oil

1 or more lemons, juiced

2 carrots, shredded

1 teaspoon orange peel zest

1/4 teaspoon fennel seeds, ground with mortar and pestle

Herbamare®, sea salt or Bragg Liquid Aminos to taste

DIRECTIONS

Discard any discolored or tough escarole leaves. Combine all the ingredients in a bowl and mix well. Let the salad sit for a little while before serving. The lemon juice and salt will marinate the escarole, giving it a nice, tangy flavor.

Weird Salad

BY RHIO

ADVANCED PREP: Optimal 5 to 8 days for sprouts   **IMMEDIATE PREP:** 15 min

SERVES 2 to 4   **SPECIAL EQUIPMENT** None

INGREDIENTS

2 cucumbers, cut into thin strips

1 ripe pear, cubed

1 banana, sliced and quartered

1/3 cup thinly sliced fennel

1/2 medium onion, sliced

handful sunflower seeds or sunflower sprouts

1/4 to 1/2 cup raw carob powder (or more) to taste

DIRECTIONS

Combine the cucumber, pear, banana, fennel, onion, and sunflower seeds in a bowl and toss everything together well.

Add the carob powder to taste and mix well before serving.

Wild Rice Salad

By Rose Lee Calabro

Advanced prep: 3 to 5 days for sprouts   **Immediate prep:** 20 min

Serves 2 to 4   **Special Equipment** None

INGREDIENTS

1 1/2 cups wild rice, soaked 3 to 5 days

1/2 cup finely chopped red bell pepper

1/4 cup corn

1 carrot, shredded

2 stalks celery, finely chopped

1/4 red onion, finely chopped

2 tablespoons parsley finely chopped

1 tomato, diced

4 tablespoons cold-pressed olive oil

2 tablespoons lemon juice

1/2 teaspoon Celtic sea salt

DIRECTIONS

Combine all of the ingredients in a mixing bowl and mix well.

Winter Salad

By John Fielder

Advanced prep: None   **Immediate prep:** 20 min

Serves 3   **Special Equipment** None

INGREDIENTS

1 beet

1 3/4-inch piece fresh ginger

1 clove garlic

1 bunch basil

3 sprigs coriander (cilantro)

1 carrot, grated

1 stalk celery, chopped

lettuce leaves

3 tomatoes

3/4 cup pumpkin seeds

DIRECTIONS

Grate the beet and ginger very finely. Chop the garlic, basil, and coriander finely and mix together well. Add grated carrot, chopped celery, tomatoes, and some lettuce leaves. Mix well and sprinkle pepita seeds on top.

Yammy Sea Salad

BY JOHN LARSEN

ADVANCED PREP: 20 min for soaking   **IMMEDIATE PREP:** 20 min

SERVES 6   **SPECIAL EQUIPMENT** Spiral slicer

INGREDIENTS

For the salad:

2 large yams, peeled

2 cups dried hiziki, soaked for 20 minutes in warm water

For the dressing:

1/2 cup extra virgin olive oil

1/4 cup raw apple cider vinegar

7 large cloves garlic, minced

1/4 cup nama shoyu

1 large bunch of basil, stems removed, minced

1/2 teaspoon cayenne pepper

DIRECTIONS

Grate the yams into thin noodles with a Saladacco® or spiralizer.

Chop the hiziki into 1-inch-long strips.

Mix all of the ingredients except vinegar and nama shoyu together in a large bowl. Adjust the quantity of vinegar and nama shoyu to taste.

I Can't Believe It's Not Waldorf Salad

By Shazzie

Advanced prep: None   **Immediate prep:** 35 min

Serves 1   **Special Equipment** Coffee mill or blender

INGREDIENTS

For the dressing:
10 macadamia nuts, halved
1 clove garlic, peeled and finely chopped
1 stalk celery, roughly chopped, divided
2 inches cucumber, chopped
2 teaspoons hemp oil

For the salad:
3 stalks celery, roughly chopped, divided
1 sweet dessert apple, cored and roughly diced
4 inches cucumber, chopped
1/2 cup walnuts

DIRECTIONS

Combine the macadamias, garlic, hemp oil, 1 stalk of chopped celery, and about 2 inches of chopped cucumber in a coffee mill, and blend until smooth. Depending on the power of your blender, you may have to pause for a minute during blending so the dressing doesn't get hot. This dressing turns a beautiful pale green color. It should be a bit thicker than whipping cream. If it's too thin, add more nuts. If it's too thick, add more oil or cucumber. In a large bowl, combine the apple with the remainder of the chopped celery and cucumber. Pour the dressing into the bowl and mix so that all the vegetables are coated. Sprinkle with walnuts and serve.

Contributor's note: This salad is so tasty that it's really a meal on its own. Just right for when you need to sink your teeth into something.

Dressings

Almond Dressing

BY RHONDA MALKMUS
ADVANCED PREP: 6 to 8 hours for soaking   **IMMEDIATE PREP:** 10 min
YIELDS 2 cups   **SPECIAL EQUIPMENT** Blender

INGREDIENTS

2/3 cup distilled water

1/3 cup fresh lemon juice

3/4 cup almonds, soaked overnight and drained

1 garlic clove, peeled (or 1 teaspoon garlic powder)

1/2 teaspoon dried dill weed

2 teaspoons dried parsley flakes

Celtic sea salt to taste (optional)

DIRECTIONS

Blend the water with the lemon juice and almonds. Add the garlic, dill, parsley, and sea salt, if using. Stir to mix well. Cover and chill.

Asian Dressing

BY NOMI SHANNON
ADVANCED PREP: None   **IMMEDIATE PREP:** 15 min
YIELDS 3/4 cup   **SPECIAL EQUIPMENT** Blender

INGREDIENTS

5 tablespoons water, or more, to taste

4 tablespoons tamari, soy sauce or nama shoyu

1/4 cup minced scallions

2 tablespoons raw tahini

2 tablespoons sesame oil

1 tablespoon honey, 2 teaspoons maple syrup, *or* 1 pitted date

1 tablespoon grated ginger

1 clove garlic, pressed

1/4 teaspoon Chinese five-spice powder

1 pinch *each* cayenne and cumin

DIRECTIONS

Stir everything together until well-mixed.

Creamy Cumin Salad Dressing

BY ELAINA LOVE

ADVANCED PREP: 6 to 8 hours for sprouts   **IMMEDIATE PREP:** 15 min

SERVES 6 to 8   **SPECIAL EQUIPMENT** None

INGREDIENTS

- 1 cup soaked sunflower seeds, almonds, or sesame seeds (3/4 cup before soaking)
- 1 1/2 cloves garlic, peeled
- 1/2 cup cilantro leaves
- 1 teaspoon Celtic sea salt
- 3 tablespoons lemon juice (about 1 lemon) or 1 1/2 teaspoons apple cider vinegar
- 1/8 cup flax, hemp or olive oil
- 1/2 teaspoon cumin powder

DIRECTIONS

Thoroughly blend all ingredients with 1 cup water. Serve over a fresh green salad. This dressing may thicken in your refrigerator, so you may need to add more water later. It will keep for up to 2 weeks in the refrigerator.

Creamy Italian Dressing

By John Larsen
Advanced prep: None   **Immediate prep:** 15 min
Yields 4 cups   **Special Equipment** Blender

INGREDIENTS

1/4 cup nama shoyu
1/2 cup olive oil
1/4 cup fresh basil
3/4 cup raw apple cider
1/4 cup fresh oregano
1/2 teaspoon cayenne pepper

4 cloves garlic, chopped
1 tablespoon granulated kelp
2 bell peppers, chopped
2 tablespoons nutritional yeast
1 cup sunflower seeds
1 to 1 1/2 teaspoons dulse flakes

DIRECTIONS

Blend all the ingredients together with 2 cups of water until creamy.

Creamy Mac Ranch Dressing

By Karie Clingo
Advanced prep: None   **Immediate prep:** 10 min
Yields 2 cups   **Special Equipment** Blender

INGREDIENTS

1/2 to 1 full cup raw macadamia nuts
1/3 cup raw apple cider vinegar or
  lemon juice
2/3 cup cold-pressed olive oil

1 teaspoon sea salt
Italian seasoning to taste
1/2 tablespoon sage

DIRECTIONS

Blend the macadamia nuts with 1/4 to 1/2 cup of water (depending on the thickness desired).

Add the apple cider vinegar, olive oil, sea salt, Italian seasoning and sage. Blend thoroughly.

Dragon's Dressing

BY JEREMY SAFRON

ADVANCED PREP: 45 min for soaking   **IMMEDIATE PREP:** 20 min

SERVES 2 to 4   **SPECIAL EQUIPMENT** Blender

INGREDIENTS

1 cup miso

1 cup black tahini

1 Medjool date, soaked and pitted

1/4 cup lemon juice

1/4 cup ginger juice

1/4 cup olive oil or garlic chili flax oil

DIRECTIONS

Blend all the ingredients with 2 cups of water until creamy.

Green Onion Dressing

BY JALISSA LETENDRE

ADVANCED PREP: None   **IMMEDIATE PREP:** 10 min

YIELDS 2 to 3 cups   **SPECIAL EQUIPMENT** Blender

INGREDIENTS

3 green onions

1 cup olive oil

1/3 cup raw apple cider vinegar

1/3 cup honey

1 1/2 teaspoons Herbamare® or sea salt

DIRECTIONS

Place all the ingredients in a blender and mix until creamy.

High Vibe Dressing

BY SHAZZIE

ADVANCED PREP: None   **IMMEDIATE PREP:** 10 min (20 min if juicing)

YIELDS 1 1/2 cups   **SPECIAL EQUIPMENT** Coffee grinder or blender

INGREDIENTS

4 tablespoons unsoaked sunflower seeds, ground to fine powder

1 cup cucumber juice (optional)

4 sprigs mint, finely chopped

minced garlic, onion or herbs (optional)

DIRECTIONS

In a coffee grinder, blend ground sunflower seeds with 1/2 cup water or cucumber juice until smooth. Add more water or cucumber juice to desired thickness (if the coffee grinder is too small, you may have to transfer the mixture to a blender, or mix in the rest of the ingredients by hand).

Add the mint and blend again until smooth. Add minced garlic, onion, or other strong herbs and spices to the dressing if you like. Enjoy as a dip or over a leafy green salad.

Hiziki Salad Dressing

BY RITA ROMANO

ADVANCED PREP: None   **IMMEDIATE PREP:** 10 min

YIELDS 2 cups   **SPECIAL EQUIPMENT** Blender

INGREDIENTS

1 cup macadamia nuts

1 large lime, juiced

2 tablespoons dried hiziki

1 large clove garlic, peeled

1 tablespoon mellow yellow miso

pinch cayenne (optional)

DIRECTIONS

Put all ingredients in blender with 1/2 cup water and whip into a creamy dressing. Serve over greens or vegetables.

Variation: Substitute almonds for the macadamias.

Honey Mustard Dressing with Poppy Seeds

By Elaina Love

Advanced prep: None   **Immediate prep:** 15 min
Yields 1 1/2 cups   **Special Equipment** Blender

INGREDIENTS

- 1/4 cup prepared Dijon mustard
- 1/4 cup honey
- 1 teaspoon Celtic sea salt
- 1/4 cup lemon or lime juice
- 1 tablespoon poppy seeds

DIRECTIONS

Blend all ingredients with 1/3 cup water until well mixed. May be stored in a glass jar in the refrigerator for up to 2 weeks.

Indian Mango Curry Dressing

By Quintessence Restaurant

Advanced prep: None   **Immediate prep:** 15 min
Yields 1 to 2 cups   **Special Equipment** Blender

INGREDIENTS

- 1 medium mango, pitted
- 1 tablespoon yellow curry powder
- 1 tablespoon garam masala
- 1 teaspoon cardamom
- 1 teaspoon sea salt
- 1/4 cup cold-pressed olive oil from a dark bottle

DIRECTIONS

Blend all the ingredients in a high-speed blender until creamy and smooth.

Oil-Free Dressing

BY JACKIE AYALA AND DAVID STEINBERG

ADVANCED PREP: None   **IMMEDIATE PREP:** 20 min
YIELDS 5 to 6 cups   **SPECIAL EQUIPMENT** Blender

INGREDIENTS

1 to 2 cups spring water

1/3 cup black radish

1 whole cucumber, chopped

1 handful Italian parsley

4 tablespoons fresh herbs, such as basil and rosemary, chopped

1/2 cup citrus juice blend (lemon/lime)

1 tablespoon Celtic sea salt

2 large cloves garlic, with skin

1 inch piece of ginger, diced small

1 teaspoon cayenne pepper

3 tablespoons cumin powder

1 tablespoon turmeric

1/3 cup raw honey

10 Italian olives, diced

1 large avocado (ripe and firm), peeled with pit removed

DIRECTIONS

Blend the spring water, radish, cucumber, parsley, fresh herbs, citrus juice, sea salt, garlic, ginger, cayenne, cumin, turmeric, and honey. Add the olives and avocado, and blend a little longer until smooth. The dressing should be ultra green and creamy, like soup. Serve with a large green salad, and enjoy.

Pineapple Anise Dressing

BY QUINTESSENCE RESTAURANT

ADVANCED PREP: None   **IMMEDIATE PREP:** 15 min
YIELDS 2 to 3 cups   **SPECIAL EQUIPMENT** Blender

INGREDIENTS

2 cups chopped fresh pineapple

1 whole pitted peach

1 tablespoon anise seeds

1/4 cup cold-pressed olive oil from a dark bottle

1/2 teaspoon sea salt

DIRECTIONS

In a high-speed blender mix all the ingredients until creamy and smooth.

Premier French Dressing

By Nomi Shannon

Advanced prep: None   **Immediate prep:** 10 min

Serves 1   **Special Equipment** None

INGREDIENTS

- 4 tablespoons flaxseed oil
- 2 tablespoons lemon juice or balsamic vinegar
- 1/2 to 1 teaspoon maple syrup (optional)
- 1 1/2 teaspoons soy sauce, tamari or a pinch of sea salt
- few drops sesame oil (optional)

DIRECTIONS

Whisk all the ingredients together with a fork and immediately pour over a salad.

Contributor's note: This dressing is a great way to enjoy flaxseed oil, which contains important essential fatty acids.

Robert's Hemp Lemon Caesar Dressing

By Robert Yarosh and Lisa Soto

Advanced prep: None   **Immediate prep:** 15 min

Yields 3 to 4 cups   **Special Equipment** Blender

INGREDIENTS

- 1 cup olive oil
- 1 cup lemon, peeled
- 1/2 teaspoon black pepper
- 1/3 cup white onion
- 4 cloves garlic
- 1/2 teaspoon Celtic sea salt
- 1/3 cup ground sesame seeds or hemp seeds
- 1 heaping tablespoon tahini
- 1 heaping tablespoon miso
- 1/4 cup almond pulp (optional)
- 1/4 teaspoon dry oregano
- 10 pitted Kalamata olives and juice

DIRECTIONS

Blend all the ingredients together in a Vita-Mix for a rich and creamy dressing.

Sweet Basil Oil Salad Dressing

BY MATT AMSDEN
ADVANCED PREP: None   IMMEDIATE PREP: 20 min
YIELDS 3 cups   SPECIAL EQUIPMENT Blender

INGREDIENTS

1 cup Thai coconut water

1/2 cup organic, cold-pressed olive oil

1 cup fresh organic basil leaves, stems removed

1 to 2 cloves organic garlic, peeled

1/4 cup fresh, organic lemon juice

1/8 cup nama shoyu

pinch Celtic sea salt

1/4 cup organic dates, pits removed

DIRECTIONS

Combine all ingredients in a blender and mix well. Serve over your favorite mixed greens.

Variation: The basil in this recipe can be substituted by mint, dill, cilantro, or tarragon, for a different flavor.

Tahini Dressing

BY JINJEE AND STORM TALIFERO
ADVANCED PREP: None   IMMEDIATE PREP: 15 min
SERVES 4   SPECIAL EQUIPMENT None

INGREDIENTS

1 jar raw organic sesame tahini (about 2 1/2 cups)

4 lemons or limes, juiced

2 to 3 cloves garlic, pressed

Celtic sea salt to taste

DIRECTIONS

Mix the tahini and lemon juice in a bowl. Add the garlic and sea salt to taste. Transfer the mixture into a jar and spoon the remainder into a bowl.

Mix 2 tablespoons of the mixture with 1 tablespoon of water and you have your salad dressing.

Adjust the amount of water to the desired thickness of dressing.

Variation 1: For a tahini dip, just add less water.

Variation 2: For a tahini "cheese," omit the water. Spread it on celery, optionally with a sprinkle of cayenne.

Wild Live Undressing

By Jackie and Gideon Graff

Advanced prep: 12 to 48 hours for soaking　**Immediate prep:** 30 min

Serves 8　**Special Equipment** Food processor

INGREDIENTS

2 garlic cloves, chopped fine

1 cup Brazil nuts, washed, soaked for 2 hours, and drained

1/4 cup nama shoyu

2 tablespoons fresh rosemary

2 tablespoons fresh sage, chopped fine

sea salt to taste

2 tablespoons unpasteurized miso

2 cups wild rice, washed, soaked for 12 to 48 hours, and drained

1 onion, chopped fine

3 stalks celery, chopped fine

1/2 cup fresh cranberries, for garnish

DIRECTIONS

Place the garlic in the food processor and process well. Add the Brazil nuts and process to a rice-like texture.

Add the nama shoyu, rosemary, sage, sea salt, and miso, and blend well. Transfer the mixture to a bowl and add the wild rice, onions, and celery. Stir well, and garnish with fresh cranberries.

8

Soups

Abeba & Anna's It's Really Soup!

By Abeba Wright and Anna Fisk
Advanced prep: None   **Immediate prep:** 30 min
Serves 8 to 10   **Special Equipment** Blender

INGREDIENTS

10 to 11 fresh Roma tomatoes, chopped
1/2 red or yellow onion, peeled and chopped
4 cloves garlic, peeled
fresh basil to taste
fresh dill to taste
2 tablespoons lemon juice
Celtic salt to taste
2 tablespoons olive oil
1/8 to 1/4 cup raisins
1 to 2 red bell peppers
1/4 jalapeño pepper (optional)
1 cup sun-dried tomatoes, finely chopped (divided)
1 avocado, cubed
1 ear of corn, cut from cob
1/2 sweet yellow pepper
finely chopped parsley, for garnish

DIRECTIONS

In a blender, combine 6 of the tomatoes with the onion, garlic, basil, dill, lemon juice, sea salt, olive oil, raisins, red bell pepper, jalapeño (if using), and 1/2 cup water. Blend well.

Add 1/2 cup of the sun-dried tomatoes, a little at a time. Blend well.

In a large bowl, combine the avocado, remaining fresh and dried tomatoes, corn, and the sweet yellow pepper. Pour the blended mixture over the chopped vegetables, and stir well. Garnish with parsley.

Contributor's note: This recipe was created at a 2002 Raw Chef's Training Retreat conducted by Victoria Boutenko. This soup was a hit—the students were scraping the bowl and begging for the recipe.

African Spicy Sesame Soup

BY SHAZZIE

ADVANCED PREP: None   IMMEDIATE PREP: 15 min

SERVES 4   SPECIAL EQUIPMENT Coffee grinder, blender

INGREDIENTS

1 teaspoon *each* coriander, cumin, and cardamom seeds

1/2 cup sesame seeds

1/2 cup tahini

1 cup finely chopped tomatoes

2 stalks celery, finely chopped

1 large onion, finely chopped

1-inch piece fresh ginger, finely chopped

2 cloves of garlic, peeled and finely chopped

1/2 teaspoon cayenne pepper

1 teaspoon turmeric

1/2 cup sweet corn

1 dessertspoon sesame oil

DIRECTIONS

Grind the coriander, cumin, cardamom and sesame seeds in a coffee grinder.

In a blender, combine the tahini with the ground seeds, tomatoes, celery, onion, ginger, cayenne, and turmeric. Blend this until smooth. Pour into serving dishes, and pile equal amounts of sweet corn in the middle of each dish. Sprinkle on a little more cayenne for decoration.

Contributor's note: This soup is based on traditional African flavors.

Avo Soup

BY STEPHEN ARLIN

ADVANCED PREP: None   IMMEDIATE PREP: 15 min

SERVES 2 to 3   SPECIAL EQUIPMENT Blender

INGREDIENTS

2 large avocados, skins and pits removed

1 medium cucumber, chopped

1 medium tomato, chopped

1 tablespoon fresh cilantro

distilled water

1 cup chopped zucchini

1/2 cup corn

1/4 cup chopped green onion

DIRECTIONS

Combine 1 to 1 1/2 avocados with the cucumber, tomato, and cilantro in a blender. Blend, adding distilled water to reach desired consistency and pour into a bowl.

Chop the remaining 1/2 avocado into small cubes and stir into the soup, along with the zucchini, corn, and onions.

Blended Salad

By Paul Nison

Advanced prep: None   **Immediate prep:** 5 min

Serves 1   **Special Equipment** Blender

INGREDIENTS

1 handful leafy greens (lettuce or spinach are best for this recipe)

1/2 cucumber

1 stalk celery

1/2 lemon, juiced

1 handful sunflower sprouts (optional)

1/2 red pepper (optional)

1 avocado

1 teaspoon flaxseed or olive oil (optional)

1 tomato

DIRECTIONS

Blend all ingredients and serve.

Borscht

By Victoria Boutenko

Advanced prep: None   **Immediate prep:** 20 min

Serves 7 to 10   **Special Equipment** Blender or Vita-Mix

INGREDIENTS

3 beets, peeled

1 small root ginger, sliced

3 to 4 cloves garlic, peeled

6 to 7 bay leaves

2 carrots, chopped

2 stalks celery

2 tablespoons apple cider vinegar

1 tablespoon honey

3 to 4 oranges, peeled, seeds removed

1 cup olive oil

sea salt to taste

1/2 cup walnuts

1/4 head cabbage, diced or grated

1 to 2 carrots, diced or grated

1 bunch parsley, diced or grated

DIRECTIONS

Blend the beets, ginger, garlic, and bay leaves with 2 cups water in a blender or Vita-Mix. Pour the mixture into a big bowl.

Blend the carrots, celery, apple cider vinegar, oranges, honey, olive oil, and sea salt with 2 cups water about 30 seconds. Stop the blender; add the walnuts and blend on low speed very quickly, so they break into small pieces but do not blend. Pour in the same bowl and stir. Add the cabbage, carrots, and parsley to the blended mixture. Stir and serve.

Broccoli Soup

By Jalissa Letendre

Advanced prep: None   **Immediate prep:** 10 min

Serves 4   **Special Equipment** Blender

INGREDIENTS

1 cup raw unsalted cashews

2 cups broccoli

2 tablespoons chopped onions

1/4 cup fresh cilantro

1/4 avocado, skin and pit removed

1 1/2 teaspoons Herbamare® to taste

DIRECTIONS

Blend ingredients with 3 cups of water until creamy.

Butternut Squash Soup

By Eddie D. Robinson
ADVANCED PREP: None   **IMMEDIATE PREP:** 20 min
YIELDS 5 to 6 cups   **SPECIAL EQUIPMENT** Vita-Mix or food processor

INGREDIENTS

1 cup grated zucchini

1 cup grated butternut squash

4 fresh basil leaves

1 teaspoon flaxseed oil

1/4 teaspoon cayenne pepper

1 tablespoon almond butter

1/2 cup grated carrots

2 green onions, chopped

1 tablespoon parsley or cilantro

1 tablespoon Bragg Liquid Aminos

1 cup purified water

1 tablespoon maple syrup (optional)

DIRECTIONS

Blend all the ingredients in a Vita-Mix or food processor until creamy.

Carrot/Orange/Pumpkin Soup

By Sharon Elam
ADVANCED PREP: None   **IMMEDIATE PREP:** 20 min
SERVES 2   **SPECIAL EQUIPMENT** Blender

INGREDIENTS

1 rounded cup organic pumpkin, puréed and fresh

1 1/2 cups organic carrots, puréed

poultry seasoning or powdered vegetable "chicken" broth powder, to taste

1 1/2 teaspoons garlic powder, to taste

1 1/2 teaspoons onion powder, to taste

3/4 to 1 inch fresh ginger, puréed

Celtic salt to taste

Water

DIRECTIONS

Blend all ingredients. Add any other seasoning of your choice to taste.

Serve at room temperature.

Shelly and Ray's Cauliflower Soup

CONTRIBUTED BY JULIE RODWELL
ADVANCED PREP: None **IMMEDIATE PREP:** 10 min
SPECIAL EQUIPMENT Blender **SERVES** 3–4

INGREDIENTS

For the base:
2–3 cups water
1/2 cup nuts
1/2 red pepper
1/2 jalapeno pepper
1/4 to 1/2 cup raisins
1/2 bunch dill
1/3 teaspoon salt

In the base/ cut into bowls:
1/4 avocado
1 cup cauliflower

DIRECTIONS

First blend water and nuts. Then blend in red pepper, jalapeno pepper, avocado, raisins, dill, and salt. Add cauliflower last to thicken. To blended mixture add chopped avocado and cauliflower

Celery Chowder

BY RHONDA MALKMUS
ADVANCED PREP: None   **IMMEDIATE PREP:** 30 min
SERVES 3 to 4   **SPECIAL EQUIPMENT** Blender, Juicer

INGREDIENTS

4 stalks celery, divided
4 green onions, diced, divided
1 small zucchini, diced, divided
1/2 bell pepper, diced, divided
1 clove garlic, minced

1 cup carrot juice
1/2 cup celery juice
1 tablespoon parsley, minced
Celtic sea salt to taste (optional)

DIRECTIONS

Blend half of the celery, onions, zucchini, and pepper with the garlic, carrot juice, and celery juice. Add the remaining vegetables, minced parsley and Celtic sea salt to taste. Mix well and enjoy!

Cold Nectarine Dessert Soup

BY VITA-MIX
ADVANCED PREP: None   **IMMEDIATE PREP:** 10 min
YIELDS 3 1/2 cups   **SPECIAL EQUIPMENT** Vita-Mix

INGREDIENTS

4 nectarines or peaches, pitted
1/2 cup cold white grape juice
1 tablespoon sugar or other sweetener
   to taste

1/2 lemon, juiced
1/8 teaspoon cinnamon
mint leaves, for garnish

DIRECTIONS

Place all the ingredients in your Vita-Mix in the order listed. Select VARIABLE, speed #1. Turn on the machine and quickly increase the speed to #10; then to HIGH. Run for 1 minute or until smooth. Garnish with mint leaves and serve immediately.

Corn Bell Pepper Soup

BY **MARY RYDMAN**

ADVANCED PREP: 6 hours to soak nuts   **IMMEDIATE PREP:** 15 min

SPECIAL EQUIPMENT Blender   **SERVES** 2–4

INGREDIENTS

2 ears corn, cut off cob

2 large red or yellow bell peppers, chopped in big chunks

1/2 cup almonds, soaked

2 teaspoons miso

1/2 clove garlic

young coconut milk or water to blend

DIRECTIONS

Blend all ingredients, adding water to desired thickness.

Contributor's note: Sweet, Simple and Tasty!

Creamy Bell Pepper Soup

BY **QUINTESSENCE RESTAURANT**

ADVANCED PREP: None   **IMMEDIATE PREP:** 20 min

YIELDS 8 cups   **SPECIAL EQUIPMENT** Vita-Mix

INGREDIENTS

2 medium sized red or yellow bell peppers, stems removed, chopped

2 medium cucumbers, chopped

1/2 medium red onion, chopped

1/4 cup cold-pressed olive oil from a dark bottle

1 teaspoon sea salt

1 teaspoon caraway seeds

2 medium cloves garlic

3 cups filtered water

DIRECTIONS

Combine all the ingredients in a high-speed blender and blend until creamy and smooth.

Cream of Shiitake Soup

BY SHAZZIE

ADVANCED PREP: None if almond milk is on hand, otherwise 1/2 day

IMMEDIATE PREP: 15 min if served cold; 1 1/2 hr if served warm using dehydrator

SERVES 2   **SPECIAL EQUIPMENT** Blender, dehydrator for warming

INGREDIENTS

1 cup fresh shiitake mushrooms, hard stems removed

1 tablespoon raw almond butter

2 cups Almond Milk (page 182, 184)

1/2 red onion, finely chopped

1/2 cup parsley

1 cup celery, finely chopped

1/2 cup spinach, tightly packed and finely chopped

1 teaspoon sesame oil

dash sea salt

dried mushrooms, for garnish

DIRECTIONS

Combine the mushrooms, almond butter, and almond milk in a blender; blend well. Add the onion and the parsley; stir well. Pour the soup into serving bowls.

Mix the celery and spinach with the sesame oil (and a little sea salt if you like). Place a small pile of this mixture in the middle of the soup, and sprinkle some dried mushrooms on top. If you are serving this warm, add the spinach and celery after heating. Chinese leaves make a great "bread" for this soup.

Delhi Express Soup (five star)

BY MAYA ADJANI

ADVANCED PREP: None   **IMMEDIATE PREP:** 20 min

SPECIAL EQUIPMENT Champion juicer, blender   **SERVES** 4

INGREDIENTS:

For the base:

5 carrots

4 stalks celery

2" slice of beet

1 apple

2 avocados, peeled and de-pitted

1 red bell pepper, seeded and chopped

2+ teaspoons curry powder

1 clove fresh garlic, pressed

1 teaspoon salt or to taste

For serving:

1 avocado, peeled, pitted and cubed

2 tomatoes, cubed

1/2 cucumber, cubed
   Cilantro and finely chopped onion for garnish

DIRECTIONS

Juice the carrots, celery, beet and apple. Pour juice into blender and add the other base ingredients. Blend until smooth. Chop the serving ingredients into four bowls. Pour soup from blender into bowls and garnish with cilantro and finely chopped onion.

Rose and Neal's "Dilliflower" Soup

CONTRIBUTED BY JULIE RODWELL

ADVANCED PREP: None **IMMEDIATE PREP:** 20 min

SPECIAL EQUIPMENT Blender **SERVES** 4

INGREDIENTS

For the base:

1/3 cup each walnuts, pine nuts and almonds

2 cloves of garlic

1 chili pepper

1/2 red bell pepper

1/2 cup cauliflower

1/2 cup grape seed oil

2 small (Roma) tomatoes

1 teaspoon salt

small bunch of dill

1/4 onion

1/2 avocado

1 tsp coriander seed

3 cups water

juice of 1 lemon

In the base/ cut into bowls:

2 tomatoes, cut in 1/4" chunks

1/2 cup cauliflower cut in bite size pieces

1/2 cup bell pepper cut in bite size pieces

For the garnish:

Dill weed

Grated lemon rind

DIRECTIONS

Mix all base ingredients in blender. Pour into bowl and add small chunks of tomato, cauliflower, bell pepper, dehydrated mushrooms, dill. Garnish with grated lemon rind.

Fresh Corner Gazpacho

By Karyn Calabrese

Advanced prep: None   **Immediate prep:** 30 min

Serves 8   **Special Equipment** Blender

INGREDIENTS

- 5 tomatoes, diced
- 1 small red bell pepper, cored, seeded and diced
- 1 small yellow bell pepper, cored, seeded and diced
- 1/4 large zucchini, diced
- 1/2 large cucumber, quartered lengthwise and thinly sliced
- 1/4 onion, diced

- 1 tablespoon chopped garlic
- 1/2 cup olive oil
- 1/4 teaspoon or less cayenne pepper, to taste
- 1/4 bunch parsley, washed, dried and coarsely chopped
- 3 tablespoons balsamic vinegar
- 2 tablespoons Spike

DIRECTIONS

In a large bowl, combine the tomatoes, red and yellow peppers, zucchini, cucumber, onion and garlic. Mix well.

In a small bowl, combine the olive oil, cayenne, parsley, balsamic vinegar and Spike. Whisk together and pour over the vegetables.

Ladle 1 1/2 cups of this mixture into your blender and blend on high until Gazpacho has liquefied. Pour into bowl and stir together. Refrigerate until ready to serve.

Full Monty Raw Soup

BY **MAYA ADJANI**

ADVANCED PREP: None   **IMMEDIATE PREP:** 30 min

SPECIAL EQUIPMENT Champion juicer, blender   **SERVES** 4

INGREDIENTS

For the base:
5 carrots
5 celery sticks
2" ginger root
2" slice beet (approx 1/2 med beet)
1 celery root
1 avocado, peeled and pitted
1 red bell pepper, cored and seeded
1 clove garlic, pressed
1 + teaspoon salt, to taste
1/2 teaspoon ground pepper

For serving:
2 tomatoes
1 avocado
1 yellow pepper
1/2 cucumber
parsley for garnish

DIRECTIONS

Juice the carrots, celery, ginger root, beet and celery root. Use the pulp in another recipe or add it to your compost pile.

Pour juice in blender and blend in the avocado, red bell pepper and seasonings. Chop the tomatoes, the second avocado, yellow bell pepper and cucumber into 4 bowls.

Pour blender contents into bowls and garnish with fresh parsley. Enjoy!

Gazpacho

By VICTORIA BOUTENKO
ADVANCED PREP: None   IMMEDIATE PREP: 20 min
SERVES 4 to 5   SPECIAL EQUIPMENT Blender

INGREDIENTS

1/4 cup extra virgin olive oil

5 large ripe tomatoes, chopped

2 cloves garlic or spicy pepper to taste

1 tablespoon raw honey (dates or raisins work just as well)

1/4 cup lemon juice

1/2 teaspoon sea salt

1 bunch fresh basil

1 large avocado, cut into 1/4-inch cubes

1 medium bell pepper, cut into 1/4-inch cubes

5 stalks celery, cut into 1/4-inch cubes

1 small onion, cut into 1/4-inch cubes

chopped parsley

DIRECTIONS

Blend the olive oil, tomatoes, garlic, honey, lemon juice, sea salt and basil with 1/2 cup of water until smooth.

Pour the soup into a large bowl, and add the chopped avocado, bell pepper, celery and onion.

Mix all the ingredients together and sprinkle with chopped parsley.

Mango Soup

By SHANNON ISLEY SCHNIBBE
ADVANCED PREP: None   IMMEDIATE PREP: 30 min
SERVES 6 to 8   SPECIAL EQUIPMENT Blender, Juicer

INGREDIENTS

3 large organic tomatoes, chopped

2 organic avocados, pits removed

2 organic mangoes, sliced, pits removed

1-inch piece fresh ginger root

1 tablespoon fresh thyme leaves, loosely packed, plus extra for garnish

20 organic carrots, juiced

DIRECTIONS

Blend the tomatoes, avocados, mangoes, ginger, and thyme with enough carrot juice to cover. Slowly add the rest of carrot juice while blending. Serve with a few thyme leaves on top.

Mushroom Soup or Gravy

BY NOMI SHANNON

ADVANCED PREP: None   **IMMEDIATE PREP:** 15 min

YIELDS 1 cup   **SPECIAL EQUIPMENT** Blender

INGREDIENTS

1/4 cup almond butter

1/2 cup water

2 cups quartered mushrooms

1 tablespoon minced onion or shallot (optional)

2 teaspoons nama shoyu or 1/2 teaspoon Celtic sea salt

4 tablespoons finely chopped mushrooms (for soup only)

DIRECTIONS

Blend the almond butter and 1/2 cup water. Gradually add the quartered mushrooms, onion, and nama shoyu, and blend until smooth. For soup, top with finely chopped mushrooms.

Contributor's note: This mixture is very rich, so keep the portions small for soup. It is also a delicious topping for Sun Garden Burgers (page 275).

Raspberry Cream Soup

BY ELYSA MARKOWITZ

ADVANCED PREP: None   **IMMEDIATE PREP:** 10 min

SERVES 2   **SPECIAL EQUIPMENT** Green Power / Star Machine, blender

INGREDIENTS

3 cups orange juice (from about 8 to 12 oranges)

1 1/2 cups raw cashews

1 box raspberries

1 orange, sliced

DIRECTIONS

In a blender, make the stock by blending the orange juice with the cashews, adding half the box of raspberries last.

Float the remaining raspberries and orange slices in the broth.

Serve in a fancy bowl, garnished with orange slices.

Hint: If you want a thicker broth, start out blending with only 2 cups of juice and add the last cup of juice slowly until the desired consistency is achieved.

Contributor's note: This soup is great on a warm day, or as a dip for parties. Another fun idea is to serve it as a fondue with the soup in the middle and the fruit arranged on a platter around it.

Graham and Doris' Rawsome Tomato Soup

CONTRIBUTED BY JULIE RODWELL

ADVANCED PREP: None   **IMMEDIATE PREP:** 15 min

SPECIAL EQUIPMENT Blender   **SERVES** 3–4

INGREDIENTS

For the base:

5 small tomatoes (approx. 1.5 cups)

1/4 cup cucumber

1/4 cup sundried tomato

1 tablespoon fresh basil

1/2 cup tahini

4 cloves garlic

1 hot pepper (cayenne)

1/2 bell pepper (use rest for garnish)

juice of 1/2 lemon

1/4 cup celery

1/8 cup fresh onion

1/8 cup dried onion

1 teaspoon salt

Approx. 1 cup water

For the garnish (choose some or all):

parsley

tomatoes

bell peppers

dried onion

purple onion

garlic

flowers

DIRECTIONS

Blend all soup base ingredients, divide into individual bowls and add garnish.

Raw Thai Lemon Coconut Soup

By Jinjee and Storm Talifero

Advanced prep: None   **Immediate prep:** 30 min

Serves 4   **Special Equipment** Juicer, citrus juicer

INGREDIENTS

1 to 2 large squash, juiced

milk of 1 coconut

1 to 4 lemons, juiced, to taste

5 mushrooms, chopped

2 carrots, sliced

DIRECTIONS

Mix all the ingredients together in a large bowl, and heat on a low flame until warm, if desired.

Seaweed Chowder

By Matt Amsden

Advanced prep: 60 min   **Immediate prep:** 15 min

Serves 2 to 3   **Special Equipment** Blender, citrus juicer

INGREDIENTS

2 ounces dried wakamé seaweed

3 cups filtered, distilled or spring water

1 cup raw, organic pine nuts

2 to 3 cloves organic garlic, peeled

1/4 cup fresh, organic lemon juice

1/2 teaspoon Celtic sea salt

DIRECTIONS

In a medium bowl, soak the seaweed in the water for 15 to 60 minutes.

Drain the seaweed and transfer to a bowl.

In a blender, combine the water, pine nuts, garlic, lemon juice and sea salt. Blend thoroughly. Pour into a bowl and serve with pieces of the soaked seaweed.

Aletha and Bonnie's Spicy Rainbow Garlic Soup

CONTRIBUTED BY JULIE RODWELL

ADVANCED PREP: None   **IMMEDIATE PREP:** 15 min

SPECIAL EQUIPMENT Blender   **SERVES** 4

INGREDIENTS

For the base:
1/2 to 3/4 cup pine nuts
2 tablespoons or more olive oil
juice of 1/2 lemon
6–8 small tomatoes (cherry or other)
6–8 cloves garlic
salt
2 dried cayenne peppers

In the base/ cut into bowls:
Avocado, cucumber, red and yellow bell pepper (cut into small chunks) (reserve a little for garnish)

DIRECTIONS

Mix all base ingredients in blender. When blended, stir in or cut into bowls small chunks of avocado, cucumber, red and yellow bell pepper. Decorate top(s) with same!

Squash and Kumquat Soup

By Shazzie

Serves 2   **Special Equipment** Juicer, blender

Advanced prep: None if almond milk is on hand; otherwise 1/2 day to 12 hr

Immediate prep: 30 min

INGREDIENTS

1/2 acorn squash (or whatever squash you can find)

6 kumquats

1 carrot

1 yellow or orange bell pepper

1 teaspoon freshly peeled lemon rind

1 small hot chili

1 tablespoon fresh coconut meat

1 clove garlic

5 dried apricots, soaked 2 to 12 hours

1 sun-dried tomato

1 cup sunflower or Almond Milk
   (page 205, 206)

DIRECTIONS

If you don't have a juicer, chop the squash, kumquats, carrot, bell pepper, lemon rind, chili, coconut meat, garlic, apricots, and sun-dried tomatoes, and place the chopped vegetables in a blender. Blend to a liquid with 1 cup sunflower or almond milk, then strain. If you want a thicker soup, add in some of the pulp.

If you own a juicer, juice the kumquats, bell pepper, coconut meat, and apricots, then add all the ingredients to the blender and blend to a liquid.

Serve this soup with a little grated squash, some sunflower seeds and some chopped green onions on top.

Sweet China Soup

BY ROSE LEE CALABRO

ADVANCED PREP: One week for sunflower sprouts **IMMEDIATE PREP:** 30 min

SERVES 2 to 4 **SPECIAL EQUIPMENT** Blender

INGREDIENTS

2 large carrots, tops removed, chopped

2 stalks celery, chopped

2 Fuji apples, cored and chopped

1/2 avocado, peeled and pitted

1/2 small beet, peeled and chopped

2 tablespoons lemon juice

2 tablespoons unpasteurized raw miso

1/2 teaspoon Chinese five-spice

1/4 teaspoon Celtic sea salt

1 cup sunflower sprouts

2 cups water

DIRECTIONS

In a blender, combine all the ingredients and blend until smooth.

Sweet Potato Soup

BY ROBERT YAROSH AND LISA SOTO

ADVANCED PREP: Overnight

IMMEDIATE PREP: 10 min or 1–1 1/2 hr if warmed in dehydrator

SERVES 2 **SPECIAL EQUIPMENT** None

INGREDIENTS

1 sweet potato (shredded and soaked overnight)

1/4 red onion, chopped

1/2 small clove of garlic

1 apple, chopped

1/2 teaspoon Chinese five-spice

1/2 teaspoon cinnamon

1/2 teaspoon Celtic sea salt

DIRECTIONS

Blend all the ingredients with 1 cup of water until smooth. Serve warm if desired.

Thai Coconut Curry Soup

By Elaina Love

Advanced prep: None   **Immediate prep:** 30 min
Yields 8 cups   **Special Equipment** Blender

INGREDIENTS

- 5 shitake mushrooms, thinly sliced
- 1 1/2 limes, juiced
- pinch sea salt
- 3 young Thai coconuts (save water from 1)
- 1 1/2 teaspoons grated or zested fresh ginger
- juice of 1 lime (about 2 tablespoons)
- 1/2 cup olive oil
- 3 dates, pitted
- 1 teaspoon Celtic sea salt
- 1 tablespoon tamari
- 2 cloves garlic, peeled
- 1 teaspoon curry powder
- 1 teaspoon Thai chili
- 3 scallions, thinly sliced

DIRECTIONS

Marinate the mushrooms in the juice of 1/2 a lime and a pinch of salt.

Blend the meat from all the coconuts with the water from 1 coconut until smooth (this may take a couple of minutes if the coconuts are cold). Add the ginger, juice of 1 lime, olive oil, dates, sea salt, tamari, garlic, curry powder, and Thai chili, and blend until smooth.

Stir in the marinated mushrooms and scallions.

Carefully warm this soup on the stove if desired or serve as is. This soup will keep in the refrigerator for up to 5 days.

Thai Soup

By Rhio

Advanced prep: None   **Immediate prep:** 30 min
Serves 4   **Special Equipment** Blender

INGREDIENTS

water from 3 young Thai coconuts

2 large tomatoes, chopped

1 1/2 large avocados

1 tablespoon chopped fresh ginger

3 to 4 cloves garlic, pressed

1/2 to 1 red jalapeño pepper, chopped

large handful mixed fresh herbs: rosemary, oregano, basil and tarragon (tarragon
   gives it a special flavor)

1 tablespoon nama shoyu or 1 teaspoon Celtic sea salt

1 red bell pepper, diced

1/2 red onion, diced

1/2 bunch cilantro, finely chopped

handful parsley, finely chopped

extra-virgin olive oil to taste

DIRECTIONS

To make the soup base, pour 1 cup coconut water into the blender. Add the
tomatoes, 1/2 avocado, ginger, garlic, jalapeño, mixed herbs, and nama shoyu
or Celtic sea salt. Mix until the herbs are well blended. Add the remainder of the
coconut water and blend again.

Pour the soup base into individual bowls and add the chopped red bell pepper,
onion, cilantro, parsley, and the remainder of the cubed avocado. Drizzle with
olive oil and serve immediately or on the same day.

Tomato Wild Rice Soup

By Chad Sarno

Advanced prep: 3 to 5 days to sprout wild rice & soak tomatoes

Immediate prep: 30 min   **Serves** 4   **Special Equipment** Vita-Mix

INGREDIENTS

1 1/2 cups diced portobello mushrooms

2 tablespoons nama shoyu

1/2 cup sun-dried tomato, soaked overnight (reserve the water)

1 tablespoon garlic, minced

3 cups chopped fresh tomato

1/2 cup chopped parsley

1/3 cup chopped basil

1 zucchini, chopped

2 tablespoons minced oregano

1/2 apple, cored

1/2 tablespoon Celtic sea salt

1/4 teaspoon cayenne or minced hot pepper

dash white pepper

2 cups wild rice, sprouted

DIRECTIONS

Marinate the mushrooms in the nama shoyu for 10 to 15 minutes.

In a Vita-Mix, blend the sun-dried tomatoes and 1 cup of their soaking water with the garlic until smooth. Add the fresh tomatoes, parsley, basil, zucchini, oregano, apple, sea salt, cayenne, white pepper, and 2 additional cups of water (use the soak water if you have any left).

Blend on low until the mixture is slightly chunky. Add the rice and blend on low for another 10 to 20 seconds. Serve warm topped with marinated mushrooms and Rosemary Croutons, if available (page 196).

Editors Note: Some brands of sundried tomatoes are extremely salty, in which case, discard the soak water and use fresh filtered water instead, and/or adjust the salt in your recipe.

Udon Noodle Soup with Green Onion

By Chad Sarno

Advanced prep: None   **Immediate prep:** One hour

Serves 4   **Special Equipment** Blender, mesh strainer or milk bag

INGREDIENTS

    3 cups coconut water

    1/2 tablespoon nama shoyu

    1 teaspoon Celtic sea salt

    1 teaspoon toasted or raw sesame oil

    1/2 tablespoon garlic

    1 tablespoon fresh ginger, chopped

    1 tablespoon lemon grass, chopped

    5 kefir lime leaves

    1/2 cup coconut meat, cut into thin strips

    1/3 cup snow peas, cut into thin strips

    1/4 cup red bell pepper confiture

    3 tablespoon green onion, diced small, plus extra for garnish

DIRECTIONS

In high-speed blender, blend the coconut water, nama shoyu, sea salt, sesame oil, garlic, ginger, lemon grass, and lime leaves until liquefied.

Pour the mixture through a fine mesh strainer in an even stream, collecting it in a bowl. Add the coconut meat, snow peas, red bell pepper, and onion to the soup.

Serve warm. Garnish with diced green onion.

Vern's Gazpacho

ADVANCED PREP: None   **IMMEDIATE PREP:** 20 min
YIELDS 5-6 servings

INGREDIENTS

For the soup liquid:
2 pounds tomatoes, chopped
5–6 cloves garlic
1/8 to 1/4 lemon, including peel
1/2 teaspoon salt, preferably Celtic sea salt
2 tablespoons olive oil
1/2 cup sunflower seeds

For the whole chunks:
1 bag frozen corn, thawed (preferably organic baby corn)
3 avocados, pitted and chopped into 1/2 inch cubes

DIRECTIONS

Blend all but the sunflower seeds in a high speed blender or food processor. If the latter, start with solid ingredients and add liquids (and tomatoes) only slowly to avoid mixture whirling out. Add the sunflower seeds last and spin some more till smooth.

Add the whole chunks, chill and serve. Note: if the corn is not quite thawed, pour the soup over it and that will thaw it out and chill the soup while you chop the avocados.

Vitality Soup

BY CHERIE SORIA

ADVANCED PREP: None   **IMMEDIATE PREP:** 10 min

SERVES 2   **SPECIAL EQUIPMENT** Blender

INGREDIENTS

1 cup non-chlorinated water

1/2 cup fresh orange juice

1/4 cup lemon juice

6 ounces greens (such as spinach, sunflower or kale)

1 medium apple, quartered and cored

1/2 to 1 full medium avocado, quartered, peeled and pitted

1 cucumber, chopped

1 garlic clove, crushed

1 green onion, chopped

1/4 habanero chili (optional)

1/8 to 1/4 teaspoon ground kelp or dulse

1 tablespoon unpasteurized light miso

sea salt to taste

DIRECTIONS

Combine all the ingredients in a blender and purée until smooth. Adjust flavors to taste and serve at room temperature.

Watercress Pear Soup

BY QUINTESSENCE RESTAURANT

ADVANCED PREP: 2 hrs to soak pecans   **IMMEDIATE PREP:** 10 min

YIELDS 4 to 6 cups   **SPECIAL EQUIPMENT** Blender

INGREDIENTS

2 pears

1/2 cup soaked pecans

1 tablespoon allspice

2 tablespoons pumpkin seed oil

1/2 bunch watercress

sea salt to taste

1/4 cup olive oil

1 cup filtered water, or more if desired

DIRECTIONS

Blend all the ingredients together in a high-speed blender. Add 1 cup water and blend until smooth and creamy. Continue slowly adding water and blending until desired consistency is achieved.

9

Snacks & Sides

Ants in a Canoe

By Stephen Arlin
Advanced prep: 12 hours   **Immediate prep:** 30 min
Serves 2   **Special Equipment** Juicer

INGREDIENTS

    2 large apples
    2 cups almonds, soaked for 12 hours
    2 ounces raisins (with seeds)

DIRECTIONS

Grind the almonds through a Champion or Green Power / Star Juicer, using the blank plate. This will make almond butter.

Cut the apples into quarters; remove and discard the seeds and core.

Spread the almond butter on the apples, and then cover them with raisins.

Contributor's note: This is a great snack when you're on the go.

Ants on a Log

By Karie Clingo
Advanced prep: None if using commercial almond butter, or see previous recipe
Immediate prep: 5–20 min depending on age of child   **Special Equipment** None

INGREDIENTS

    celery
    raw almond butter
    raisins

DIRECTIONS

Cut celery into "logs." Spread raw almond butter into the celery logs. Let a child put the "ants," or raisins, onto the log and enjoy!

Chili Pistachios

BY CHAD SARNO
ADVANCED PREP: 12 hours + 14 hrs   IMMEDIATE PREP: 15 min
YIELDS 2 cups   SPECIAL EQUIPMENT Dehydrator

INGREDIENTS

2 cups pistachios, soaked 10 to 12 hours
2 tablespoons chili powder
1 1/2 tablespoons onion powder
1 tablespoon cumin
1 tablespoon Celtic sea salt

DIRECTIONS

In a mixing bowl, toss the nuts together with the spices. Spread the nuts on a dehydrator sheet and dehydrate at 110°F for 12 to 14 hours or until crisp. Serve with Fajita Vegetables (see recipe page 237).

Chunkey Monkey

BY JULIAN HUERTA
ADVANCED PREP: None   IMMEDIATE PREP: 15 min
SPECIAL EQUIPMENT None   YIELDS 1 large serving

INGREDIENTS

1/2 cup zucchini (chopped into chunks)
1/2 cup cucumber (chopped into chunks)
1/2 cup avocado (chopped into chunks)
1/4 cup cold pressed olive oil
1/8 teaspoon sea salt (more or less to your taste)
1/4 teaspoon paprika
1/8 teaspoon tarragon

DIRECTIONS

Mix all above. Let the avocado get a little bruised when mixing; it adds to the overall dish.

Now, even though this is chunky, and you may feel like a monkey afterwards, if you really want to take it over the edge . . . shape it into a monkey head!

For monkey face (optional):

Mouth: Cut off 1 inch of the end of the cucumber and zucchini. Then cut it so that you have 2 wedges. **Eyes:** circles from the cucumber, zucchini and add 2 tablespoons chopped olives. Mix everything together.

Layered Portobello with thick Pine Nut and Sesame Cream

BY JULIAN HUERTA

ADVANCED PREP: None   IMMEDIATE PREP: 1 hour

SPECIAL EQUIPMENT Blender   SERVES 2

INGREDIENTS

2 large portobello mushrooms

15 Kalamata olives finely diced (e.g. cut into thin rings, then quarter)

Reserve 1 teaspoon for garnish.

2 1/2 tablespoon green onion (thin green rings)

Reserve 1 teaspoon for garnish

Portobello Marinade

3 tablespoons olive oil

1 tablespoon Kalamata olive juice

dash sea salt

1/4 teaspoon black pepper

1/2 teaspoon dried basil

Thick Cream

1/2 cup pine nuts

1/4 cup sesame

1/8 cup spring water

1 teaspoon lemon juice

2 tablespoons olive oil

few dashes sea salt

1 teaspoon minced garlic

1/4 teaspoon black pepper

DIRECTIONS

Take portobello mushrooms, and thinly slice them across their top. When you get to the gills, stop. Save them for another recipe. Be careful not to break the slices. You want to end up with several wide pieces as they will become the layers, like a lasagna, with the cream in between. Next, Mix the marinade together, and then pour over the portobello slices. Make sure that all of the portobello surface areas have touched the marinade. Set aside.

Thick Cream: Blend ingredients on a medium-low setting. Let it be a little chunky. It will add some texture to the food. Next, one slice of the portobello and lay it in the middle of a plate. Spoon about 1 1/4 tablespoon of cream on top. Add 3/4 teaspoon of the finely diced kalamata olives evenly on top, followed by 1/2 teaspoon green onion rings. Put a slice of a portobello on a new plate, and repeat. Go back to the first plate, and add another portobello slice, followed by 1 1/2 tablespoon cream, 3/4 teaspoon Kalamata olives, 1/2 teaspoon green onion rings. Repeat process until all is used up. Probably will result in about 3 layers. I recommend the last layer being finished with a portobello with no cream on top.

Garnish: 1/4 teaspoon green onion on top of each. Sprinkle around each plate 1/4 tsp green onion, and 1/2 teaspoon finely diced Kalamata olives

Serving Suggestion: Bowl of baby spinach greens, lightly tossed in olive oil and a few dashes of sea salt or Kalamata olive juice. Keep the flavors light as the main dish is so rich.

Mustard-Ginger Pumpkin Seed Crunchies

By Elaina Love

Advanced prep: 1 to 2 days for sprouting + 24–36 hours for dehydrating

Immediate prep: 30 min   **Serves** 12 to 14   **Special Equipment** Dehydrator

INGREDIENTS

- 1 pound or 5 cups dry pumpkin seeds, sprouted
- 1/4 cup tamari, Bragg Liquid Aminos®, or 2 to 4 teaspoons Celtic sea salt
- 1/4 cup honey, maple syrup or Rapadura®
- 1 1/2 tablespoons apple cider vinegar
- 1/2 teaspoon ginger powder or 1 tablespoon zested ginger root
- 1 teaspoon mustard powder or 1 tablespoon Dijon mustard
- 1 teaspoon garlic powder or 1 clove crushed garlic (optional)
- 1/2 teaspoon curry powder
- 1 tablespoon dried herbs (such as basil, dill, tarragon, or Italian seasoning)

DIRECTIONS

Mix everything together in a bowl.

Spread on a dehydrator tray lined with a Teflex sheet.

Dehydrate for 4 to 6 hours at 105°F.

Flip and remove the Teflex sheet.

Continue to dehydrate until crunchy (12 to 24 hours). Store in a glass jar on your counter or in the refrigerator.

Naked Nuts

BY SHANNON ISLEY SCHNIBBE

ADVANCED PREP: 8–12 hours for soaking, 12–24 hours for dehydrating
IMMEDIATE PREP: under 5 min   **SPECIAL EQUIPMENT** None

INGREDIENTS

Almonds or cashews

DIRECTIONS

Soak nuts overnight; drain and rinse. Dehydrate 12 to 24 hours or until crunchy.

Contributor's notes: Soaking and dehydrating give these nuts an amazing crunch. They are very satisfying by themselves, especially the almonds. You can also try them in salads, wraps and other creations.

Olive Buckwheat Snacks

BY SHANNON ISLEY SCHNIBBE

ADVANCED PREP: 2 to 3 days for sprouting + 12 hours for dehydrating
IMMEDIATE PREP: 30 min   **YIELDS** 24 crackers   **SPECIAL EQUIPMENT** Cuisinart, spice or coffee grinder, dehydrator

INGREDIENTS

3 medium carrots

4 cloves garlic

1/4 cup olive oil

1 medium onion, chopped

1 medium tomato, chopped

1/3 cup loosely packed chopped thyme

1 cup loosely packed chopped parsley

1 tablespoon Celtic sea salt

2 cups buckwheat groats, soaked 10 hours and sprouted 1 to 2 days

2 cups flax seeds

10 olives, pitted and chopped

DIRECTIONS

Process the carrots in a Cuisinart fitted with the shredding blade. Change to the "S" blade and process the carrots with garlic, olive oil, onion, tomato, thyme, parsley, and sea salt.

Add the buckwheat and process again.

Grind the flaxseed in a spice or coffee grinder. Add to the buckwheat mixture and process, slowly adding 1 cup water.

Transfer mixture to a bowl and mix in the olives by hand. Spread the mixture onto 2 dehydrator trays. Dehydrate at 105°F for 12 hours, or to desired consistency. Enjoy with an avocado, raw pesto, or raw marinara sauce.

Contributor's note: This is a great raw alternative to olive bread.

Portobello Mushroom— Marinated and Stuffed

BY SHARON ELAM

ADVANCED PREP: 3 to 5 hours   **IMMEDIATE PREP:** 15 min

SERVES Serves 12   **SPECIAL EQUIPMENT** None

INGREDIENTS

24 portobello mushrooms, washed and stemmed

For the marinade:
1 pint olive oil
1 small onion
2 to 4 cloves garlic
1 to 2 tablespoons lemon juice
2 tablespoons chopped dill
1/2 teaspoon fresh ground pepper
1 teaspoon mustard seed
1 1/2 teaspoon Celtic salt

For the stuffing:
seed spread or nut cheese (see p.)
sliced tomatoes
lettuce
sprouts
onion

DIRECTIONS

Wash and stem the portobello mushrooms, then place them, topside down, in a marinating dish. Pierce the mushroom top and bottom to allow the marinade to properly soak in.

Blend marinade ingredients together, then pour over the mushrooms and in the stem indentation area. Let stand for several hours for best absorption.

When serving the mushrooms, spread your favorite seed spread or nut cheese in the mushroom. Serve with sliced organic tomatoes, lettuce leaf, sprouts, red onion slices, and whatever else may sound delicious to you.

Spicy Almonds

BY VERN CURTIS
ADVANCED PREP: 12 hours to soak almonds + 2 days for dehydrating
IMMEDIATE PREP: 30 min
SERVES 10 to 12   **SPECIAL EQUIPMENT** Dehydrator

INGREDIENTS

2 tablespoons tamari
2 to 3 tablespoons cayenne pepper
2 tablespoons sea salt
garlic powder and/or pressed fresh garlic to taste
apple juice to taste
1 pound raw organic almonds, soaked overnight and drained
psyllium powder as needed (optional)

DIRECTIONS

Mix the tamari, cayenne, and sea salt with the garlic and apple juice in a large bowl.

Add the almonds, toss to coat well. A little psyllium powder can be added to help the marinade adhere.

Spread the almonds onto dehydrator trays lined with Teflex sheets. Dehydrate at 105°F until crunchy (24 to 36 hours).

Contributor's note: Use your imagination and try different seasonings.

Spicy Party Mix

BY RHIO

ADVANCED PREP: 1 day for sprouting + 2 days for dehydrating

IMMEDIATE PREP: 30 min   **YIELDS** 2 cups   **SPECIAL EQUIPMENT** Dehydrator

INGREDIENTS

2 1/2 cups sunflower seeds, sprouted 1 day

1 cup red lentils, sprouted 1 day

1 medium to large onion, diced small

1 tablespoon dried minced garlic

1 teaspoon flax garlic chili oil

1 tablespoon nama shoyu

2 pinches habanero powder (be careful with this—it's very hot)

DIRECTIONS

Mix all ingredients together in a bowl; adjust the seasonings to taste.

Spread on dehydrator trays lined with Teflex sheets and dehydrate at 95°F for 24 to 36 hours or until completely dry. Spicy Party Mix can be stored at room temperature for a month or two. It must be kept dry.

Caution: Wash your hands after using habanero—do not touch your eyes!

Contributor's note: This crunchy snack also makes a zippy addition to salads and soups.

Spicy Seed Mix

BY JONATHAN WEBER
ADVANCED PREP: 36 hours for sprouting + 2 days for dehydrating
IMMEDIATE PREP: 30 min   **YIELDS** 4 quarts
SPECIAL EQUIPMENT Blender, dehydrator

INGREDIENTS

8 cups raw sunflower seeds, soaked overnight and sprouted 24 hours

3 cups raw pumpkin seeds, soaked overnight and sprouted 24 hours

2 cups sun-dried tomatoes, soaked overnight

1 bulb garlic, cloves separated and peeled

1 tablespoon Mexican spice or chili powder

2 teaspoons chili flakes or 1 teaspoon cayenne powder

2 teaspoons cumin

1/2 cup nama shoyu (or sea salt or seasoning salt to taste)

1/2 cup raisins, soaked (optional)

DIRECTIONS

To make the sauce, blend the sun-dried tomatoes, garlic, Mexican spice, chili flakes, cumin, nama shoyu and raisins (if using). The sauce should be thick and not too watery.

Place sprouted seeds in a large bowl and pour sauce over them. Mix well, so that all the seeds are completely coated with the sauce.

Spoon the seed mixture directly onto dehydrator screens, spreading it thinly and evenly. Do not use Teflex sheets.

Dehydrate at 95°F for 15 to 20 hours or until crunchy and crisp. Store in glass jars.

Contributor's note: This makes a great snack on the road and also works well on salads.

Spicy Sunflower Seed Snacks

BY JULIAN HUERTA
ADVANCED PREP: 3-4 days for sprouting   **IMMEDIATE PREP:** variable
SPECIAL EQUIPMENT None, dehydrator (optional)

INGREDIENTS

sunflower seeds

cayenne powder

chili powder

sea salt

DIRECTIONS

Sprout sunflower seeds (as many as you want) Stick in a mesh strainer for a day or two in the fridge until they dry a bit, then Sprinkle with Cayenne, Chili, and a salt and Voilà! Store in fridge unsealed to continue drying and store. You could also dehydrate.

Tasty Sea Snacks

BY JOHN LARSEN
ADVANCED PREP: 8 hours for soaking + 12 hours for dehydrating
IMMEDIATE PREP: 25 min   **SERVES** 4 to 6
SPECIAL EQUIPMENT Food processor, dehydrator

INGREDIENTS

2 cups almonds, soaked for 8 hours

8 cloves garlic, minced

1 package nori sheets

1/2 cup nama shoyu

DIRECTIONS

Process the almonds, garlic, and nama shoyu to a grainy paste. Cut the nori sheets into quarters. Place 1 spoonful of the nut mixture onto each piece of nori. Roll the nori up, moistening the edge with a little water to seal it.

Dehydrate rolls at 105°F for 12 hours or until crispy.

Watermelon Mountains

By Karie Clingo

ADVANCED PREP: None   IMMEDIATE PREP: 15 min

SPECIAL EQUIPMENT None

INGREDIENTS

watermelon
seedless grapes

DIRECTIONS:

Slice watermelon into triangles. Put a long toothpick into the pointed end of each triangle. Slide some grapes the ("mountain climbers") onto the toothpick.

Eat the "mountain climbers" at the top of the mountain and then eat the whole mountain! If the watermelon is seeded, eat the seeds or have a seed-spitting contest!

Contributor's note: The more you involve your children's imaginations into these creations, the more success you will have in getting them to eat more fresh fruits and vegetables. These recipes are fun for the whole family!

Side Dishes

Cheese Pierogi

BY MATT AMSDEN

ADVANCED PREP: None   **IMMEDIATE PREP:** 45 min

YIELDS 30 pierogi   **SPECIAL EQUIPMENT** Mandolin slicer, blender

INGREDIENTS

1 organic jicama, peeled

1/4 cup fresh, organic lemon juice

2 to 3 cloves organic garlic, peeled

1/4 cup nama shoyu

1/2 organic red bell pepper, seeded and chopped

1/2 cup raw organic macadamia nuts

1/2 cup raw organic pine nuts

DIRECTIONS

Using a deli slicer or mandolin, slice the jicama into paper-thin rounds.

Combine the lemon juice, garlic, nama shoyu, red bell pepper, macadamia nuts, and pine nuts in a blender, and mix until thick and creamy.

Place approximately 1/2 teaspoon of the blended "cheese" on one half of the jicama rounds.

Fold the other half over to create a "pouch" and serve.

Crispy Spring Rolls

By Shazzie
Advanced prep: 4 days for sprouts; 1 1/2 days for soaking
Immediate prep: 35 min   **Serves** 4   **Special Equipment** None

INGREDIENTS

2 cups soft dark greens (such as spinach or watercress)

2 avocados, peeled and pitted

1 clove garlic, peeled

1-inch piece fresh ginger root

1 cup almonds, soaked for 12 hours and sprouted for 1 day

8 Chinese cabbage leaves

1 cup bean sprouts

1/2 cup chives

1/2 cup green onions, cut into thin strips

DIRECTIONS

Mince the dark greens with the avocado, garlic, ginger and sprouted almonds until smooth but still chunky.

Cut the Chinese leaves so that you're only using the top 4-inch portion.

Spread some of the mixture onto the top of a Chinese leaf. Place the bean sprouts, chives and spring onions on the leaf lengthwise.

Roll up the leaf so it overlaps. Place the spring rolls open side down on a plate. Serve with Sweet Apricot Sauce (page 303).

Crunch Fries with Ketchup

By SERGEI AND VALYA BOUTENKO

ADVANCED PREP: 2 hours for soaking   **IMMEDIATE PREP:** 35 min

SERVES 5   **SPECIAL EQUIPMENT** None

INGREDIENTS

For the Crunch Fries:

1 pound jicama, sliced to look like french fries

2 tablespoons extra virgin olive oil

1 tablespoon paprika

1 tablespoon onion powder

sea salt to taste

1/4 cup onion powder

For the Ketchup:

1/2 cup dried tomatoes, soaked for 2 hours and drained

1/4 apple cider vinegar

1/4 cup raisins

1 tablespoon salt

DIRECTIONS:

For the fries, combine the sliced jicama with the olive oil, paprika, 1 tablespoon of the onion powder, and sea salt to taste.

For the ketchup, blend together the tomatoes, vinegar, raisins, salt and onion powder. Dip fries in ketchup and enjoy.

Contributor's note: These look as real as if you got them at the drive-thru window.

Dolmades

By SHAZZIE

ADVANCED PREP: 3 to 7 days for sauerkraut + 5 to 10 min for soaking

IMMEDIATE PREP: 35 min   **SERVES** 4   **SPECIAL EQUIPMENT** None

INGREDIENTS

1 packet wakamé seaweed

2 shallots or 1/4 red onion, finely chopped

1/4 cup fresh mint, finely chopped

1 cup avocado, peeled and pitted

1 cup Sauerkraut (page 128 to 129), finely chopped

DIRECTIONS

Soak the wakamé for 5 to 10 minutes prior to use. It will become soft very quickly, but won't fall apart if you soak it longer.

Combine the onions, mint, avocado and Sauerkraut in a bowl. Mix thoroughly until it becomes a paste.

Select large pieces of wakamé and place them on a chopping board. If there are no wide pieces, place a few side by side and then one across the center to strengthen it.

Put a tablespoon of the paste in the middle of the wakamé. Roll up the sides of the wakamé, and then roll up the ends, so that the stuffing is wrapped up like a parcel. No extra adhesive is necessary; the dolmades will self-seal immediately.

Continue to make dolmades until you have used all the mixture.

Tip: You can make these as big or as small as you like, but their size is often dictated by the size of the seaweed strips.

Contributor's note: The sauerkraut in the stuffing gives this variation of the Greek favorite its spicy Middle Eastern taste.

Eddie's Spring Rolls

BY EDDIE D. ROBINSON
ADVANCED PREP: 40 min for marinating   **IMMEDIATE PREP:** 45 min
SERVES 2   **SPECIAL EQUIPMENT** None

INGREDIENTS

For the Spring Rolls:
2 carrots, shredded
1/2 red cabbage, shredded, plus several leaves whole (for the wraps)
3 tablespoons hiziki, soaked 30 minutes
1 large zucchini, cut in thin strips
1 red bell pepper, cut in thin strips
olive oil

Bragg Liquid Aminos, to *taste*
1 tablespoon lemongrass
dulse flakes, to taste

For the Dipping Sauce:
nama shoyu
dried ginger
scallions, chopped

DIRECTIONS

Marinate the whole cabbage leaves for 40 minutes or more in olive oil and Bragg Liquid Aminos.

Wrap the shredded vegetables and veggie strips in the marinated cabbage leaves. Tie rolls with chive or carrot shreds.

To make the dipping sauce, mix nama shoyu with dried ginger and chopped scallions to taste. Serve in a small bowl with Spring Rolls.

Fresh Spring Rolls in Romaine Leaves

BY ELAINA LOVE

ADVANCED PREP: 5 to 6 days for sprouts   **IMMEDIATE PREP:** 20 min

SERVES 4 to 6   **SPECIAL EQUIPMENT** None

INGREDIENTS

2 romaine leaves, stems removed and cut in half lengthwise or 4 Spring Roll Wraps (page 131)

12 whole basil leaves

12 whole spearmint leaves

40 bean sprouts

1/2 avocado or meat of 1 young coconut cut into thin strips (divided into 4)

1/2 pound sunflower greens, buckwheat greens, pea shoots or baby greens (divided into 4)

DIRECTIONS

Place the romaine halves (or spring rolls) on a cutting board.

Close to one end of each leaf half, place 4 basil leaves, 4 spearmint leaves, 10 bean sprouts, 1/4 of the reserved avocado, and 1/4 of the greens.

Roll up the ingredients and place a toothpick through the middle to hold it together.

Place the rolls upright on a plate (as you would a nori roll). You may need to trim the ends to get them to stand up.

"Fried" Mushrooms

By Karen Knowler

Advanced prep: 4 hours for dehydrating   **Immediate prep:** 20 min

Serves 2   **Special Equipment** Dehydrator

INGREDIENTS

10 medium portobello mushrooms, sliced into 1/4-inch strips

olive oil

1 lemon, juiced

garlic, chopped, to taste (optional)

DIRECTIONS

Mix the olive oil, lemon juice, and chopped garlic (if using) in a bowl.

Pour the dressing over the mushrooms, making sure they are well coated.

Place the mushrooms on dehydrator trays and dehydrate at 105°F for at least 4 hours.

Remove excess oil from mushrooms, patting them with a paper towel. Serve as a side dish.

Marinated Veggies

By Karen Knowler

Advanced prep: 2 hours for marinating   **Immediate prep:** 20 min

Serves Depends on quantities used   **Special Equipment** None

INGREDIENTS

olive oil

lemon juice

fresh herbs of your choice

vegetables, such as: mushrooms, zucchini, tomatoes, bell peppers, onion, eggplant, leek, okra (any that will soak up the marinade)

Blend some olive oil with lemon juice and fresh herbs of your choice.

Cut a selection of raw veggies into strips and mix them into the dressing. Make sure everything is well coated, and marinate for at least 2 hours.

Use as a topping for a pizza or mix into a green leafy salad with some creamy avocado. Very versatile and yummy too!

Mesquite Melts

BY SHAZZIE

ADVANCED PREP: 1 to 2 hours for marinating + 6 to 12 hours for dehydrating
IMMEDIATE PREP: 20 min   **SERVES** 4   **SPECIAL EQUIPMENT** Mandolin, dehydrator

INGREDIENTS

- 2 sweet potatoes
- 1 lemon, juiced
- 2 tablespoons olive oil
- 1 teaspoon sea salt
- 1 tablespoon mesquite powder

DIRECTIONS

Cut the sweet potatoes into fine chips; a mandolin slicer is great for this. Put the potato chips in a wide-bottomed bowl.

Add the lemon juice, olive oil, and sea salt. Marinate for 1 to 2 hours, then drain the liquid from the potatoes.

Add the mesquite powder to the potatoes, and mix well to make sure it's evenly spread.

Place the potatoes on dehydrator trays, making sure they aren't overlapping. Dehydrate at 115°F for 6 to 12 hours, depending on the thickness of the chips, turning them once.

Contributor's note: This is a variation on the recipe for Curly Crisps (page 201)

Onion Bhajis

By Shazzie

Advanced prep: 2 hours for soaking + 8 to 24 hours for dehydrating
Immediate prep: 40 min   **Serves** 4   **Special Equipment** Food processor or juicer, dehydrator

INGREDIENTS

2 cups walnuts, soaked for 1 hour and drained

1 cup portobello mushrooms

4 sun-dried tomatoes, soaked at least 2 hours and drained (reserve juice for another recipe or as sweetener)

2 teaspoons paprika

20 to 30 stalks fresh cilantro

10 to 20 stalks fresh parsley

1 clove garlic, finely chopped

1 red pepper, seeds and stalks removed, chopped

1 dessertspoon garam masala

pinch cayenne pepper

2 cups finely chopped red onion, divided

DIRECTIONS

Combine the walnuts, mushrooms, sun-dried tomatoes, paprika, cilantro, parsley, garlic, red pepper, garam masala, cayenne, and 1 cup of the red onion in a food processor, and process.

Transfer to a bowl and use a hand blender to achieve a finer consistency. If you have a Champion or other juicer, use the blank plate to process until smooth.

Add the remaining onions and mix thoroughly.

Roll small amounts of the mixture into 3/4-inch balls. Place them in a dehydrator at 115°F for 8 to 24 hours, making sure to turn them several times.

Contributor's note: These are great served with cauliflower florets and Sweet Mango Chutney (page 293) as an appetizer.

Pepper-Corn Boats

BY DAVID KLEIN

ADVANCED PREP: None   **IMMEDIATE PREP:** 15 min

SERVES 4   **SPECIAL EQUIPMENT** None

INGREDIENTS

- 2 avocados, peeled and pitted
- 2 or more fresh ears of corn kernels, cut from cob
- 2 large red or yellow bell peppers, seeds and stems removed, cut in half lengthwise

DIRECTIONS

Mash the avocados together with the corn in a bowl. Spoon the avocado-corn mixture onto the bell pepper halves and enjoy.

Pesto Mushrooms

BY JOHN LARSEN

ADVANCED PREP: 3 hours for dehydrating   **IMMEDIATE PREP:** 35 min

SERVES 4   **SPECIAL EQUIPMENT** Food processor, dehydrator

INGREDIENTS

- 1 bunch fresh basil, coarsely chopped
- 1/2 cup lemon juice
- 3 large cloves garlic, pressed
- 1 teaspoon black peppercorns
- 2 cups walnuts
- 3/4 teaspoon sea salt to taste
- 1/4 cup olive oil
- 20 Crimini mushrooms, stems removed

DIRECTIONS

Combine the basil, lemon juice, garlic, peppercorns, walnuts, sea salt and olive oil in the food processor and process to a thick paste.

Fill the mushroom caps with the pesto. Dehydrate on Teflex sheets at 105°F for 3 hours. Enjoy as a main dish or as an appetizer.

Roasted Bell Pepper Cheese & Mushroom Risotto

BY QUINTESSENCE RESTAURANT

ADVANCED PREP: None   **IMMEDIATE PREP:** 30 min

SERVES 4 to 6   **SPECIAL EQUIPMENT** Blender, food processor

INGREDIENTS

    2 whole red or yellow bell peppers

    1/4 cup cold-pressed olive oil from a dark bottle

    4 teaspoons sea salt

    2 to 3 dried chipotle peppers, (for less heat remove seeds)

    1 cup pine nuts

    1 cup macadamia nuts

    3 1/2 to 4 cups chopped yellow squash

    2 cups sliced button or Crimini mushrooms

    chopped parsley, for garnish

DIRECTIONS

Blend the bell peppers, olive oil, sea salt and chipotle peppers together in a high speed blender. Add the pine nuts and macadamia nuts and blend to a thick cream. Set aside.

To make the rice, process the chopped yellow squash in a food processor fitted with the "S" blade and pulse-chop to a rice-like consistency.

Transfer the bell pepper cream and the "rice" to a mixing bowl and add button or Crimini mushrooms. Mix well and garnish with chopped parsley before serving.

Romaine Roll-Ups

By Shazzie

Advanced prep: 5 days for sprouts   **Immediate prep:** 20 min
Serves 2   **Special Equipment** None

INGREDIENTS

    1 large head of romaine lettuce
    3 large tomatoes, finely chopped
    1 avocado, peeled, pitted, and finely chopped
    1 handful alfalfa sprouts
    2 tablespoons fresh cilantro, finely chopped
    basil, oregano or mint, finely chopped
    onion and/or garlic, finely chopped (optional)

DIRECTIONS

Separate the leaves of the romaine lettuce and place on a plate.

In a bowl, mix together the tomatoes, avocado, alfalfa, cilantro, basil, oregano or mint, onion and garlic (if using) to make the filling.

Spoon a generous dollop of the filling at one end of each lettuce leaf. Roll the sides of the leaf over, fold it in half. Continue until you have used all the filling and then eat like a sandwich.

Sauerkraut

By Shazzie

Advanced prep: 3 to 7 days to ferment   **Immediate prep:** 40 min
Yields 3 to 4 cups   **Special Equipment** None

INGREDIENTS

    1 to 4 heads red or white (or mixed) cabbages

DIRECTIONS

Remove some of the outer leaves from the cabbage heads and set them aside.

If you have a Champion juicer, roughly chop the cabbage into manageable portions and process it all using the blank blade. If you don't have a Champion, use a food processor to chop the cabbage until it is very fine (you might need to do this in batches). If all you have is a blender, finely chop about half of the cabbage, and put the other half through the blender. Add enough water to get the blender going and blend until very fine. Combine the finely chopped and blended cabbage.

Place the cabbage into a big bowl and mix thoroughly. If the cabbage seems dry, add some water, and mix again.

Press the cabbage down, as far as it will go. It should not be watery, just moist. Put the saved cabbage leaves on top, and press it down again. Put a layer of plastic wrap on top and press it all down again. Put a weight on top, such as a bag of unopened lentils, which form to the shape of a bowl well.

Cover the bowl with a tea towel and place it somewhere in the house where you don't go very often. The cabbage has a strong odor during fermentation.

In 3 days, check to see whether you have sauerkraut. You will know when it's kraut, because it will smell pickled, and the cabbage will have a translucent appearance. If it still isn't ready, leave it for another day or so. It will soon be sauerkraut.

Transfer the sauerkraut to clean jars with tight lids and press it down so no air is trapped. Use it immediately, or store it in the fridge for a few months and use it as needed.

Variation: Add layers of cucumber, carrots, zucchini, pepper slices, or onion rings to the cabbage before fermentation. You will receive wonderful pickled vegetables as a result, which make lovely crisp additions to salads.

Contributor's note: In just 3 to 7 days you will be rewarded with delicious, vinegary sauerkraut. There's lots of good bacteria in this, so if you have stomach problems, you should give it a try. It's very good blended with soaked sunflower seeds for a lovely pâté, or in a salad. Sauerkraut takes 3 to 5 days to ferment, but after that it will keep in a jar in your fridge for a couple of months.

Savory Neat Balls

BY **MARY RYDMAN**

ADVANCED PREP: 6 hours to soak nuts
IMMEDIATE PREP: 20 min, 1–2 hours dehydrating time
SPECIAL EQUIPMENT Food processor, dehydrator   **SERVES** 5–6

INGREDIENTS

1 stalk chopped celery
1/4 cup sliced leeks
1/4 cup chopped carrots
1 cup almonds, soaked and well drained
3/4 cup walnuts, soaked and well drained
1 teaspoon Krystal Salt brine or 1/4 teaspoon granules
2 teaspoons Nama Shoyu, or to taste
pinch sage
pinch thyme

DIRECTIONS

Put vegetables in food processor first then add the remaining ingredients. Process, adding a bit of water to help it turn over, if necessary. Be careful to add only a bit of water—you will need to keep scraping down the sides for it to all incorporate. If there is too much liquid you will not be able to form balls. Form into 1 1/2 inch balls and dehydrate at 145 degrees for 1 hour. If they are not dry enough, continue dehydrating at 110 degrees until they have a slight crust on the outside but are soft on the inside.

Serve warm, fresh from the dehydrator on pre-warmed plate with Tomato Sauce

Contributor's note: Serve these and you will feel like a raw gourmet!

Scrumptious Samosas

By Michal Adi

Advanced prep: 3 hours for dehydrating **Immediate prep:** 45 min

Serves 10 **Special Equipment** Juicer, dehydrator

INGREDIENTS

6 cups cashews

4 cups macadamias

3 heads cauliflower

meat from 2 young Thai coconuts

1 large jicama

3 carrots

4-inch piece turmeric root (optional)

3 teaspoons Celtic sea salt

6 cloves garlic, minced

1 teaspoon turmeric (2 teaspoons if you did not add the fresh turmeric root)

1 teaspoon ground cumin

3 teaspoons curry powder

2 cups fresh sweet peas

2 red pepper, diced

DIRECTIONS

Homogenize the cashews, macadamias, cauliflower, coconut meat, jicama, carrots and turmeric root (if using) in a heavy-duty juicer. (Champion, Green Life, and the Omega 8001 all have the homogenizer attachment.)

Add the sea salt, garlic, turmeric, ground cumin, curry powder, peas, and red peppers. Mix everything together very well with your hands.

Form the dough into triangles about 3 inches thick to create delightful hors d'oeuvres.

Dehydrate at 110°F for 3 hours or until the samosas are light brown. Serve with Spicy Cilantro Chutney (page 290) and Sweet Mango Chutney (page 293).

Contributor's note: This is an amazing raw version of the deep-fried Indian Classic. Make a lot—you'll want more!

Spring Rolls

BY ROBERT YAROSH AND LISA SOTO
ADVANCED PREP: 4 days for sprouts   **IMMEDIATE PREP:** 25 min
SERVES 4 to 6   **SPECIAL EQUIPMENT** Grater

INGREDIENTS

1/2 cup shredded red cabbage
1/2 cup shredded yellow cabbage
5 carrots, shredded
1/2 red pepper, cut into thin strips
1/2 cup fresh mint, chopped

1 cup Mung bean sprouts
1 pack spring roll sheets

DIRECTIONS

Mix all ingredients together in a large bowl.

Spoon a small amount of the mixture onto one end of each spring roll sheet and roll into a cone shape.

Note: For totally raw spring rolls, use nori sheets instead.

Spring Roll Wraps

BY ELAINA LOVE
ADVANCED PREP: 6 to 9 hours for dehydrating   **IMMEDIATE PREP:** 30 min
YIELDS 28   **SPECIAL EQUIPMENT** Blender, dehydrator

INGREDIENTS

4 large carrots, chopped
2 avocados, skins and pits removed
1 teaspoon Celtic sea salt
1 tablespoon lemon juice
1 1/2 cups flax meal (1 cup whole seeds before grinding)

Easy Pad Thai By Elaina Love

Cashew Yogurt and Berry Parfaits By Cherie Soria

DIRECTIONS

Blend carrots with 1 cup water until smooth. Add the avocados and sea salt and blend until smooth.

Pour into a mixing bowl. Add flax meal and mix by hand.

Place 1 1/4 cups of the batter on a 16- x-16 Excalibur dehydrator tray lined with a Teflex sheet and spread it thinly and evenly.

Score the tray of batter into 4 strips in one direction and 2 sections in the other direction.

Dehydrate at 105°F for 1 to 2 hours.

Flip the wraps and remove the Teflex sheet. Continue to dehydrate until the wraps are still moist but dry enough to store. Store in a Ziploc bag at room temperature for up to a week, or in the refrigerator for months.

Tip: If the wraps seem too dry when you take them out of the dehydrator, simply place them in a Ziploc bag with a moist unbleached paper towel and seal it. Leave the bag in a warm place and the wraps will be soft within 20 minutes.

Thai Cannelloni Bites with Pine Nut-Herb Pâté

BY CHAD SARNO

ADVANCED PREP: 10 to 12 hours for soaking + 6 to 9 hours for dehydrating

IMMEDIATE PREP: 45 min   **SERVES** 4 to 6   **SPECIAL EQUIPMENT** Food processor, dehydrator

INGREDIENTS

2 cups almonds or cashews, soaked 10 to 12 hours

1 cup pine nuts

2 tablespoons olive oil

2 tablespoons lime or lemon juice

1/2 teaspoon Celtic sea salt

1/2 teaspoon black pepper

1 tablespoon garlic

1 1/2 tablespoons ginger, minced

1 tablespoon minced lemongrass (optional)

1 tablespoon curry powder

1/2 teaspoon cayenne

1/2 cup sun-dried black olives, pitted and minced

2 tablespoons minced cilantro

2 tablespoons minced basil

3 zucchini, sliced thin lengthwise with mandolin

DIRECTIONS

Place the almonds or cashews, pine nuts, olive oil, lemon or lime juice, sea salt, pepper, garlic, ginger, lemongrass, curry powder, cayenne and 3 tablespoons water in the food processor and blend to a smooth, thick paste. Pulse in the olives, cilantro, and basil.

To assemble the cannelloni, place two zucchini strips side by side. Spoon a small amount of pâté near the end of the strips facing you. Fold over zucchini and roll until the pâté actually holds together. Slice off excess zucchini. Place directly on the screen of dehydrator trays and dehydrate at 110°F for 6 hours or until firm.

These are delicious with a curry sauce.

Tomato Cocorella Appetizer

BY MICHAL ADI

ADVANCED PREP: None **IMMEDIATE PREP:** 20 min

SERVES 4 **SPECIAL EQUIPMENT** None

INGREDIENTS

    meat from 1 to 2 coconuts medium young coconuts (meat should be
       at least 1/2-inch thick)
    2 fresh heirloom tomatoes
    bunch fresh basil
    organic olive oil, to taste
    Celtic sea salt, to taste
    fresh ground black pepper, to taste

DIRECTIONS

Spoon the coconut meat out in 1- by 2-inch ovals. Slice the tomatoes into 1/3-inch-thick slices .

Layer the ingredients in the following order: tomato, coconut, basil, tomato, coconut, basil, and tomato.

Top with a generous drizzle of olive oil, Celtic sea salt, and fresh ground black pepper to taste. Garnish with two large basil leaves.

Vern's Specials

Makes 4–6 dehydrator trays

ADVANCED PREP: None　　**IMMEDIATE PREP:** 30 min

SPECIAL EQUIPMENT Food processor, dehydrator

INGREDIENTS

Step 1:

1 quart sprouted sunflower seeds

1 quart sprouted raw peanuts (make sure they are organic!)

2 cups raisins

1 pint to 1 quart water

2 tablespoons cinnamon

2 tablespoons vanilla

Step 2:

4 cups raisins

5 cups nuts (your favorite ones, or a combination, such as cashews,
    Brazil nuts, and almonds)

6 cups rolled oats

DIRECTIONS

Put the quart of sunflower seeds in the food processor with 1 cup of the raisins and as much water as necessary for it to turn over. Blend well. Put in a big bowl. Do the same with the peanuts and remaining cup of raisins, cinnamon, and vanilla. Put this into the same big bowl and mix everything together.

Spread out on teflex sheets and dehydrate for 4–6 hours at 110°. Flip, score and continue drying until desired consistency. Store in tightly lidded jars.

Zucchini Cashew Sour Cream Treats

By shannon Isley Schnibbe
Advanced prep: 8 hours for Sour Cream + 15 min for marinating zucchini; + 12 hours for dehydrating   **Immediate prep:** 40 min

Serves 4   **Special Equipment** Blender, dehydrator

INGREDIENTS

   1 cup cashews
   dash sea salt
   4 to 5 zucchinis, sliced into pieces 1/8- to 1/2-inch-thick
   1 teaspoon cayenne pepper
   1 cup tamari

DIRECTIONS

To make the sour cream, blend the cashews with 1 cup water and a dash of sea salt, starting with about 1/2 cup water, and slowly adding more until it reaches the consistency of heavy cream.

Pour into a pint jar. Cover with cheesecloth, or something similar, to allow air to circulate freely. Let sit for 8 hours or more. The cream is ready once it tastes sour and tart, and is covered in a gray film. Skim the film off with a spoon, then cover and refrigerate the sour cream.

Marinate the zucchini in cayenne, tamari, and enough water to cover, for at least 15 minutes.

Spread the zucchini slices onto dehydrator trays, and top with a dollop of sour cream. Dehydrate 12 hours at 105°F or to desired consistency. They won't get crunchy, but should be nice and firm.

Contributor's note: You may want to double this recipe; these go fast!

10
Smoothies, Shakes, & Juices

Banana Tahini Drink

BY PAUL NISON

ADVANCED PREP: None   **IMMEDIATE PREP:** 5 min

SERVES 1   **SPECIAL EQUIPMENT** Blender

INGREDIENTS

1 banana

2 tablespoons tahini

DIRECTIONS

Blend the banana and tahini with 1 cup of water and serve.

A Berry Delicious Drink

BY ELYSA MARKOWITZ

ADVANCED PREP: 20 min for soaked dates   **IMMEDIATE PREP:** 15 min

SERVES 2   **SPECIAL EQUIPMENT** Blender

INGREDIENTS

1 to 2 bananas

3 to 5 pitted dates, soaked in 1 cup water for 20 minutes (save soak water)

1 cup fresh or frozen strawberries

1/2 cup fresh or frozen raspberries

1 cup fresh orange juice

DIRECTIONS

In a blender, purée at least 1 banana, the dates with their soaking water, the fresh or frozen strawberries and raspberries, and the orange juice. Thin the mixture with more water or thicken it with more banana to suit your taste.

Serve in attractive glasses.

Contributor's note: This refreshingly sweet drink will help balance your electrolytes in warm weather.

Better than V8 Juice

BY PHILIP MCCLUSKEY
ADVANCED PREP: None   IMMEDIATE PREP: 10 min
SPECIAL EQUIPMENT Juicer (Green Star, Champion or Breville)   SERVES 1–2

INGREDIENTS

romaine (3 small heads)
1 bunch parsley
1 small celery heads
1 cucumber
1/2 bunch radish (w/ leaves)
2 tomatoes

1 lemon (w/ skin)
1–2 garlic cloves
1/4 teaspoon cayenne
1 teaspoon maca (optional)
1 teaspoon mesquite (optional)

DIRECTIONS

Cut all the ingredients in half and juice. After juicing is finished sprinkle in cayenne, maca, and/or mesquite to taste into your juice. Enjoy!

Blueberry Smoothie

BY JULIE RODWELL
ADVANCED PREP: None   IMMEDIATE PREP: 10 min
SPECIAL EQUIPMENT Blender   SERVES 1

INGREDIENTS

1/2 bunch organic parsley, washed and picked over
1/2 to 3/4 cup frozen blueberries
1/2" piece ginger root (cut finely to

reduce the "hairs")
1/4" organic lemon piece, including rind but not seeds
1/2 cup filtered water

DIRECTIONS

Spin all in a high powered blender such as a Vitamix until smooth and creamy. Drink for breakfast to get a zing to your day!

Broccoli, Kale and Celery Juice

BY VITA-MIX

ADVANCED PREP: None   **IMMEDIATE PREP:** 10 min

YIELDS 1 1/2 cups   **SPECIAL EQUIPMENT** Vita-Mix

INGREDIENTS

2 broccoli floretes

1/2 kale leaf

1/2 celery stalk

2 small carrots, tops and tails removed

1/4 apple, cored

1/2 cup ice cubes

DIRECTIONS

Place all the ingredients in your Vita-Mix container in the order listed. Add 1/4 cup of cold water and secure the 2-part lid. Select VARIABLE, speed #1. Turn the blender on and quickly increase speed to #10; then to HIGH. Run for 1 minute until smooth. Serve immediately.

Brutus is Scared

BY SHAZZIE

ADVANCED PREP: None   **IMMEDIATE PREP:** 15 min

SERVES 2   **SPECIAL EQUIPMENT** Juicer

INGREDIENTS

4 cups of spinach, tightly packed

2 large carrots, tops removed

4 tomatoes

1/4 lemon

1 cucumber, peeled if not organic

DIRECTIONS

Juice all the ingredients, mix well, and enjoy.

Contributor's note: This will turn you into Popeye!

Cabbage and Carrot Juice

BY SHAZZIE

ADVANCED PREP: None   **IMMEDIATE PREP:** 15 min

SERVES 1   **SPECIAL EQUIPMENT** Juicer

INGREDIENTS

4 outer or 6 to 8 inner cabbage leaves

6 carrots, tops and tails removed

1/2 inch piece of ginger root

DIRECTIONS

Juice all the ingredients and serve immediately.

Captain's Powerhouse

BY STEPHEN ARLIN

ADVANCED PREP: None

YIELDS 1 to 2 cups   **SPECIAL EQUIPMENT** Vita-Mix or blender

INGREDIENTS

1 young Thai coconut (reserve water)

1 large avocado, peeled and pitted

2 handfuls wild or organic greens

DIRECTIONS

Drain the coconut water into a Vita-Mix or blender. Crack the coconut in half, scoop out the soft meat, and add it to the Vita-Mix. Add the avocado and the greens, and blend until smooth.

Cardamom Cooler

By Shazzie

Advanced prep: 8 to 12 hours for soaked almonds + 15 min for almond milk
Immediate prep: 10 min   **Serves** 2   **Special Equipment** Blender

INGREDIENTS

    4 cardamom pods
    1 papaya, peeled and seeded
    2 1/2 cups Almond Milk (page 182)

DIRECTIONS

Split the cardamom pods open and scoop the black seeds into the blender. Add
the papaya and almond milk, and blend all the ingredients until smooth.

Chocolate Drink with Xoçai™

By Peggy Kenney

Advanced prep: 24 hours for soaking
Immediate prep: 10 min   **Special Equipment** Blender

INGREDIENTS

    1 raw carrot
    8 oz coconut milk
    1 oz Xoçai™ Activ™
    1 quart cold water
    dash cinnamon

DIRECTIONS

One raw coconut with its milk, broken into small pieces. Add cold water and let
stand in refrigerator for 24 hours.

Place in blender and blend until mixed thoroughly. Pour through fine filter.

Add Xoçai™ Activ™ and mix. Pour into glass and sprinkle with cinnamon.
Serve cold.

Chocolate Smoothie

BY PEGGY KENNEY

ADVANCED PREP: None   **IMMEDIATE PREP:** 5 min
SPECIAL EQUIPMENT Blender   **SERVES** 2

INGREDIENTS

2/3 cup almonds

1 ripe banana

1 1/3 cups mango slices

1 tablespoon Activ™ Powder

1 1/2 cups water

DIRECTIONS

Place all ingredients into the blender and mix thoroughly.

Chockie Milkshake

BY SHAZZIE

ADVANCED PREP: 2 to 9 hours for soaked nuts   **IMMEDIATE PREP:** 15 min
SERVES 1   **SPECIAL EQUIPMENT** Blender

INGREDIENTS

20 Brazil nuts, soaked at least 2 hours

2 Medjool dates or 4 smaller ones

1 banana, peeled

1 inch of vanilla pod

2 to 4 teaspoons raw carob powder

DIRECTIONS

Blend the Brazil nuts and dates with 2 cups of water, and strain. (Use the nut fiber for another recipe.) Return the milk to the blender. Add the banana, vanilla, and carob powder and blend until smooth.

Variation: For a thicker shake, use a sliced, frozen banana.

Contributor's note: This shake is so rich and creamy, you won't want to share it!

Citrus Explosion

BY PHILIP McCLUSKEY
ADVANCED PREP: None **IMMEDIATE PREP:** 10 min
SPECIAL EQUIPMENT Juicer (Green Star, Champion or Breville) **SERVES** 1–2

INGREDIENTS

3 grapefruit
6 clementines
3 blood Oranges
3 carrots

DIRECTIONS

Peel all the citrus fruits, then juice all the produce. Enjoy!

Coconut Drink

BY SHAZZIE
ADVANCED PREP: None **IMMEDIATE PREP:** 20 min
SERVES 1 to 2 **SPECIAL EQUIPMENT** Blender, juicer

INGREDIENTS

1/2 coconut and all of its water
1 banana, peeled
1/2 lime, juiced
1-inch piece fresh vanilla
2 oranges, juiced

DIRECTIONS

Combine all the ingredients in a blender and blend until smooth. You may strain this for a smoother texture or drink it as is. If you have a juicer, juice the coconut and banana, and add the juice to the mixture. Add as much pulp back as you like for the consistency you desire.

Cranberry "Wine"

BY ELAINA LOVE

ADVANCED PREP: None   **IMMEDIATE PREP:** 25 min

SERVES 15   **SPECIAL EQUIPMENT** Juicer

INGREDIENTS

1 pound fresh cranberries

1 red beet

6 pounds apples

1 head celery

1/2 lemon, including peel

DIRECTIONS

Put all the ingredients through a juicer in batches. Mix well and serve in several large pitchers.

Cucumber Number

BY SHAZZIE

ADVANCED PREP: None   **IMMEDIATE PREP:** 15 min

SERVES 2   **SPECIAL EQUIPMENT** Juicer

INGREDIENTS

1 cucumber

1 teaspoon lemon peel

3 apples, cored

DIRECTIONS

Juice all of the ingredients and mix well. Serve immediately.

Energized Smoothie

BY VIKTORAS KULVINSKAS

ADVANCED PREP: None   **IMMEDIATE PREP:** 15 min

YIELDS 1 to 2 cups   **SPECIAL EQUIPMENT** Blender

INGREDIENTS

1 organic apple, cored and chopped

1 handful of your favorite organic greens

1 teaspoon grated fresh ginger

1 ripe Haas avocado

pinch sea salt

DIRECTIONS

Blend the apple with the greens, ginger, avocado, sea salt, and 1/2 cup water. Transfer to a bowl and sprinkle with your favorite sprouts, a spoonful of seed cheese and a handful of dulse or nori flakes. If you want something more filling, serve with dehydrated crackers (see chapter 5).

Fractal Fortnight

BY SHAZZIE

ADVANCED PREP: None   **IMMEDIATE PREP:** 15 min

SERVES 2   **SPECIAL EQUIPMENT** Juicer

INGREDIENTS

2 teaspoons E3Live

1 cup kale or Savoy cabbage, tightly packed

4 pears, peeled and cored

4 stalks celery

DIRECTIONS

Juice all of the ingredients and mix well.

Contributor's note: Drink this juice every fortnight (2 weeks) to clear your head and sharpen your thoughts. The E3Live in this juice forms beautiful shifting fractal patterns when you look at it closely. It's a kaleidoscope in a cup!

Frozen Choc-Shake

BY KAREN KNOWLER

ADVANCED PREP: 4 to 8 hours for soaking   **IMMEDIATE PREP:** 15 min
SERVES 2   **SPECIAL EQUIPMENT** Vita-Mix or blender

INGREDIENTS

1 cup organic almonds, soaked 4 to 8 hours and drained

12 small dates or 5 large Medjool dates

3 tablespoons carob powder

4 frozen bananas, broken into pieces

DIRECTIONS

Pour one cup water into a Vita-Mix or blender with the almonds. (Organic almonds taste superior to non-organic, often with a marzipan-like flavor). Blend on high speed until nuts are completely broken down to almond milk.

Pour the almond milk through a strainer or mesh bag (such as a sprouting bag), and collect strained milk in a jug or bowl. Rinse Vita-Mix or blender jug to remove remains from nuts.

Pour the newly strained almond milk back into the blender. Add another cup of water, all the dates, the carob, and the banana pieces. (If not using a Vita-Mix, allow the frozen bananas to thaw for a while first to avoid damaging your blender.)

Blend all ingredients thoroughly until thick, whipped ice-cream-like consistency is achieved. Pour into two tall glasses and enjoy! (The remaining almond pulp can be used in cakes or cookies later).

Variation 1: Add some vanilla instead of the carob, or any other flavoring of your choice.

Variation 2: This shake is also delicious with just bananas, nut milk, and dates.

Contributor's note: Everyone who has tasted this rich drink loves it. It's even better than the thick chocolate shakes we used to slurp on in fast food restaurants—not to mention much healthier!

FUN (Fast, Unusual, Natural) CEO Meal

BY VIKTORAS KULVINSKAS
ADVANCED PREP: 8 to 12 hours for soaking   **IMMEDIATE PREP:** 10 min
YIELDS 2 to 3 cups   **SPECIAL EQUIPMENT** Blender

INGREDIENTS

1/2 cup almonds, soaked overnight

1 handful fresh strawberries (frozen work well, too)

1 banana, peeled

1 teaspoon Blue Green Algae or Spirulina

1 cup water or fruit juice

pinch of your favorite spices

1 teaspoon vanilla

pinch sea salt

DIRECTIONS

Blend all the ingredients to a cream. Sip slowly and rule the world.

Contributor's note: This drink is a meal of its own—and a major time saver.

Ginger Ale

BY DAVID KLEIN
ADVANCED PREP: 2 hours for refrigerating   **IMMEDIATE PREP:** 10 min
YIELDS 2 cups   **SPECIAL EQUIPMENT** Juicer

INGREDIENTS

white grapes

2 stalks celery

1/4-inch piece fresh ginger root

DIRECTIONS

Juice the white grapes, celery and fresh ginger root. Mix well, chill, and enjoy.

"Give Me Greens!" Sweet Milkshake

By Elaina Love

Advanced prep: 8 to 12 hours for soaking + 15 min for almond milk

Immediate prep: 10 min   **Yields** 3 cups   **Special Equipment** Blender

INGREDIENTS

- 3 cups Almond Milk (page 208)
- 1 ripe banana, fresh or frozen
- 1 teaspoon vanilla extract (or another extract of choice)
- 1 tablespoon green powder (Chlorella, Spirulina, Blue Green Algae, Nature's First Food, Pure Synergy, or Barley Green)
- dash nutmeg (optional)

DIRECTIONS

Blend the Almond Milk with the banana and vanilla until frothy.

Add the green powder and quickly blend again.

Pour the shake into a glass and top with a sprinkle of nutmeg.

Contributor's note: This is a great drink to start your day with, or gulp down any time you need some extra energy.

Grape-Celery Cooler

By David Klein

Advanced prep: None   **Immediate prep:** 10 min

Yields 2 to 3 cups   **Special Equipment** Juicer

INGREDIENTS

- sweet grapes
- 1 to 2 celery stalks (per glass)
- mint for garnish (optional)

DIRECTIONS

Juice your favorite sweet grapes with 1 or 2 celery stalks.

Stir and serve. Garnish with fresh mint leaves if desired.

Green Lemonade

By John Larsen

Advanced prep: None **Immediate prep:** 20 min

Yields 5 cups **Special Equipment** Juicer

INGREDIENTS

10 large apples, each cut into slices that will fit in juicer

1 bunch of kale, cut into 2-inch pieces

4 stalks celery, cut into 2-inch pieces

1 large lemon, cut into slices

DIRECTIONS

Process all the ingredients through a juicer, alternating between the apple, kale, celery, and lemon. Enjoy this delicious, refreshing sweet and sour drink.

Heavenly Chai

By Michal Adi

Advanced prep: 8 to 12 hours for soaking **Immediate prep:** 15 min

Yields 8 cups **Special Equipment** Blender

INGREDIENTS

meat from 2 young Thai coconuts

3 cups young coconut water

1/2 cup cashews, soaked

1/2 cup macadamias, soaked

5 to 7 dates

1-inch piece fresh ginger root

1/2 teaspoon cinnamon

1/4 teaspoon cardamom

1/4 teaspoon black pepper

1/8 teaspoon ground cloves

DIRECTIONS

Blend all the ingredients until smooth and creamy. Strain for an extra silky smooth texture.

Hint: For superior flavor and fragrance buy the cinnamon, cardamom, black pepper, and cloves whole and grind them in a coffee grinder. Be sure to remove the green shell from the cardamom and grind only the seed.

Hopping Wild

BY SHAZZIE

ADVANCED PREP: None   **IMMEDIATE PREP:** 15 min

SERVES 2   **SPECIAL EQUIPMENT** Juicer

INGREDIENTS

  10 to 20 big wild leaves from your garden (such as dandelion, dock, or plantain)
  2 apples, peeled and cored
  5 stalks celery

DIRECTIONS

Juice all of the ingredients and mix well. Increase the amount of wild greens as you get used to their strength. If you find them too strong at first, use only 5 leaves and gradually build up to more.

Variation: If you don't have a garden, and there are no wild plants near you, use kale, spinach, watercress or herbs.

Malted Vegetable Juice

By Jameth and Kim Sheridan

Advanced prep: None **Immediate prep:** 15 min
Yields 1 to 2 cups **Special Equipment** None

INGREDIENTS

1 cup fresh or frozen (and thawed) raw carrot juice
celery juice to taste (optional)
beet juice to taste (optional)
1 to 2 tablespoons HealthForce® Greener Grasses
1 to 2 teaspoons lecithin powder or granules

DIRECTIONS

Mix the fresh carrot juice with celery juice and/or beet juice to taste (if using). Add the Greener Grasses and lecithin (if using). Mix together well and enjoy.

Variation: For warm malted juice, (also known as Hot Chocolate) heat the juice in a saucepan on the stove's lowest setting until it reaches 105°F to 110°F. Stir the juice well while warming it, and remove it from the heat as soon as it is warm enough.

Hint: We recommend you start by adding 1 tablespoon Greener Grasses, rather than 2, and adding 2 teaspoons of lecithin powder or granules. The lecithin gives a creamier texture. You can gradually increase the Greener Grasses to 1 1/2 or 2 tablespoons per cup of carrot juice if you want.

Hint: Use your own finger to judge the temperature as you warm the juice. Your body temperature is approximately 98.6°F. When you put your finger into the mixture, notice if it feels cool, the same, or warmer. If it feels cool, it is less than 98.6°F. If it feels the same, it is approximately 98.6°F. If it feels slightly warmer than your finger, it is only slightly above 98.6°F and the perfect temperature for drinking. If is feels quite a bit warmer, it may be hot enough to cause or start to cause enzyme destruction. Try not to heat the juice to enzyme-destructive temperatures, as doing so will lessen its nutritional benefits.

Hint: Another method for warming the juice is to put it in a waterproof container such as a glass or bottle with a lid or top. Then fill up a container, or your sink, with very warm water. Immerse the glass or bottle in water until it is warmed (usually about 5 minutes, depending on the temperature of the water, and the amount of juice to be warmed).

Contributor's note: This is a wonderful tasting and deeply nourishing combination.

Molotov Cocktail

BY DAVID WOLFE

ADVANCED PREP: None   **IMMEDIATE PREP:** 10 min

SERVES 1   **SPECIAL EQUIPMENT** Blender

INGREDIENTS

4 apples

1 clove garlic

1/4 slice onion root

1 red jalapeño pepper

1 slice fresh ginger root

DIRECTIONS

Blend all ingredients well. Drink two cups of this each day: one in the morning and one in the evening.

Morning Glory

BY DAVID KLEIN

ADVANCED PREP: None   **IMMEDIATE PREP:** 15 min

YIELDS 2 to 3 cups   **SPECIAL EQUIPMENT** Citrus press or other citrus juicer

INGREDIENTS

several sweet oranges

1 pomegranate

DIRECTIONS

Slice the oranges and pomegranate in half. Use a citrus press or other citrus juicer to juice the fruits. Mix the juices together and enjoy!

Pink Elephant

BY JEREMY SAFRON

ADVANCED PREP: None   **IMMEDIATE PREP:** 20 min

SERVES 2 to 4   **SPECIAL EQUIPMENT** Juicer, blender

INGREDIENTS

5 large green prickly pear cacti

2 medium purple prickly pear cacti or 1 cup black raspberries

1 cup frozen cherimoya, peeled and seeded

DIRECTIONS

Carefully peel and juice the green and purple prickly pears (or berries if no purple prickly pears are available). Blend the prickly pear juice with the frozen cherimoya and serve.

Pucker Up Passion Juice

BY PHILIP McCLUSKEY

ADVANCED PREP: None   **IMMEDIATE PREP:** 6 min

SPECIAL EQUIPMENT Juicer (Green Star, Champion, Breville)   **SERVES** 1–2

INGREDIENTS

2 grapefruit

4 apples

1 lemon (w/ skin)

7 small carrots

1/2 teaspoon cinnamon

1 teaspoon maca *(optional)

1 inch piece ginger *(optional)

DIRECTIONS

Cut all the ingredients in half and juice. After juicing is finished sprinkle in cinnamon and/or maca into your juice. Enjoy!

Persimmon Nog

By John Larsen

Advanced prep: 8 to 12 hours for soaked almonds   **Immediate prep:** 15 min

Yields 6 cups   **Special Equipment** Blender; nut milk bag, cheesecloth or fine strainer

INGREDIENTS

2 cups almonds, soaked

6 dates, pits removed

3 cups purified water

3 persimmons, peeled, seeds removed

1/2 teaspoon each nutmeg, cinnamon

1/4 teaspoon each ginger, cardamom

DIRECTIONS

Blend the almonds, dates and water until creamy and smooth (about 2 minutes).

Strain the liquid through a nut milk bag, cheesecloth, or fine strainer. Apply pressure to squeeze out all the liquid. Save the pulp for another recipe and pour the almond milk back into the blender.

Add the persimmons along with the nutmeg, cinnamon, ginger, and cardamom and blend for 30 seconds. Enjoy!

Red Desire

By Philip McCluskey

Advanced prep: None   **Immediate prep:** 5 min

Special Equipment Juicer (Green Star, Champion, Breville)   **Serves** 1–2

INGREDIENTS

1/4 beet

2 pears

2 apples

1/2 pineapple

1 inch piece ginger

DIRECTIONS

Cut all the ingredients in half and juice. Enjoy!

Seaside Smoothie

BY SHAZZIE

ADVANCED PREP: None   **IMMEDIATE PREP:** 10 min

SERVES 1 to 2   **SPECIAL EQUIPMENT** Blender

INGREDIENTS

3 bananas, peeled

2 pears, peeled

2 stalks celery, finely chopped

1 teaspoon Superfood

DIRECTIONS

Combine the bananas, pear, and celery in a blender with 1 cup of water and blend for a few seconds. Add the Superfood and blend until smooth.

Contributor's note: The celery in this smoothie makes for a healthy rounded taste.

Spicy Pear

BY SHAZZIE

ADVANCED PREP: None   **IMMEDIATE PREP:** 10 min

SERVES 1   **SPECIAL EQUIPMENT** Juicer

INGREDIENTS

4 pears, cored

4 stalks celery

1/4 teaspoon cinnamon powder

DIRECTIONS

Juice the pears and celery. Run the cinnamon through your juicer between ingredients, and stir it in afterward. Serve immediately.

Strawberry Patch

BY SHAZZIE

ADVANCED PREP: None   **IMMEDIATE PREP:** 15 min

SERVES 1   **SPECIAL EQUIPMENT** Juicer

INGREDIENTS

4 cups strawberries

1 head little gem lettuce

2 cups blueberries

DIRECTIONS

Juice all of the ingredients, mix well, and serve immediately.

Sunrise

BY SHAZZIE

ADVANCED PREP: None   **IMMEDIATE PREP:** 15 min

SERVES 2   **SPECIAL EQUIPMENT** Blender

INGREDIENTS

2 Pakistani or Indian mangoes (other mangoes will do, but you may want to add a couple of dates for sweetness)

water from 1 young coconut

meat from 1 young coconut

1 banana, plus extra slices for garnish

DIRECTIONS

Blend all of the ingredients together. Pour into long glasses and decorate with a slice of banana. If the coconut meat is a bit tough, and you don't have a high-power blender, omit it.

Contributor's note: This drink is great to wake up to. Make it when you know it's going to be a hot day, take it to the beach or to a lovely green hill, and sip it as the sun comes up.

Sun Tea

By Sergei and Valya Boutenko

Advanced prep: 8 hours for brewing tea   **Immediate prep:** 10 min

Yields 1 gallon   **Special Equipment** None

INGREDIENTS

- 1 bunch peppermint
- 1 bunch spearmint
- 1 bunch lemon balm

DIRECTIONS

Place all the ingredients in a gallon jar and fill with filtered water. Let it sit in the sun for 8 hours or more until it becomes a rich, golden color.

Contributor's note: This is a great drink on a hot summer day. Sun tea is a good substitute for black teas, green teas, and coffee.

The Candy Floss Tart

By Shazzie

Advanced prep: None   **Immediate prep:** 15 min

Serves 1 to 2   **Special Equipment** Blender

INGREDIENTS

- 3 pink grapefruits
- 2 limes
- 2 soft ripe pears
- 2 cups watermelon

DIRECTIONS

Remove the citrus peels from the fruit and juice all the ingredients. Combine everything in a blender and blend until smooth. Strain this drink for a smoother texture if you like.

Contributor's note: This drink is such a sugary pink color, it almost glows!

Vanilla and Sesame Shake

By Karen Knowler
Advanced prep: 4 to 6 hours for soaking   **Immediate prep:** 15 min
Yields 5 to 6 cups   **Special Equipment** Blender or Vita-Mix

INGREDIENTS

1/2 cup sesame seeds, soaked

2 cups pure water

10 dates (fresh, or soaked if dry)

4 bananas, peeled

2 teaspoons vanilla powder or alcohol-free extract

DIRECTIONS

Make sesame milk by blending the sesame seeds with the water. Add more or less water to achieve desired consistency. Strain through a nut milk bag, cheese cloth or fine strainer.

Add the dates, bananas, and vanilla to the strained milk and blend well in a Vita-Mix or blender until smooth and creamy.

Hint: Add crushed ice for a much cooler drink.

Wake Up, Ginger

By Shazzie
Advanced prep: None   **Immediate prep:** 15 min
Serves 2   **Special Equipment** Juicer

INGREDIENTS

2 inch piece fresh ginger

4 oranges

1 cup berries (such as red currants, strawberries, or black currants)

DIRECTIONS

Juice all of the ingredients and mix well. Serve immediately.

Wandering Monotrome

By Jeremy Safron

Advanced prep: 8 to 12 hours for soaking   **Immediate prep:** 15 min

Serves 2 to 4   **Special Equipment** Blender

INGREDIENTS

1 apple, cored

1/2 cup raisins, soaked

1/2 cup dates, soaked (reserve water)

1/2 cup almonds, soaked

1/2 cup coconut meat

2 teaspoons cinnamon

1 teaspoon ginger juice

dash ground cloves

dash of nutmeg

2 cups coconut water or date soak water

DIRECTIONS

Place all the ingredients in a blender and blend until smooth.

Warm Apple Punch

BY SHAZZIE

ADVANCED PREP: 1 hour for marinating   **IMMEDIATE PREP:** 15 min

SERVES 2   **SPECIAL EQUIPMENT** Juicer

INGREDIENTS

- 8 apples, cored
- 1/2 vanilla pod, roughly chopped
- 1 cinnamon stick, broken into pieces
- 4 slices lemon
- 4 slices orange
- 1 teaspoon of Chinese five-spice powder

DIRECTIONS

Juice the apples and pour the juice into a pitcher. Add the vanilla, cinnamon, lemon, orange, and five-spice to the juice, and let it marinate for 1 hour in the sunshine. If you have no sunshine, place the juice in a cupboard or somewhere else warm (but not hot).

11

Breads, Crackers, & Chips

Breads

Almond Cinnamon Bread

By Elaina Love
Advanced prep: 6 hours for soaking + 4 hours for dehydrating
Immediate prep: 25 min   **Serves** 12   **Special Equipment** Dehydrator

INGREDIENTS

6 cups almond pulp (left over from making almond milk)

2 cups flaxseed meal, from 1 1/2 cups flax seeds

1 cup olive or coconut oil

1/2 cup date paste, honey, or maple syrup

1 teaspoon cinnamon

1 cup raisins or currants

2 teaspoons Celtic sea salt

DIRECTIONS

Mix the almond pulp and flaxseed meal together by hand in a large mixing bowl. Add the olive or coconut oil, date paste or other sweetener, cinnamon, raisins or currants, and sea salt and mix well with your hands.

Press onto a dehydrator tray lined with a Teflex sheet. The dough should be about 1/4-inch thick. Use your hands to smooth it flat. Flip the bread using another dehydrator tray, and remove the Teflex sheet. Dehydrate at 105°F for about 4 hours. Store in the refrigerator for up to a week, or freeze in a Ziploc bag and remove pieces of bread as needed.

Apple Cinnamon Bread

By Rose Lee Calabro

Advanced prep: 12 to 48 hours for soaking + 12 to 48 hours for dehydrating
Immediate prep: 40 min **Yields** 3 loaves **Special Equipment** Coffee grinder or blender; food processor; dehydrator

INGREDIENTS

  2 cups golden flax seeds, ground
  1 cup almonds, soaked 12 to 48 hours
  1 cup raisins, soaked 4 to 6 hours
  2 apples, grated
  1 teaspoon vanilla
  1 tablespoon cinnamon
  1 teaspoon Celtic sea salt

DIRECTIONS

Grind the flax seeds in a coffee grinder or a blender. (Do not over-grind them—the thicker the mixture, the better the bread).

Process the almonds to a meal in a food processor fitted with the "S" blade.

Process the raisins in a blender until smooth, adding some of the raisin soak water to blend.

Combine the ground flax seeds, almonds, and raisins in a mixing bowl, and add the grated apples, vanilla, cinnamon, and sea salt. Mix well.

Form into 3 loaves approximately 4- by 8- by 1-inch, and dehydrate at 105°F for 12 to 14 hours or until desired consistency is obtained.

Corn Bread

BY ELAINA LOVE
ADVANCED PREP: 4 to 8 hours for soaking + 6 hours for dehydrating
IMMEDIATE PREP: 45 min   **YIELDS** 2 dehydrator trays (16- x 16-inch)
SPECIAL EQUIPMENT Blender, dehydrator

INGREDIENTS

2 cups raw almonds, soaked 4 to 8 hours (1 1/4 cups before soaking) and drained

2 cups raw cashews or 1 cup raw cashew butter

1 cup pine nuts

1 ten-ounce bag of frozen corn or fresh corn off the cob

1/4 cup raw honey or maple syrup

2 teaspoons Celtic sea salt

2 cloves garlic

1 1/2 cups dry golden flax seeds ground into meal or soaked 4 to 8 hours and ground in a Vita-Mix blender

DIRECTIONS

Place the almonds in the blender with enough water to cover, and blend until creamy.

Blend the cashews as you did the almonds or add the cashew butter to the bowl.

Blend the pine nuts, corn, honey or maple syrup, sea salt, and garlic in the blender until creamy. The corn can remain a little chunky if you like. You may need to add a little water to blend.

Combine all the ingredients together in a bowl and mix well. Let it sit for 15 minutes.

Spread the batter onto a 16- x 16-inch dehydrator tray covered with a Teflex sheet. Make the bread about 1/4-inch thick. Score into 25 squares with the edge of your spatula or a butter knife. This should fill at least 2 trays. Dehydrate at 105°F for about 3 hours.

Flip the bread and remove the Teflex sheets.

Dehydrate for another 3 hours or until the bread is still moist, but easy to lift. Store in the refrigerator for up to 1 week.

Corn Chips

CONTRIBUTED BY JULIE RODWELL

ADVANCED PREP: 24–36 hours for dehydration

IMMEDIATE PREP: 20 min **SPECIAL EQUIPMENT** Food processor

INGREDIENTS

4 cups of corn off the cob

1/2 cup olive oil

1/4 cup water

1 1/2 teaspoons salt

1/2 cup ground flax seeds (in coffee grinder or food processor)

2 chili peppers

1 tablespoon honey

1/4 bunch cilantro

DIRECTIONS

Blend the cilantro, peppers and water first; add in all but flax; mixture will be somewhat thick; add flax to thicken further while blender is running. Spread thinly on teflex sheets, dehydrate at 110°; turn and mark in triangles after a few hours; dehydrate until crisp. Store in a tightly lidded jar.

Garlic Rosemary Sourdough Bread

BY JOHN LARSEN

ADVANCED PREP: 8 to 12 hours for soaking + 7 to 10 hours for fermenting + 11 hours for dehydrating **IMMEDIATE PREP:** 30 min

SERVES 8 to 10 **SPECIAL EQUIPMENT** Food processor, dehydrator

INGREDIENTS

2 cups oat groats, soaked, rinsed, and strained

1 cup almonds, soaked, rinsed, and strained

1 cup kamut, soaked, rinsed, and strained

1 tablespoon olive oil

1 teaspoon sea salt

5 cloves garlic, minced

1/4 cup fresh rosemary, minced

DIRECTIONS

Process the soaked nuts and grains in food processor using s blade along with olive oil and sea salt for 30 seconds. Mix in the garlic and rosemary by hand and let the dough sit, covered, overnight at room temperature.

Spread the dough 1/2-inch-thick on Teflex sheets, and dehydrate for 5 hours at 100°F.

Turn the bread and score it into 6-inch squares. Dehydrate for 6 hours more, or to desired texture.

Sun-Dried Tomato Pesto Nut Loaf

BY JOHN LARSEN

ADVANCED PREP: 8 to 10 hours for soaking; 5 hours for dehydrating
IMMEDIATE PREP: 45 min   **SERVES** 6 to 8   **SPECIAL EQUIPMENT** Coffee grinder or Vita-Mix, food processor, dehydrator

INGREDIENTS

2 cups almonds

1 cup sunflower seeds

1 1/2 teaspoons sea salt

1 teaspoon marjoram

1 teaspoon chili powder

2 tablespoons nutritional yeast

1 cup oat groats, soaked and drained

1 medium yellow onion, chopped

5 green onions, chopped

1 red bell pepper, chopped

1 yellow bell pepper, chopped

4 carrots, chopped

1 head broccoli, chopped

3 fresh sage leaves

2 bay leaves

1/3 cup olive oil

1/8 cup nama shoyu

1 portobello mushroom, chopped

DIRECTIONS

Grind the almonds and sunflower seeds in a coffee grinder or Vita-Mix. Add the sea salt, marjoram, chili powder and nutritional yeast and set aside.

Grind the soaked oat groats in the Vita-Mix with 1 cup water until creamy; set aside.

In a food processor combine the chopped yellow and green onions, peppers, carrots, broccoli, sage and bay leaves with the olive oil and nama shoyu. Process to a grainy paste.

Place the chopped mushrooms and all the other ingredients in a large mixing bowl. Mix everything together well and form into loaves 2 inches thick on a Teflex sheet. Dehydrate at 105°F for 3 hours. Turn over the loaves and continue to dehydrate for 2 hours more. Top with your favorite pesto and dehydrate for 1 hour more.

Zucchini Bread

BY ROSE LEE CALABRO

ADVANCED PREP: 6 to 8 hours for soaking + 8 to 10 hours for dehydrating
IMMEDIATE PREP: 40 min   YIELDS 3 loaves   SPECIAL EQUIPMENT Coffee grinder or blender, food processor, dehydrator

INGREDIENTS

2 cups golden flax seeds, ground

1 cup pecans, soaked 6 to 8 hours and drained

1 1/2 cups raisins, soaked 4 to 6 hours and drained (reserve soak water)

1 cup zucchini

2 teaspoons cinnamon

1 teaspoon vanilla

1/2 teaspoon nutmeg

1/4 teaspoon cardamom

1 teaspoon Celtic sea salt

DIRECTIONS

Grind the flax seeds in a coffee grinder or blender. (Do not over-grind them—the thicker the mixture, the better the bread).

Process the pecans to a meal in a food processor fitted with the "S" blade.

In a blender, process the raisins and zucchini until smooth. Add some of the raisin soak water to blend. Combine the ground flax seeds, pecans, raisins, and zucchini in a mixing bowl, and add the cinnamon, vanilla, nutmeg, cardamom, and sea salt. Mix well.

Form into 3 loaves approximately 4- x 8- x 1-inch and dehydrate at 105°F for 8 to 10 hours or to desired consistency. The bread should be dry and crispy on the outside and firm on the inside.

Crackers

Almond Flax Crackers

By Rose Lee Calabro

Advanced prep: 12 to 48 hours for soaking + 14 hours for dehydrating
Immediate prep: 40 min   **Yields** 9 full trays (14- x 14-inch)   **Special**
Equipment Champion juicer or food processor, dehydrator

INGREDIENTS

- 3 cups almonds, soaked 12 to 48 hours
- 4 cups carrot pulp
- 6 cups flax seeds, soaked 4 to 6 hours (not drained)
- 1 cup fresh parsley, finely chopped
- 4 stalks celery, finely chopped
- 1 red bell pepper, finely chopped
- 1 red onion, finely chopped
- 2 tablespoons Celtic sea salt or to taste
- 1/2 to 1 teaspoon cayenne or 1 tablespoon curry powder and 2 teaspoons cumin powder (optional)

DIRECTIONS

Process the drained almonds and carrots through a Champion juicer with the blank plate or in a food processor fitted with the "S" blade. Combine all the ingredients in a large mixing bowl and mix well. Spread the dough out about 1/4-inch thick onto a Teflex sheet in the dehydrator.

Score the dough with a knife into small squares. Dehydrate at 105°F for 6 hours. Turn over the crackers, remove the Teflex sheets, and continue dehydrating for 6 to 8 hours or until desired consistency is obtained. Store the crackers in glass jars.

Editor's Note: Whenever you soak flax seed, the water becomes thick and mucilaginous. This is a nutritious, high protein liquid and becomes part of your recipe—don't attempt to drain soaked flax seed!

Buckflax Savory Crackers

BY JONATHAN WEBER

ADVANCED PREP: 1 to 2 days for sprouting and soaking + 16 to 20 hours for dehydrating   **IMMEDIATE PREP:** 1 hour   **YIELDS** 65 to 80 crackers
SPECIAL EQUIPMENT Food processor, dehydrator

INGREDIENTS

4 large fresh tomatoes, chopped, or 1 cup sun-dried tomatoes, soaked overnight and drained

2 red bell peppers or 1/2 cup dried red bell pepper, soaked overnight and drained

1 large bunch celery, chopped

1/4 cup seaweed, such as wakamé, kelp, or aramé, broken up and soaked overnight then drained

1/2 cup dulse seaweed flakes

2 cups raisins, soaked overnight and drained (reserve soak water)

3 to 4 cups brown flax seeds, soaked overnight in 6 to 7 cups water (not drained)

3 to 4 cups buckwheat groats, soaked, then sprouted 1 to 2 additional days

2 medium red onions, chopped

1 whole bulb garlic, chopped

1/2 cup dill weed

1 teaspoon cayenne

2 tablespoons caraway seed

1 tablespoon coriander powder

1 tablespoon sea salt or seasoning salt (or more if desired)

pulp remaining from making nut or seed milks (optional)

soaked nuts or seeds, such as almonds, sunflower seeds, or walnuts (optional)

fresh herbs, such as oregano, basil, or parsley to taste (optional)

DIRECTIONS

Process all the ingredients in 3 or 4 batches in a large food processor fitted with the "S" blade. Begin each batch with fresh or soaked vegetables. Add the celery, seaweed, and raisins and process until well broken up. Add 1/3 of the soaked flax to this mixture and process for 2 minutes. Add some of the buckwheat and process again until creamy. Transfer the mixture to a large mixing bowl.

Repeat the steps above until all the ingredients are processed. Collect the entire mixture in a large mixing bowl. Add the onions and garlic, and mix everything together well. The dill, cayenne, caraway, coriander, and sea salt can either be added to the mixture in the bowl and mixed in by hand, or processed along with the other ingredients.

Taste the mixture to test its flavor and texture. Some of the sprouted buckwheat can be included without processing for crackers with more texture. If the batch is too moist, add a cup or two of ground dry flax seeds and mix in well. Allow 1/2 hr.

Place 2 or more cups of the mixture on Teflex sheets in your dehydrator and spread it out evenly with a spoon, knife, or bowl scraper. This batch is enough to fill 7 to 8 large dehydrator trays (15- x 15-inch), depending on the thickness of the crackers. Dehydrate at 95°F for 10 to 12 hours.

Flip the crackers over and remove the Teflex sheets. Score the dough with a plastic knife into cracker sizes and shapes of your choice. Sprinkle the moist side of the crackers with sesame seeds and additional seasonings if desired. Continue dehydrating to desired consistency—moist or crispy (another 6 to 8 hours). Break the crackers and store them in a sealed container. Enjoy!

Variation: For fermented sourdough crackers, cover the bowl of dough before dehydrating and set it aside for 2 to 4 days. Stir well once a day. The dough will rise slightly as the fermentation occurs. Stir the dough to keep it down and taste it periodically.

Corn Off the Cob Crackers

By Jonathan Weber

ADVANCED PREP: 1 to 2 days for sprouted buckwheat + 16 to 20 hours for dehydrating   **IMMEDIATE PREP:** 50 min

YIELDS 65 to 80 crackers   **SPECIAL EQUIPMENT** Food processor, dehydrator

INGREDIENTS

   3 cups buckwheat groats, soaked and sprouted 2 to 3 days, then drained
   2 1/2 cups yellow flax seeds, soaked overnight in 4 cups water (not drained)
   2 medium red or yellow onions, chopped
   1 to 2 whole bulbs of garlic, chopped
   2 to 3 large fresh tomatoes
   6 to 8 cups fresh corn, cut from cob
   1 tablespoon sea salt or organic seasoning salt
   2 teaspoons chili powder
   1 teaspoon cayenne powder
   2 cups ground yellow flax seeds (dry and unsoaked)

DIRECTIONS

Place portions of all the ingredients except the ground flax seeds into a large food processor and process with the "S" blade to desired texture. Transfer the mixture to a large bowl.

Repeat the steps above 2 or 3 more times until all the ingredients are processed. Collect the entire mixture in a large mixing bowl and mix well, adding the dry ground flax seeds at the end. Mix well.

The salt, chili powder, and cayenne can either be added to the mixture in the bowl and mixed in by hand, or processed along and blended with the other items.

Place 2 or more cups of the mixture onto Teflex sheets in your dehydrator and spread it out evenly with a spoon, knife, or bowl scraper. This batch is enough to fill 7 to 8 large dehydrator trays (15- x 15-inch), depending on the thickness of the crackers.

Dehydrate at 95°F for 10 to 12 hours.

Flip Teflex sheets over on the trays and peel off the cracker mixture. Sprinkle the moist side of the crackers with herbs of your choice for additional seasoning and spice.

Score the crackers into sizes and shapes of your choice. Continue dehydrating until the crackers are dry and crisp or remain slightly chewy (another 6 to 8 hours).

Break the crackers into individual pieces and store the crisp ones in a sealed container. Moist or chewy crackers are best kept in Ziploc bags in the refrigerator.

Variation: For a tangy sourdough flavor, let the dough remain in a large plastic bowl or bucket covered with a towel for a day or two prior to dehydrating.

Jameth and Kim's Original Flax Crackers

BY JAMETH AND KIM SHERIDAN

ADVANCED PREP: 5 to 7 hours for soaking; 24 hours for dehydrating
IMMEDIATE PREP: 15 min   **SERVES** 6   **SPECIAL EQUIPMENT** Dehydrator

INGREDIENTS

1 cup flax seeds, soaked in purified water for 5 to 7 hours
1 1/4 to 1 1/2 cups purified water

DIRECTIONS

Mix the flax slurry with the additional water.

Spoon the soaked flax seeds and water mixture onto dehydrator trays, spreading it to a uniform 1/8- to 1/4-inch thickness.

Using a butter knife, slice lines through the flax mixture for the cracker shapes you choose (such as squares). Dehydrate at 110°F for about 24 hours or until crispy. At "half time," turn the dehydrator trays around 180° to ensure full dehydration. Peel off the trays and enjoy!

Variation 1: Mix 2 tablespoons Bragg Liquid Aminos and 2 teaspoons Italian seasoning with the flaxseed mixture before dehydrating for savory "pizza" flavored crackers.

Variation 2: Blend 4 to 5 cloves garlic with the purified water before soaking the flax seeds in it. After soaking the flaxseed for 5 to 7 hours, add 3/8 cup celery juice and 3 tablespoons fresh lemon juice to the mixture. Mix thoroughly and dehydrate for delicious crispy crackers.

Contributor's note: Keep in mind that dehydration time is slightly longer for crackers with seasonings.

Corn Tortillas

BY SHAZZIE

ADVANCED PREP: 8 to 12 hours for dehydrating   **IMMEDIATE PREP:** 25 min
YIELDS 20 to 40 tortillas   **SPECIAL EQUIPMENT** Food processor, dehydrator

INGREDIENTS

    4 cobs sweet corn kernels, cut from cobs
    1 clove garlic, crushed
    1 red onion
    1 bunch coriander
    1 tablespoon flaxseed, ground fine

DIRECTIONS

Combine all the ingredients in the food processor and grind until everything is broken down. Continue blending until mixture becomes doughy. If the mixture remains crumbly, add a tomato or two.

Spread the mixture onto Teflex sheets in your dehydrator, and flatten the dough to about 1/4-inch thick (it will get much flatter as it dries). Score the tortillas where you want to snap them, and dehydrate at 115°F for 4 hours.

Turn over the tortillas at least once during dehydration, and remove the dehydrator sheets. Dehydrate until crisp.

Contributor's note: These are great with soups and salads. They're also a lovely snack on their own.

Flax and Corn Crackers

By Shazzie
Advanced prep: 6 to 12 hours for dehydrating   **Immediate prep:** 30 min
Yields 20 to 40 crackers   **Special Equipment** Food processor, dehydrator

INGREDIENTS

    2 cobs sweet corn, de-cobbed
    1 clove garlic, crushed
    2 cups flax seeds, ground
    4 teaspoons sesame oil

DIRECTIONS

Combine all the ingredients in a food processor and blend until the mixture is fluffy. Spoon out the mixture onto dehydrating trays, and flatten to about 1/2-inch thick (it will get much flatter as it dries). Dehydrate at 115°F for 6 to 12 hours, depending on thickness of crackers.

Variation: Add ingredients such as chopped herbs (chives are really good), sea salt, chopped tomatoes, peppers, chili, onion, mushroom or mustard powder to the mixture. Try dividing the mixture into different bowls and adding different flavors to each one.

"Pizza" Crackers

BY JULIE RODWELL

ADVANCED PREP: 3 to 5 days for sprouts and soaking + 28 hours for dehydrating
IMMEDIATE PREP: 1 hour   **YIELDS** 6 to 7 dehydrator trays full
SPECIAL EQUIPMENT Coffee grinder, Champion juicer, dehydrator

INGREDIENTS

2 to 3 dried or fresh cayenne or dried Thai devil peppers

1/2 cup or more fresh or dried desert sage, rosemary, tarragon, parsley, or other herbs

4 cups chickpeas (garbanzos), soaked overnight and sprouted for 3 to 5 days (they will triple in volume)

2 cups flaxseed or 1 cup flaxseed mixed with 1 cup sesame seeds, soaked for 8 hours but not drained

4 stalks celery, chopped (to reduce strings) (optional)

4 to 5 large red bell peppers, chopped

1 red onion, chopped

2 pounds tomatoes, chopped (cherry tomatoes are best)

3 to 8 cloves garlic

1/2 to 1 teaspoon sea salt (not optional to most tastes)

other bland raw green veggies, such as broccoli stalks or zucchini (avoid additional onions, scallions, leeks, and the like, as the blend will be too strong)

DIRECTIONS

Grind the dried hot peppers and the sage or other dried herbs in a coffee grinder until powdered (this isn't essential but prevents nasty surprise mouthfuls).

Run the chickpeas (garbanzos), flax, celery, bell peppers, onion, tomatoes, garlic, and ground hot peppers and herbs through a Champion juicer using the blank plate. Blend all ingredients well. Spread the mixture onto Teflex sheets, making sure it is at least 1/4-inch thick all over. The dough should fill 6 to 7 sheets. Dehydrate at 105°F for 3 to 4 hours.

Turn over the crackers, and score them into squares with a knife, spatula, or cracker cutter. Dehydrate another 24 hours or more, to desired crispness. Store the crackers in an airtight container.

Hint: Using a wire coil eggbeater to mix the batter will help remove any celery "strings," as does chopping the celery finely.

Contributor's note: This is a crunchy cracker that was derived from the Boutenkos' "Everybody's Favorite Cracker" recipe. They are very popular and Julie has people begging her to make them commercially.

Raw Tortillas

By Elaina Love

Advanced prep: 6 to 12 hours   **Immediate prep:** 25 min
Yields 16 tortillas   **Special Equipment** Blender, dehydrator

INGREDIENTS

2 large carrots, chopped

2 zucchini (green or yellow), chopped

2 avocados, peeled and pitted

1 teaspoon Celtic sea salt

1 tablespoon lemon juice

1 teaspoon onion powder (optional)

1 teaspoon garlic powder (optional)

dash cayenne (optional)

2 cups flax meal (1 1/2 cup whole seeds before grinding)

DIRECTIONS

Blend the carrots and zucchini with 1 cup water until smooth.

Add the avocado, sea salt, lemon juice, onion powder, garlic powder, and cayenne and blend until smooth. Pour into a mixing bowl. Add the flax meal, and mix by hand.

Divide the batter into 4 sections, and spread each section on a 16- x 16-inch Excalibur dehydrator tray lined with a Teflex sheet. Score each tray into 4 tortillas, and dehydrate at 105°F for 1 to 2 hours.

Flip the tortillas and remove the Teflex sheets. Continue to dehydrate until the tortillas are still moist but seem dry enough to store. Store in a Ziploc bag at room temperature for up to a week, or in the refrigerator for months.

Really Veggie Crackers

BY ELAINA LOVE

ADVANCED PREP: 8 to 12 hours for soaking + 24 hours for dehydrating
IMMEDIATE PREP: 35 min   **SERVES** 12 to 16   **SPECIAL EQUIPMENT** Food processor, dehydrator

INGREDIENTS

1/2 onion, chopped

2 to 5 cloves garlic

1 head spinach

1 cup fresh herbs (such as dill, basil, sage, oregano, rosemary, or thyme), chopped

3 teaspoons Celtic sea salt

1/4 cup lemon juice

2 zucchini, shredded

2 carrots, shredded

2 cups flax seeds, soaked 8 to 12 hours but not drained

2 cups flax seeds, ground

DIRECTIONS

Purée the onions, garlic, spinach, and herbs with the sea salt and lemon juice in food processor. Transfer the mixture to a bowl, and add the zucchini, carrots, and soaked flax seeds.

Mix everything together well, adding the flax meal and 1 or more cups water at the very end. The batter should be thick and easy to spread.

Spread the batter onto Teflex sheets in a dehydrator, and dehydrate for 8 hours at 105°F.

Flip the crackers, and remove the Teflex sheets. Continue to dehydrate another 16 hours or until the crackers are crunchy.

Rosemary Croutons

BY CHAD SARNO

ADVANCED PREP: 6 to 8 hours for soaking + 12 to 16 hours for dehydrating
IMMEDIATE PREP: 1 hour   **YIELDS** 8 to 9 dehydrator trays   **SPECIAL EQUIPMENT**
Food processor, dehydrator

INGREDIENTS

- 2 cups golden flax seeds, soaked in 3 cups filtered water for 4 to 6 hours
- 2 cups sunflower seeds (or almonds), soaked in filtered water for 6 to 8 hours and drained
- 4 carrots, chopped
- 1/3 cup chopped leek
- 1 cup chopped red bell pepper
- 1/4 cup dried rosemary
- 3 tablespoons garlic powder or 3 cloves fresh garlic
- 2 tablespoons dried Italian seasoning
- 1/2 teaspoon cayenne
- 1 1/2 tablespoons Celtic sea salt
- freshly cracked black pepper to taste

DIRECTIONS

In a food processor, blend the soaked flax and sunflower seeds to a pâté. Transfer to a large mixing bowl.

Combine the carrots with the leek, bell pepper, rosemary, garlic powder, Italian seasoning, cayenne, sea salt, and black pepper in the food processor and blend until finely minced. Add this to the seeds and mix together thoroughly.

Spread a 1/2-inch even layer of the mixture onto Teflex sheets in a dehydrator. Score the dough into even squares as small as you want the croutons to be. Dehydrate at 110°F for 12 to 16 hours. Remove the Teflex sheets about halfway through dehydrating, and break apart the croutons.

Rosemary Croutons will keep for about 1 month in a sealed container.

Rye Bread Sticks with Avocado Sauce

By Elysa Markowitz

Advanced prep: 8 to 10 hours for soaking + 4 to 8 hours for dehydrating
Immediate prep: 40 min **Yields** 24 to 36 bread sticks and 1 1/2 cups sauce **Special Equipment** Blender, food processor, or Green Power / Star juicer with Bread Stick Maker

INGREDIENTS

1 cup rye, soaked overnight and drained

1/8 cup flax seeds, soaked overnight (not drained)

1/8 cup caraway seeds, soaked overnight and drained

1/2 cup sunflower seeds, soaked overnight and drained

1 to 2 tablespoons soy sauce (Osawa or nama shoyu) or sea salt to taste

For the avocado sauce:

1 avocado

1 tomato

2 green onions

1 teaspoon mustard powder

DIRECTIONS

Soak the grains and seeds together in a large bowl. Rinse in a strainer with small holes to keep from losing the caraway seeds.

In a high-power blender or food processor fitted with an "S" blade, process the soaked rye, flax, caraway, and sunflower seeds with 1/2 to 1 cup water. (Use less water if you want a thicker bread stick; more would make a cracker.)

Stir in the soy sauce or sea salt and roll out the bread sticks so they are 1/2 inch in diameter and 6 to 8 inches in length.

Place the bread sticks on dehydrator trays. Dehydrate at 105°F for 4 to 8 hours, or to desired crispiness.

Purée the avocado, tomato, green onions, and mustard powder in a blender to a smooth consistency. Serve as a spicy dipping sauce for the bread sticks.

Tip: The easiest way to make Rye Bread Sticks is to use the Green Power / Star juicer with the Bread Stick Maker in place.

Sweet Golden Crackers

BY KARIE CLINGO

ADVANCED PREP: 5 to 7 hours for soaked golden flax + 20 hrs for dehydrating   **IMMEDIATE PREP:** 30 min   **YIELDS** 2 1/2 dehydrator trays full
SPECIAL EQUIPMENT Vita-Mix or coffee grinder, dehydrator.

INGREDIENTS

1 to 2 cups golden flaxseed, soaked (or grind the dry seeds in a Vita-Mix or coffee grinder and add an equal amount of liquid)

1/2 cups raw honey or 8 soaked blended dates for sweetener

1 teaspoon cinnamon (to taste)

pinch Celtic sea salt

DIRECTIONS

Combine the ground flaxseed with the honey or dates, cinnamon, and sea salt, and mix well. Dehydrate at 110°F overnight, flip, and continue to dehydrate for half a day.

Hint: Add more seasoning than you think you will need!

Chips

Abeba's Corn Chips

By Abeba Wright

Serves 10   **Special Equipment** Food processor or blender, dehydrator

INGREDIENTS

- 6 to 8 ears worth of corn kernels, cut from the cobs
- 3/4 cup sunflower seeds, soaked overnight
- 1/3 to 1/2 red onion, chopped
- 1/4 teaspoon cumin
- 1/3 cup ground flaxseed
- dash cayenne pepper
- Celtic sea salt to taste

DIRECTIONS

Mix corn, sunflower seeds, and onion in blender or food processor (For more crunch, use a food processor.)

Add the cumin, ground flaxseed, cayenne, sea salt, and mix well. Spoon onto dehydrator trays lined with Teflex sheets. Dehydrate at 105°F for 8 hours. Flip the corn chips and remove the Teflex sheets. Continue to dehydrate until crisp.

Barbecue Chips

By Abeba Wright

Advanced prep: 30 min for soaking + 8 to 10 hours for dehydrating
Immediate prep: 40 min   **Serves** 10 to 12   **Special Equipment** Blender, dehydrator

INGREDIENTS

2 carrots, chopped

1 to 2 dates or 12 raisins, soaked 30 minutes and drained (reserve soak water)

3/4 teaspoon chili powder

1 celery stalk, chopped

2 tomatoes

1/2 cup sun-dried tomatoes, soaked for 30 minutes, drained and chopped (reserve soak water, test for saltiness)

cayenne pepper to taste

nama shoyu or Celtic sea salt to taste

1/4 to 1/2 medium beet (optional)

2/3 cup flax seeds, soaked 3 hours or overnight

DIRECTIONS

Combine the carrots, dates, chili powder, celery, tomatoes, sun-dried tomatoes, cayenne, nama shoyu, beet (if using), and 1 1/2 cups of water in a blender. Blend well and adjust the seasonings.

Add the flax seeds and blend well. The mixture should be thick but pourable. If mixture is too thick, crackers will be chewy, not crunchy—add a little water if necessary to keep it runny.

Spoon the dough onto dehydrator trays lined with Teflex and dehydrate at 105°F degrees for 8 to 10 hours.

Remove the Teflex sheets and flip the chips. Continue to dehydrate until crisp.

Curly Crisps

By Shazzie

Advanced prep: None   **Immediate prep:** 20–40 min

Special Equipment Spiral slicer, dehydrator

INGREDIENTS

vegetables such as sweet potatoes, pumpkin, zucchini, or carrots
sea salt and seaweed flakes (optional)

DIRECTIONS

Using a spiral slicer on the curly setting, slice the vegetables.

Add salt or ground seaweed flakes if desired.

Place the curls on a dehydrator tray and dehydrate at 115°F for 6 to 12 hours, depending on the thickness of the chips.

Variation 1: After slicing, marinate the vegetables overnight in an herby dressing, and then dehydrate.

Variation 2: For savory crisps, thinly slice vegetables such as eggplant, beets, tomato, rutabaga, or zucchini and dehydrate until crisp. Add sea salt or ground seaweed flakes if desired. Also, try variation 1 with any of these vegetables.

Variation 3: For sweet crisps, slice apples, pineapples, pears, or bananas and dehydrate until crisp. Try squeezing some lemon juice over the fruits before dehydrating for a fresh new flavor.

Contributor's note: These fun snacks go well with all dips and look beautiful on top of soups.

Joe's Chip Shop Chips

BY SHAZZIE
ADVANCED PREP: None   **IMMEDIATE PREP:** 15 min
SERVES 2   **SPECIAL EQUIPMENT** None

INGREDIENTS

2 avocados, ripe but firm
1 bag (about 1/2 cup) poppy seeds

DIRECTIONS

Slice the avocados in half and carefully remove each pit without damaging the avocado. Cut into quarters, then eighths. Gently peel off the skin off and discard.

Place the poppy seeds on a flat-bottomed dish, and roll the avocados in the seeds until they're fully covered. Place on an attractive serving dish.

Contributor's note: My friend Joe came up with this, and I'm very grateful to him for allowing it to be shared!

Hemp Corn Chips

BY MATT SAMUELSON
ADVANCED PREP: 5 to 7 hours for soaking + 24 to 30 hours for dehydrating
IMMEDIATE PREP: 40 min   **YIELDS** approximately 175 chips
SPECIAL EQUIPMENT Food processor, dehydrator

INGREDIENTS

6 cups fresh or frozen corn
10 cups sunflower seeds, soaked (6 cups before soaking)
1 cup hemp seeds
1 1/2 cups flax seeds, ground into meal
1 1/2 tablespoons Celtic sea salt
1 lime, juiced

DIRECTIONS

Purée the corn in a food processor until creamy. Place in a mixing bowl. Purée the sunflower seeds with 2 3/4 cups water until creamy; add to the mixing bowl. Add the hemp seeds, ground flax seeds, sea salt, and lime juice; mix well.

Spread 2 1/2 cups of the batter on a 16- x 16-inch dehydrator tray covered with a Teflex sheet. Cut into shapes, such as triangles, squares, or circles. Dehydrate for 24 to 30 hours at 105°F until crispy. Remove the Teflex sheets after about 10 hours.

Nut Chips

BY JALISSA LETENDRE
ADVANCED PREP: 8–10 hours for soaking + 12 hours for dehydrating
IMMEDIATE PREP: 40 min   **MAKES** about 40 chips   **SPECIAL EQUIPMENT** Food processor, dehydrator

INGREDIENTS

2 cups hazelnuts, soaked overnight and drained

1 cup sesame seeds, soaked overnight and drained

1/3 cup chopped fresh cilantro

1/2 cup chopped red onion

1 lemon, juiced

1/2 tablespoon dried basil

1/2 tablespoon garlic powder

2 tablespoons honey

2 teaspoons Herbamare® or sea salt

paprika for garnish

DIRECTIONS

Blend the hazelnuts and sesame seeds in a food processor, slowly adding 2 cups water to the mixture. Stop the processor once in a while to scrape the sides of the bowl.

In a large bowl, combine all the ingredients, including the ground nuts and seeds, and mix well.

Divide the mixture in half and spread over 2 Teflex sheets to dehydrate. Using a spatula, cut the mixture into triangles, and sprinkle with paprika. Dehydrate for 5 hours at 105°F.

Remove the Teflex sheets and dehydrate for 7 more hours.

12

Raw Milk & Cheese Substitutes

Milk

Almond Milk

BY ELAINA LOVE

ADVANCED PREP: 8 to 12 hours for soaking   **IMMEDIATE PREP:** 15 min
YIELDS 3 to 4 cups   **SPECIAL EQUIPMENT** Blender, The Amazing Nut Milk, Juice and Sprout Bag

INGREDIENTS

    1 cup almonds, soaked (1/2 cup before soaking) and drained
    2 pitted dates (optional)
    1 teaspoon vanilla (optional)

DIRECTIONS

Blend all the ingredients with 3 cups water on high until well blended.

Pour through The Amazing Nut Milk, Juice and Sprout Bag to strain. Store the milk in a glass jar in the refrigerator for up to 4 days.

Contributor's note: Almonds are packed with calcium, fiber, folic acid, magnesium, potassium, riboflavin, and Vitamin E. Drain off the first soak water, which will be brown.

Almond Milk

BY AMY YOCKEL

ADVANCED PREP: 4 hours for soaking   **IMMEDIATE PREP:** 15 min
SPECIAL EQUIPMENT Blender   **SERVES** 4   **YIELDS** 6 cups

INGREDIENTS

- 2 cups almonds soaked and drained
- 4 cups pure water
- 3 tablespoons honey
- 1 1/2 teaspoons vanilla bean extract
- 1 teaspoon ground cinnamon
- 1 teaspoon ground nutmeg
- 1/4 teaspoon ground cloves
- 1 teaspoon Celtic sea salt or to taste (optional)

DIRECTIONS

Place 2 almonds in blender with 4 cups water blend until smooth. Line pitcher with sprout bag, pour mixture into bag, and squeeze out all liquid into pitcher.

***Keep the pulp for crackers or bread or throw away.

Add honey, vanilla bean extract, ground cinnamon, ground nutmeg, ground cloves, and Celtic sea salt (optional)

Blend all ingredients in blender and serve.

Almond Cheese or Yogurt

BY SHARON ELAM

ADVANCED PREP: 2 1/2 days   **IMMEDIATE PREP:** 40 min

YIELDS 6 to 8 cups   **SPECIAL EQUIPMENT** Blender, Sieve, Draining Bags

INGREDIENTS

2 to 3 cups almonds

basil, chopped, to taste

garlic, minced, to taste

lemon juice, to taste

Celtic salt, to taste

DIRECTIONS

Soak almonds for 12 to 24 hours (the longer soaked, the easier to skin). They will double in size. Discard soak water.

Boil a pot of water. Using a wire sieve, blanch a cupful of almonds at a time by immersion for 7 seconds. Skin each batch as you go.

Blend 4 cups skinned almonds with 4 cups water in a Vita-Mix or blender. Pour into quart canning jars and set in a warm place for approximately 12 hours. The mixture will grow and there will be lots of air holes throughout. There will also be about 3⁄4 to 1 inch of yellow liquid at the bottom of the container.

Pour the mixture into draining bags. You can also use nylon painter bags—quart or gallon size. Twist and knot bags. Hang over the sink or a bowl for about 12 hours.

Add chopped basil, garlic, lemon juice, and Celtic salt. Use your imagination and create your own favorite spreads.

Almond, Hazel, or Sunflower Milk

BY SHAZZIE

ADVANCED PREP: 6 hours for soaking   **IMMEDIATE PREP:** 10 min

YIELDS 3 cups   **SPECIAL EQUIPMENT** Blender

INGREDIENTS

> 2 cups raw almonds, hazelnuts or sunflowers, or a mixture of these, soaked for at least 6 hours and drained
>
> 2 Medjool dates, or 4 other dates, pits removed

DIRECTIONS

Combine all the ingredients in your blender with 1 1/4 cups water. Blend for as long as possible, to break down the solid ingredients.

Pour the mixture through a strainer into a bowl. Add the solid bits back into the blender with another 1 1/4 cups water, blend again, and strain. Store the milk in the fridge, and use within 2 days. Don't worry if it separates; just shake it before use.

Contributor's note: Always make enough almond or sunflower milk for 2 days and keep it in the fridge. Drink it any time by itself, or add some to a blender with a piece of fruit for a quick and filling drink.

Brazil Nut Mylk Magic

BY KAREN PARKER

ADVANCED PREP: 4 hours for soaking   **IMMEDIATE PREP:** 20 min

YIELDS 6 to 7 cups   **SPECIAL EQUIPMENT** Blender, Nut Mylk bag

INGREDIENTS

1 1/2 cups brazil nuts, unsoaked

1/2 cup white sesame seeds, soaked up to 4 hours

3 cups young coconut water

1/2 teaspoon celtic sea salt

1 tablespoon mesquite meal

5 drops liquid stevia (optional)

DIRECTIONS

Combine all the ingredients in a high-powered blender and mix until smooth.

Strain the mylk by pouring it through a nylon mesh nut mylk bag, catching the liquid in a pitcher and squeezing the remaining liquid from the bag. Serve immediately.

Cashew Yogurt

BY CHERIE SORIA

ADVANCED PREP: 6 to 12 hours for soaking+ 2 days for rejuvelac

YIELDS 1 quart   **SPECIAL EQUIPMENT** Blender, sprout bag, glass jar

INGREDIENTS

2 cups raw cashews, soaked in purified (non-chlorinated) water for 6 to 12 hours and drained

2 or more cups rejuvelac (recipe on page 9)

1/4 cup pure maple syrup or date paste, to taste

1 teaspoon vanilla extract or 1/8 teaspoon almond extract

DIRECTIONS

Place the cashews in a blender with the rejuvelac. Blend until smooth and creamy, adding more rejuvelac, if necessary.

Pour into a sprout bag and allow to drain for 1 to 2 hours.

Pour into a glass jar, place in a warm (not hot) location and let ferment for another 8 to 12 hours.

Add the maple syrup and extract to the yogurt and blend well. Pour the yogurt into a glass jar and store in the refrigerator.

Serving suggestion: Layer with berries or other fruit for a beautiful parfait. If you omit the sweetener and extracts, you can use Cashew Yogurt as a base for creamy salad dressing, soups, and sauces.

Green Hemp Milk

By Shazzie

Advanced prep: 8 to 10 hours for soaking   **Immediate prep:** 15 min

Serves 2   **Special Equipment** Blender

INGREDIENTS

4 carrots

4 cups spinach

1 orange, peeled

2 stalks celery, finely chopped

sprig rosemary or sage

1 cup hemp seeds, soaked overnight

DIRECTIONS

Combine all the ingredients in a blender, and blend until smooth. Place a clean cloth such as muslin inside a strainer, and place over a bowl. Pour the mixture into the cloth, and wring the cloth to squeeze out all the juice.

Quickest Tahini Milk

By Shazzie

Advanced prep: None   **Immediate prep:** 10 min

Yields 3 cups   **Special Equipment** Blender

INGREDIENTS

1/2 cup raw tahini

2 Medjool or 4 other dates, pits removed

DIRECTIONS

Blend the tahini and dates with 2 1/2 cups of water and enjoy.

Variation: Add raw carob, banana, strawberries or raspberries to the blender for a tasty, protein-rich milkshake.

Contributor's note: Children love this sweet drink. It's very useful if you need a nut milk and have no soaked nuts to make it with.

Cheeses

Chedda Sauce

By Rhio

ADVANCED PREP: 8 to 10 hours for soaking   **IMMEDIATE PREP:** 35 min

YIELDS 1 1/4 cups   **SPECIAL EQUIPMENT** Blender

INGREDIENTS

- 3/4 cup pine nuts, soaked overnight or for at least 2 hours, rinsed and drained
- 1/2 cup sunflower seeds, soaked overnight or for at least 2 hours, and rinsed and drained
- 1 large red bell pepper, seeds removed
- juice of 1/2 lemon
- 1 1/2 tablespoons nutritional yeast flakes
- 1 small clove garlic (optional)
- 2 teaspoons nama shoyu

Combine all ingredients in a blender and mix well. If the bell pepper doesn't liquefy readily, add a little water. Chedda Sauce will keep for 2 to 3 days in the refrigerator.

Variation 1: For those who don't appreciate the flavor of pine nuts, make the recipe with 1 cup sprouted, blanched almonds, and reduce the amount of sunflower seeds to 1/4 cup. For a creamier sauce, add 1 to 2 tablespoons soaked macadamia nuts. All other ingredients remain the same.

Variation 2: This sauce can also be made into a cheddar-type cheese by dehydrating it. Spread the sauce 1/4-inch thick on a Teflex-lined dehydrator tray and dehydrate at 95° F for 1 to 2 days. The resulting sheet can then be cut into pieces or crumbled and used like grated cheese. It will keep for more than 2 weeks in the refrigerator.

Contributor's note: Great on finely chopped broccoli or brussels sprouts.

Cheddary Cheeze Spread

BY SHAZZIE
ADVANCED PREP: 2 hours for soaking   **IMMEDIATE PREP:** 20 min
YIELDS 3 cups   **SPECIAL EQUIPMENT** Hand blender, dehydrator

INGREDIENTS

    3 cups pine nuts, soaked for 2 hours
    4 sun-dried tomatoes, soaked for 2 hours
    1/2 small orange or yellow pepper, seeds and core removed
    1 lemon, juiced
    1 clove garlic, chopped

DIRECTIONS

Blend all the ingredients with a hand blender until very smooth. Spread on dehydrated crackers and enjoy.

Variation: To make cheddary cheeze squares, spread the mixture out 1/4-inch thick onto Teflex-lined dehydrator trays. Dehydrate at 115°F for 6 to 24 hours, until firm. Cut the cheeze into squares, peel them apart and turn them over. Dehydrate the cheeze for another 2 to 4 hours, and serve with veggie or Walnut Burgers (see recipe page 279), on crackers, or with your favorite meal.

Herbed Cream Cheese

BY KAREN PARKER
ADVANCED PREP: 1/2 hour for cooling in refrigerator
IMMEDIATE PREP: 25 min   **YIELDS** 2 to 3 cups   **SPECIAL EQUIPMENT** Blender

INGREDIENTS

    1 1/3 cups Brazil, macadamia or pine nuts, unsoaked
    1/4 cup olive oil
    3 tablespoons lemon juice
    1 1/2 teaspoons salt
    1 teaspoon freshly cracked peppercorns
    2 tablespoons fresh dill, minced
    1 tablespoon fresh sage, minced

DIRECTIONS

Combine the nuts, lemon juice, salt, olive oil, and 1/3 cup water in high-powered blender, mixing until smooth.

Transfer the mixture to a bowl. Hand mix in the remaining ingredients. Cool in the refrigerator for half an hour before serving.

Macadamia Cream

BY SHAZZIE
ADVANCED PREP: None   **IMMEDIATE PREP:** 15 min
YIELDS 1/2 cup   **SPECIAL EQUIPMENT** Coffee grinder, citrus juicer

INGREDIENTS

    10 macadamia nuts
    1 orange, juiced
    2 Medjool or 4 other dates, pits removed

DIRECTIONS

Combine all ingredients in a coffee mill and blend until totally smooth. This might take several runs depending on the power of your mill.

Contributor's note: *Add this to soup, dressings and smoothies, or spoon it on top of your favorite fruit.*

Macadamia Nut Cream Cheese

BY ELAINA LOVE

ADVANCED PREP: 8 to 12 hours for fermenting   **IMMEDIATE PREP:** 25 min

YIELDS 2 to 3 cups   **SPECIAL EQUIPMENT** Blender

INGREDIENTS

- 2 cups macadamia nuts
- 1 lemon, juiced (about 3 tablespoons)
- 2 probiotic capsules (Kio-dophilus or any good acidophilus)

DIRECTIONS

Blend the macadamia nuts with the lemon juice, adding just enough water to cover the nuts.

Once the mixture is creamy, add the powder from the capsules and blend until mixed.

Pour the mixture into a colander or a stack of 3 strawberry baskets lined with a cheesecloth and drain.

Cover the cheese with the cheesecloth. Let it sit in a warm spot (70°F or warmer) for 8 to 12 hours.

Test the cheese. When it tastes the way you like it, put it in a glass container and refrigerate for up to 5 days.

Variation: You may also dehydrate this mixture to make a dry cheese to sprinkle on pasta or pizza.

Mild Almcheddar
Cheese Crumbs

By Viktoras Kulvinskas

Advanced prep: 12 hours for fermenting   **Immediate prep:** 30 min

Yields 3 to 4 cups   **Special Equipment** Food processor

INGREDIENTS

2 cups blanched almonds

1/2 cup sesame for sharp taste (optional)

4 capsules acidophilus or other bacteria mix (optional)

DIRECTIONS

Place half the nuts and sesame seeds in a dry blender pitcher; blend on high speed. Grind the nuts for about 30 seconds, and then begin adding water slowly. Blend the nuts and seeds to a cream. This might take as long as 2 minutes.

Blend in the acidophilus.

Transfer the mixture to a wide-mouth glass jar. Let it sit for at least 8 hours. Bubbles will form and it will have a sour, lemonish, odor and taste.

Drain off the water by pouring the mixture through a sprout bag or cheesecloth, gently squeezing out as much of the liquid as you can. Let the cloth hang over your kitchen sink for 4 hours or more.

Place the cheese in an airtight container or Ziploc bag in the refrigerator to store. Wash out the sprout bag and let it dry.

Contributor's note: Serve the cheese with salad, or with fresh fruit such as bananas, pears, or peaches, or mix 2 cups of the Almcheddar with 1 teaspoon of Celtic sea salt. Spread the cheese on dehydrator trays lined with Teflex sheets. Dehydrate at 118°F for 12 hours or until dry. Break into crumbs. Store in an airtight container or Ziploc bag.

13

Breakfast, Lunch, & Dinner Entrées

Early Bird Specials

Banana Bites

By Shazzie

Advanced prep: None   **Immediate prep:** 20 min

Serves 2   **Special Equipment** None

INGREDIENTS

2 bananas, peeled, with the end cut off

12 raisins, dry

12 walnut halves, dry

DIRECTIONS

Slice each banana into 6 equal discs (12 pieces total).

Push one raisin down into the top of each banana round. Sit a walnut half on each banana round, and serve.

Contributor's note: *You'll absolutely love these little easy-to-eat treats!*

Granola

By Rose Lee Calabro

Advanced prep: 12 to 48 hours for soaking   24 hr for dehydrating

Immediate prep: 30 min

Yields 5 cups   **Special Equipment** Food processor, dehydrator

INGREDIENTS

2 cups almonds, soaked 12 to 48 hours and drained

1 cup raw pumpkin seeds, soaked 8 hours and drained

1 cup sunflower seeds, soaked 4 to 6 hours and drained

2 apples, chopped with seeds and stem removed

1 tablespoon cinnamon

1 teaspoon Celtic sea salt

1/2 cup raisins (optional)

DIRECTIONS

Process the almonds in a food processor fitted with the "S" blade into small chunks and transfer to a mixing bowl. Process the pumpkin seeds and sunflower seeds until roughly ground and combine with the almonds.

Process the apples and add them to the nuts and seeds. Add the cinnamon and sea salt and mix well.

Spread mixture onto a dehydrator tray lined with a Teflex sheet and dehydrate for 20 to 24 hours at 105°F or to desired crunchiness. Be sure to dehydrate until all the water is removed from the granola. Add 1/2 cup raisins to the granola after dehydrating (if using). Store in a glass jar. This granola will last up to 3 months, so make lots! Serve with Almond Milk (page 208).

Grawnola

BY RHIO

ADVANCED PREP: 2 to 3 days for sprouting and soaking, + 24 to 36 hours for dehydrating   **IMMEDIATE PREP:** 45 min   **YIELDS** approximately 1 1/2 quarts
SPECIAL EQUIPMENT Blender, dehydrator

INGREDIENTS

1 1/2 cups almonds, sprouted 1 day
2 1/2 cups oat groats, sprouted 2 to 3 days
1 cup sunflower seeds, sprouted 1 day
1 cup buckwheat, sprouted 1 to 2 days
1 1/3 cups dates, pitted and soaked overnight

DIRECTIONS

With a sharp knife, cut the almonds into long slivers and place in a bowl with the sprouted oats, sunflower seeds and buckwheat. Toss to mix, and set aside.

Put the soaked and pitted dates into the blender with a little of the soak water and blend to a thick purée.

Pour the date purée over the grains, seeds and almonds and toss everything together well.

Spread the Grawnola onto dehydrator trays lined with Teflex sheets and dehydrate at 95° F for 24 to 36 hours. Store in a glass jar at room temperature. Grawnola keeps well when thoroughly dehydrated. You can also store in a plastic container in the freezer.

Variation: Put 1/2 to 1 cup Basic Grawnola Mix into a large bowl and add the following ingredients:

1 banana, sliced

1/2 cup fresh berries, mango or other fruit of your choice

1 tablespoon raisins or currants

sprinkle of vanilla powder (ground vanilla bean)

Almond Milk (page 182) or another nut or seed milk.

Maple Hemp Nut Bars

BY ROBERT YAROSH AND LISA SOTO

ADVANCED PREP: 8 hours for dehydrating **IMMEDIATE PREP:** 45 min
YIELDS 24 bars **SPECIAL EQUIPMENT** Food processor, dehydrator

INGREDIENTS

2 cups hemp nut seeds

1 cup Brazil nuts

1 cup ground rolled oats

1 cup ground sunflower seeds

1 cup raisins

1 cup carob chips (optional)

1 1/2 cups maple syrup or honey

1 tablespoon vanilla

1 cup olive oil

DIRECTIONS

Blend the hemp nut seeds, Brazil nuts, rolled oats, sunflower seeds, raisins, and carob chips (if using) to powder. Add the maple syrup or honey, vanilla, and olive oil. Blend well, and roll mixture onto oiled Teflex sheets.
Dehydrate at 115°F for 4 hours. Flip over and dehydrate for another 4 hours.

Marvelous Muësli

By Karen Knowler

Advanced prep: None   **Immediate prep:** 10 min

Serves 1   **Special Equipment** None

INGREDIENTS

2 handfuls nuts of your choice (chopped if larger than a hazelnut)

handful small berries (strawberries, raspberries, or blueberries), chopped

1 apple, diced

1 banana, sliced into discs and halved

any other fresh fruit

1/3 cup dried fruit (such as dates, figs, raisins, or apricots)

sprinkling of coconut flakes

sprinkling of sesame seeds (optional)

DIRECTIONS

Mix together all the nuts, berries, and fruit in a bowl, and top with coconut flakes and sesame seeds, if using. If you want milk, simply blend a handful of your favorite raw nuts with 3 to 4 cups of pure water, and strain well. Add the milk to your muësli and enjoy!

Oatmeal

BY **SHANNON ISLEY SCHNIBBE**

ADVANCED PREP: 8–12 hours for soaking
IMMEDIATE PREP: 5–10 min   **SPECIAL EQUIPMENT** None

INGREDIENTS

steel cut oats, 1/2 cup or so, cover with water to about 1 finger above oats, soak overnight

cinnamon, a dash

agave or date syrup, to taste

sea salt, a dash

almond butter, heaping tsp, (optional)

flax seeds, 1 teaspoon or more, ground in coffee grinder (optional)

berries (optional)

DIRECTIONS

Blend everything together until smooth and perhaps lightly warm. You may need to add water while blending. You can add the berries while blending and/or sprinkle a few on top once it is in the serving bowl.

Contributor's note: I've even added carob powder to this mixture. Feel free to play with it!

Pink Porridge

BY SHAZZIE

ADVANCED PREP: 6 hours for soaking   **IMMEDIATE PREP:** 10 min
SERVES 2   **SPECIAL EQUIPMENT** Blender

INGREDIENTS

2 cups almonds, soaked at least 6 hours, and drained
2 cups fresh or frozen raspberries
6 to 8 dried apricots, soaked 1 hour, and drained

DIRECTIONS

Place all the ingredients in a blender with 1 cup water and process to a porridge consistency. Add water slowly to keep the porridge from becoming too runny.

Spiced Strawberry Granola Crunch

BY KAREN PARKER

ADVANCED PREP: 12 hours for soaking + 12 hours for dehydrating   **IMMEDIATE PREP:** 35 min   **SERVES** 4 to 6   **SPECIAL EQUIPMENT** Food processor, dehydrator

INGREDIENTS

2 cups almonds, soaked 12 hours or more and drained
1 cup macadamia nuts, unsoaked
1 cup young Thai coconut meat
2 tablespoons Tree of Life mesquite flour

2 cups strawberries, chopped
1 teaspoon cinnamon
1 teaspoon nutmeg
1 teaspoon allspice
1/2 teaspoon Celtic sea salt

DIRECTIONS

Chop the almonds and macadamia nuts for 30 to 45 seconds in a food processor. Transfer the ground nuts to a large mixing bowl.

Chop the coconut meat into tiny pieces in a food processor. Add the coconut to the mixing bowl and stir in the strawberries, cinnamon, nutmeg, allspice, and sea salt. Mix well.

Spoon mixture onto dehydrator trays lined with Teflex sheets. Dehydrate for 12 hours at 95°F or until thoroughly dry and crunchy. Store the granola in a sealed, glass container in the refrigerator, and eat within one month.

Viktoras' Secret Raw Horamola

By Viktoras Kulvinskas

ADVANCED PREP: 30 hours for sprouting **IMMEDIATE PREP:** 30 min

YIELDS 6 to 7 cups **SPECIAL EQUIPMENT** Food processor, dehydrator

INGREDIENTS

- 5 cups buckwheat, sprouted
- 5 teaspoons honey
- 5 teaspoons Sucanat® raw sugar
- 5 teaspoons vanilla
- 3 teaspoons cinnamon
- 2 teaspoons sea salt
- 1 cup raisins
- 1/2 cup dates, chopped

DIRECTIONS

Partially process all the ingredients in a food processor to a sticky consistency. Do not cream the mixture.

Spread the mixture directly on dehydrator screens (no Teflex sheet) and dehydrate until crunchy.

Contributor's note: This makes a great—and sweet—trail mix!

Vanilla Bean Porridge

By Karen Parker

Advanced prep: 12 hours for soaking   **Immediate prep:** 15 min

Serves 4 to 6   **Special Equipment** High-power blender

INGREDIENTS

- 2 cups almonds, soaked 12 hours or more and drained
- 2 cups young coconut meat (reserve water)
- 1 1/4 cups young coconut water
- 1 teaspoon Celtic sea salt
- 1-inch piece vanilla bean
- 1 teaspoon raw coconut butter
- 3 drops liquid stevia (optional)

DIRECTIONS

Rinse the almonds well to remove tannic acid and other enzyme inhibitors and discard the soaking water.

Combine all the ingredients in a Vita-Mix or other high-powered blender. Process until smooth and creamy.

Italian-Style Favorites

Double Stuffed Tomatoes

By Shazzie

Advanced prep: 6 hours for soaking   **Immediate prep:** 35 min

Serves 4   **Special Equipment** Hand blender

INGREDIENTS

4 beefsteak or other large tomatoes, with stems intact

3 cups sunflower seeds, soaked at least 6 hours and drained

1 cup sun-dried tomatoes, roughly chopped, soaked for at least 6 hours and drained

1/2 teaspoon paprika

1/2 cup fresh basil, chopped, plus extra leaves for garnish

1 clove garlic

5 pitted black olives

DIRECTIONS

Cut off the tops of the tomatoes, leaving the stalk on the top, and set aside. Scoop out the seeds and the flesh of the tomatoes. Use the discarded tomato middles in another recipe such as Gazpacho Soup (see recipe on page 99).

Using a hand blender, blend the sunflower seeds with the sun-dried tomatoes and paprika until smooth. Mix in the chopped basil, garlic, and olives.

Stuff the tomatoes with the mixture until they overflow. Top with some extra basil leaves, and place the "lids" of the tomatoes back on top. Serve with your favorite salad.

Variation: For party hors d'oeuvres, use the same filling, but stuff tiny cherry tomatoes instead.

Eggplant Pizza

By Elysa Markowitz

Advanced prep: 20 min for soaking + 2 hours for dehydrating
Immediate prep: 45 min   **Serves** 2 to 4   **Special Equipment** Blender or Vita-Mix, dehydrator

INGREDIENTS

1 eggplant, peeled and cut into 1/2-inch-thick slices

For the sauce:
1/2 cup sun-dried tomatoes, soaked for 20 minutes in enough warm water to cover (reserve soak water)
2 to 3 tablespoons olive oil
1 clove garlic
1/4 cup fresh basil
2 to 4 pitted dates

For the toppings, choose from:
1 avocado, sliced
1 cup grated yellow squash
1/2 cup grated carrot
4 tablespoons chopped fresh parsley

DIRECTIONS

Place the eggplant slices in a dehydrator at 105°F.

To make the sauce, pour the sun-dried tomato soaking water into a blender along with the sun-dried tomatoes. Add the olive oil and crushed garlic, and purée.

Add the basil and pitted dates, and purée again until creamy.

Spread the sauce on top of the sliced eggplant, and let dehydrate for 1 to 2 hours.

Decorate the eggplant slices with your selected toppings. Return to the dehydrator for 5 to 10 minutes, and serve warm.

Variation: Toppings can be changed to suit your taste. You can use black olives, onion slices, basil, or mushrooms, just as you would on a regular pizza.

Contributor's note: This flourless pizza will thrill wheat-sensitive eaters.

Italian Rawsage

By Sergei and Valya Boutenko

Advanced prep: None   **Immediate prep:** 25 min

Serves 8   **Special Equipment** Food Processor

INGREDIENTS

- 1 cup pumpkin seeds
- 1/2 head lettuce
- 1/2 cup olive oil
- 5 cloves garlic
- 1/2 cup onion powder
- 1 tablespoon caraway seeds
- 1 tablespoon dried sage
- 1/2 bunch fresh basil

DIRECTIONS

Blend all ingredients in a food processor. Form into sausage shaped patties. (If preferred dehydrate at 110 degrees until firm on outside.)

Contributor's note: These raw "sausages" have a delicious nostalgic flavor.

Italian-Style Zucchini Pasta Pesto

By Cherie Soria

Advanced prep: 1 hour for soaking   **Immediate prep:** 45 min

Serves 4   **Special Equipment** Food processor, spiral slicer, or hand shredder

INGREDIENTS

For the pesto:
- 1 large bunch fresh basil leaves, washed and spun dry
- 1/4 cup olive oil
- 1/4 cup pine nuts
- 2 garlic cloves, crushed
- 1/4 tablespoon or to taste sea salt

For the pasta:
- 2 medium zucchini, cut into thin strips or shredded lengthwise to resemble pasta
- 8 to 10 mushrooms, chopped
- 2 to 3 tablespoons pesto
- 4 to 6 sun-dried tomatoes, soaked until soft and cut into thin strips

DIRECTIONS

To make the pesto, combine the basil leaves, olive oil, pine nuts, garlic, and sea salt in a food processor or blender and pulse to a paste.

Mix the zucchini, mushrooms, and pesto together with 1/4 cup water. Serve chilled on a bed of greens and garnish with the sun-dried tomatoes prior to serving.

Hint: To make zucchini resemble pasta, use a food processor with a julienne attachment, spiral slicer, or a hand shredder, and shred lengthwise to create long, fine, linguine-like strands. Warm it gently, and it will soften to the texture of *al dente* pasta.

Karie's Lasagna

BY KARIE CLINGO
ADVANCED PREP: 1 hour for dehydrating   **IMMEDIATE PREP:** 45 min
SERVES 4 to 8   **SPECIAL EQUIPMENT** Food Processor, dehydrator

INGREDIENTS

For the red marinara sauce:
4 to 6 ounces sun-dried tomatoes
2 to 3 fresh tomatoes
fresh Italian herbs, such as basil or oregano, to taste
Celtic sea salt
olive oil

1/2 soft date, pitted
3 to 5 cloves fresh garlic, to taste

For the layers:
1 to 2 cups pine nuts, macadamias, or Brazil nuts
2 bunches organic spinach leaves, washed

DIRECTIONS

To make the sauce, blend sun-dried tomatoes with fresh tomatoes, fresh herbs, sea salt, 1 tablespoon olive oil, date, and 2 to 3 cloves of fresh garlic.

To make the cheese, place the nuts in a food processor or blender with about 1/2 teaspoon Celtic sea salt and 2 to 3 cloves fresh garlic. Blend lightly so it remains crunchy.

In a glass dish, layer the ingredients in the following order: spinach leaves, red marinara sauce, and then the white nut cheese. Follow this with another layer. Drizzle cold-pressed olive oil over the dish if you choose, and sprinkle with fresh Italian herbs. To serve, warm the lasagna in a dehydrator at 110°F for 1 hour or so until warm. Enjoy!

Variation: Add sliced mushrooms on top of the spinach layer, or add other items such as red peppers.

Variation: Use thin zucchini slices instead of spinach.

Living Pizza

BY **SHARON ELAM**
ADVANCED PREP: 2 to 4 days for sprouts and soaking   **IMMEDIATE PREP:** 45 min
SERVES 6 to 8   **SPECIAL EQUIPMENT** Food Processor, Blender

INGREDIENTS

For the crust:
6 cups kamut berries, soaked and
  sprouted
4 cloves garlic
1 medium onion
3 tablespoons pizza seasoning
3 to 4 stalks celery
2 cups garbanzo beans, sprouted
  (chickpeas)
Celtic salt, to taste

For the pizza sauce:
2 cups dried tomatoes
1 cup water
onion powder, to taste
garlic powder, to taste
pizza seasoning, to taste
2 to 4 dates, puréed
almond cheese (page 183) (optional)

Soak the dried tomatoes in the water for 30 to 40 minutes. Saving the water, remove the tomatoes and place into a Vita-Mix or blender with the other sauce ingredients.

Blend to a thick, paste-like consistency. Thin this paste as needed with the soak water. Store in a canning jar.

Process the kamut in a food processor, potentially in a couple of batches. I suggest using a smaller food processor to do the onion, celery, and garlic, then add to the grain along with the Celtic salt and the pizza seasoning. You may also add a small portion of carrot and carrot juice to give the crust a bit of color.

Dollop the mixture onto teflex sheets, flatten to about 7" diameter and dehydrate until they are the consistency you prefer (chewy or crisp).

Spread the crust with almond cheese or any other spread. Top with the sauce and any other ingredients. Avocado is excellent.

Mock Spaghetti

BY JAMETH & KIM SHERIDAN
ADVANCED PREP: None   **IMMEDIATE PREP:** 10–20 min
SERVES 4 to 6   **SPECIAL EQUIPMENT** V-Slicer or another shredding device

INGREDIENTS

> any summer squash, such as zucchini, crookneck, or sunburst
> fresh-squeezed lemon juice, or any sauce or dressing of your choice (optional)

DIRECTIONS

Shred the squash lengthwise into long "spaghetti" strands using a V-Slicer or other shredding device. The longer the squash is, the longer the "spaghetti" will be. Sunburst squash will make shorter strands, more like "noodles."

Eat as is, or top with lemon juice and/or any sauce or dressing of your choice.

Pickled Zucchini, Eggplant

CONTRIBUTED BY JULIE RODWELL
ADVANCED PREP: None   **IMMEDIATE PREP:** 20 min
SPECIAL EQUIPMENT Vita-Mix   **SERVES** 6   **YIELDS** 1 Gallon

INGREDIENTS [MISSING QUANTITIES]

> eggplant, green zucchini, yellow zucchini (cut in 1" slices)
> 1 1/2 cup water
> garlic
> 2 teaspoons salt
> 2 tablespoons honey
> fresh oregano
> fresh thyme
> 1/2 cup apple cider vinegar

DIRECTIONS

Cut eggplant thinner. Put all eggplant and zucchini in gallon jar. Put in water, garlic, salt, honey, fresh oregano, and fresh thyme into Vitamix; add apple cider vinegar. Pour in jar, mix by hand in jar. Let sit 3 days. Don't use any liquid remaining after finished with veggies; compost or toss.

Raw-Violi

By Robert Yarosh & Lisa Soto

Advanced prep: 30 min for soaking   **Immediate prep:** 45 min

Serves 2 to 4   **Special Equipment** Saladacco, Vita-Mix

INGREDIENTS

rutabaga, daikon, or turnip

For the cheese:
1/4 cup pine nuts
1/4 cup macadamia nuts
1/4 teaspoon Celtic sea salt
1/4 cup olive oil
2 cloves garlic, minced
1 lemon, juiced

For the sauce:
3 Roma tomatoes, chopped

7 large fresh basil leaves
1/4 teaspoon Celtic sea salt
5 Medjool dates, soaked
1/4 cup olive oil
1/2 cup sun-dried tomatoes, soaked
1/2 cup chopped red pepper
1/4 cup chopped red onion
3 cloves garlic
1 tablespoon Italian seasoning
1 teaspoon apple cider vinegar

DIRECTIONS

Slice the rutabaga, daikon, or turnip into small thin discs with your Saladacco.

To make the cheese, purée all the cheese ingredients in a blender or food processor.

Place 1 teaspoon of the filling onto each disc, then fold in half to make the Raw-Violi.

Blend all the tomato sauce ingredients in a Vita-Mix and cascade the sauce over the Raw-Violi.

Walnut Stuffed Peppers

BY SHAZZIE

ADVANCED PREP: 30 min for soaking + 6 hours for dehydrating   **SERVES** 4
SPECIAL EQUIPMENT Champion juicer or food processor, dehydrator, spiral slicer, hand blender

INGREDIENTS

8 red peppers, divided

4 cups walnuts, shelled

For the peppers:
4 sun-dried tomatoes, soaked, and drained
plus extra for garnish

2 small red onions, finely chopped

2 zucchinis, spiral sliced

For the TK:
fresh cilantro leaves for garnish

walnuts, for garnish

olive oil

DIRECTIONS

Chop 4 peppers, and put them in a food processor. Add the walnuts and sun-dried tomatoes and process to a pâté. If you have a hand blender, transfer the mixture to a bowl and finish it with the hand blender for a smoother finish. If you have a Champion juicer, use it with its blank plate for the above stages.

Mix the chopped onion into the pâté, but don't blend it. Cut off the tops of the remaining 4 peppers, and remove the seeds. Transfer equal amounts of pâté into each pepper. Replace the lids, and place each on a serving plate. Place the zucchini spirals around each pepper. Finish by adding some extra-finely sliced sun-dried tomatoes, a few fresh cilantro leaves, some walnuts and a drizzle of olive oil to the zucchini. If you want, dehydrate the stuffed peppers for around 6 hours to soften them slightly. Add the zucchini after dehydrating.

Variation 1: Instead of stuffing peppers, use the pâté as a dip to spread on vegetable rounds, or serve with crudités.

Variation 2: Stuff nori instead of peppers.

Youktoras Have A Heart Pizza

By Viktoras Kulvinskas

Advanced prep: 12 hours for Almcheddar Cheese; 1 hour for dehydrating
Immediate prep: 1 hour 15 min **Makes** one 10 to 12-inch pie **Special Equipment** Vita-Mix, dehydrator

INGREDIENTS

For the crust:
1 cup carrot pulp
1/2 cup flax seed, soaked for a few hours but not drained
1 cup almonds, soaked and drained
1 tablespoon olive oil
1 teaspoon Celtic sea salt
1 tablespoon Sucanat®

For the sauce:
2 cups chopped Roma tomatoes
1/2 cup dried pineapple chunks
1/4 cup peeled and chopped beet
1 teaspoon grated fresh ginger root
2 cloves garlic, crushed
1/2 cup chopped red bell pepper
1/4 cup fresh oregano or 2 tablespoons dried
1 cup olive oil
1/2 cup lemon juice

1/2 cup sun-dried tomatoes, soaked 1 hour
1/4 cup unpasteurized soy sauce (Yamaki organic) or sea salt to taste
1/4 cup finely chopped onion

For the toppings:
1 large Roma tomato, thinly sliced
1 red bell pepper, sliced in rings
1 small red onion, sliced in thin rings
fresh herbs (such as oregano, rosemary, basil, thyme), chopped
1/4 cup sun-dried tomatoes
1 portobello mushroom, diced and soaked in Yamaki organic soy sauce
2 tablespoons jalapeño pepper, diced
1/2 cup finely sliced carrots
1 cup Mild Almcheddar Cheese Crumbs (page 190)
1 lemon, juiced

DIRECTIONS

Using a Vita-Mix, process all the crust ingredients to a dough. Shape the crust into a heart, or whatever shape you choose, and dehydrate overnight.

Excluding the onion, process all the ingredients for the sauce in a food processor. Add the onion as you shut off the unit.

Place the almond crust on a Teflon sheet. Spread the sauce on top, and arrange the tomatoes, bell pepper, onion, basil, oregano, rosemary, thyme, sun-dried tomatoes, mushrooms, and jalapeño. Sprinkle with sliced carrots, Almcheddar Cheese Crumbs see page 215, and lemon juice.

Dehydrate for at least 1 hour before serving. Place the pizza on a pan, and use a cutting wheel to cut the pie into 8 slices.

Platos de Mexico y España

Avocado Burritos

BY DAVID WOLFE

ADVANCED PREP: None   **IMMEDIATE PREP:** 20 min

SERVES 4   **SPECIAL EQUIPMENT** None

INGREDIENTS

2 avocados

2 jalapeño peppers

4 tomatoes

1 orange, juiced

8 lettuce leaves

DIRECTIONS

In a medium bowl, mash and mix together the avocados, peppers, and tomatoes. Squeeze in some orange juice for sweetness. Divide mixture among lettuce leaves and roll up burrito style.

Tip: Omit the jalapeño pepper if you're serving this dish to young children, or others who don't enjoy hot food.

Calabasa Relleno with Pico de Gallo

By Quintessence

Advanced prep: None   **Immediate prep:** 1 hour

Serves 5   **Special Equipment** Food processor

INGREDIENTS

5 sunburst squash

For the stuffing:
1/2 cup pine nuts
1 cup Brazil nuts
1/4 cup macadamia nuts
3 sun-dried tomatoes
1 1/2 tablespoons olive oil
1 1/2 tablespoons cumin powder
1 1/2 tablespoons chili powder
1/4 tablespoon cayenne powder
1 clove garlic
sea salt, to taste
1/2 bell pepper

1/4 bunch green onions
1/2 bunch cilantro

For the sauce:
1 large tomato
1 ounce sun-dried tomato
1 clove garlic
1 ounce lemon juice
1/4 cup filtered water
1/4 medium onion, minced
1/2 bunch green onions, minced
1/4 bunch cilantro, minced
2 tablespoons olive oil

DIRECTIONS

To prepare the Calabasa Relleno, remove the tops of the squash and set them aside. Hollow out the squashes, and save the insides. If you want, dehydrate the squash at 95°F degrees for 4 to 5 hours to soften.

Process the nuts, sun-dried tomatoes, olive oil, cumin, chili powder, cayenne, garlic, and sea salt in a food processor. Blend until lumpy and transfer to a bowl.

In the food processor, pulse-chop to mince the meat from the 5 squash together with the bell pepper, green onion, and cilantro. Mix together with the nut stuffing and set aside.

To prepare the Pico de Gallo, blend half of the fresh tomato with the sun-dried tomato, garlic, lemon juice, and filtered water. Transfer to a mixing bowl.

Chop the remainder of the fresh tomato. Add the minced onion, green onion, cilantro, olive oil, and the chopped tomato to the sauce, and mix well.

Fill each individual squash with the stuffing, and replace the squash caps. If you want, place them in the dehydrator to warm until serving. When ready to serve, spoon sauce onto plates and place each squash on top.

Chili Rellenos

By Robert Yarosh and Lisa Soto

Advanced prep: 2 hours for dehydrating   **Immediate prep:** 50 min

Serves 6 to 8   **Special Equipment** Food processor, dehydrator

INGREDIENTS

For the pâté:

1/2 cup pumpkin seeds, soaked and drained

1/2 cup almonds, soaked and drained

1/2 cup walnuts, soaked and drained

1/2 cup chopped red peppers

1/2 onion, chopped

1 1/2 tablespoons Mexican seasoning

1/2 cup fresh cilantro

3 cloves garlic

1/2 teaspoon Celtic sea salt

1 tablespoon yellow miso

6 to 8 Hatch chili peppers

For the cheese:

1 teaspoon yellow miso

1 teaspoon tahini

For the salsa:

3 tomatoes

2 mangos, diced

2 avocados, diced

1/2 red pepper, diced

1/2 cup papaya, diced

1/4 jalapeño, diced

2 cloves garlic

3 green onions, chopped

1/4 teaspoon Celtic sea salt

1/4 cup olive oil

1/4 cup fresh lime juice

1/2 bunch fresh cilantro, chopped

1/2 teaspoon chili powder

DIRECTIONS

Combine the pumpkin seeds, almonds, walnuts, red peppers, onion, Mexican seasoning, cilantro, garlic, sea salt, and yellow miso in a food processor and blend to a chunky pâté.

Stuff the chili peppers with the pâté. Place the chilis in your dehydrator at 115°F for 2 hours.

To make the cheese, combine the yellow miso with 1 teaspoon tahini and 2 teaspoons water in a bowl and mix well.

Mix together all the salsa ingredients in a bowl. Top the warm rellenos with the salsa and cheese. Enjoy!

Fajita Vegetables with Chili Pistachios

By Chad Sarno

Advanced prep: Chili Pistachios (12 hr) 1 hour for marinating or 2 hours for dehydrating **Immediate prep:** 15 min

Serves 6 **Special Equipment** None

INGREDIENTS

1 1/2 cups thin strips of red bell pepper

1 cup thin strips of yellow bell pepper

1 cup thin strips of zucchini

1 tablespoon minced garlic

1/4 cup chopped fresh cilantro

3 tablespoons minced oregano

3 tablespoons lemon juice

3 tablespoons olive oil

1 1/2 tablespoons chili powder

1 teaspoon cumin

1 1/2 teaspoons Celtic sea salt

DIRECTIONS

Toss all the ingredients together in a bowl. Marinate for up to 1 hour, or dehydrate for 2 hours to soften and warm. Serve with Chili Pistachios (page 125).

Haiku Burritos

By Juliano

Advanced prep: None **Immediate prep:** 25 min

Serves 2 **Special Equipment** None

INGREDIENTS

1 cup mashed avocado

2 teaspoons jalapeño, minced

2 teaspoons minced garlic

2 teaspoons minced fresh ginger

2 teaspoons fresh lemon juice

2 large romaine lettuce leaves

2 teaspoons organic stone-ground mustard

1 pickle, sliced lengthwise into strips

1/3 cup wakamé seaweed, thinly sliced

1/2 cup grated burdock

1/3 cup chopped onion

1/3 cup chopped red bell pepper

1/4 cup corn kernels, cut from cob

2 tablespoons nama shoyu

In a mixing bowl, stir together the avocado, jalapeño, garlic, ginger, and lemon juice. On each lettuce leaf, spread half the avocado mixture, mustard, pickle, seaweed, burdock, onion, red bell pepper, corn, and nama shoyu. Wrap like a burrito and devour.

From *Raw: The UnCook Book* (New York: ReganBooks, 1999.)

Mexican Stuffed Peppers

By Rose Lee Calabro

Advanced prep: 12 to 48 hours for soaking   **Immediate prep:** 45 min

Serves 8   **Special Equipment** Champion juicer or food processor, blender

INGREDIENTS

For the filling:

1 cup almonds, soaked 12 to 48 hours

1 cup sunflower seeds, soaked 6 to 8 hours and drained

1/2 cup pumpkin seeds, soaked 6 hours and drained

1/2 cup lentils, sprouted

1/2 cup finely grated carrots

1/2 cup finely chopped celery

1/2 cup finely chopped cilantro

2 tablespoons lemon juice

4 Anaheim chilis or red bell peppers, rinsed, seeds removed

1 tablespoon chili powder

1 tablespoon cumin

1 teaspoon Celtic sea salt

For the sauce:

2 red bell peppers, chopped

2 to 3 pitted dates, chopped

1 tomato, chopped

1 tablespoon carob powder

1 tablespoon lemon juice

1 teaspoon Celtic sea salt

1/2 teaspoon chili powder

dash cayenne

For serving:

bed of sprouts

DIRECTIONS

To make the filling, process the almonds, sunflower seeds, pumpkin seeds, and lentils through a Champion juicer using the blank plate or in a food processor fitted with the "S" blade.

In a large bowl, combine the processed nuts, seeds, and lentils with the carrots, celery, cilantro, lemon juice, chili powder, cumin, and sea salt. Mix well. Stuff the peppers with the filling and serve on a bed of sprouts.

To make the sauce, combine all the sauce ingredients in a blender. Blend well, adding water until desired consistency is reached. Serve on the side with stuffed peppers.

Soft Tacos

BY MATT AMSDEN

ADVANCED PREP: None   **IMMEDIATE PREP:** 35 min

SERVES 2   **SPECIAL EQUIPMENT** Food processor

INGREDIENTS

For the filling:

3 cups ground raw organic walnuts

1 teaspoon organic cumin seed powder

1 teaspoon organic coriander seed powder

1/3 cup nama shoyu

For the salsa:

3 cups organic tomatoes, chopped

1/2 cup chopped organic green or yellow onions

1/4 cup fresh, organic lime or lemon juice

1 organic bell pepper, chopped

1 cup fresh organic cilantro, chopped

with stems removed

1/4 cup organic cold-pressed olive oil

3 cloves organic garlic, peeled and crushed or minced

organic cayenne powder to taste

1/2 teaspoon Celtic sea salt

1 teaspoon organic cumin seed powder

For the taco shell:

organic collard green leaves

For the topping:

organic romaine lettuce, shredded

1 avocado, cubed

DIRECTIONS

To make the taco filling, combine the filling ingredients in a bowl and mix well.

In another bowl, combine the salsa ingredients and mix well.

To assemble the tacos, lay the collard green leaves flat. Spread the taco filling lengthwise. Add a layer of lettuce and top with the salsa and avocado.

Vegetable Paella

BY SHAZZIE

ADVANCED PREP: 2 to 3 days for sprouting and soaking + 4 days for marinating   **IMMEDIATE PREP:** 35 min   **SERVES** 4   **SPECIAL EQUIPMENT** None

INGREDIENTS

    1 red pepper, cut into thin strips
    1 yellow pepper, cut into thin strips
    1 cup chopped young tender asparagus
    2 white onions sliced into fine rings
    5 cloves garlic, crushed
    4 stalks celery, juiced
    2 lemons, juiced
    4 tablespoons olive oil
    2 cups quinoa, sprouted and rinsed
    4 ripe tomatoes, finely chopped
    4 sun-dried tomatoes, soaked at least 2 hours, drained and finely chopped
    1/2 cup black olives, pitted and finely chopped
    1 teaspoon saffron threads or 1/2 teaspoon saffron powder
    1 teaspoon paprika
    fresh herbs, edible flowers, and spices of your choice

DIRECTIONS

Place the peppers, asparagus, onions, and crushed garlic in a wide bowl. Mix the celery and lemon juice with the olive oil, and pour it over the chopped vegetables. Let the vegetables marinate for 1 to 3 days, until soft and juicy.

Meanwhile, sprout the quinoa overnight in water as in the Herby Stir Fry recipe (page 247). In a bowl, combine the fresh and sun-dried tomatoes, olives, saffron, and paprika.

Rinse the quinoa well, and place in an attractive serving dish. Pour the tomatoes and olives over the rice. Add the marinated vegetables, and stir the whole dish well.

Pour on a few tablespoons of the marinade, and leave the dish to stand in a non-refrigerated spot for 12 to 24 hours before serving. Serve with a generous helping of fresh chopped herbs, spices, and flowers scattered over the top.

Wild Mushroom Fajitas

By Shazzie

Advanced prep: 20 min for "It's Not Really Mayonnaise" + 4 hours for dehydrating   **Immediate prep:** 40 min   **Serves** 2 to 4   **Special Equipment** None

INGREDIENTS

1 white onion, finely chopped

1 yellow or orange pepper, cut into thin slices

2 cloves garlic, finely chopped

2 cups chopped portobello and/or shitake mushrooms

1 teaspoon cumin powder

1 teaspoon cayenne

2 tablespoons olive oil

1 lemon, juiced

4 to 6 Savoy cabbage leaves

handful spinach, chopped into fine strands

salsa

It's Not Really Mayonnaise (page 287)

handful chives, finely chopped (save flowers for decoration)

DIRECTIONS

In a large bowl, combine the onion, pepper, garlic, mushrooms, cumin and cayenne.

Mix the olive oil and lemon juice together and pour over the vegetables. Dehydrate at 105°F for 4 to 6 hours.

Arrange cabbage leaves on a big plate, and cut out any hard stems. Place equal amounts of the mushroom mixture on each. Top with spinach, and add the salsa and It's Not Really Mayonnaise. Sprinkle the fajitas with chives and add flowers for decoration just before serving.

Contributor's note: This is a healthy and tasty variation of the traditional Mexican favorite. Serve with guacamole, salsas and a big green salad with lots of fresh sweet corn in it.

Asian Delights

Beggin' For Bangkok Broccoli Bombast Bonanza

By Jackie Ayala and David Steinberg

Advanced prep: None   **Immediate prep:** 40 min

Serves 4 to 6   **Special Equipment** Vita-Mix

INGREDIENTS

For the salad:

1 cup diced broccoli

1/2 cup diced bok choy

1/2 cup diced fresh turmeric

1 cup Asian-cut celery

2 large cloves garlic, sliced thin

4 tablespoons ginger, diced

meat from 1 young coconut

1/2 cup red bell pepper, cut into thin strips

1/2 cup diced Fuji apple

1 yellow squash

1 cup Asian-cut zucchini

1/2 cup fresh herbs, such as parsley, cilantro, and rosemary, diced

For the dressing:

1/2 cup citrus juice blend (3/4 orange and 1/4 lemon or lime)

1/3 cup Moroccan olive water (or 2 teaspoons salt)

1 large clove garlic, with skin

1 whole hot pepper

1/2 cup stone-crushed olive oil

DIRECTIONS

In a bowl combine the broccoli, bok choy, 1/4 cup turmeric, celery, 1 clove garlic, 2 tablespoons ginger, coconut, bell pepper, apple, squash, zucchini, and fresh herbs.

In a Vita-Mix, combine the citrus juice blend and olive water with the remaining garlic and ginger, hot pepper, and turmeric. Blend until smooth. Add the olive oil with the blender still running. Pour the dressing over the salad, and enjoy. This dish will keep for up to 5 days in the refrigerator.

Chinese Wild Rice with Tender Vegetables

By Elaina Love

Advanced prep: 48 hours for soaking; 1 hour for marinating **Immediate prep:** 35 min **Serves** 6 **Special Equipment** Food processor

INGREDIENTS

1/2 head purple cabbage

1 onion

3 large cloves garlic

3 tablespoons fresh ginger

1 red bell pepper, cut into thin strips

2 heads broccoli, including stems, cut into small pieces

2 carrots, cut into thin strips

1 bunch cilantro, stems removed, chopped

1 bunch flat leaf parsley, chopped

1/2 cup lemon juice

3/4 cup olive oil

3/4 cup sesame oil

zest of 1 orange

1/4 cup nama shoyu

1 1/2 teaspoons Celtic sea salt

1/4 teaspoon ground habanero powder (dehydrate peppers and grind in spice or coffee grinder) or 1/2 teaspoon cayenne

1/2 pound wild rice, soaked 48 hours

DIRECTIONS

Pulse the cabbage, onion, garlic and ginger in a food processor until minced.

Transfer to a bowl, and add the bell pepper, broccoli, carrots, cilantro, parsley, lemon juice, olive oil, sesame oil, orange zest, nama shoyu, sea salt, habanero or cayenne, and the rice. Mix all the ingredients well, and let it sit for 1 hour or more before serving to let the flavors meld.

Hint: Pulse the dry wild rice in your food processor before soaking to help it absorb the water more quickly.

Curried Kofta Balls in Cashew Tomato Curry Sauce

BY MICHAL ADI

ADVANCED PREP: 2 to 3 hours for dehydrating   **IMMEDIATE PREP:** 50 min

SERVES 8   **SPECIAL EQUIPMENT** Food processor, dehydrator, blender

INGREDIENTS

For the Kofta Balls:

3 cups sunflower seeds, soaked and sprouted

1 cup almonds, soaked and peeled

handful fresh parsley

handful fresh cilantro

2 teaspoons curry powder

1 teaspoon cumin

1/2 teaspoon cayenne

1 zucchini

4 cloves garlic

1/2 teaspoon Celtic sea salt

1/2 teaspoon coriander

1-inch piece fresh ginger root

pinch nutmeg

1 teaspoon honey

For the sauce:

1 cup sun-dried tomatoes, soaked 2 hours and drained (reserve water)

2 to 3 plum tomatoes

1/2 zucchini

1 cup cashews

1 teaspoon curry powder

1/4 teaspoon cayenne

3 cloves garlic

1/2 teaspoon paprika

handful fresh cilantro, plus extra for garnish

1/2 teaspoon Celtic sea salt

2 tablespoons honey

2 tablespoons lime juice

DIRECTIONS

Process the Kofta Ball ingredients in a food processor fitted with the "S" blade. Form into medium-size balls and dehydrate for 2 to 3 hours on each side at 110°F.

Combine the Curry Sauce ingredients in a blender. Blend until smooth, adding just enough soak water from the sun-dried tomatoes for a thick and creamy sauce. Serve over the Kofta Balls.

Serve in the traditional Indian way as a soup by placing 2 to 3 Kofta balls in a bowl and filling the bowl with the sauce, or serve as an entrée over spiralized zucchini "noodles." Garnish with fresh cilantro.

Easy Pad Thai

By Elaina Love
Advanced prep: Pad Thai Sauce (2 hours) 1/2 hr for marinating
Immediate prep: 30 min   **Serves** 4   **Special Equipment** Spiral slicer or vegetable peeler

INGREDIENTS

For the Pad Thai:
3 zucchini, shaved into noodles with a spiral slicer or vegetable peeler
1 package (3 1/2 ounces) Enoki mushrooms, trimmed and separated
3 green onions, thinly sliced
1 red bell pepper, cut into thin strips
10 snow peas, cut into thin strips
1/2 pound mung bean sprouts
1/2 lime, juiced
1/2 teaspoon Celtic sea salt
1 tablespoon Bariani® olive oil

For the topping:
1 cup dehydrated almonds, chopped
1/4 cup cilantro, chopped
handful bean sprouts
Pad Thai and Thai Wild Rice Sauce (p. 301)

DIRECTIONS

Place all the ingredients in a bowl except the toppings and let the Pad Thai marinate for 1/2 hour.

Place the Pad Thai on a platter and cover with 1 cup of the Pad Thai and Thai Wild Rice Sauce (see recipe page 301), chopped almonds, cilantro, and bean sprouts, or put the sauce and toppings on the side and let individuals serve themselves.

If you want, warm the dish in a dehydrator at 110°F before serving.

Easy Sushi

By Shazzie

ADVANCED PREP: Variable   **IMMEDIATE PREP:** 30 min

SERVES Depends on quantities used   **SPECIAL EQUIPMENT** None

INGREDIENTS

For Green Sushi:
Guacamole (page 274)
sun-dried tomatoes, soaked and cut
    into thin strips
mustard cress

For Nutter Sushi:
raw almond butter
carrot, cut into thin strips
your favorite sprouts
fresh coriander leaves

For Earth and Fire Sushi:
"Fried" Mushrooms (page 123)
wasabi powder, mixed to paste with
    water
celery, cut into thin strips

For Cheeze and Onion Sushi:
Cheddary Cheeze Spread (page 188)
scallions, spring onion, cut into thin
    strips
zucchini, cut into thin strips

DIRECTIONS

Fold several sheets of black nori in half. Cut them with scissors along the fold. Cut them so each is in strips of 4, then cut them again in the opposite direction. You should end up with 8 little strips per sheet. Have a glass of water handy.

Pick up one nori strip, and put about a teaspoon of the soft filling along half of the strip. Add small slices of the other ingredients so they sit in the middle of the soft filling. Arrange them so they poke out of one end, but not the other, as you need a flat base to stand the rolls up.

Gently hold the fillings in place with one finger, and roll up the sheet so the ends overlap with one another. Brush the ends with a little water to firm them down. Once all the sushi is made, place it on a serving dish and garnish as you choose.

Hint: Here's a shortcut, if you don't feel confident doing all that. Put the soft ingredient in before rolling the sushi up, and then add the other ingredients once the sushi is standing.

Contributor's note: Easy Sushi is a delicious main course, and great for parties, starters, nibbles, packed lunches, and side dishes. Serve with thin slices of ginger, wasabi sauce, or your favorite side dishes. Use the suggested ingredients from one of the recipes below, or invent your own.

Herby Stir-Fry

By Shazzie

Advanced prep: 2 to 3 days for sprouts; (Plum Sauce 8 hours)

Immediate prep: 30 min; (Plum Sauce 10 min) **Serves** 4 **Special Equipment** Food processor

INGREDIENTS

1 carrot

1 tablespoon coconut meat

1 cup parsnip pieces

2 cups quinoa, sprouted 24 hours

1 cup broccoli florets

1 cup cauliflower florets

4 green onions, thinly sliced

1 cup alfalfa sprouts

10 sun-dried tomatoes, cut into slivers

1 bunch chives

1 bunch cilantro

1 bunch parsley

1 tablespoon olive oil

4 peaches, peeled and pitted

Plum Sauce (p. 300)

DIRECTIONS

In a food processor, process the carrot, coconut meat and parsnip into small rice-sized pieces. Transfer to a bowl, and mix with the sprouted quinoa.

Add the broccoli, cauliflower, onions, alfalfa sprouts, and sun-dried tomatoes, chives, coriander, parsley and olive oil. Mash the peaches and add them to the bowl. Mix well. Serve with Plum Sauce (page 300).

Hint: Drain and rinse the quinoa 3 to 4 times during the day and watch the little tails appear! Once you see tails, it's ready to eat.

Contributor's note: This really does come out like a stir-fry.

Roast Tofu with Satay Sauce

By Shazzie

Advanced prep: 10 to 20 min for marinating; 4 to 6 hours for dehydrating
Immediate prep: 40 min   **Serves** 4   **Special Equipment** Dehydrator, coffee grinder

INGREDIENTS

For the Tofu:
4 portobello mushrooms, skins, stems and gills removed
3 cloves garlic, minced
2 stalks celery, juiced
1 lemon, juiced
2 tablespoons olive oil
pinch sea salt

For the sauce:
1 cup raw peanuts
2 tablespoons almond butter
1/2 teaspoon cayenne
1/4 cup coconut meat
4 dates, soaked

DIRECTIONS

Cut the skinned mushrooms into 1-inch cubes to make the "tofu." In a bowl, combine the garlic, celery juice, lemon juice, olive oil, and salt.

Add the mushroom cubes and mix so all sides are thoroughly coated. Allow them to marinate for 10 to 20 minutes, then put them in a dehydrator. Keep the rest of the marinade for the sauce. Dehydrate the mushrooms at 105°F for 4 to 6 hours.

To make the Satay Sauce, put the peanuts, almond butter, cayenne pepper, coconut, dates and the leftover marinade into a coffee mill and grind to a sauce. If you need more liquid, add a little water at a time.

Serve the "tofu" cubes on skewers and covered with the Satay Sauce.

Thai Wild Rice with Spring Vegetables

By Elaina Love

Advanced prep: 2 to 4 days for soaking (Pad Thai Sauce 30 min)

Immediate prep: 30 min (Pad Thai Sauce 20 min)   **Serves** 6 to 8   **Special Equipment** None

INGREDIENTS

1 1/4 cups or 1/2 pound dry black wild rice, soaked 2 to 4 days in 4 cups water

4 stalks celery, thinly sliced

1 zucchini, cut in thin strips

4 green onions, thinly sliced

8 leaves dinosaur or red Russian kale, thinly sliced including stems

20 basil leaves, sliced into thin ribbons

20 spearmint leaves, sliced into thin ribbons

Pad Thai and Thai Wild Rice Sauce (page 301)

DIRECTIONS

Place all the ingredients in a large bowl and cover with 1 cup Pad Thai and Thai Wild Rice Sauce (page 265). Enjoy immediately or store in the refrigerator for up to 5 days.

Hint: Pulse the wild rice in a food processor to reduce the soaking time. Rinse once a day.

Other Classic Entrées

Assorted Vegetables with Almond Chili Sauce and Bean Sprouts

By Chad Sarno

Advanced prep: 2 to 3 hours for dehydrating   **Immediate prep:** 40 min

Serves 6   **Special Equipment** Blender, dehydrator

INGREDIENTS

- 1/2 cup almond butter (see p. 110 Ants in a Canoe)
- 1 tablespoon chopped fresh ginger
- 1 1/2 tablespoons lemon juice
- 2 tablespoons sweetener (such as dates, raisins or prunes)
- 2 cloves garlic, peeled
- 1 1/2 teaspoons Celtic sea salt or 1 1/2 tablespoons nama shoyu
- 1 1/2 tablespoons chopped lemongrass
- 1 teaspoon diced serrano pepper (optional)
- 1 zucchini, cut into thin strips
- 1 cup thin strips red bell pepper
- 2 carrots, cut into thin strips
- 1 cup broccoli florets
- 1/2 cup cilantro, chopped
- 1 cup Asian bean sprouts
- 6 lime wedges

DIRECTIONS

To make the sauce, blend the almond butter, ginger, lemon juice, sweetener, garlic, sea salt, lemongrass, serrano pepper and 1/3 cup of water in a high-speed blender until smooth. Add more water to desired consistency.

Toss the sauce in a large mixing bowl with the zucchini, red pepper, carrots, broccoli, and cilantro.

Dehydrate the vegetables on Teflex sheets at 105°F for 2 to 3 hours to soften and warm.

To serve, place a handful of the mixture in the middle of each plate, and top with a generous amount of bean sprouts. Garnish each plate with a wedge of lime.

Hint: A great option is to serve over a bed of coconut noodles.

'Bello Burger

BY MARY RYDMAN

ADVANCED PREP: 6 hours to soak nuts, 3 1/2 hours dehydrating time
IMMEDIATE PREP: 20 min
SPECIAL EQUIPMENT Food processor, dehydrator   **SERVES** 3–4

INGREDIENTS

1/2 large red bell pepper, chopped
2 medium portobello mushroom caps, chopped
1 small carrot, cut into 1/2 inch slices
1 cup almonds, soaked
2 tablespoons onion, chopped
1 small clove garlic, sliced
1 1/2 tablespoons mild flavored miso
1 teaspoon lemon juice
1/4 tsp dried basil

DIRECTIONS

Process all in food processor to smooth consistency. You will need to keep scraping down the sides and may need to add a couple tablespoons water, but be careful not to add too much. Drop by 1/4 cups-full onto Teflex sheets and form into patties about 3/4 inch thick. Dehydrate 2 hours at 145 degrees (Excalibur dehydrator only), then about 1 1/2 hours at 110 degrees to moist burger consistency. Serve warm from dehydrator. Serve with your favorite sauce and sliced tomatoes. They will keep a day in the refrigerator if necessary.

Contributor's note: Moist and meaty, these will amaze you!

Broccoli with Chedda Sauce

By Rhio

Advanced prep: 6 hours for soaking; 2 to 4 hours for dehydrating

Immediate prep: 40 min   **Serves** 3 to 4   **Special Equipment** Blender, dehydrator

INGREDIENTS

3 cups finely chopped broccoli

For the sauce:

1 large red bell pepper, chopped with seeds and stem removed

3/4 cup pine nuts, soaked overnight or for at least 2 hours and drained

1/2 cup sunflower seeds, soaked overnight or for at least 2 hours and drained

1/2 lemon, juiced

1 1/2 tablespoons nutritional yeast flakes

1 small clove garlic (optional)

2 teaspoons nama shoyu

For the marinade:

1 tablespoon olive or flaxseed oil

1 lemon or lime, juiced

1 to 2 teaspoons nama shoyu or dash Celtic sea salt

DIRECTIONS

Toss the broccoli with all the marinade ingredients until it is well coated. Cover and let marinate overnight in the refrigerator.

To make the sauce, place the red bell pepper in the blender first. (It releases liquid so you won't have to add any water.)

Rinse the soaked pine nuts and sunflower seeds and add to the blender. Add the lemon, yeast flakes, garlic, and nama shoyu and blend well. If the red bell pepper doesn't liquefy readily, add a little water (not too much).

Mix the broccoli with some of the sauce; serve as is or dehydrate for 2 to 4 hours at 95°F and serve warm.

Variation 1: For those who don't care for the flavor of pine nuts, you can make the recipe with 1 cup sprouted, blanched almonds, and reduce the amount of sunflower seeds to 1/4 cup. You may also add 1 to 2 tablespoons soaked macadamia nuts for a creamier sauce. All other ingredients remain the same.

Variation 2: This sauce can also be made into a cheddar-type cheese by dehydrating it. Spread the sauce 1/4-inch thick on a Teflex-lined dehydrator tray and dehydrate at 95°F for 1 to 2 days. The resulting sheet can then be cut into pieces or crumbled with your hands and used like grated cheese. It will keep for more than 2 weeks in the refrigerator.

Broccoli with Red Pepper Dressing

By Rita Romano

Advanced prep: None   **Immediate prep:** 25 min

Serves 4   **Special Equipment** Cuisinart or heavy-duty food processor

INGREDIENTS

2 red peppers, chopped

1 young yellow squash, chopped

1 large clove garlic, minced

1/2 red onion, chopped

4 tablespoons tahini

1 teaspoon curry powder

1 teaspoon maple syrup (optional)

1/4 teaspoon cayenne (optional)

Bragg Liquid Aminos or yellow miso, to taste

1 bunch broccoli florets

DIRECTIONS

Combine the red peppers, squash, garlic, onion, tahini, curry powder, maple syrup (if using), and cayenne (if using) in a Cuisinart and process using the "S" blade. Blend the mixture and add enough water to create a thick dressing. Add more miso or Bragg Liquid Aminos to taste.

Coat the broccoli with the dressing. It sticks to the florets and gives the crunchy broccoli a great flavor.

Buttery Peas and Corn (Fast Food Raw Food)

BY JULIAN HUERTA

ADVANCED PREP: None   IMMEDIATE PREP: 10 min

SPECIAL EQUIPMENT None   SERVES 1

INGREDIENTS

1/2 cup corn (I use the frozen kind and warm them with warm water)

1/2 cup peas (same as corn)

3 teaspoons cold pressed organic olive oil

dashes of salt

1/8 tsp cayenne powder

1/8 tsp basil (optional)

DIRECTIONS

. . . Mix it up . . . Yeah!

This is one of my favorite fast foods for its ease, simplicity, tastiness, and easily accommodates other ingredients that I have on hand that I want to add. It will fill you up if you want to feel full.

Coconut Rice

BY RHIO

ADVANCED PREP: 4 days for sprouting and soaking   **IMMEDIATE PREP:** 25 min

SERVES 4   **SPECIAL EQUIPMENT** None

INGREDIENTS

1 1/2 cups Manitok wild rice, sprouted (or any wild rice, sprouted) or a combination of 3/4 cup sprouted wild rice and 3/4 cup sprouted sweet brown rice

1 cup shredded carrots

1 cup shredded fresh coconut (light brown shell)

1/4 cup unhulled sesame seeds, soaked overnight, and drained

1/4 cup raisins or currants

3/4 tablespoon olive oil

3/4 tablespoon flaxseed oil

1 teaspoon cinnamon

1/2 teaspoon ground cumin

1/2 teaspoon ground black mustard

pinch ground cloves (optional)

pinch fresh ground white pepper (optional)

Celtic sea salt to taste

DIRECTIONS

Mix the rice, carrots, coconut, sesame seeds, and raisins together in a bowl, and set aside.

In a small bowl, stir oil and spices together. Pour onto the coconut/rice mixture and toss well. Taste the rice and adjust the seasonings.

Variation: For a savory version of this recipe, eliminate the raisins and cinnamon, and add pressed garlic, to taste.

Corn with Sweet Cream and Peas

BY JULIAN HUERTA

ADVANCED PREP: 10 min   IMMEDIATE PREP: 10 min
SPECIAL EQUIPMENT Blender   SERVES 1

INGREDIENTS

1/2 cup corn (OK, I usually cheat, I use sweet frozen corn. It's the raw equivalent of microwaveable food!

Just put the frozen corn in a bowl and run warm tap water over it and let it sit in the warm tap water until the corn defrosts.)

1/2 cup sweet peas (um . . . I use the frozen peas here too. But they are organic :)

1/4 cup Sweet Cream (See Bountiful Berry Medley)

DIRECTIONS

Mix it all up! And dance while doing it. I bet you'll feel happy and you are making it happen. Be happy for yourself. You did it!

Endive Cups with Ragoût of Wild Mushrooms and Chili Tamarind Sauce

BY CHAD SARNO

ADVANCED PREP: 1 hour for marinating   **IMMEDIATE PREP:** 30 min

SERVES 4 to 6   **SPECIAL EQUIPMENT** None

INGREDIENTS

    3 cups assorted wild mushrooms, sliced thin
    3 tablespoons minced green onion
    1/4 cup diced red bell pepper
    1/4 cup thick tamarind juice
    2 tablespoons maple syrup or date paste
    2 tablespoons minced fresh ginger
    1 1/2 teaspoons lime zest
    2 1/2 tablespoons nama shoyu
    2 tablespoons olive oil
    1 teaspoon Celtic sea salt
    18 small Belgian endive leaves

DIRECTIONS

In a medium bowl, toss together the mushrooms, onions and bell peppers, setting aside 1 tablespoon of green onions.

In a separate bowl, whisk together the tamarind, maple syrup or date paste, ginger, lime zest, nama shoyu, olive oil and sea salt. Toss with the mushrooms and let marinate for up to 1 hour.

Place 2 tablespoons of the marinated mushroom mixture on each of the endive leaves. Arrange the endive leaves in a tree and garnish with minced onion.

Erie Ojibwa Rice

By Jeremy Safron

Advanced prep: 4 days for sprouting; 1 hour for marinating
Immediate prep: 25 min **Serves** 4 **Special Equipment** None

INGREDIENTS

3 cups black long grain wild rice, sprouted
1 red pepper, diced
1 yakon root (or jicama), diced
1 ear corn, kernels cut from cob
1/2 cup shredded carrot
1/2 cup cilantro, loosely packed
1/2 cup dry sunflower seeds
1 teaspoon caraway seeds
1/2 cup flaxseed oil
2 teaspoons sea salt

DIRECTIONS

Mix all the ingredients together in a large bowl and let sit for 1 hour before serving.

Contributor's note: Black, long grain, wild rice grows throughout the Great Lakes, where native people of the Ojibwa and Chippewa tribes still harvest the grain-like seed by hand. One of the only sprouts to grow without oxygen, black long grain wild rice also takes the longest to grow (up to 7 days). Remember to enjoy the rich earthy smell when you change the soaking water twice daily.

Falafels

BY ROSE LEE CALABRO

ADVANCED PREP: 8 hours for soaking   **IMMEDIATE PREP:** 40 min

SERVES 6 to 8   **SPECIAL EQUIPMENT** Champion juicer or food processor, dehydrator

INGREDIENTS

- 1 1/2 cups chickpeas, soaked, drained and sprouted for 8 hours
- 1 cup sunflower seeds, soaked 6 to
    8 hours and drained
- 1 medium red onion, finely chopped
- 1 to 2 cloves garlic, pressed
- 1/4 cup fresh parsley, finely chopped
- 2 tablespoons lemon juice
- 1/4 cup cold-pressed olive oil
- 1 teaspoon ground coriander
- 1 teaspoon ground cumin
- 1/4 to 1/2 teaspoon cayenne
- 1 teaspoon Celtic sea salt

DIRECTIONS

Process the chickpeas and sunflower seeds in a Champion juicer using the blank plate or in a food processor fitted with the "S" blade. Transfer the mixture to a bowl.

Add the onion, garlic, parsley, lemon juice, olive oil, coriander, cumin, cayenne, and sea salt. Mix well.

Form the mixture into small patties about 2 inches wide and 1/2 inch thick, and place on Teflex sheets in the dehydrator. Dehydrate for 16 to 18 hours at 105°F. Falafels can be served wrapped in lettuce leaves, Napa cabbage leaves, or red or green cabbage. Also add some sprouts, tomatoes, or cucumbers.

Fennel 'Shroom Disco

BY JULIAN HUERTA

ADVANCED PREP: 15 min   **IMMEDIATE PREP:** 15 min

SPECIAL EQUIPMENT Food Processor   **SERVES** 2

INGREDIENTS

1 1/2 cups fennel

1 1/2 cups marinated mushrooms (marinate in equal amounts of shoyu and olive oil for at least 15 min, or just leave in the fridge)

1 1/2 tablespoons of diced Marinated onions (marinate same as Marinated Mushrooms)

1/2 cup broccoli florets and/or the inside of the stem of the broccoli diced up

1 1/2 tablespoons shredded fresh basil or 1 1/2 tsp dried basil

Mixing Cream

2 tablespoons pine nuts

2 tablespoons walnuts

dashes of salt

1 tsp fresh basil or 1/2 tsp dried basil

DIRECTIONS

Food process the cream, and then mix all ingredients together. Do a little dance!

Fig Stew

By Shazzie

Advanced prep: 8–10 hours for soaking; 1 hour for marinating

Immediate prep: 25 min (Macadamia Cream 20 min)   **Serves** 2

Special Equipment blender

INGREDIENTS

2 cups berries, such as blueberries, raspberries, strawberries, or blackberries

4 fresh figs (or 4 dried figs, soaked overnight), finely chopped

2 Medjool dates (or 4 dates, soaked overnight), finely chopped

1 tomato, finely chopped

1/2 red pepper, finely chopped

1 apple, cored

handful raisins or sultanas (golden raisins)

pinch of cinnamon

Macadamia Cream (page 189)

DIRECTIONS

Blend 1 cup berries, and finely chop those that remain. Mix together the berries, figs, dates, tomato, and pepper, and let marinate for at least an hour.

Transfer the mixture to a serving dish. Grate the apple on top. Sprinkle the raisins over the apple and add a pinch of cinnamon. Serve with Macadamia Cream (page 213).

Live Gardenburgers

By Victoria Boutenko

Advanced prep: None   **Immediate prep:** 40 min

Serves 10   **Special Equipment** Food processor

INGREDIENTS

1 pound of your favorite nuts, unsoaked and ground

1 pound carrots, chopped

1 medium onion, chopped

1 tablespoon sweetener (such as honey, very ripe banana, or raisins)

1 tablespoon olive oil

1 to 2 tablespoons poultry seasoning (or other seasoning) such as Herbamare®

2 to 3 tablespoons nutritional yeast (optional)

sea salt to taste

paprika

DIRECTIONS

Grind the nuts in a food processor. Set aside. Combine the carrots, onion, sweetener, oil, seasoning, yeast (if using) and sea salt and grind in a food processor.

Mix everything together well. If mixture isn't firm enough, add one or two of the following thickeners: dill weed, dried garlic, dried onion, dried parsley flakes, nutritional yeast, psyllium husk powder, ground flax seed.

Form into balls, cutlets, or fillets, and sprinkle with paprika before serving.

Variation: To make "fishburgers" add seaweed (such as dulse, kelp, or nori) to the mixture.

Lotus Manitok

By Juliano

Advanced prep: 4 days for sprouts   **Immediate prep:** 35 min

Serves 2   **Special Equipment** None

INGREDIENTS

- 1 cup thin strips red bell pepper
- 1 cup thin strips carrots
- 1/2 cup zucchini strips (shaved with a vegetable peeler)
- 1/2 cup thin strips red beets
- 1/4 cup sliced chiogga beets
- 1/2 cup sliced yams
- 1/4 cup quartered walnuts
- 1/4 cup black Manitok rice, sprouted
- 1/4 cup chopped dill
- 1/2 cup thin strips apples
- 1 cup maple syrup
- 2 cups fresh-squeezed orange juice
- 1/4 cup fresh-squeezed lemon juice
- 1/4 cup olive oil
- 1/4 cup balsamic vinegar
- 1/4 cup nama shoyu
- 1 tablespoon ginger, minced
- 2 1/2 teaspoons garlic, minced
- 2 1/2 teaspoons jalapeño, minced
- 1 tablespoon fresh cranberries
- 1/4 cup sliced sunchokes
- 1 tablespoon grated lemon rind
- 1 tablespoon grated orange rind

DIRECTIONS

Combine all the ingredients together in a serving bowl, mix well, and serve. It's like nothing you've ever tried before!

From *Raw: The UnCook Book* (New York: ReganBooks, 1999.)

Miss Lill's Down Home Marinated Greens

By Lillian Butler

Advanced prep: 2 days for marinating   **Immediate prep:** 20 min

Serves 8   **Special Equipment** None

INGREDIENTS

2 bunches collards

1 bunch kale or mustard greens

olive or flax oil to coat greens

1 tablespoon garlic powder

1 tablespoon onion powder

1 tablespoon chili powder

1 tablespoon cajun seasoning

1 tablespoon lemon juice

1/2 tablespoon cayenne

nama shoyu, to taste

DIRECTIONS

Wash and cut the greens. Coat greens with oil, add the seasonings, and mix well. Let the greens marinate and soften in refrigerator for 2 days, tossing each day.

Neat Balls

By Jalissa Letendre

Advanced prep: 8–10 hours for soaking; 8–12 hours for dehydrating

Immediate prep: 50 min

Yields 70 Neat Balls   **Special Equipment** Champion Juicer, dehydrator

INGREDIENTS

4 cups almonds, soaked overnight and drained

2 cups sunflower seeds, soaked overnight and drained

3 medium carrots, chopped

3 lemons, juiced

1 red onion, chopped

2 celery stalks, finely chopped

2 tablespoons sage powder

1 tablespoon dried basil

1 tablespoon dried oregano

1 tablespoon dried rosemary

1 tablespoon garlic powder

1 tablespoon Herbamare or sea salt

DIRECTIONS

Run the soaked almonds, sunflower seeds, and carrots through a juicer in "sorbet" mode. You should have a dry paste. Collect the paste in a bowl and add the rest of the ingredients to it. Mix well with your hands.

Form into about 70 little balls. Arrange the balls on Teflex sheets and dehydrate for 8 to 12 hours at 105°F.

The balls should be dry on the outside but soft on the inside. Enjoy!

NutMeat

BY JEREMY SAFRON

ADVANCED PREP: None   **IMMEDIATE PREP:** 25 min

SERVES 2 to 4   **SPECIAL EQUIPMENT** Small blender or mini food processor

INGREDIENTS

2 cups dry walnuts

1 cup sun-dried tomatoes, soaked

1 clove garlic, peeled

1/4 cup olive oil

2 tablespoons Bragg Liquid Aminos or nama shoyu

DIRECTIONS

In a small blender or mini food processor, grind the dry walnuts into powder.

Blend the sun-dried tomatoes, garlic, olive oil, and Bragg Liquid Aminos (or nama shoyu) in a separate blender jar.

Stir the wet mixture into the dry walnut powder and use as a filling for raw burritos, lasagna, or stuffed porcini mushrooms.

Contributor's note: This recipe has a rich oil flavor and is very hearty and filling.

Nutmeat Stroganoff

BY ELIZABETH BAKER

ADVANCED PREP: 10 min for peroxide soak   **IMMEDIATE PREP:** 20 min (Pine Nut Sour Cream 15 min)

SERVES 4   **SPECIAL EQUIPMENT** Blender

INGREDIENTS

4 large or 6 medium white mushrooms, chopped

1 teaspoon sea salt

1/2 cup Pine Nut Sour Cream
   (page 276)

dash pepper

3/4 cup chopped walnuts

green onions, finely chopped
   (for garnish)

DIRECTIONS

Blend all the ingredients together with 1 cup water, adding the nuts last. Set blender bowl in very hot water until the stroganoff is hot. Serve garnished with fine chopped green onions.

Hint: Before making this dish, remove any mold from the nuts: Pour 1/2 cup water and 1/4 cup hydrogen peroxide over the nuts and let sit 10 minutes. Pour off the fizzy water, wash 2 or 3 times and chop.

Oh My Chili

By Abeba Wright

Advanced prep: None   **Immediate prep:** 35 min

Serves 12   **Special Equipment** Blender

INGREDIENTS

- 8 to 10 Roma tomatoes, plus 1/2 cup chopped tomatoes
- 1 cup unsoaked sun-dried tomatoes
- 1/2 red onion
- 1/2 cup cilantro, divided
- 4 stalks celery, chopped and divided
- 2 tablespoons olive oil
- 2 red bell peppers, chopped and divided
- 3 cloves garlic

- 1 tablespoon lemon juice
- Celtic sea salt, to taste
- jalapeño to taste
- 1/2 teaspoon cumin
- 1/4 cup unsoaked raisins
- 1 1/2 cups barley, soaked 3 days (without draining or rinsing)
- 1/3 cup chopped green onion
- 1 to 2 ears corn (optional)
- 1 teaspoon dill flakes (optional)

DIRECTIONS

Blend 8 to 10 fresh tomatoes, the sun-dried tomatoes, red onion, 1/4 cup cilantro, 2 celery stalks, olive oil, 1 red bell pepper, garlic, lemon juice, Celtic sea salt to taste, jalapeño, raisins, and 1 cup water in a blender.

If the blended ingredients are too thin, purée 2 carrots in the food processor and add these to blended the mixture. Do not blend again.

Rinse and drain barley well. Pour the mixture into a bowl with the barley and add: 1/2 cup chopped tomato, 2 chopped celery stalks, 1/4 cup chopped cilantro, 1 chopped red bell pepper, and 1/3 cup chopped green onion. For thicker chili, add the corn and dill flakes.

Pecan Almond Stuffed Mushrooms

By Rita Romano

Advanced prep: 24 hours for soaking

Serves 6 **Special Equipment** Food processor

INGREDIENTS

1 cup pecans, soaked for 24 hours and drained

1 cup almonds, soaked for 24 hours and drained

2 tablespoons almond butter

1 cup chopped celery

1/2 cup chopped red onion

1 1/2 cups finely chopped carrots

2 teaspoons poultry seasoning

6 large mushroom caps (or more)

seedless cucumbers and baby greens, for garnish

DIRECTIONS

Combine the pecans, almonds, almond butter, celery, onion, carrots, and poultry seasoning in food processor fitted with "S" blade and pulse to a chunky pâté. Don't over-blend. Leave some texture in the carrots.

Clean and rinse the mushrooms, then stuff each with the pâté. Garnish with seedless cucumbers and baby greens.

Hint: Serve stuffed mushrooms with lots of greens, sprouts, and sliced cucumbers.

Variation 1: For an added dimension, marinate the mushroom caps several hours in garlic flavored Bragg Liquid Aminos and lemon juice. The mushrooms will soften and absorb some of the flavor. Rinse the mushroom caps before stuffing.

Variation 2: Stuff zucchini, peppers, or endives instead of mushrooms.

Editor's note: *Add the mushroom stems into the pâté to use them up too.*

Purple Lotus Wraps with Almond Fig Sauce

BY MAYA ADJANI

ADVANCED PREP: None   **IMMEDIATE PREP:** 20 min

SPECIAL EQUIPMENT Blender,   **SERVES** 4

INGREDIENTS

For the fig sauce:

4 cups dried black mission figs, soaked in warm water

4 tablespoons raw almond butter

juice of 1 lemon

3" piece of ginger, chopped

1 clove of garlic

1 teaspoon dulse flakes (optional)

1 teaspoon sea salt or 1 tablespoon mellow white miso

For the wraps:

4–8 purple cabbage leaves

1 cup sprouts (any kind)

I avocado, sliced

1/2 beet, shredded

1 carrot, shredded

1 cup other chopped or shredded veggies (optional)

DIRECTIONS

Place figs and soaking water in blender with other ingredients, adding more water as needed and blend until creamy. Smooth Almond Fig Sauce into purple cabbage leaves and add sprouts, avocado, shredded beets, carrots, and any veggies you enjoy. This dish is both aesthetically gorgeous and deeply satisfying.

Raw Ratatouille

By Jinjee and Storm Talifero

Advanced prep: None   **Immediate prep:** 15 min

Serves 4   **Special Equipment** None

INGREDIENTS

For the Ratatouille:
- 1 avocado, peeled, pitted and chopped
- 2 tomatoes, chopped
- 1/4 cup chopped cilantro
- 2 cloves garlic, peeled and chopped
- 1 squash, chopped

For the sauce:
- 1 tablespoon tahini
- 1 teaspoon honey
- Celtic sea salt, to taste

DIRECTIONS

Combine the avocado with the tomatoes, cilantro, garlic, and squash in a large bowl.

Mix the tahini and honey together, adding sea salt to taste. Pour the dressing over the vegetables.

Serve immediately or chill in the refrigerator.

Seeded Noodles

By Shazzie

Advanced prep: None   **Immediate prep:** 20 min

Serves 2   **Special Equipment** Spiral slicer

INGREDIENTS

- 2 cups butternut squash cubes
- 1 cup chopped zucchini
- 1 tablespoon tahini

- 2 limes, juiced
- 1 teaspoon celery seed
- 1 teaspoon poppy seeds

DIRECTIONS

Spiral slice the squash and marrow on the spaghetti setting to make the noodles. Mix the tahini with lime juice in a small bowl until watery. Add the seeds, pour over the noodles, and enjoy!

Shiitake Croquettes with Purée of Yellow and Red Peppers

By Chad Sarno
Advanced prep: 10 to 12 hours for soaking; 5 to 7 hours for marinating
Immediate prep: 1 hour   **Serves** 8   **Special Equipment** Blender

INGREDIENTS

For the Croquettes:
1 1/2 cups shiitake mushrooms, sliced paper thin
1 1/2 tablespoons nama shoyu
2 tablespoons olive oil
2 1/2 cups walnuts, soaked 10 to 12 hours
1 cup pine nuts
1 cup diced red and yellow bell pepper
1 1/2 tablespoons fresh ginger, minced fine
2 cloves garlic, minced

1 1/2 tablespoons lemon juice
1 cup broccoli florets
1 1/2 teaspoons Celtic sea salt
3 tablespoons basil, shredded fine
1/4 cup cilantro, chopped fine

For the purée:
2 bell peppers, chopped
1 tablespoon olive oil
1/2 tablespoon ginger
1/2 tablespoon ground cumin
1/4 teaspoon Celtic salt

DIRECTIONS

Marinate the mushrooms in the nama shoyu and olive oil for 10 to 20 minutes.

Mix the walnuts and pine nuts together, and add the remaining croquette ingredients by hand, including the mushrooms.

Form the mixture into half-dollar-size burgers and dehydrate for 5 to 7 hours at 110°F.

To make the bell pepper purée, blend the chopped bell peppers, olive oil, ginger, cumin, and sea salt in a high-speed blender until smooth.

To serve, pour a small amount of red and yellow bell pepper purée on each side of the plate so that they meet in the middle. Place 2 to 3 croquettes in the middle of the purée, and top with microgreens or sweet pea shoots.

Snappy Unfried Peas

BY JACKIE AND GIDEON GRAFF

ADVANCED PREP: 30 min for marinating   **IMMEDIATE PREP:** 25 min

SERVES 8   **SPECIAL EQUIPMENT** Food processor

INGREDIENTS

2 cups sliced mushrooms

2 tablespoons nama shoyu, plus extra for mushroom marinade

2 cups mung beans

3 tablespoons Celtic sea salt

1/4 cup plus 1 tablespoon lemon juice, divided

2 cups filtered water

3 cloves garlic, peeled

3 drops lemon oil

1/4 cup extra virgin olive or flax oil

1 cup coarsely chopped fresh basil

1 tablespoon lemon zest

4 cups sugar snap peas or snow peas, sliced thin on a diagonal

DIRECTIONS

Marinate the mushrooms in nama shoyu for 30 minutes.

Marinate the mung beans in 2 tablespoons sea salt, 1 tablespoon lemon juice, and the filtered water. Place the garlic in a food processor and chop well. Add the lemon juice, lemon oil, olive oil, sea salt, basil, nama shoyu, and lemon zest, processing well.

Pour the dressing over the sugar snap peas, mushrooms, and mung beans. Mix well and serve immediately.

Spinach and Potato Latkes

By Jackie and Gideon Graff

Advanced prep: 8 hours for soaking; 2–3 days for rejuvelac
Immediate prep: 40 min **Serves** 8 **Special Equipment** Blender, dehydrator

INGREDIENTS

- 1 cup macadamia nuts, soaked 8 hours and drained
- 2 cloves garlic, minced
- 2 teaspoons Celtic sea salt
- 1/2 cup lemon juice, freshly squeezed
- 1 cup rejuvelac (page 9) or filtered water
- 1 cup pine nuts, soaked 2 hours and drained
- 6 cups spinach, chopped fine
- 1 sweet onion, chopped fine
- 6 small red potatoes, grated
- 1/2 cup ground flaxseed
- 1 teaspoon paprika powder

DIRECTIONS

Place the macadamia nuts, garlic, salt, lemon juice, and rejuvelac or water in a blender and blend until smooth. Add the pine nuts and blend well.

Fold the nut mixture into the spinach and add the onion and potato, stirring well.

Add the flaxseed. Stir well, and let sit for 15 minutes. If the mixture separates, add more flaxseed.

Spoon onto Teflex sheets and pat down into latkes. Sprinkle paprika on the latkes and dehydrate for 6 to 8 hours.

Turn over the latkes and dehydrate for 6 hours more. They should be dry but slightly moist.

Sun-Dried Tomato Bliss Pâté

BY MAYA ADJANI

ADVANCED PREP: None   **IMMEDIATE PREP:** 10–15 min

SPECIAL EQUIPMENT Food processor   **YIELDS** about 4 cups

INGREDIENTS

2 cups cashews

1 red bell pepper, cored and seeded

juice of 1 lemon

1 cup soaked sun-dried tomatoes
(w/soaking water)

basil, dill, garlic, rosemary to taste

2 tablespoons mellow white miso

2 tablespoons raw tahini

DIRECTIONS

Add water as needed and blend until smooth.

To serve: Eat on crackers or with vegetable sticks or scoop pâté into portobello mushrooms and garnish with sliced avocado, olives, carrots, etc.

Sun Garden Burgers

BY NOMI SHANNON

ADVANCED PREP: 4 to 8 hours for dehydrating **IMMEDIATE PREP:** 45 min
(Mushroom Gravy 15 min)

SERVES 6 **SPECIAL EQUIPMENT** Electric coffee grinder, juicer, blender, dehydrator

INGREDIENTS

6 tablespoons flax seeds, ground in electric coffee grinder

3/4 cup water

2 cups sunflower seeds, ground in electric coffee grinder

2 cups carrot pulp (from 4 to 6 large carrots, juiced)

1 cup finely minced celery

3/4 cup finely minced onion

4 tablespoons finely minced parsley

4 tablespoons finely minced red pepper

1 tablespoon tamari, nama shoyu, or 1 teaspoon Celtic sea salt, plus 1 tablespoon water

cabbage leaves (for buns)

Mushroom Gravy (page 300)

DIRECTIONS

Make the carrot pulp by juicing carrots in a heavy-duty juicer.

In a blender, blend the ground flax seed and water. Pour the mixture into a bowl and set aside. Immediately rinse the blender container before mixture thickens.

In a medium size bowl, thoroughly stir together the carrot pulp, ground sunflower seeds, celery, onion, parsley, red pepper, and tamari. Add the flaxseed mixture and mix thoroughly. Add more water if necessary for burger consistency.

Form the mixture into six 1/2-inch-thick patties. Dehydrate the patties for 4 to 8 hours, or leave in the sun until warm. Serve in a leafy cabbage bun or make balls rather than burgers and serve with tomato sauce or Mushroom Gravy (page 100) on the side.

Tip: To ensure equal sized burgers, first make 6 balls of equal size, then flatten into burgers.

Super Asparagus Wraps

BY SHAZZIE

ADVANCED PREP: None   **IMMEDIATE PREP:** 30 min

SERVES 2   **SPECIAL EQUIPMENT** None

INGREDIENTS

- 1 avocado
- 1 teaspoon Superfood
- 1 small hot chili, finely chopped
- 2 stalks celery, sliced thin on diagonal
- 2 green onions, sliced thin
- 6 stalks young asparagus, sliced thin on diagonal

- 1/2 cup pumpkin seeds, plus extra for garnish
- 2 large soft cabbage leaves
- 1 tomato, finely sliced
- squeeze of lemon juice
- lemon wedges, for garnish

DIRECTIONS

In a bowl, mash the avocado with the Superfood and chili. Add the celery, onion, and sliced asparagus stalks. Set the asparagus tips aside.

Squeeze some lemon juice into the mixture, and add the pumpkin seeds.

Roll the cabbage leaves into cones, so there's a wide mouth at one end and the other end is closed. Add half of the diced tomatoes to each, then fill each cone with the green stuffing.

Place the asparagus tips inside, so they stick out the top of each cabbage cone. Garnish with pumpkin seeds and lemon wedges.

Super Broccoli Quiche

BY SHAZZIE

ADVANCED PREP: None   **IMMEDIATE PREP:** 25 min

SERVES 4   **SPECIAL EQUIPMENT** None

INGREDIENTS

- 2 creamy avocados, mashed
- 1 tablespoon seaweed flakes
- 1 tablespoon Superfood

1 head broccoli florets, broken into small pieces

pinch sea salt (optional)

1 tablespoon sunflower seeds

4 stalks celery, finely chopped

DIRECTIONS

Mix the mashed avocados with the seaweed, Superfood, broccoli and sea salt. Sprinkle sunflower seeds on top, and place the finely chopped celery in the center of the dish. Serve in individual ramekin dishes with a light salad, or use this mixture as a filling for a simple pecan nut and date base if you like.

Thai Crane's Nest in Coconut Curry

By Cherie Soria

Advanced prep: 1 to 2 days for sprouts   **Immediate prep:** 40 min

Serves 4   **Special Equipment** None

INGREDIENTS

1 cup coconut milk

1 teaspoon Thai red curry paste

1 clove garlic, minced

1 tablespoon lemon juice

4 cups shredded butternut squash or carrots

2 cups shredded jicama or cucumber

4 cups Napa or Asian cabbage, cut into fine shreds

4 ounces spinach leaves, cut into fine shreds

2 large fresh basil leaves, cut into fine shreds

1/2 cup cilantro, cut into fine shreds

2 green onions, finely sliced

1/8 cup chopped peanuts or cashews, sprouted

DIRECTIONS

Warm coconut milk to no more than 105°F. Add the curry and garlic; stir well.

Toss the coconut curry with the lemon juice, squash, jicama, cabbage, spinach, basil and cilantro.

Form nests in individual shallow bowls or serving dishes and garnish with peanuts and onions. Serve at room temperature or gently warmed in a dehydrator or oven.

Hint: To shred leaves, such as basil and spinach, stack one on top of the other and roll them tightly from stem to tip. Holding them firmly in this rolled position, cut thin slices, starting at one end and working over to the other side.

Toona

BY RHIO
ADVANCED PREP: 8 to 10 hours for soaking   **IMMEDIATE PREP:** 40 min
SERVES 6   **SPECIAL EQUIPMENT** Champion or Green Power juicer, food processor, dehydrator (optional)

INGREDIENTS

3 cups walnuts, soaked overnight or for at least 3 hours, drained and rinsed

3 cups chopped carrots

1 cup chopped celery, with leaves

1 to 2 garlic cloves (to your taste), peeled

1/4 to 1/2 medium onion

1/2 cup parsley or cilantro

1/2 cup fresh basil (or another fresh herb, such as dill)

2 ounces lemon juice

nama shoyu and/or Celtic sea salt, to taste

DIRECTIONS

Process the walnuts and carrots to a pâté through a Champion or Green Power juicer, with the blank plate in place. If you don't have one of these machines, process in a food processor until smooth. You may have to add a little water. Set aside in a bowl.

Cut the celery into 1-inch pieces, then pulse-chop the garlic, onion, celery, herbs and lemon juice in a food processor until well chopped. Add this mixture to the carrot and walnut pâté and mix well. Add nama shoyu and Celtic sea salt to taste.

Hint: This dish goes well with crudités.

Variation 1: In place of celery, use fennel for a different flavor.

Variation 2: Use as a stuffing for nori rolls, adding clover sprouts and matchstick-cut pieces of cucumber and tomato.

Eddie's Spring Rolls By Eddie D. Robinson

Mango Tart with Pecan Fig Crust and Rambutan Coulis By Chad Sarno

Variation 3: This recipe also makes delicious dehydrated crackers. Dehydrate the mixture at 95°F for 1 1/2 to 2 days.

Walnut Burgers

BY SHAZZIE

ADVANCED PREP: 2 to 6 hours for soaking + 8 to 24 hours for dehydrating
IMMEDIATE PREP: 45 min   **SERVES** 8   **SPECIAL EQUIPMENT** Blender, hand blender, dehydrator

INGREDIENTS

6 cups walnuts, soaked for 2 hours

2 cups carrots, topped, tailed, and chopped

2 cups chopped portobello mushrooms

2 cloves garlic

2 teaspoons paprika

1 teaspoon dried pizza herbs

1 teaspoon dried parsley

1 1/2 cups chopped red onion, divided

1 cup fresh herbs, such as parsley, basil, and coriander, tightly packed

1/2 red pepper, chopped with seeds and stalk removed

6 sun-dried tomatoes, soaked for 2 to 6 hours and finely chopped

romaine lettuce (for buns)

mustard cress (optional)

extra slices of onion (optional)

DIRECTIONS

Blend the walnuts, carrots, mushrooms, garlic, paprika, pizza herbs, dried parsley, and half the onions in a food processor.

Transfer to a large bowl and continue blending with a hand blender for a smooth consistency.

Very finely chop the fresh herbs, red pepper, sun-dried tomatoes and remaining red onion and add these to the bowl. Mix well.

Divide the mixture into 8 or 10 equal portions. Form into burger shapes and dehydrate at 115°F for 8 to 24 hours.

Wrap the burgers in large romaine leaves and add a little mustard cress and some thinly sliced onion rings. Top with your choice of Tomato Sauce, "Fried" Mushrooms, Mango Chutney (pages 305-306, 141, and 293, respectively). Serve with Joe's Chip Shop Chips (page 202) and a smile on your face.

What's for Dinner Loaf

By Rhonda Malkmus

Advanced prep: None   **Immediate prep:** 40 min

Serves 4 to 6   **Special Equipment** Food processor, juicer

INGREDIENTS

- 1/2 cup almonds
- 1 1/2 cups flaxseed
- 1/2 cup pumpkin seeds
- 1 cup celery, juiced (discard pulp)
- 1/2 cup red onion, minced
- 4 cloves garlic, pressed
- 1 cup finely shredded carrots
- 1 teaspoon Celtic sea salt (optional)
- 1 tablespoon rosemary
- 1 tablespoon sage

DIRECTIONS

Process the almonds, flaxseed, and pumpkin seeds to a meal in a food processor. Combine the ground nuts and seeds with the celery juice, onion, garlic, carrots, sea salt, rosemary and sage in a bowl. Mix together thoroughly and set aside for 3 to 4 hours for flavors to blend.

Form the mixture into a loaf and serve.

Hint: The longer it sits, the stronger the flavors become.

14

Spreads, Sauces, & Dips

Spreads

Awesome Pistachio Pâté

BY JULIAN HUERTA

ADVANCED PREP: None   **IMMEDIATE PREP:** 15 min

SPECIAL EQUIPMENT Food Processor   **SERVES** 4

INGREDIENTS

1 1/2 cups raw pistachios unsoaked, or 2 cups soaked pistachios

1/2 cup extra virgin olive oil (maybe more)

5 leaves fresh basil or 2/3 tsp dried basil

1 tablespoon lime juice (If you end up storing the pâté and not using it all at once, you may want to add more lime juice when you pull it out because the flavor mellows out)

1 tablespoon nama shoyu (or less if you like less salt)

1 clove garlic

1/8 teaspoon cayenne powder

few dashes of chili powder

1/8 teaspoon cumin

DIRECTIONS

Food process everything above.

Contributor's note: I like dipping this with slices of cucumber because they have a cooling effect for me with this herbed up pâté. I also sometimes use baby spinach leaves to dip in if I want something really quick or easy. But, in general, I usually just see what I have in the fridge that I am attracted to. Maybe I'll see a carrot. I'll just rinse it off and dip and bite. I won't even cut it up if I don't feel like it. Same goes for peppers, celery, tomatoes, zucchini, etc . . . And/or Raw Buckwheat crackers. I wonder what else you can find to dip in it?

Variation: Mix in 1/2 cup raisins to hit your tongue with surprising bursts of sweetness!

Best Ever Almond Nut Pâté

By Rose Lee Calabro

Advanced prep: 12 to 48 hours for soaking   **Immediate prep:** 35 min
Serves 6 to 8   **Special Equipment** Juicer or food processor

INGREDIENTS

- 2 cups almonds, soaked 12 to 48 hours
- 1 cup sunflower seeds, soaked 4 to 6 hours
- 3 carrots
- 3 stalks celery, finely chopped
- 1 red bell pepper, finely chopped
- 1/2 finely chopped red onion
- 1/2 cup fresh parsley, finely chopped
- 2 tablespoons fresh lemon juice
- 1 teaspoon Celtic sea salt, or to taste
- 1/4 teaspoon cayenne or 1 to 2 teaspoons curry powder (optional)

DIRECTIONS

Process the almonds, sunflower seeds, and carrots through a Champion juicer using the blank plate or in a food processor fitted with the "S" blade.

Transfer to a mixing bowl and add the celery, bell pepper, red onion, parsley, lemon juice, salt, and cayenne or curry powder (if using). Mix well. Serve with vegetable slices or spread on raw crackers. Enjoy!

Carrocado Mash

BY DAVE KLEIN
ADVANCED PREP: None   **IMMEDIATE PREP:** 25 min
YIELDS 2 to 4 cups   **SPECIAL EQUIPMENT** Juicer

INGREDIENTS

6 large fresh carrots

1 large or 2 small ripe avocados

1 to 2 cups of broccoli florets
(optional)

1 ounce whole dulse leaf, rinsed
(optional)

1 large red or yellow bell pepper
(optional)

DIRECTIONS

Run the carrots through a Champion juicer using the blank plate. Collect the juicy pulp in a bowl. Remove the skin from the avocado(s) and, using a fork, mash the avocado into the carrot pulp.

Variation 1: Run broccoli through a Champion juicer and add the juicy pulp into the carrot and avocado mix.

Variation 2: Add the dulse and chopped bell pepper to the mixture.

Variation 3: Scoop out a bell pepper and stuff with the mixture.

Carrot and Tomato Spread

BY SHAZZIE
ADVANCED PREP: None   **IMMEDIATE PREP:** 15 min
YIELDS 1 1/2 cups   **SPECIAL EQUIPMENT** Coffee mill or hand blender

INGREDIENTS

2 carrots, finely chopped

1/2 avocado, chopped

1 tomato, chopped

DIRECTIONS

Process the chopped carrots in a coffee mill if you have one, or with a hand blender. The coffee mill will give the best results for this recipe.

Add the chopped tomato and avocado, and process until everything is mixed. You may need to take the mill off the processor and shake it from time to time. This is a lovely light dip, but very satisfying.

Contributor's note: Spread this on strong Batavia or romaine lettuce, top with some chopped green onion, fold and enjoy!

Heart Warmin' Fruit Spread

BY VITA-MIX
ADVANCED PREP: None **IMMEDIATE PREP:** 15 min
YIELDS 4 cups **SPECIAL EQUIPMENT** Vita-Mix

INGREDIENTS

2 cups fresh, canned, or frozen pears, thawed

1 cup fresh or canned pineapple

1/4 cup hot or mild green chilis

1/2 cup to 1 cup sugar or other sweetener, to taste

1 teaspoon fruit fresh or lemon juice

DIRECTIONS

Place all the ingredients in your Vita-Mix container in the order listed. Secure the 2-part lid. Select VARIABLE, speed #1. Turn on machine and quickly increase speed to #10; then to HIGH. Run for 3 minutes. Store this spread in an airtight container in your refrigerator.

Honey Butter

BY ELAINA LOVE
ADVANCED PREP: None   **IMMEDIATE PREP:** 10 min
YIELDS 1 cup   **SPECIAL EQUIPMENT** Blender

INGREDIENTS

1/2 cup coconut oil (butter)
2 tablespoons honey
1/8 teaspoon sea salt

1/2 teaspoon butter extract
small dash turmeric, for color

DIRECTIONS

Mix all the ingredients together in a small bowl with a firm spatula or fork.

Spread on Almond Cinnamon Bread (page 159), or on a slice of Corn Bread (page 161). Store at room temperature in a glass jar.

Tip: Butter extract is available from Frontier Herbs at www.frontiercoop.com

Horseradish

BY VITA-MIX
ADVANCED PREP: None   **IMMEDIATE PREP:** 35 min
YIELDS 1 cup   **SPECIAL EQUIPMENT** Vita-Mix

INGREDIENTS

1 cup horseradish root, peeled and cut in pieces
1/2 cup vinegar
1 tablespoon sugar or other sweetener
1/4 teaspoon salt

DIRECTIONS

Place the empty container on its base. Secure the 2-part lid. Select VARIABLE, speed #1. Turn on the machine and quickly increase speed to #5. While the machine is running, remove the lid plug and drop in the pieces of horseradish until all the pieces are grated.

Stop the machine. Scrape down the sides of container with spatula. Select VARI-ABLE, speed #1. Turn on the machine and quickly increase the speed to #8. Add the remaining ingredients. Run for 15 to 20 seconds or until well mixed. Refrigerate in an airtight container.

It's Not Really Mayonnaise

BY SHAZZIE

ADVANCED PREP: None   **IMMEDIATE PREP:** 20 min
YIELDS 4 cups   **SPECIAL EQUIPMENT** Juicer, blender

INGREDIENTS

2 cups macadamia nuts

1/2 cucumber, juiced

5 stalks celery, juiced

1 lemon, juiced

1 teaspoon paprika

1/2 cup olive oil

DIRECTIONS

Combine all the ingredients in a blender. If you're using a Vita-Mix, simply blend until you have mayonnaise. If you're using a regular blender, transfer the mixture to a blending bowl once the nuts are broken down. Finish off with a hand blender for a smoother mayonnaise.

Mediterranean Black Olive & Walnut Tapenade

BY CHERIE SORIA

ADVANCED PREP: None   **IMMEDIATE PREP:** 15 min

YIELDS 1 cup   **SPECIAL EQUIPMENT** Food processor

INGREDIENTS

1 cup black Niçoise or Greek olives, pitted

1/2 cup walnuts, ground

1 clove garlic, crushed

3 tablespoons capers

1 tablespoon flax oil or extra-virgin olive oil

2 teaspoons lemon juice

1/2 teaspoon crushed oregano

1/4 teaspoon ground thyme

1/4 teaspoon ground basil

DIRECTIONS

Combine all of the ingredients in a food processor and pulse, removing the lid several times to scrape the sides with a spatula. The mixture should be smooth, but not totally puréed.

Pico de Gallo

BY SHAZZIE

ADVANCED PREP: None   **IMMEDIATE PREP:** 20 min

YIELDS 1 1/2 cups   **SPECIAL EQUIPMENT** None

INGREDIENTS

2 tomatoes, skinned, seeds removed, and chopped into 1/4-inch chunks

1 red onion, peeled and chopped into 1/4-inch chunks

1 red pepper, seeds removed and chopped into 1/4-inch chunks

1 lime, juiced

1 clove of garlic, finely chopped

2 stalks of celery, finely chopped

DIRECTIONS

Place the tomato chunks between several sheets of paper towel and press tightly. Squeeze the juice out of them.

Mix the chopped tomatoes, onions, and pepper in a bowl. Squeeze the lime juice over the top and add the garlic and celery. Add sea salt if desired, but it is a good idea to taste it first.

Mix everything together well, cover, and let marinate a few hours before serving.

Pine Nut Dressing/Sauce

BY MARY RYDMAN
ADVANCED PREP: none or 6 hours to soak almonds
IMMEDIATE PREP: 10 min
SPECIAL EQUIPMENT Blender   **SERVES** 3–4

INGREDIENTS

1 cup pine nuts (or 1/2 cup pine nuts, 1/2 cup soaked almonds)
1 large red bell pepper, cut in large pieces
1 tablespoon miso
1 clove garlic
1 teaspoon Krystal Salt brine or 1/4 teaspoon salt
pinch cayenne (optional)
water to blend to desired consistency

DIRECTIONS

Blend all in blender to smooth consistency.

Contributor's Note: Rich and creamy, this one will please everyone!

Pumpkin Stuffing

Amy Yockel

Advanced prep: None **Immediate prep:** 10 min
Special Equipment Food processor **Serves** 7–8

INGREDIENTS

1 cup raw macadamia nuts

2 tablespoons ground flax seeds

3 heaping cups of pumpkin, chopped in large chunks

1 cup celery cut in chunks

1/2 cup onion cut in chunks

2 tablespoons fresh basil (handful)

1 tablespoon fresh oregano (half handful)

1 1/2 teaspoons dulse or Celtic sea salt

1/2 cup honey or to taste

DIRECTIONS

Grind the nuts in a food processor until fine, add all other ingredients and process. Use this stuffing in nori rolls and serve with cranberry sauce.

Spicy Cilantro Chutney

By Michal Adi

Advanced prep: None **Immediate prep:** 15 min
Yields 1 cup **Special Equipment** Food processor

INGREDIENTS

4 bunches cilantro

4 jalapeño peppers

1 to 1 1/2 teaspoons Celtic sea salt

3 tablespoons olive oil

DIRECTIONS

Process the cilantro, jalapeños and sea salt in a food processor using the "S" blade. Gradually add the olive oil. Use as a condiment.

Sunny Dill Seed Spread

BY SHARON ELAM

ADVANCED PREP: 5 to 8 days for sprouts   **IMMEDIATE PREP:** 25 min

YIELDS 4 cups   **SPECIAL EQUIPMENT** Food Processor

INGREDIENTS

- 3 cups sunflower seeds, sprouted
- 2 tablespoons lemon juice
- Braggs Liquid Aminos, to taste
- 1 small red onion, well chopped by hand or in small food processor
- 1/4 cup parsley, freshly chopped
- 1/4 to1/2 cup fresh dill
- 4 cloves garlic
- dash of cayenne, or more to taste

Process sunflower seeds, lemon juice and Aminos in food processor. Process remaining ingredients in small food processor and then add to first ingredients.

Sunny Pâté

By NOMI SHANNON

ADVANCED PREP: 12 to 16 hours for sprouts   **IMMEDIATE PREP:** 35 min

YIELDS 8 cups   **SPECIAL EQUIPMENT** Food processor, heavy-duty juicer or blender

INGREDIENTS

- 3 cups sunflower seeds, soaked 8 to 12 hours and sprouted 2 to 4 hours
- 1 cup fresh-squeezed lemon juice
- 1/2 cup roughly chopped scallions
- 1/2 cup raw tahini
- 2 tablespoons nama shoyu or 1 teaspoon Celtic sea salt and 3 to 4 tablespoons water
- 2 to 4 slices red onion, cut in chunks
- 4 to 6 tablespoons coarsely chopped parsley
- 2 to 3 medium cloves garlic, coarsely chopped
- 1/2 teaspoon cayenne pepper, or more to taste (optional)

DIRECTIONS

In a food processor, process the sunflower seeds, lemon juice, scallions, tahini, nama shoyu, onion, parsley, garlic and cayenne (if using) to a smooth paste. Adjust the seasonings to taste. The pâté will develop a stronger garlic flavor after a few hours. This recipe tastes best after several hours to a day in the refrigerator, when all the flavors have had a chance to meld.

Note: If you do not have a food processor or heavy-duty juicer, this recipe can also be made using a heavy-duty blender (K-Tec HP3 or Vita-Mix). If you use a heavy-duty blender, you may have to add additional liquid to keep from straining the blender motor. Keep in mind that your results may have a wetter consistency.

If your food processor is not large enough, make this recipe in batches. It can also be made with a heavy-duty juicer such as a Champion or Green Star using the blank plate. (Put all ingredients except the tahini and dried spices through the juicer, then stir in the tahini and spices.)

Variation 1: Add 1 to 2 tablespoons ginger juice or chopped fresh ginger and 1 teaspoon cumin for a spicier version of this recipe.

Variation 2: Asian pâté goes well with salads containing snap peas, snow peas and other Asian-type vegetables, such as bok choy, Napa cabbage, or mung bean sprouts. Asian pâté is also delicious stuffed in red peppers, or in nori rolls (yields 3 to 4 cups).

Into 3 cups Sunny Pâté stir in any or all of the following:

1/4 cup finely chopped mild onions or shallots

1/4 cup minced parsley

1/2 red pepper, finely chopped

cilantro, minced celery, snow peas, or leeks, finely chopped

Moisten with Asian Dressing (page 86–87).

Variation 3: Mexican Flavor Pâté (yields 4 to 6 cups)

Into 3 cups of Sunny Pâté stir in some or all of the following:

1/2 cup very finely minced carrots

1/2 cup minced celery

1/2 cup minced zucchini

1/2 cup onion, minced

1 cup finely chopped cilantro

1 to 2 garlic cloves, finely minced

2 teaspoons dried oregano

3/4 teaspoon cayenne pepper or more to taste

1/2 cup minced red or yellow pepper

lemon juice to taste

1 minced habanera pepper or 1 chili pepper (if you enjoy spicy food)i

Sweet Mango Chutney

By Michal Adi

Advanced prep: None   **Immediate prep:** 15 min

Yields 3 cups   **Special Equipment** Blender

INGREDIENTS

- 4 ripe mangoes
- 4 pieces dried papaya, unsweetened and unsulphured
- 4 pieces dried mango, unsweetened and unsulphured
- 1/2 teaspoon ground cloves
- 1/8 teaspoon ground cardamom

DIRECTIONS

Blend all ingredients together in a blender using just enough water to create a thick pudding-like texture. Use as a condiment.

Walnut Pâté

BY KARYN CALABRESE

ADVANCED PREP: None   IMMEDIATE PREP: 20 min

YIELDS 4 cups   SPECIAL EQUIPMENT Food processor

INGREDIENTS

6 cups walnuts

4 stalks celery, minced

1/2 onion

fresh dill, to taste

Bragg Liquid Aminos, to taste

curry powder, to taste

DIRECTIONS

Grind the walnuts into a paste in a food processor. Add the celery, onion, dill, Bragg Aminos, and curry powder and pulse until mixed.

Spoon into a loaf pan and cover with plastic wrap. Chill in the refrigerator until ready to eat.

Sauces

Already-Alive Atomic Really All Right Astounding Alfredo Sauce

BY JACKIE AYALA AND DAVID STEINBERG

ADVANCED PREP: None **IMMEDIATE PREP:** 30 min

YIELDS 2 to 3 cups **SPECIAL EQUIPMENT** Vita-Mix

INGREDIENTS

1/2 cup organic stone-crushed olive oil

1 drop *each* therapeutic grade basil, thyme, and oregano essential oils

water and meat of 1 young Thai coconut

1/3 cup citrus juice blend

1 tablespoon Celtic sea salt

2 large cloves garlic (with skins)

1/2 cup macadamia nuts

DIRECTIONS

In a glass bowl combine the olive oil and essential oils (the oils will soothe and inspire you as you prepare the sauce).

In a Vita-Mix, combine the coconut water and meat, citrus juice blend, salt, and garlic. With the Vita-Mix set on 5, blend until the mixture is smooth. Slowly add the macadamia nuts while the machine is still running, and increase the speed to 9. Scrape the sides to make sure everything is well blended. Turn the variable speed down to 7, add the olive oil, and continue to blend for another 5 seconds.

Variation: The main reason for using the essential oils is to maintain the white color of the sauce. If you want a green alfredo sauce, you may substitute 1/4 cup chopped fresh basil, oregano, or thyme.

Better-Than-Fish Sauce

By Matt Samuelson

Advanced prep: 20 min for soaking **Immediate prep:** 10 min

Yields 3/4 cups **Special Equipment** Blender

INGREDIENTS

3 tablespoons hiziki seaweed, soaked in 1/3 cup water (reserve water)

1 1/2 teaspoons sesame oil

2 tablespoons dulse flakes

1/2 large date

1/4 teaspoon apple cider vinegar

1 1/2 teaspoons nama shoyu

DIRECTIONS

Blend all the ingredients including the soak water together until smooth.

Bon Apricot Sauce

By Elysa Markowitz

Advanced prep: None **Immediate prep:** 20 min

Yields 2 cups **Special Equipment** Green Power / Star juicer or blender

INGREDIENTS

1 cup dried apricots or 4 to 6 fresh
    apricots

2 fresh bananas

1 frozen banana

1 fresh apple, cored

juice of 1 lemon

DIRECTIONS

To make the sauce, alternate putting the 2 fresh bananas, 1 frozen banana, dried or fresh apricots, and the apple through your Green Power / Star juicer with the open blank in place, or blend in a bowl. Add lemon juice to taste. Serve in a fancy bowl or on top of fresh fruit or greens.

Hint: You can peel or leave the skin on the apple. If it is a waxed apple, definitely peel it. Otherwise, the skin adds a flavor and a texture that some prefer, plus a good deal of nutrition.

Hint: If the dried apricots are hard, you might want to soak them for a short while in warm water. This will make the sauce a bit creamier.

Contributor's note: If you can find Turkish apricots, you are in for a real treat. They are so succulent.

Date Syrup

BY SHANNON ISLEY SCHNIBBE
ADVANCED PREP: None   IMMEDIATE PREP: 10 min
YIELDS 2 cups   SPECIAL EQUIPMENT Blender

INGREDIENTS

1 cup dates, pitted
1 cup water

DIRECTIONS

Blend the dates with 1 cup of water. Pour into a pint jar and refrigerate.

Contributor's note: Make a batch or two of this and keep it on hand—you never know when you'll need sweet syrup.

Eastern Kung-Foo Cashew Sauce

BY JACKIE AYALA AND DAVID STEINBERG
ADVANCED PREP: None   IMMEDIATE PREP: 20 min
YIELDS 1 to 2 cups   SPECIAL EQUIPMENT Vita-Mix

INGREDIENTS

1 cup cashews, soaked
1/3 cup lime juice
1/4 cup orange juice
1 teaspoon Celtic sea salt

1/2 cup diced mango
1 date, pitted
1 tablespoon diced fresh ginger
1 large clove garlic

DIRECTIONS

Blend all the ingredients together until creamy. Pour over a fresh salad or tasty raw pasta.

Golden Applesauce

BY ELYSA MARKOWITZ

ADVANCED PREP: None   **IMMEDIATE PREP:** 15 min

SERVES 2   **SPECIAL EQUIPMENT** Blender or Vita-Mix

INGREDIENTS

1/4 to 1/2 cup raisins

3 apples

2 to 4 Calimyrna figs (or any nonsulphured fig)

cinnamon, to taste

fresh nutmeg, to taste

fresh ginger, to taste (optional)

apple, pear, apricot, peach, plums or any fresh fruit

celery, lettuce, hemp seed oil, pecans, walnuts (optional)

DIRECTIONS

Place the raisins in a blender with about 1/2 cup water (enough to blend them), and blend to a sauce-like consistency. Add the apples and figs, and blend to desired consistency.

Spice with cinnamon, fresh nutmeg, and/or ginger (if using), to taste. Be careful how much ginger you add; it tastes hot and can dominate the flavor. Use a small slice without the skin, and add a little at a time. You can always add more.

If you want the sauce to be warm, either use hot water when you blend or place the sauce in saucepan and warm it over a very low flame for a very short time. Use your finger to test the temperature. If it gets too warm, turn off the heat.

Serve in an attractive bowl surrounded by sliced fruit chips.

Variation 1: Add currants or cranberries for a more tart applesauce.

Variation 2: Use dates instead of raisins and figs. With the right date, this can taste almost like caramel applesauce.

Variation 3: For some, adding nuts and/or greens tempers the fruit sugar and makes it easier to eat without the sugar highs and lows. Just line the bowl with lettuce leaves or shredded lettuce and put the sauce on top, sprinkled with crushed walnuts or pecans.

Variation 4: Celery can be added for crunch with the fruit chips, making this like a Waldorf salad without the mayonnaise.

Variation 5: For a creamier sauce, add a bit of hemp oil to the blender (up to 1/2 teaspoon) before blending.

Contributor's note: A deliciously warmed applesauce with fruit chips to dip into on a cool morning.

Jali's Tomato Sauce

By Jalissa Letendre
Advanced prep: 20 min for soaking   **Immediate prep:** 20 min
Yields 3 cups   **Special Equipment** Blender

INGREDIENTS

2 cups chopped fresh tomatoes

2 cloves garlic, peeled

1/2 cup fresh basil

1/4 cup chopped onion

1/2 cup raisins

2 teaspoons dried oregano

2 tablespoons olive oil

2 teaspoons paprika

2 teaspoons Herbamare® or sea salt

1/2 cup sun-dried tomatoes, soaked

1/8 cup fresh cilantro (optional)

1/8 cup fresh parsley (optional)

DIRECTIONS

In a blender, combine the fresh tomato with the garlic, basil, onion, raisins, oregano, olive oil, paprika, and Herbamare® or sea salt. Blend well.

Add the sun-dried tomatoes to the mixture and blend again, slowly adding 1 1/2 cups water for desired consistency.

Pour the sauce into a container and add the cilantro and parsley. Mix well with a spoon.

Mushroom Gravy

BY SHAZZIE
ADVANCED PREP: 1 to 8 hours for marinating   **IMMEDIATE PREP:** 20 min
YIELDS 3 cups   **SPECIAL EQUIPMENT** Juicer, blender

INGREDIENTS

2 cups portobello mushrooms, finely chopped
1 lemon, juiced
1 small onion, finely chopped
6 stalks celery, juiced
1 clove garlic, finely chopped
1/2 teaspoon paprika

DIRECTIONS

Combine all the ingredients in a bowl and allow to marinate for 1 to 8 hours.
Transfer to a blender and process until smooth.

Plum Sauce

BY SHAZZIE
ADVANCED PREP: 8 hours for soaking   **IMMEDIATE PREP:** 10 min
YIELDS 1 cup   **SPECIAL EQUIPMENT** Blender

INGREDIENTS

6 plums, pitted and peeled
2 Medjool dates, pitted
2 to 4 pieces dried papaya, soaked 8 hours minimum
2 cardamom pods

DIRECTIONS

Remove the seeds from the cardamom pods, and discard the pods. Blend all the
ingredients together and enjoy as a delicious condiment.

Contributor's note: The plums must be sweet and ripe for this recipe to work. Plum Sauce makes a lovely and surprising addition to Herby Stir Fry (page 247).

Pad Thai and Thai Wild Rice Sauce

BY ELAINA LOVE
ADVANCED PREP: 2 to 3 hours for soaking   **IMMEDIATE PREP:** 20 min
SERVES 4 to 6   **SPECIAL EQUIPMENT:** Blender

INGREDIENTS

1 tablespoon hiziki seaweed soaked for 30 minutes or more in enough water to cover

1/2 cup almond butter

1/2 cup sun-dried tomatoes, soaked 2 hours

1 lime, chopped (including peel if organic)

4 cloves garlic, peeled

7 dates, pitted

1/4 cup olive oil

2 small Thai chilies or 1 jalapeño (do not remove seeds if you like it hot!)

1 1/2 tablespoons shredded or zested fresh ginger

1 to 2 tablespoons tamari, plus extra if desired

1 1/2 teaspoons Celtic sea salt, plus extra if desired

1 cup cilantro, loosely packed (for Thai Wild Rice)

juice of 1/2 lemon or lime or about 1 1/2 tablespoons (for Thai Wild Rice)

1 tablespoon maple syrup or date paste (for Thai Wild Rice)

DIRECTIONS

Blend the hiziki, almond butter, sun-dried tomatoes, lime, garlic, dates, olive oil, chilies, ginger, tamari, and sea salt with 1/2 cup water until creamy.

For the Thai Wild Rice, blend 1 cup of the sauce with the cilantro, lemon or lime juice, maple syrup or date paste, and extra salt or tamari if desired.

Spicy Ginger Marinara

BY CHAD SARNO

ADVANCED PREP: 2 to 3 hours for soaking   **IMMEDIATE PREP:** 30 min

YIELDS 4 cups   **SPECIAL EQUIPMENT** Blender

INGREDIENTS

2 cups chopped red bell pepper

1 cup chopped tomato

1/2 cup sun-dried tomato, soaked for 2 to 3 hours

1/2 cup chopped apple

2 cloves garlic

2 tablespoons chopped fresh ginger

4 kefir lime leaves (optional)

2 tablespoons olive oil

Celtic sea salt, to taste

1/2 teaspoon black pepper, cracked

cayenne to taste (optional)

3 tablespoons fresh chopped basil

2 tablespoons fresh chopped chives

DIRECTIONS

In a blender, mix the red pepper, tomato, sun-dried tomato, apple, garlic, ginger, lime leaves, olive oil, salt, pepper and cayenne to a smooth consistency.

Pulse in the fresh basil and chives. Make sure not to blend fully; leave small pieces of herbs in the sauce. Serve over Thai Cannelloni (page 133), or with any raw vegetable pasta.

Variation: Try using 2 cups tomatoes instead of 2 cups bell peppers. With excess leftovers, simply add a bit of olive oil and apple cider vinegar for a salad dressing.

Spinach Pesto

BY SHAZZIE

ADVANCED PREP: Mushroom Gravy 2 to 3 hours   **IMMEDIATE PREP:** 20 min
(Mushroom Gravy 30 min)   **YIELDS** 3 cups   **SPECIAL EQUIPMENT** Hand
blender or food processor

INGREDIENTS

- 1 cup fresh basil, tightly packed
- 1/2 cup fresh parsley, tightly packed
- 1 cup chopped spinach, tightly packed

- 1 clove garlic
- 1/2 teaspoon salt
- 1 cup pine nuts
- 1 cup Mushroom Gravy (page 100)

DIRECTIONS

Blend all ingredients together with a hand blender or food processor.

Contributor's note: This goes perfectly with Courgetti or other spiralized squashes.

Sweet Apricot Sauce

BY SHAZZIE

ADVANCED PREP: 8 to 10 hours for soaking   **IMMEDIATE PREP:** 10 min
YIELDS 1/2 cup   **SPECIAL EQUIPMENT** none

INGREDIENTS

- 10 dried apricots, soaked overnight
- 1/2 teaspoon anise seed
- 1/2 teaspoon fennel seed

DIRECTIONS

Blend all the ingredients together, and serve with Crispy Spring Rolls (page 137).

Sweet Miso-Ginger Sauce

BY ELAINA LOVE

ADVANCED PREP: None   **IMMEDIATE PREP:** 15 min

YIELDS 1 1/2 cups   **SPECIAL EQUIPMENT** Blender

INGREDIENTS

1/2 cup sesame or olive oil

1 teaspoon toasted sesame oil (optional)

1 large clove garlic, peeled (optional)

2 tablespoons fresh ginger, chopped or shredded

1 tablespoon raw apple cider vinegar or 2 tablespoons lemon juice

1/4 cup honey, maple syrup or date paste (dates and water blended)

2 tablespoons light miso paste

1 tablespoon tamari or Bragg Liquid Aminos

1/8 teaspoon cayenne, or to taste

DIRECTIONS

Blend all ingredients together until creamy.

Sweet and Spicy Chili Sauce

BY ELAINA LOVE

ADVANCED PREP: None   **IMMEDIATE PREP:** 15 min

YIELDS 4 to 5 cups   **SPECIAL EQUIPMENT** Blender

INGREDIENTS

1 pound red bell peppers (about 2) or for more heat, fresh cayenne peppers, seeds removed, chopped

4 green or red jalapeños or 1 habanero pepper, chopped

6 medium soft dates, pitted

3 medium cloves garlic

1 teaspoon Celtic sea salt

1 teaspoon raw apple cider vinegar or 2 teaspoons lemon or lime juice

DIRECTIONS

Place all the ingredients in a blender, and blend on high until mixture is mostly smooth, but a little chunky.

Pour into a pint-size glass jar. Cover and store in the refrigerator for 2 or more months. Enjoy with a number of recipes as a topping or side condiment.

Tomato Sauce

BY SHAZZIE

ADVANCED PREP: 2 hours for soaking   **IMMEDIATE PREP:** 15 min

YIELDS 2 1/2 cups   **SPECIAL EQUIPMENT** Hand blender

INGREDIENTS

6 sun-dried tomatoes, soaked 2 hours minimum

2 cups chopped fresh tomatoes

10 basil leaves

4 Medjool dates, soaked 2 hours minimum

pinch paprika

1 red pepper, seeds and core removed

DIRECTIONS

Using a hand blender, blend all the ingredients until smooth. The sauce will keep for two days in the fridge if you cover it.

Contributor's note: Perfect with Walnut Burgers (page 279) and Joe's Chip Shop Chips (page 202)

Tomato Sauce

BY **MARY RYDMAN**
ADVANCED PREP: 2 hours to soak dried tomatoes
IMMEDIATE PREP: 15 min
SPECIAL EQUIPMENT Blender   **YIELDS** 3–4 cups

INGREDIENTS

2 cups tomatoes, chopped
1/2 cup dried tomatoes, soaked
1/4 cup fresh basil leaves or 1 teaspoon dried
1/4 cup fresh oregano or 1 teaspoon dried
1/4 cup red or white wine (or water)
5 pitted raw olives
juice of 1/2 lemon
1/2 teaspoon peeled, chopped ginger
1 clove garlic
3 teaspoons Krystal Salt Brine or 3/4 teaspoon salt

DIRECTIONS

Soak dried tomatoes in just enough water to cover for 2 or more hours. Place all ingredients in blender including tomato soak water and blend all until well combined, adding more water if necessary. Store leftover sauce in a glass jar in refrigerator. Keeps for a week or so.

Contributor's note: Makes a great sauce for pizza, nut loaves or patties—or use as a cracker topping.

White Sauce / Salad Dressing

BY AMY YOCKEL

ADVANCED PREP: None   **IMMEDIATE PREP:** 15 min

SERVES 7   **SPECIAL EQUIPMENT** Food processor or blender

INGREDIENTS

1 cup cashews or pine nuts

1 cup macadamia nuts

1/2 cup fresh lemon juice

1 clove garlic

1/2 teaspoon ground peppercorns

1 1/2 teaspoons Celtic sea salt (or dulse)

splash coconut water (optional)

DIRECTIONS

Blend all the ingredients together in a food processor, adding a little water (or coconut water) for desired consistency. Serve over zucchini pasta or with raw crackers (see chapter 5).

Dips

Carrot and Cilantro Dip

BY SHAZZIE

ADVANCED PREP: None **IMMEDIATE PREP:** 15 min

YIELDS 1 1/2 cup **SPECIAL EQUIPMENT** Hand blender

INGREDIENTS

1/2 mild onion, peeled and diced

bunch cilantro, finely chopped

1 lime, juiced

2 large carrots

1/2 avocado, peeled, pitted and diced

1 clove garlic, peeled and chopped

DIRECTIONS

Combine the onion and cilantro, and set aside in a bowl with the juice of half the lime.

Blend the carrots, avocado, and garlic together using a hand blender. Once smooth, pour into the onion and cilantro mixture, and blend thoroughly. Serve with crudités of your choice and the other lime half on the side.

Carrot-Corn Salsa

By Abeba Wright
Advanced prep: None **Immediate prep:** 20 min
Yields 1 1/2 cups **Special Equipment** Food processor

INGREDIENTS

3 carrots
1 garlic clove
1/4 red onion
1/4 cup chopped green onion
1/2 red bell pepper
1 tablespoon lemon juice

1/4 cup cilantro
1/2 teaspoon cumin
1 tablespoon olive oil
1 tablespoon nama shoyu
1 to 2 ears corn, kernels cut from
   the cob

DIRECTIONS

Process the carrots, garlic, red and green onions, pepper, lemon juice, and cilantro in a food processor until fine. Add the cumin, olive oil, and nama shoyu.

Pour into a bowl and add the corn. Adjust the seasonings to taste and serve with Abeba's Krazy Corn Chips (page 309).

Creamy Herb Dip

By Shazzie
Advanced prep: 1 hour for soaking **Immediate prep:** 15 min
Yields 2 1/2 cups **Special Equipment** Juicer, food processor, hand blender

INGREDIENTS

1 lemon, juiced
2 teaspoons olive oil
2 stalks celery, juiced
3 cloves garlic

1/2 cup fresh parsley, tightly packed
1 dessertspoon (about 2 teaspoons)
   dried dill
1/2 teaspoon oregano
1 cup cashew nuts, soaked at least
   1 hour

DIRECTIONS

Process all ingredients in a food processor. Transfer to a bowl and blend to a creamy dip using a hand blender. If you have a Vita-Mix, simply blend the ingredients to a dip. If it's too thick, add more celery juice. If it's too thin, add more cashews.

Contributor's note: Everyone loves this fresh, wholesome flavor, and it complements many spicy recipes to perfection.

Dahl

By John Fielder

Advanced prep: None   **Immediate prep:** 25 min

Serves 4   **Special Equipment** None

INGREDIENTS

400 grams (about 1 pound) butternut pumpkin

2 small tomatoes

7 tablespoons sesame seed, sun-flower seed, and almond mixture

1/2 small coconut

1 hot radish

4 small mustard leaves

1 stalk celery

1 large onion

8 garlic chives

6 sprigs parsley

2 level teaspoons cumin

1 two-inch piece fresh ginger

2 tablespoons curry leaves

DIRECTIONS

Chop all ingredients into 1-inch strips. Toss together in a bowl and feed through a corn mill, cast iron meat mincer, or grinder. Stir thoroughly and decorate with tomato and parsley. Mixture should be smooth and creamy.

Guacamole

By Shazzie

Advanced prep: None   **Immediate prep:** 15 min
Yields 2 cups   **Special Equipment** Food processor

INGREDIENTS

2 avocados, peeled and pitted
1 or 1/2 medium red chili, seeds removed and chopped
1 clove of garlic, chopped
2 tomatoes

DIRECTIONS

Process the avocado, chili, garlic, and tomatoes in a food processor until they're smooth, but still a little chunky. For a chunkier guacamole, don't process one of the avocados. Instead, dice it and mix it in afterward.

Variation 1: Fruit—Add the juice of 1 orange to the ingredients before blending. This gives the guacamole a lovely sweet mellow flavor.

Variation 2: Sweetie—Add a banana to the ingredients before blending. This gives it a sweet and substantial flavor.

Variation 3: Manly—Leave out the tomatoes and add a cup of watercress or spinach.

Variation 4: Herbie—Adding cilantro, mint or basil to the ingredients before blending gives it a summery and hearty flavor.

Variation 5: Bertie Bassett—Mix any of the above for a different guacamole each time. Don't let this selection limit you: add other herbs, spices and fruit.

Keep Your Guacamole Fresh: If you're making guacamole a few hours in advance, add the juice of a lemon to the ingredients before blending and place the avocado stones in the middle of the guacamole. Some say the added pits will keep it fresh.

Contributor's note: Guacamole is the most beautiful of all processed foods and has so many variations I can put only a few here.

Loveliest Live Almond Hummus

BY MICHAL ADI

ADVANCED PREP: 24 hours for soaking   **IMMEDIATE PREP:** 20 min

YIELDS 4 cups   **SPECIAL EQUIPMENT** Food processor

INGREDIENTS

3 cups almonds, soaked 24 hours and peeled

1/2 cup tahini

juice of 2 lemons

3 cloves garlic

1 teaspoon cumin

3/4 teaspoon Celtic sea salt

3 tablespoons olive oil

fresh thyme or za'atar mixture for garnish

1 diced tomato, for garnish

olive oil

DIRECTIONS

Combine all ingredients in the food processor and process using the "S" blade. Garnish with fresh thyme or za'atar mixture, diced tomato, and olive oil. Serve with sliced cucumbers.

Papaya Macadamia Nut Salsa

BY JEREMY SAFRON

ADVANCED PREP: None   **IMMEDIATE PREP:** 20 min

YIELDS 3 to 4 cups   **SPECIAL EQUIPMENT** Food processor

INGREDIENTS

2 cups ripe diced papaya

1 cup diced tomato

1/2 cup diced onion, rinsed

1/2 cup cilantro, loosely packed

1 chipotle pepper, soaked

7 macadamia nuts

1/4 cup lime juice

1 tablespoon sea salt or to taste

DIRECTIONS

Mix the papaya, tomato, and onion together in a large bowl. Grind the cilantro, pepper, and macadamia nuts in a food processor. Stir the ground nuts and spices into the papaya mixture. Add the lime juice and sea salt and mix thoroughly.

Pine Nut Sour Cream

By Elaina Love

Advanced prep: 1 hour for soaking **Immediate prep:** 15 min

Serves 8 **Special Equipment** Blender

INGREDIENTS

- 1 1/4 cups pine nuts, soaked 1 hour or more
- 1/2 cup young coconut meat or 1/2 additional cup of pine nuts
- 1 teaspoon raw apple cider vinegar
- 1/2 teaspoon unpasteurized light miso paste
- 1/4 teaspoon Celtic sea salt
- 1/2 lemon, juiced (about 1 1/2 tablespoons)

DIRECTIONS

Blend all the ingredients together in a blender until smooth and creamy. Pine Nut Sour Cream will keep for up to 2 weeks in the refrigerator.

Ranch Dip or Dressing

By Elaina Love

Advanced prep: None **Immediate prep:** 15 min

Yields 18 ounces **Special Equipment** Blender

INGREDIENTS

- 1 1/2 cups raw cashews
- 4 teaspoons lemon juice or 2 1/2 teaspoons raw apple cider vinegar
- 1 teaspoon Celtic sea salt
- 1 teaspoon onion powder
- 1 teaspoon garlic powder
- 1 teaspoon dried dill weed
- 1 teaspoon Italian seasoning
- 1 basil leaf, minced

DIRECTIONS

Blend the cashews, lemon juice, sea salt, onion and garlic powder with 1 cup purified water until smooth and creamy. You may need to add more lemon juice if the lemons you are using are not sour enough. Pour into a bowl.

Add the dill, Italian seasoning, and basil leaf by hand to the blended dressing. Serve as a dip or salad dressing. Store in a glass jar in the refrigerator for up to 2 weeks.

Raw Hummus

BY JONATHAN WEBER

YIELDS 4 to 5 cups   **SPECIAL EQUIPMENT** Food processor

INGREDIENTS

2 cups chickpeas, soaked 24 hours and sprouted 72 hours
4 cloves garlic, chopped
1/2 cup raw tahini (or to taste)
2 tablespoons nama shoyu or 1/2 teaspoon sea salt
2 lemons, juiced (to taste)
1 cup fresh parsley or more, to taste
red onion, chopped, for garnish
chives, for garnish
parsley, for garnish
extra-virgin olive oil

DIRECTIONS

Combine chickpeas, garlic and 1/2 cup water in a food processor and process until well mixed.

Add tahini, nama shoyu or sea salt, lemon juice and parsley and process until very smooth.

Adjust consistency with more water if necessary, and add seasonings and lemon juice as desired.

Garnish with chopped red onion, chives, or parsley and drizzle with extra-virgin olive oil.

Salsa Fresca

By Matt Samuelson
Serves 2 to 4   Special Equipment None

INGREDIENTS

2 large tomatoes, diced

1/2 medium red onion, finely minced

2 cloves garlic, crushed

1/2 jalapeño or more to taste, finely minced

1 lemon or lime, juiced

1/2 cup chopped cilantro leaves

1/2 teaspoon Celtic sea salt, or more, to taste

1 teaspoon apple cider vinegar (optional)

2 tablespoons sun-dried tomatoes, puréed (optional)

DIRECTIONS

Mix all the ingredients together in a bowl. For best results, let the salsa sit for 1 hour or more before serving so the flavors can meld.

Tahitian Almond Dipping Sauce

By Robert Yarosh and Lisa Soto
Yields 1 1/2 cups   Special Equipment Blender

INGREDIENTS

1 cup raw almond butter

1/2 cup pine nuts

1/2 cup chopped cilantro

1 clove garlic

1/4 cup fresh orange juice

1 1/2 tablespoons honey

DIRECTIONS

Blend all ingredients together until smooth. Serve with your favorite raw crackers and fresh fruit.

Tomatillo Salsa

BY VITA-MIX

ADVANCED PREP: None   **IMMEDIATE PREP:** 15 min

YIELDS 2 cups   **SPECIAL EQUIPMENT** Vita-Mix

INGREDIENTS

16 tomatillos

4 scallions

2 jalapeños, seeded

1 clove garlic

1/4 cup lime juice

1 cup cilantro leaves

1 teaspoon salt

DIRECTIONS

Place all the ingredients in your Vita-Mix container in order listed. Secure the 2-part lid. Select VARIABLE, speed #1. Turn on machine and quickly increase speed to #5. Run for 10 seconds or just until chopped. If necessary, use the tamper to push the ingredients into the blades while processing. Do not over-mix. Serve as a dip or as an accompaniment.

Xocolat Covered Berries

BY PEGGY KENNEY

ADVANCED PREP: none   **IMMEDIATE PREP:** 30 min

SPECIAL EQUIPMENT double boiler with thermometer   **SERVES** 1–2

INGREDIENTS

6 Xoçai™ Nuggets

1/2 lb organic strawberries

DIRECTIONS

In a double boiler heat water to 100°F. Remove from heat. Place Xoçai™ Nuggets in the top of boiler. Place the lid on the pan and let stand for 20 minutes. The nuggets are fine Belgian chocolate and will melt easily.

When the chocolate is melted, stir until smooth. Place your berries on the end of a fork and swirl in the Xoçai™ chocolate until covered.

Place on a clean surface to dry.

TIP: With smaller fruit pieces you can spear them with a toothpick, over them with chocolate and stick the tooth pick into an apple for display. It's fun and healthy!

Xoçai™ Fondue Fruit Dip

BY PEGGY KENNEY

ADVANCED PREP: None   IMMEDIATE PREP: 20 min
SPECIAL EQUIPMENT Fondue pot   SERVES 2–4

INGREDIENTS

16 Xoçai™ Nuggets
Selected fruit cubed and arranged on a plate.

DIRECTIONS

Place your fondue pot on the lowest setting.

Unwrap the Xoçai™ Nuggets and place in the fondue bowl and cover.

Let warm for 10 minutes.

Stir and dip with fruit of choice.

Xoçai™ Topping

BY PEGGY KENNEY

ADVANCED PREP: none   **IMMEDIATE PREP:** 2–5 min
SPECIAL EQUIPMENT none   **SERVES** 1

INGREDIENTS

2 oz Xoçai™ Activ™
Fruit medley of your choice

DIRECTIONS

Drizzle Xoçai™ Activ™ over your favorite fruit bowl and enjoy.

15

Cookies & Other Sweets

Apple Raisin Cookies

BY ROSE LEE CALABRO

ADVANCED PREP: 6 to 8 hours for soaking + 8 to 12 hours for dehydrating
IMMEDIATE PREP: 30 min   **YIELDS** 24 cookies   **SPECIAL EQUIPMENT** Champion juicer, dehydrator

INGREDIENTS

2 cups sunflower seeds, soaked 6 to 8 hours and rinsed

2 Fuji apples, cored

2 large bananas, peeled

1/2 cup honey dates, pitted

1 teaspoon vanilla

1 teaspoon cinnamon

1 cup raisins

1 cup walnuts, soaked 6 to 8 hours and chopped

DIRECTIONS

Process sunflower seeds, apples, bananas, and dates through a Champion juicer using the blank plate. Spoon into a large bowl, and add the vanilla, cinnamon, raisins, and walnuts. Spoon the dough onto a dehydrator tray lined with a Teflex sheet, and form into small round cookies. Dehydrate at 105°F for 4 to 6 hours, and then turn cookies over and remove Teflex sheet. Continue dehydrating for another 4 to 6 hours to desired consistency.

Blueberry Snow Cookies

By Elaina Love

ADVANCED PREP: 8 hours for dehydrating   **IMMEDIATE PREP:** 40 min

YIELDS 60 cookies   **SPECIAL EQUIPMENT** Food processor, Champion or Green Power / Star juicer; dehydrator

INGREDIENTS

4 apples

3 carrots

2 cups dates, pitted and packed

4 cups almonds, soaked

1/2 cup coconut butter or olive oil

3 cups raisins

4 cups shredded coconut

2 cups frozen blueberries or cranberries

3 cups walnuts or pecans, soaked and dehydrated

2 cups flaxseed, soaked and ground into a meal

1 teaspoon Celtic sea salt

3/4 teaspoon stevia (optional)

2 cups dried apples, finely chopped (optional)

DIRECTIONS

Purée the apples, carrots, dates and almonds in a food processor or run through a Champion juicer or Green Power / Star juicer, alternating the nuts with the wetter items.

If you are using coconut butter, warm it until it becomes liquid before adding to the batter.

Add the warm coconut butter or olive oil, raisins, shredded coconut, walnuts or pecans, berries, flaxseed, sea salt, stevia, and dried apples (if using). Mix well.

Shape into 2-ounce round cookies using a 1/4 cup measuring cup.

Dehydrate at 105°F for approximately 8 hours until desired consistency is reached. Keep refrigerated if you plan to keep the cookies for more than 4 days.

Bountiful Berry Medley

BY JULIAN HUERTA

ADVANCED PREP: none   IMMEDIATE PREP: 20 min

SPECIAL EQUIPMENT Blender   SERVES 2

INGREDIENTS

1/4 cup blueberries

1 large peach

2/3 cup raspberries

1/3 cup soaked raisins

1/2 tsp ground flaxseed

Sweet Cream

1 1/2 cup of soaked macadamia nuts or truly raw cashews

2–3 soaked dates

3 dashes salt

DIRECTIONS

Baked fruit pie filling often has some glaze in it (some fruity syrup) which comes from cooking the fruit with sugar and some of the water being released. I create a glaze here by putting 2 teaspoons of each fruit except raisins, in the blender along with the raw thickening agent: ground flaxseed. Toss the glaze with the berries and fruits.

Sweet Cream: Blend.

Serve by layering the fruit with the cream in the middle of a small plate.

Variation: Substitute other fruits or berries.

Carob-Cherry Thumbprint Cookies

BY ELAINA LOVE

ADVANCED PREP: 8 to 12 hours for soaking + 20 to 26 hours for dehydrating
IMMEDIATE PREP: 45 min   SERVES 10 to 12   SPECIAL EQUIPMENT Blender, dehydrator

INGREDIENTS

For the cookie:

2 medium zucchini, chopped (peel first for a white cookie)

1 cup soaked almonds

1 1/2 cups carob powder

1 cup raisins or dried, pitted cherries

3 cups shredded coconut

3/4 cup honey or Rapadura

2 teaspoons cherry extract

1 teaspoon vanilla extract or 1/4 whole vanilla bean (use soft pulp from center)

1 1/2 tablespoons lemon juice

1/2 teaspoon Celtic sea salt

dash of cayenne

For the filling:

1/2 cup berries

1/4 cup honey or Rapadura®

DIRECTIONS

Blend zucchini and 1/8 cup water until smooth.

Add the almonds and blend again until smooth. Spoon into a large bowl, and add the carob powder, raisins, coconut, 3/4 cup honey or Rapadura, cherry and vanilla extracts, lemon juice, Celtic sea salt, and cayenne.

Using a tablespoon, scoop batter and shape into thick round circles. Use your thumb to make a deep indentation in each. Place on a dehydrator tray lined with a Teflex sheet.

To make the filling, blend together 1/2 cup berries and 1/4 cup honey or Rapadura®. Fill the center of each cookie.

Dehydrate for 8 hours. Flip and remove the Teflex sheet. Dehydrate another 12 to 18 hours or until crunchy. Store in a glass jar.

Chewy Apricot Cookies

By John Larsen

Advanced prep: 8 to 10 hours for soaking + 7 hours for dehydrating
Immediate prep: 40 min   **Yields** 20 cookies   **Special Equipment** Vita-Mix, dehydrator

INGREDIENTS

2 cups oat groats, soaked

10 dates, pitted and chopped

1/2 cup raisins, soaked

1 1/2 cups fruit soak water

1/4 cup raw honey

1 cup golden flaxseed, ground

1 1/2 cups dried apricots, chopped

1 cup walnuts, chopped

DIRECTIONS

In a Vita-Mix blender, combine the oat groats, dates, raisins, soak water, and honey. Grind flaxseed in a coffee grinder and add to blender for 20 seconds. Pour contents of blender into a bowl.

Stir in chopped apricots and walnuts. Form into cookies on Teflex sheets and dehydrate at 100°F for 4 hours. Turn over and continue dehydrating for 3 more hours. These are especially delicious when eaten warm from the dehydrator.

Chocolate Chia Cookie

By Peggy Kenney

Advanced prep: 30 min for standing, 24 hours for dehydrating
Immediate prep: 20 min
Special Equipment food dehydrator   **Serves** 4

INGREDIENTS

1/4 cup chia seeds

2 1/4 cup water

2 oz Xoçai™ Activ™ Chocolate

3 each Xoçai™ finely grated nuggets

DIRECTIONS

Add Chia seeds to water and mix with wire whisk. Wait 10 min and whisk again.

Add Xoçai™ Activ™ chocolate and mix well.

Let mixture stand for 30 minutes.

Using the plastic sheet in your food dehydrator, spread the mixture over the sheet. Sprinkle the grated Xoçai™ nuggets on the top and dehydrate for 24 hours.

Fruity-Mint Patties

BY JULIE RODWELL

ADVANCED PREP: 6 to 8 hours for dehydrating + 6 to 8 hours for refrigerating and mixing   **IMMEDIATE PREP:** 40 min

SERVES 6 to 8   **SPECIAL EQUIPMENT** Dehydrator (optional)

INGREDIENTS

1/2 to 2/3 cup thin honey

2 small lemons, juiced

1 cup dates, chopped, pitted and well-packed

1 cup raisins

1 cup dried apricots, chopped and well-packed

1 1/2 cups walnuts, coarsely chopped

1 teaspoon mint essence

2 teaspoons cinnamon

1 teaspoon sea salt

2 to 6 tablespoons psyllium powder

1/2 to 3/4 cup coconut flakes, unsweetened

DIRECTIONS

Mix together the honey, lemon juice, dates, raisins, dried apricots, walnuts, mint essence, cinnamon, and sea salt. Cover and let sit overnight in the fridge.

Next day, add enough psyllium to create a firm dough. Roll heaping teaspoonfuls of the dough by hand into patties, dusting with coconut flakes. Dehydrate for 6 to 8 hours at 105° (optional). Will keep for weeks in the fridge!

Contributor's note: These are a pleasant surprise to the palate because of the mint. The mixture is soaked overnight so that the dried fruits soften and expand.

Gooey Mint Cookies

BY DAVE KLEIN
ADVANCED PREP: 8 to 12 hours for soaking   **IMMEDIATE PREP:** 20 min
SERVES 6 to 8   **SPECIAL EQUIPMENT** Champion juicer

INGREDIENTS

2 cups dried Black Mission figs (soak in water if they are not pliable)
1 cup soaked almonds
several fresh mint leaves, shredded

DIRECTIONS

Process or run the figs, almonds, and mint through a Champion juicer using the blank plate. Mix together. Form the mixture into cookies or balls. Enjoy!

Haystacks

BY ELAINA LOVE
ADVANCED PREP: 10 min for warming coconut oil   **IMMEDIATE PREP:** 30 min
YIELDS 20 pieces   **SPECIAL EQUIPMENT** Blender

INGREDIENTS

3/4 cup coconut oil
1/2 cup Rapadura®, Sucanat® (whole dehydrated cane juice) or honey
1/2 cup carob powder or organic cocoa powder
1/8 vanilla bean or 1 teaspoon vanilla extract
3 cups shredded coconut (more or less as needed)

DIRECTIONS

Place the coconut oil in a bowl of hot water, or put it in your dehydrator for 10 minutes to liquefy it.

If using Rapadura or Sucanat, mix in a blender until it becomes powder.

Add the coconut oil, carob or cocoa powder, and vanilla. If using a vanilla bean, cut the bean open and use the black pulp inside. Blend on high until the batter emulsifies.

Mix the batter in with the shredded coconut in a mixing bowl.

Form into haystack shapes on a tray lined with wax paper. Let set in the refrigerator or freezer before serving. The haystacks will be soft at temperatures over 60°F, but they'll last 6 to 12 months in the refrigerator or freezer.

Meltaway Peppermint Patties

By Elaina Love

Advanced prep: 10 min for freezing **Immediate prep:** 50 min

Yields 3 to 4 cups **Special Equipment** Blender

INGREDIENTS

For the mint layer:

3 cups dry, raw shredded coconut

1/3 cup honey or maple syrup

1/2 teaspoon mint extract or 3 drops peppermint essential oil

For the chocolate or carob layer:

3 cups dry, raw shredded coconut

1/3 cup honey or maple syrup

1/8 cup organic cocoa powder or raw carob powder

1/2 teaspoon vanilla extract

dash cayenne pepper

1/8 teaspoon Celtic sea salt

DIRECTIONS

For the mint layer, blend 3 cups coconut in a dry blender on low speed with the lid off. Use a spatula to keep things moving until it becomes the consistency of butter. Make sure you do not blend so long as to separate all the oil from the coconut. This takes a powerful blender such as a Vita-Mix. You can still do this if you don't have a Vita-Mix, but you may need to separate the coconut into 2 batches.

Remove the coconut and transfer to a mixing bowl. Add 1/3 cup honey or maple syrup and mint extract. Use a spatula to mix well. Set aside.

For the chocolate layer, blend 3 cups shredded coconut by hand with 1/3 cup honey or maple syrup, the vanilla, cayenne pepper, and sea salt. Add 1/8 cup organic cocoa powder or raw carob powder until mixture reaches desired color.

Separate the chocolate mixture into 2 halves. Press one half into the bottom of a

4- x 4-inch baking dish or Tupperware. Put it in the freezer for 5 minutes until it is solid.

Remove dish from the freezer and add all of the mint layer. Place in the freezer again for a couple of minutes.

Add the second half of the chocolate mixture to the top of the mint layer. Freeze again until solid or refrigerate.

Pop the meltaways out of the container by twisting it (if it is plastic) or use a spatula to pry them up. Place on a cutting board and cut your meltaways into whatever shape you like using a sharp, thin knife.

Put the patties in candy papers, or arrange them on an attractive serving dish. They will keep at room temperature for a few days, or in the refrigerator.

Contributor's note: Have an outrageously healthy and delicious snack in less than an hour!

Pecan Fudge

BY **MARY RYDMAN**

ADVANCED PREP: 2 or 3 hours to soak dates   **IMMEDIATE PREP:** 30 min
SPECIAL EQUIPMENT High speed blender to grind nuts, hand blender
SERVES about 26

INGREDIENTS

1 cup pecans, not soaked or soaked then dried
1/2 cup walnuts, not soaked or soaked then dried
1/2 cup carob powder
1/4 cup raw cocoa powder
3/4 cup dates, pitted and soaked until soft in just enough water to almost cover*.
1 tablespoon vanilla extract
1 teaspoon almond flavor
1/2 teaspoon Krystal Salt brine (or pinch granulated salt)
1/2 cup pine nuts
About 1/2 cup sesame seeds

DIRECTIONS

Grind pecans and walnuts as fine as possible, preferably in dry carafe or Vitamix. In large bowl, stir nut meal, carob and cocoa powder together, smashing any lumps. In a separate small bowl, blend dates, vanilla, almond flavor and salt with hand blender. Add pine nuts and blend again using short spurts with the thick batter. Mash wet ingredients into dry ingredients using hands if necessary. Form into small balls and roll in sesame seeds. If the mixture is too soft to form easily into balls, refrigerate several hours first. The firmness will vary with how much oil is in the nuts and how much water is used to soak the dates.

Variation: Christmas Fudge—soak dates in fresh orange juice and add a half teaspoon orange zest to the wet ingredients.

*Note: to soak dates, pit and press into a jar or bowl and add only enough water to almost cover so there is no excess liquid that needs to be drained off after soaking. Soak for 2 or 3 hours.

Publisher's Notes: This recipe tastes absolutely decadent! Your friends will be impressed, even those who don't like raw foods.

Pecan Sandies

By Elaina Love
Advanced prep: 8 to 12 hours for soaking + 20 to 26 hours for dehydrating
Immediate prep: 40 min **Serves** 8 to 10
Special Equipment Blender, dehydrator

INGREDIENTS

3 yellow sunburst squash, chopped (peel for a white cookie)
1 1/2 cups soaked almonds, soaked (3/4 cup before soaking)
1 1/4 cup Rapadura® or maple syrup
3 cups shredded coconut
1 teaspoon vanilla extract or 1/4 whole vanilla bean (use soft pulp from center)
1 1/2 tablespoons lemon juice
1/2 teaspoon Celtic sea salt
1 cup pecans, coarsely chopped and soaked (1/2 cup before soaking)

DIRECTIONS

Blend the squash with 1/8 cup water until smooth. Add the almonds and blend again until smooth.

Blend in the Rapadura®. Spoon the mixture into a large bowl, add the shredded coconut, vanilla, lemon juice, and Celtic sea salt, and mix well. Shape into thin round cookies and sprinkle pecans on top.

Place on a dehydrator tray lined with a Teflex sheet, and dehydrate for 8 hours.

Flip the cookies and remove the Teflex sheet. Dehydrate for another 12 to 18 hours or until crunchy. Store in a glass jar.

Sunflower Raisin Cookies

BY SHARON ELAM

ADVANCED PREP: 5 to 8 days for sprouts + 20 to 28 hours for dehydrating
IMMEDIATE PREP: 35 min
SERVES 6   **SPECIAL EQUIPMENT** Blender, Dehydrator

INGREDIENTS

  1 cup organic kamut, sprouted
  1 cup organic sunflower seeds, sprouted
  1 cup organic raisins
  1/2 cup walnuts, chopped
  1/2 to 1 cup organic rolled oats
  1 teaspoon vanilla extract

DIRECTIONS:

Blend kamut sprouts, sunflower seed sprouts, and raisins, and vanilla extract into a nice creamy batter. Add rolled oats and chopped walnuts and stir in by hand.

Drop by spoonfuls on teflex sheets, flatten, and place in dehydrator at approximately 95 to 100 degrees.

Remove from teflex and turn when top side feels right to you. These store very well in airtight containers.

Variations on these cookies can be with 1/2 cup carob powder added to the batter.

Valya's Almond Orange Cookies

By Valya Boutenko

Advanced prep: 20 hours for dehydrating   **Immediate prep:** 35 min

Yields 10 to 12 cookies

INGREDIENTS

- 4 cups raw almonds, soaked overnight, plus extra for garnish
- 2 cups raisins, plus extra for garnish
- 1/2 cup orange peel
- 2 medium oranges, whole
- 1/2 teaspoon sea salt
- 2 apples, cored

DIRECTIONS:

Blend the almonds, raisins, orange peel, oranges, sea salt, and apples in a food processor until they are finely chopped.

When all ingredients are finely processed, use a spatula to spread cookie mixture onto a dehydrator tray. Dehydrate at 115° F for 20 hours or until dry.

Decorate each cookie with sliced nuts or raisins.

Other Sweets

Carob Fudge Brownies

By Sharon Elam

Advanced prep: 2 to 3 days for sprouts   **Immediate prep:** 35 min
Serves 6   **Special Equipment** Food Processor, Dehydrator

INGREDIENTS

1 cup kamut, sprouted

3 cups sunflower seeds, sprouted

1/2 to 1 cup walnuts, chopped

1/2 to 1 cup pure maple syrup (or sweetener of choice)

2/3 to 1 cup raw tahini

dash of oil of choice

DIRECTIONS

Place sprouted kamut and sunflower in food processor until well processed (consistency of moist to wet dough). Add carob powder, tahini, sweetener, and oil.

Chop walnuts to degree of choice; add by hand. Pat or roll (between parchment paper) to about 1/2 inches thick. Place on teflex sheet and dehydrate. The center will remain slightly moist.

These brownies keep well in an airtight container.

Carob Nut Brownies

By Shannon Isley Schnibbe

Advanced prep: 24 hours for sprouts; 12 hours for dehydrating   **Immediate prep:** 35 min

Yields 30 brownies   **Special Equipment** Cuisinart, dehydrator

INGREDIENTS

2 cups of your favorite dates, pitted

1 cup pecans

1 cup walnuts

1/2 cup carob

2 cups buckwheat groats, soaked for 12 hours, then sprouted for 12 hours

DIRECTIONS

Process the sprouted groats in a Cuisinart. Transfer to a big bowl.

Process the nuts. Once they are ground, add the dates and continue to process.

Add 1 cup water and process again. Add the carob and process. Add the buckwheat, then process again.

Spread the mixture onto dehydrator sheets. Dehydrate for 12 hours at 105°F to desired consistency.

Contributor's note: These make a nice sweet treat that all your friends will enjoy.

Carob Walnut Fudge

By Matt Amsden

Advanced prep: None   **Immediate prep:** 25 min

Serves 12   **Special Equipment** Food processor

INGREDIENTS

3 1/2 cups raw, organic walnuts

1 3/4 cups pitted, organic dates

1/2 cup raw, organic carob powder

DIRECTIONS

In a food processor, grind the walnuts until they reach a nut butter consistency.

In a bowl thoroughly mix the walnuts, carob and dates by hand. Firmly press the mixture into a square glass dish (about 3/4-inch thick). Serve as is or chill in the refrigerator. Cut into whatever shapes you choose with a sharp knife. Enjoy!

Cashew Date Frosting

BY NOMI SHANNON

ADVANCED PREP: None   **IMMEDIATE PREP:** 20 min

SPECIAL EQUIPMENT Blender

INGREDIENTS

1 cup cashews (not soaked)

1/2 teaspoon vanilla

4 to 6 soft dates, pitted (not soaked)

DIRECTIONS

Blend cashews and vanilla with enough water for the blender to work. When the mixture is smooth, add dates, one at a time, until the desired thickness and sweetness is achieved.

Christmas Balls

BY SHAZZIE

ADVANCED PREP: 4 to 24 hours for soaking   **IMMEDIATE PREP:** 35 min

YIELDS 20 to 25 balls   **SPECIAL EQUIPMENT** Food processor

INGREDIENTS

1 cup raisins

2 cups dried apricots, rehydrated for 4 to 24 hours

1/2 coconut (reserve the water)

1 cup sunflower seeds

1/2 teaspoon grated fresh ginger

1 teaspoon dried mixed spice

DIRECTIONS

Mix all the ingredients together in a food processor until the dough forms a ball. If this doesn't happen, add a little of the coconut water until the ball forms. Form the mixture into balls about 1 1/2 inches in diameter.

Variation 1: Press an almond, half a pecan, or a mint leaf on top of each ball.

Variation 2: Roll some of the balls in dried coconut, raw carob powder or ground Brazil nuts. This makes for a beautifully decorative Christmas treat (any time of the year).

Divine Truffles

BY ROSE LEE CALABRO

ADVANCED PREP: 2 to 4 hours for soaking   IMMEDIATE PREP: 35 min
YIELDS 36 truffles   SPECIAL EQUIPMENT Food processor

INGREDIENTS

  2 cups dates, pitted
  2 cups pecans, soaked 2 to 4 hours
  1 tablespoon raw carob powder
  1 teaspoon vanilla

DIRECTIONS

Process the dates, pecans, vanilla, and 1 tablespoon raw carob powder in a food processor fitted with the "S" blade until the mixture becomes smooth and forms a ball. Roll into small balls and coat with coconut, carob, or ground nuts of your choice.

Variation 1: Add an extract of your choice to give the truffles a different flavor.

Variation 2: Add 1/4 cup pine nuts to make the truffles richer and smoother. Be sure to soak the pine nuts for about 1 hour before processing.

Peanut Butter Cups with Xoçai™ Nuggets

BY PEGGY KENNEY

ADVANCED PREP: None   **IMMEDIATE PREP:** 30–40 min
SPECIAL EQUIPMENT Double boiler pan with thermometer   **SERVES** 12

INGREDIENTS

12 medium sized strawberries
18 Xoçai™ Nuggets
1 1/2 cup Peanut Butter

DIRECTIONS

Using a double boiler pan with thermometer, warm water to 110 degrees. Remove from heat. Place Xoçai™ Nuggets into the top of the double boiler pan and cover with lid. Allow to sit for 20 minutes.

This fine Belgium chocolate will melt easily. Stir until smooth.

Swirl top halves of strawberries in the melted chocolate. Place on plate to harden.

When the chocolate is hard you can easily separate the chocolate cap from the strawberry. Place formed chocolate "bowls" in small candy tin, open side up.

Take a tablespoon of fresh ground peanut butter and drop into the formed chocolate cup. After the peanut butter has been added to the cups, spoon the remaining melted chocolate over the peanut butter to seal it with chocolate.

Serve chilled.

Contributor's Note: Store-bought peanut butter is generally roasted, not raw. You can make your own raw nut butters in the juicer using the blank plate, or substitute here a different raw nut butter that can be bought commercially e.g. almond, cashew.

Use the strawberries in another recipe.

Pistachio Halvah

By Michal Adi

Advanced prep: 2 hours for refrigerating   **Immediate prep:** 30 min

Serves 8   **Special Equipment** Food processor

INGREDIENTS

2 cups tahini

1/2 cup honey

1 teaspoon vanilla extract

1/2 cup shelled pistachios

DIRECTIONS

Process the tahini, honey, and vanilla extract in a food processor fitted with the "S" blade. Mix in pistachios and shape into a loaf.

Chill in the refrigerator for 2 hours. Slice into thick pieces and serve.

Variation: You can make marble Halvah by adding 1/3 cup carob powder to half of the vanilla mixture and processing. Add the pistachios as you gently mix both flavors just enough without blending them.

Raw Candy

By David Wolfe

Advanced prep: None   **Immediate prep:** 5 min

Makes 10 pieces   **Special Equipment** None

INGREDIENTS

10 dates

10 almonds

DIRECTIONS

Pit the dates; insert an almond into the pit hole of each date.

Contributor's note: This will help any cooked chocolate lover to switch to raw foods!

Sergei's Amazing Truffles

BY SERGEI BOUTENKO

ADVANCED PREP: None   **IMMEDIATE PREP:** 25 min

MAKES 8 to 12 truffles   **SPECIAL EQUIPMENT** Food processor

INGREDIENTS

1 cup raw unsoaked walnuts

1/2 cup of your favorite dates, pitted

4 tablespoons raw carob

1/4 cup young coconut water or plain water

your favorite fruit (for decoration)

DIRECTIONS

Blend the walnuts and dates in a food processor until the mixture is smooth. Add the carob and (coconut) water.

Shape the walnut and date mix into small balls and roll the balls in the carob. Decorate with your favorite fruit.

Sesame Honey Crunch Bars

BY ELAINA LOVE

ADVANCED PREP: 1 to 2 days for sprouts and soaking + 44 hours dehydrating

IMMEDIATE PREP: 1 hour + 20 min

YIELDS 56 bars   **SPECIAL EQUIPMENT** Dehydrator

INGREDIENTS

6 cups dry brown sesame seeds, soaked 4 hours

2 cups honey

3/4 cup Rapadura

1 cup pumpkin seeds, sprouted

1 teaspoon Celtic sea salt

3 teaspoons extract of your choice,

such as almond, cherry, ginger, maple, vanilla.

1 cup whole flax seeds, ground (1 1/2 cups meal)

2 cups dried fruit, such as, cherries, mangoes, pineapples, or raisins, chopped

DIRECTIONS

Mix everything together in a large bowl. Spread the batter onto a dehydrator tray lined with a Teflex sheet.

The bars should be about 1/2-inch thick. The batter should fill 2 1/2 14- x 14-inch Excalibur dehydrator trays. Dehydrate for 8 hours at 105°F.

Flip the bars and remove Teflex. Continue to dehydrate until crunchy, about 36 hours.

Let the bars cool to check if they are crunchy. Store in a glass jar in the refrigerator for up to 6 months, or on the counter top for 2 weeks.

Sweet (blue-green) Balls

BY VIKTORAS KULVINSKAS

ADVANCED PREP: None   **IMMEDIATE PREP:** 50 min
YIELDS Forty 1-inch balls   **SPECIAL EQUIPMENT** Food processor

INGREDIENTS

- 2 cups almonds
- 1/2 cup dried pineapple, chopped
- 8 dried Black Mission figs, stems removed
- 1/2 teaspoon sea salt
- 2 tablespoons Sucanat® (sugar cane juice powder)
- 1/2 teaspoon pumpkin pie spice mix
- pinch cayenne

- 12 caps AFA algae
- 4 caps acidophilus
- 4 caps enzymes
- 4 tablespoons lemon juice
- 1 tablespoon vanilla extract
- 1/4 cup sesame seeds
- 1/2 cup raisins (optional)

DIRECTIONS

Process the almonds in a food processor until they are reduced to a fine flour. Remove the blade, and loosen any crumbs from the walls. Replace the blade.

Add the dried pineapple and figs, and reduce the mixture to a flour. Add the sea salt, Sucanat®, pumpkin pie spice, and cayenne, and empty the powder from the AFA algae, acidophilus, and enzyme caps. Process until well mixed. Slowly pour in the lemon and vanilla, and process until the mixture forms a ball. You might have to add 1 tablespoon water. Roll the mixture into balls with your hands. Roll the balls in the sesame seeds until they are coated. Refrigerate or freeze.

Vanilla Crème

BY SHAZZIE

ADVANCED PREP: None   **IMMEDIATE PREP:** 20 min

YIELDS 2 cups   **SPECIAL EQUIPMENT** Coffee mill or blender

INGREDIENTS

2 oranges, juiced

1 cup macadamia nuts

2 inch piece of fresh vanilla pod

squeeze of lemon or lime

DIRECTIONS

Place all the ingredients in a coffee mill and blend until smooth. If you're making a larger amount, a powerful blender such as the Vita-Mix will work. Add more nuts if you want a thicker cream. If you want it thinner, add more orange juice.

Vanilla Crème will keep for a couple of days in the refrigerator if you don't eat it all right away.

Variation 1: To make a cream that goes well with savory dishes, use a bit more lemon or lime and a bit less orange. Omit or halve the amount of vanilla.

Variation 2: If you have a young coconut on hand, add the meat and/or water to the cream. It adds a smooth, tropical flavor.

Contributor's note: This goes well with desserts, and is a real treat on top of the ice cream recipes!

Xoçai™ Confection

BY PEGGY KENNEY

ADVANCED PREP: 2 hours for refrigeration   **IMMEDIATE PREP:** 15 min

SPECIAL EQUIPMENT Food Processor   **SERVES** 4

INGREDIENTS

- 1/4 cup cashew
- 2 tablespoons Activ™ Powder
- 1/3 cup agave nectar
- 1 1/2 cup almonds
- 1/4 cup coconut milk
- 1/4 tsp cinnamon
- 1/4 tsp spirulina powder

DIRECTIONS

In a food processor grind cashews and almonds until fine.

Add all ingredients together and mix well.

Press into glass dish and refrigerate until cool. Cut into small individual squares.

Xocolat Coconut Confection

BY PEGGY KENNEY

ADVANCED PREP: None   **IMMEDIATE PREP:** 20 min

SPECIAL EQUIPMENT Food processor, molds   **SERVES** 4

INGREDIENTS

- 2 cups shredded coconut
- 3/4 cup of agave nectar
- 1/2 cup dry Xoçai™ Activ™ Chocolate
- 3 cups ground walnuts

DIRECTIONS

Using a food processor blend the walnuts until smooth.

Mix all of the above ingredients together.

Place mixture in small single serving form molds and place in cool place until ready to eat.

Xocolat Cookies

BY PEGGY KENNEY

ADVANCED PREP: None   **IMMEDIATE PREP:** 20 min
SPECIAL EQUIPMENT Dehydrator Tray   **SERVES** 4

INGREDIENTS

- 2 cups of almonds
- 1 1/4 cups of agave nectar
- 1 cups Xoçai™ nuggets
- 1 teaspoon vanilla
- 1 cup raisins
- 2 tablespoons cinnamon

DIRECTIONS

Place almonds in food processor and grind until finely chopped.

Unwrap whole nuggets and cut into small pieces.

Add all ingredients together and mix well.

Spread on dehydrator tray and dehydrate for approximately 24 hours.

16

Pies & Cakes

Raw Apple Pie

By Jinjee and Storm Talifero
ADVANCED PREP: 4 to 6 hours for soaking   IMMEDIATE PREP: 30 min
SERVES 4   SPECIAL EQUIPMENT Cuisinart or blender

INGREDIENTS

For the crust:
1 cup almonds, soaked for 4 to 6 hours
pinch Celtic sea salt
1/8 cup olive oil

For the filling:
4 apples, cored but not peeled
3 dates, pitted
1 teaspoon flaxseed oil
pinch Celtic sea salt

DIRECTIONS

To make the crust, blend almonds in a Cuisinart or blender until they turn to powder. Add the sea salt and olive oil. Blend well, and spoon into pie dish.

To make the filling, blend apples, dates, flaxseed oil, and sea salt.

Carob Mint Pie

By Elysa Markowitz
ADVANCED PREP: 8 to 12 hours for soaking +2 hours for refrigerating
IMMEDIATE PREP: 45 min   YIELDS one 9-inch pie   SPECIAL EQUIPMENT Food processor or Green Power/ Star juicer

INGREDIENTS

For the crust:
2 cups almonds, soaked 8 to 12 hours and rinsed
4 to 6 dates, pitted

For the filling:
4 bananas, frozen (overnight or for at least 12 hours)

3 fresh bananas, plus extra slices for garnish
3 tablespoons carob powder
1 to 2 teaspoons mint extract
spearmint leaves, for garnish
carob chips, for garnish

DIRECTIONS

To prepare the crust, alternate putting the almonds and dates through a Green Power / Star juicer, with the solid blank in place. (You can also use a Champion juicer with the solid blank plate or a food processor.) Press the base into a 9-inch pie plate and freeze for 1 to 2 hours.

To make the filling, mash the fresh banana with the carob powder and mint extract. Alternate putting the fresh and frozen bananas through the machine (or into a food processor) and into a bowl; pour this mixture into the frozen piecrust. Place the pie in the freezer for 2 to 4 hours.

When ready to serve, decorate with sliced fresh bananas, carob chips and mint leaves. Let soften in the refrigerator for 30 minutes and serve.

Hint: Use a fork to stir the carob powder with the fresh banana. The more carob powder you use, the darker the pie will be. Use whatever amount you prefer to get the desired color.

Contributor's note: This is a must for parties, especially if you like mint. It looks like a chocolate cream pie, but the carob will not interfere with calcium absorption, and the carob flavor is heavenly with the banana.

Coconut Cream Pie

BY JINJEE AND STORM TALIFERO

ADVANCED PREP: 4 to 6 hours for soaking   **IMMEDIATE PREP:** 40 min

SERVES 4   **SPECIAL EQUIPMENT** Cuisinart or blender

INGREDIENTS

For the crust:
1 cup almonds, soaked 4 to 6 hours
pinch Celtic sea salt
1/8 cup olive oil

For the filling:
4 bananas

meat of 2 young coconuts
5 dates, pitted
1/8 cup flaxseed oil
cold-packed honey, to taste
cinnamon, to taste
nutmeg, to taste
1 avocado (optional)

DIRECTIONS

To make the crust, blend nuts in a Cuisinart or blender until they turn to powder. Add the sea salt and olive oil. Blend well, and spoon into pie dish.

To make the filling, blend bananas, coconut meat, dates, flaxseed oil, honey, cinnamon, nutmeg, and avocado (if using).

Coconut Lime Tarts

BY MATT SAMUELSON

ADVANCED PREP: (Almond Pulp from Milk 12 hours)   **IMMEDIATE PREP:** 1 hour (Almond Pulp from Milk 15 min)

MAKES 24 crusts or cookies   **SPECIAL EQUIPMENT** Dehydrator, blender

INGREDIENTS

For the crust:

2 cups almond pulp (leftover from making Almond Milk, page 182)

1 1/2 cups shredded coconut, ground in blender or spice grinder to a fine powder

3 tablespoons honey or maple syrup

6 teaspoons flaxseed meal

1/4 to 1/2 teaspoon Celtic salt

1 teaspoon vanilla (optional)

1/2 cup coconut butter (warmed to a liquid)

For the filling:

1 cup coconut meat (from approximately 2 young coconuts)

juice of 3 to 4 limes

5 to 7 large dates

DIRECTIONS

Combine all the crust ingredients with 1/4 cup water in a large mixing bowl, adding the liquid coconut butter last. Mix the dough well with your hands.

Divide the dough into 24 equal portions. Using a small tart pan lined with cheesecloth, press one section of dough at a time into the pan and hollow out the middle. Gently remove from tart pan by lifting the cheesecloth. Place the crusts on mesh dehydrator trays and dehydrate at 105°F for 18 to 24 hours.

Blend the filling ingredients until smooth.

Fill the tart shells to desired fullness and chill before serving. For decoration, top with thin slices of a lime.

Variation: For greener tarts, substitute 1/2 cup avocado for 1/2 cup coconut meat.

Creamed Strawberry Pie

BY KARIE CLINGO

ADVANCED PREP: 30 min for soaking **IMMEDIATE PREP:** 40 min

SERVES 8 **SPECIAL EQUIPMENT** Blender

INGREDIENTS

For the crust:

2 cups pecans

4 to 6 Medjool dates, pitted

dash cinnamon (optional)

For the filling:

2 to 3 ripe bananas

For the topping:

3/4 cup strawberries (or other berries in season)

1 cup macadamia nuts or cashews, or 4 to 6 soaked dates

DIRECTIONS

To make the crust, combine the pecans and dates in a blender. Combine well and press into a pie dish. Sprinkle with cinnamon if desired.

Divide into 2 equal portions and shape the first layer of the pie to fit your serving dish. Add sliced bananas. Shape the second layer of the pie and place it on top.

To make the topping, blend strawberries, macadamias, dates, and just enough water to move the blender blade, 3/4 to 1 cup. Pour the mixture over the pie and decorate with fruit and berries. If you don't like nuts, use bananas instead.

Decadent Vanilla Carob Halva Pie

BY MICHAL ADI

ADVANCED PREP: 8 to 12 hours for soaking + 2 hours for refrigeration
IMMEDIATE PREP: 1 hour   **SERVES** 8   **SPECIAL EQUIPMENT** Blender, food processor

INGREDIENTS

For the crust:
3 cups almonds, soaked overnight
pinch nutmeg
pinch cloves
pinch cinnamon
1/4 teaspoon Celtic sea salt
1 to 2 tablespoons honey

For the coconut filling:
4 to 5 brown (mature) coconuts, juiced
2 oranges or 1 cup papaya meat
2 teaspoons agar-agar flakes

For the Halva topping:
2 cups tahini
1/2 cup honey
1 teaspoon vanilla extract
1/3 cup carob powder (optional)

DIRECTIONS

To make the crust, process the almonds, nutmeg, cloves, cinnamon, and sea salt using the "S" blade, gradually adding honey till a ball of dough forms. Press the mixture into a pie plate.

To make the filling, blend coconut juice with oranges or papaya meat. Add agar-agar and blend for another 45 seconds. Pour the mixture into crust and refrigerate until coconut cream sets.

To make the topping, process the tahini, honey, and vanilla in a food processor using the "S" blade. You can make marble Halva by adding carob powder to half the vanilla mixture and processing. Refrigerate Halva for 2 hours before slicing.

Top coconut cream with a 1/2-inch layer of Halva creating a pattern of your choice to mix vanilla and carob Halva flavors. For extra decadence place another layer of Coconut Cream on top of the Halva and refrigerate until it sets. Top with a final layer of Halva.

De Lime Pie

BY EDDIE D. ROBINSON

ADVANCED PREP: 4 hours for soaking + 1 hour for refrigeration   IMMEDIATE
PREP: 1 hour   MAKES 1 Pie   SPECIAL EQUIPMENT Food processor, Vita-Mix

INGREDIENTS

For the crust:

1/2 cup almonds, soaked 4 hours

1/2 cup pecans, soaked 4 hours

1/2 cup sunflower seeds, soaked
    4 hours

1/2 cup pumpkin seeds, soaked
    4 hours

6 dates, pits removed

dash of cinnamon

For the filling:

4 large limes

2 cups coconut meat (from 2 to
    3 coconuts)

1 1/2 cups dates, pits removed

1/4 cup fresh squeezed orange juice

1/4 cup fresh squeezed lemon juice

1 tablespoon lime zest

1 tablespoon agar-agar

DIRECTIONS

Process all the crust ingredients together in a food processor. Spread the mixture
into an 8-inch glass pie pan. Blend all the filling ingredients to a creamy consistency. Pour the filling into the crust, transfer to the refrigerator, and let the pie
chill for 1 hour before serving.

Fresh Strawberry Pie

BY ELAINA LOVE

ADVANCED PREP: 8 to 12 hours for soaking + 1 hour for refrigeration
IMMEDIATE PREP: 50 min   **SERVES** 8   **SPECIAL EQUIPMENT** Food processor, blender

INGREDIENTS

For the crust:
1 1/2 cups almonds, walnuts or pecans soaked 8 to 12 hours
1/2 teaspoon Celtic sea salt
pinch cayenne
3/4 cup soft dates, pitted

For the filling:
2/3 cup dates, firmly packed and pitted
1 1/3 cups berries (any kind of berry works great)
4 to 6 cups berries (slice if using strawberries)
2 tablespoons psyllium husk powder

DIRECTIONS

To make the crust, purée the nuts in a food processor to a flour-like consistency. Add the Celtic sea salt, cayenne pepper, and dates and purée until the mixture sticks together or forms a ball.

Press into a pie plate.

To make the filling, blend the dates and berries in a blender or food processor until well mixed. Add 4 cups of berries and psyllium, and mix together.

Fill the pie shell with berry mixture and refrigerate before serving.

Mango Tart with Pecan Fig Crust and Rambutan Coulis

BY CHAD SARNO

ADVANCED PREP: 2 to 3 hours for soaking + 2 hours for refrigeration
IMMEDIATE PREP: 1hr + 10 min **SERVES** 8 **SPECIAL EQUIPMENT** Food processor, high-speed blender

INGREDIENTS

For the crust:

2 cups pecans, unsoaked and finely minced

1 1/2 cups dried figs, stems removed, soaked for 1 hour

1 tablespoon fresh lemon zest

1/2 tablespoon cinnamon

1/4 teaspoon Celtic sea salt

For the filling:

2 cups dried mango, soaked for 1 to 3 hours in 2 cups orange juice until soft (reserve juice)

3 tablespoons dates, pitted

1/4 cup macadamia nuts, unsoaked

1 tablespoon coconut butter

1 tablespoon lemon juice

1 fresh mango, peeled and thinly sliced

For the Coulis: (optional)

1 cup rambutan, seeded and peeled (strawberries can be substituted)

1/2 tablespoon powdered dried ginger

1 tablespoon sweetener—Sucanat®, date sugar or maple sugar

optional chopped pecans

DIRECTIONS

In a food processor, combine pecans, figs, lemon zest, cinnamon, and sea salt and process until the mixture is fully blended and forms a ball. Transfer the mixture into a 9-inch tart pan and set aside.

In high-speed blender, blend the rehydrated mango, dates, macadamia nuts, coconut butter and lemon juice until creamy. Fold the mixture with a rubber spatula for optimum consistency.

Pour the mixture into crust and evenly spread the thinly sliced fresh mango. Chill for at least 2 hours so the tart forms and sets.

In a high-speed blender, blend the rambutan, ginger, 1/2 cup orange juice reserved from the rehydrated mangos and sweetener. Blend until smooth.

With a fine mesh strainer, strain rambutan sauce. Stir with spoon to drain the liquid and discard pulp.

To serve, cut tart into 8 slices, pour a small puddle of rambutan sauce to coat bottom of plate, and place the tart slice in middle. Drizzle a bit more rambutan sauce over the top. Serve chilled with a tropical fruit compote on the side.

Mud Pie

By Rose Lee Calabro

Advanced prep: 12 to 48 hours for soaking **Immediate prep:** 50 min
Serves 6 to 8 **Special Equipment** Juicer or food processor

INGREDIENTS

For the crust:
1 cup almonds, blanched and soaked 12 to 48 hours

1 cup sunflower seeds, soaked 6 to 8 hours

1 cup honey dates

1/2 cup raisins

1/2 cup raw carob powder

1 teaspoon vanilla

For the filling:
1 1/2 cups almonds, blanched and soaked 12 to 48 hours

4 medium bananas

1 teaspoon vanilla

For garnish:
strawberries, sliced

fresh mint leaves

DIRECTIONS

For the crust, process almonds, sunflower seeds, dates, and raisins through a Champion juicer using the blank plate or in a food processor using the "S" blade.

Add carob powder and vanilla; mix well and press into a 9-inch pie plate or tart shell pan.

To make the filling, blend almonds, bananas, and vanilla with 1/2 cup water in the blender. Pour the mixture into the piecrust and place in freezer until firm. Decorate with sliced strawberries and fresh mint leaves.

Papaya Pie

BY ROBERT YAROSH AND LISA SOTO

ADVANCED PREP: 2 hours for soaking + 1 hour for refrigeration   IMMEDIATE
PREP: 40 min   SERVES 8 to 10   SPECIAL EQUIPMENT Food processor

INGREDIENTS

For the crust:
1/2 cup hazelnuts
1/2 cup Brazil nuts
1/4 teaspoon vanilla
dash Celtic sea salt
1/2 teaspoon olive oil

For the filling:
1 cup dried papaya spears, soaked
1 cup fresh papaya
1 to 2 tablespoons honey
1 teaspoon agar-agar
dash Celtic sea salt

DIRECTIONS

To make the crust, process hazelnuts, Brazil nuts, vanilla, sea salt and olive oil
in a food processor until the mixture forms a ball. Press crust into a lightly
oiled pie plate.

To make the filling, process papaya (fresh and dried), honey, agar-agar, and a
dash of sea salt in a food processor. Process the purée using the "S" blade.

Pour filling into crust and chill before serving.

Cakes

Carrot Cake

By Elizabeth Baker

Advanced prep: 15 min for juicing   **Immediate prep:** 20 min

Serves 12 to 16   **Special Equipment** None

INGREDIENTS

2 cups oat flour (made by processing rolled oats in a blender)

2 cups pulp from 6 to 8 large juiced carrots

1/4 teaspoon salt

2 cups dates, finely chopped or ground

1 cup nuts, chopped

2 teaspoons vanilla

3 tablespoons honey

DIRECTIONS

Mix all the ingredients together well. Knead and form into 2 rolls for slicing or layers for a layer cake.

Carrot Pineapple Shortcake with Mesquite Flour and Sweet Cashew Cream Cheese

BY CHAD SARNO

ADVANCED PREP: 12 to 14 hours for soaking + 14 hours for fermenting + 2 days for rejuvelac   **IMMEDIATE PREP:** 1 hour 20 min

SERVES 8   **SPECIAL EQUIPMENT** Juicer, hand blender

INGREDIENTS

For the shortcake:
2 cups fresh shredded carrot
1 1/2 cups minced dried pineapple
1 1/2 cups pecans, unsoaked and ground into flour
1/4 cup raisins
3/4 cup dates, pitted and minced
1 1/2 tablespoons cinnamon
1 1/2 tablespoons fresh orange zest
2 tablespoons orange juice
2 tablespoons mesquite powder
1 teaspoon nutmeg
1/4 teaspoon Celtic sea salt

For the Cashew Cream Cheese:
2 cups cashews, soaked 12 to 14 hours
1/3 cup rejuvelac
1 tablespoon coconut butter
1/2 teaspoon vanilla bean, diced
2 tablespoons date paste
1/4 teaspoon Celtic sea salt

For the topping:
1/4 cup shredded coconut
fresh pineapple slices, for garnish
finely shredded carrot, for garnish

DIRECTIONS

Place the carrots, pineapple, pecan flour, raisins, dates, cinnamon, orange zest, orange juice, mesquite powder, nutmeg, and sea salt into bowl and hand mix. Mix gently but thoroughly, to make sure dates are evenly distributed.

Line the bottom of a 6-inch springform pan with plastic wrap. Press cake firmly into the pan.

To make the Cashew Cream Cheese, use a juicer to homogenize the cashews. Hand mix the rejuvelac, and allow to sit in a glass bowl or wrapped in cheese-cloth for 12 to 14 hours.

When the Cashew Cream Cheese is finished culturing, hand mix in the coconut butter, vanilla bean, date paste and sea salt.

Frost the cake with the Sweet Cashew Cream Cheese and sprinkle with shredded coconut.

To serve, place a small slice on a plate and garnish with fresh pineapple and finely shredded carrot.

Chill before serving.

Variation: Form extra cake into bars and dehydrate for 10 to12 hours at 110ºF for a great snack on the trail.

Celebrate the Good Times Cake

BY SHAZZIE
ADVANCED PREP: 12 to 24 hours for soaking   **IMMEDIATE PREP:** 1 hour
SERVES 8   **SPECIAL EQUIPMENT** Food processor

INGREDIENTS

For the base:
1 cup hazelnuts, soaked 12 to
    24 hours
pinch of cinnamon or mixed spice
1 cup raisins, soaked 12 to 24 hours
meat of 1/2 coconut, ground (save
    water for filling)

For the filling:
1/2 cup raw tahini
1 dessertspoon (about 2 teaspoons)
    raw carob power

1/2 cup raisins or dates

For the icing:
1 banana
1/2 papaya
2 tablespoons raw tahini

For garnish:
starfruit, thinly sliced
strawberries, thinly sliced
edible flowers

DIRECTIONS

To make the base, process the hazelnuts, cinnamon, and raisins. Add the ground coconut to the mixture. If the mixture isn't wet enough, add some coconut water. If too wet, add more nuts.

Mold into a circular base, about 1-inch thick.

To make the filling, mix the tahini and carob powder in a bowl with a fork; it will become very stiff.

Add coconut water to make a thick and creamy mixture. If you run out of coconut water, add drinking water. Process the raisins and/or dates until smooth.

Add the carob-tahini mixture and process all together.

Spread on top of the cake base. If it's too stiff to spread, add more water or spread with a wet knife.

To make the frosting, process the banana, papaya, and tahini. Spread on top of the cake and let some dribble down the sides. If the icing is too runny add more tahini. Garnish with thinly sliced starfruit, strawberries and flowers.

Five-Minute Raw-Berry Shortcake

BY SERGEI AND VALYA BOUTENKO

ADVANCED PREP: None   **IMMEDIATE PREP:** 5 min

SERVES 8   **SPECIAL EQUIPMENT** Blender

INGREDIENTS

For the crust:
2 cups almonds
1/2 cup honey

For the topping:
1 cup walnuts

1/4 cup honey
2 tablespoons fresh coconut butter
   (optional)

For garnish:
Fresh strawberries, sliced

DIRECTIONS

To make the crust, blend the almonds and honey until finely chopped. Spoon into a serving dish and pack down well.

To make the topping, blend the walnuts with honey and fresh coconut butter (if using) until smooth. Decorate with fresh, sliced strawberries.

Contributor's note: Of all the cakes we make, this is one of the fastest and easiest to put together—it literally takes less than five minutes to make.

Holiday Fruitcake

By Rita Romano

Advanced prep: 24 hours for soaking   **Immediate prep:** 30 min

Serves 8   **Special Equipment** Food processor

INGREDIENTS

- 1 cup cranberries, fresh or frozen
- 1 cup fresh apples, chopped
- 1 cup fresh navel oranges, chopped
- 2 tablespoons orange juice concentrate (frozen)
- 2 tablespoons fresh lemon juice
- 2 tablespoons psyllium husk powder
- 1 teaspoon pumpkin pie spice (or to taste)
- 1 cup walnuts, soaked for 24 hours
- 1/2 cup dried apricots, minced
- 1/2 cup dried figs, minced
- 1 cup currants
- 1 cup raisins

DIRECTIONS

In a large food processor, use the "S" blade to process cranberries, apples, oranges, orange juice concentrate, lemon juice, psyllium husk powder, pumpkin pie spice, and walnuts. Prepare in several small batches if necessary.

Pulse ingredients to a fine pebble consistency and mix with dried apricots, figs, currants, and raisins. Press into bundt pan and let sit several hours before removing from mold.

Kumquat and Nutmeg Cheesecake

BY SHAZZIE

ADVANCED PREP: 2 hours for soaking + 1 hour for freezing

IMMEDIATE PREP: 40 min   **SERVES** 8   **SPECIAL EQUIPMENT** Food processor

INGREDIENTS

For the crust:

3 cups almonds

2 tablespoons raw carob powder

1 cup pecans

2 cups dates, pitted and soaked 2 hours

1 vanilla pod

1 teaspoon nutmeg

1 orange, juiced

For the cheese:

5 bananas, peeled, thinly chopped and frozen overnight

4 kumquats, halved, middles discarded

1 large mango, peeled

DIRECTIONS

Cover the base of a springform pan in plastic wrap, fitting it to the pan. Cover the sides in aluminum foil.

Combine the almonds, pecans (reserve 8 for decoration), dates, 1 inch of the vanilla pod, a dash of nutmeg, carob powder, and orange juice in a food processor. Process gently to start, and continue until you get a dough-like consistency. If it's not doughy enough, add small quantities of water until you achieve the desired result. Place in the cake pan and flatten.

Clean your food processor and add the banana and kumquat skins.

Slit the vanilla pod and scrape the seeds into the processor. Carve the peeled mango away from its seed and add to the food processor along with a dash of nutmeg. Add a couple of chopped dates if you like, too. Process for several minutes, until the entire mixture turns white and fluffy.

Add the mixture to the cake tin on top of the nut base. Smooth it all down so there's no trapped air, and it's level on top. Decorate with reserved pecans and sprinkle on the remaining nutmeg.

Freeze for at least 1 hour before serving. Turn out the cake by pushing the loose base out and up. Remove the foil and place on a serving plate.

Party Carrot Cake

By Julie Rodwell

Advanced prep: 1 hour for refrigeration **Immediate prep:** 40 min

Serves 8 to 10 **Special Equipment** Juicer, coffee grinder, food processor

INGREDIENTS

For the cake:

1 generous cup walnut halves

1 generous cup dried unsweetened coconut

2/3 cups dates, pitted and ground

1/2 cup raisins, ground

1/4 cup flaxseed, ground fine in coffee grinder

5 cups carrot pulp (from about 5 pounds juiced carrots)

1/2 to 1 teaspoon cinnamon

1/2 teaspoon nutmeg

1/2 to 1 cup carrot juice

1 tablespoon psyllium husk powder (optional)

For the filling and frosting

1 cup raw cashews, soaked for up to 1 hour

1 lemon, juiced

4 to 6 tablespoons raw honey

1 teaspoon almond extract

small piece dried mango or papaya

carrot leaves

DIRECTIONS

Set aside 7 to 8 of the best-shaped walnut halves and 1 tablespoon coconut for garnish. Grind the remaining walnuts in a food processor and place in a large bowl. Add the dates, raisins, flaxseed, carrot pulp, nutmeg, and cinnamon.

Mix by hand, kneading for smoothness. Add just enough carrot juice to bind the mixture. If using psyllium, it will thicken and bind the mixture in about 5 minutes.

Divide into two equal portions and shape the first layer of the cake to fit your serving platter.

To make the frosting, process the cashews, lemon juice, honey, and almond extract in a food processor until very smooth.

Coat the first layer of cake with about a third of the frosting. Shape a second layer and place on top of the first. Coat the top and sides of the cake with remaining frosting. Press walnuts into the sides where the 2 layers meet, and sprinkle coconut on top. Decorate with pieces of mango or papaya cut in carrot shapes, and add a bit of carrot leaf to each.

Chill in the refrigerator before serving.

Wedding Cake

By Sergei and Valya Boutenko

Advanced prep: 1 hour for refrigeration   **Immediate prep:** 30 min

Serves 10 to 14   **Special Equipment** Food processor

INGREDIENTS

For the crust:
2 cups raw tahini
4 cups dry, shredded coconut
1/2 cup honey
1/2 teaspoon salt

For the frosting:
1 cup cashews
1 teaspoon mint extract
1/4 cup fresh coconut butter
2 tablespoons honey
1/2 teaspoon sea salt

For garnish:
sliced fruit of your choice

DIRECTIONS

To make the crust, using clean, bare hands, mix together the tahini, shredded coconut, honey, and sea salt until desired texture is achieved. For layers, add any sliced fruit of your choice.

Process the cashews, mint extract, coconut butter, honey, sea salt, and 1/2 cup water. (Try to use as little water as possible. The less water you use, the thicker the frosting will be).

Frost the cake and chill it in the refrigerator before serving. You may buy the wedding cake stand at any craft store.

Contributor's note: This cake does not need to be frozen because the crust is very firm. The more coconut you add, the firmer it will be.

Yummy Cake

By Abeba Wright

Advanced prep: 8 to 10 hours for soaking   **Immediate prep:** 45 min
1 cake **serves** 10 to 15   **Special Equipment** Food processor

INGREDIENTS

For the cake:
1 cup *each* almonds, walnuts, and hazelnuts (or filberts), soaked overnight
1/2 cup raw carob
1 1/2 cups Medjool dates, soaked 30 minutes
1 cup almonds, unsoaked
1/2 teaspoon vanilla or butterscotch extract

For the filling:
banana slices, or other fruit of your choice

For the frosting:
3/4 cup raw cashews, soaked 30 minutes
1/4 cup pine nuts, soaked 10 minutes
Medjool dates, pitted, or honey, as sweetener, to taste
1/2 teaspoon vanilla extract

DIRECTIONS

Chop soaked nuts in food processor until fine. Blend in carob and vanilla, and mix again. Add dates until nuts form a loose ball; check for sweetness and add more dates if necessary. Transfer mixture to a large bowl.

Chop unsoaked almonds until fine in processor and add to the bowl.

If you are making 2 layers, divide mixture into 2 equal parts and shape the first layer on the platter with half the mixture.

Add sliced bananas or other fruit of choice to the platter. Add the other half of the nut and fruit mixture to the platter (if making 2 layers).

To make the frosting, combine the cashews, pine nuts, Medjool dates or honey, vanilla extract, and 1/2 cup of water in the blender.

Frost the cake with a large knife or using a frosting nozzle.

Variation: Omit the carob from the cake, and add 1 tablespoon lemon juice to the frosting.

17

Ice Cream & Puddings

Ice Cream

Banana Ice Cream with Chocolate or Carob Syrup

BY ELAINA LOVE

ADVANCED PREP: 36 hours for freezing bananas   **IMMEDIATE PREP:** 30 min

SERVES 2   **SPECIAL EQUIPMENT** Champion juicer

INGREDIENTS

4 very ripe bananas, peeled and frozen

For the Carob Syrup:
2 heaping tablespoons organic unsweetened cocoa powder or carob powder

1/4 cup flaxseed oil

3/4 cup purified water

1 teaspoon vanilla extract

1 teaspoon maple extract (optional; use with dates only)

1/4 teaspoon cinnamon

1/4 teaspoon Celtic sea salt

1/2 cup or 1/4 pound pitted dates, packed (use fresh dates, such as Medjools, honey or barhi) or 1/2 cup maple syrup

For the Topping:
chopped nuts of your choice

DIRECTIONS

Process the frozen bananas through a Champion juicer with the blank plate in place. The bananas will come out looking and tasting like soft-serve ice cream.

You may also cut the frozen bananas into small pieces and blend them with a tiny bit of water until creamy. You can also shred them in a food processor and then purée the shreds with the "S" blade until creamy.

Blend all the syrup ingredients together until smooth. Pour over the Banana Ice Cream and top with chopped nuts. Store the sauce in a glass jar in the refrigerator for up to 4 weeks.

Cashew Gelato

BY JULIANO

ADVANCED PREP: 1 hour for freezing   **IMMEDIATE PREP:** 15 min

SERVES 2   **SPECIAL EQUIPMENT** None

INGREDIENTS

2 cups raw cashew butter

1 1/2 cups maple syrup

2/3 cup almonds, coarsely chopped

DIRECTIONS

Mix the cashew butter and maple syrup together in a bowl. Fold in the chopped almonds and mix well. Spoon the mixture into individual serving bowls and freeze. Serve frozen.

Variation: Add 1/2 cup raw carob powder for a chocolaty variation!

From *Raw: The UnCook Book* (New York: ReganBooks, 1999).

Choconilla Ice Cream

BY DAVE KLEIN

ADVANCED PREP: 36 hours for freezing bananas + 10 to 60 min for soaking

IMMEDIATE PREP: 10 min   **SERVES** 4 to 6   **SPECIAL EQUIPMENT** Champion juicer

INGREDIENTS

6 or more ripe bananas, frozen

1 cup or more dried Black Mission figs. (If they are not soft and pliable, soak them in purified water for 10 to 60 minutes.)

DIRECTIONS

Chill the rotor blade and blank plate of a Champion juicer in freezer, then install them. Run bananas, then figs, through juicer. Serve in a bowl and enjoy!

Coconut Banana Split

BY SHAZZIE

ADVANCED PREP: 36 hours for frozen bananas   **IMMEDIATE PREP:** 20 min

SERVES 4   **SPECIAL EQUIPMENT** Food processor, coffee grinder

INGREDIENTS

4 fresh bananas, peeled

1/2 coconut, and some of its water

4 Medjool dates, pitted

4 ripe figs, or the equivalent in weight of your favorite berries

4 frozen bananas, peeled and chopped

1/2 teaspoon cinnamon powder

DIRECTIONS

Split the fresh bananas lengthwise and place them (split side up) in individual serving dishes.

Peel the brown layer off the coconut, and either juice the coconut (if you have a heavy duty juicer) or process it in a food processor. Set to one side.

Blend the dates and figs or berries together in a coffee grinder to make the fruit sauce. If it's not "saucy" enough, add some coconut water and blend again.

Make the ice cream from the frozen bananas, as in the Whip the Mister recipe (see page 327). Once you have ice cream, add the cinnamon and beat the coconut into it. If you need to, put the ice cream in the freezer for 5 minutes to firm it up.

Top each banana split with three scoops of ice cream. Drizzle the fruit sauce over the top, and enjoy!

Contributor's note: This is a really attractive dessert.

Mangoes Marinated in Golden Ginger Syrup with Lychee Ice Cream

BY SHAZZIE

ADVANCED PREP: 8–10 hours for soaking   **IMMEDIATE PREP:** 15 min

SERVES 4   **SPECIAL EQUIPMENT** Hand blender, food processor

INGREDIENTS

- 2 mangoes, pitted, peeled and thinly sliced
- 6 Medjool dates, pitted and soaked for 6 hours in water with 1 dessertspoon (about 2 teaspoons) minced ginger (reserve soak water)
- 4 bananas, peeled, chopped and frozen at least overnight
- 10 lychees, peeled and pitted
- mint leaves (for garnish)
- flowers (for garnish)

DIRECTIONS

Lay the mangoes in a flat bottomed dish.

With a hand blender, blend the dates with the ginger, slowly adding soak water to make a syrup consistency. Pour over the mangoes and set aside to marinate for at least an hour.

In a food processor, process the frozen bananas with a few lychees until the ice cream turns white and fluffy. This may take a few minutes, so stop your processor for a while if it needs to rest.

Put the mango and syrup into individual bowls, and add scoops of the ice cream to serve. Decorate with mint leaves and fresh flowers for the finishing touch.

Contributor's note: This tasty dessert is heavenly!

Pistachio Raspberry Ice Cream Pie

BY RHIO

ADVANCED PREP: 8 to 12 hours for soaking + 36 hours for freezing bananas + 2 hours for freezing pie   **IMMEDIATE PREP:** 30 min

SERVES 6   **SPECIAL EQUIPMENT** Food processor, coffee grinder

INGREDIENTS

For the crust:
1/2 cup pistachios
1/2 cup almonds
1/2 cup sunflower seeds
4 dates, soaked for 1 hour

For the filling:
2 bananas
2 cups frozen raspberries

2 tablespoons raw honey (or 1/3 to 1/2 cup soaked raisins)

For the frosting:
1/2 cup macadamia nuts, soaked overnight (or at least 2 hours)
3 frozen bananas
1/2 teaspoon vanilla powder (ground vanilla bean)

DIRECTIONS

For the crust, in a food processor fitted with the "S" blade, grind the pistachios, almonds, sunflower seeds and dates to a crumb consistency. Spread three-quarters of this mixture evenly on the bottom of a 9-inch glass pie pan.

Combine the 2 bananas and frozen raspberries with the honey or soaked raisins in the food processor. Using the "S" blade, blend to a creamy consistency. Spread this filling on top of the crust.

Sprinkle the remainder of the nut/seed crumbs on top of the raspberry mixture. Store the pie in the freezer while you make the frosting.

To make the frosting, put the 3 frozen bananas, macadamias, and vanilla powder into a food processor. Using the "S" blade, blend to a creamy consistency.

Spread the frosting on top of the pie and return the pie to the freezer for a couple of hours. When ready to serve, let the pie sit at room temperature for 5 to 10 minutes before slicing. It will keep for a week or more in the freezer.

Rainbow Sherbet

BY ELYSA MARKOWITZ

ADVANCED PREP: 8 to 12 hours for freezing **IMMEDIATE PREP:** 15 min

SERVES 4 to 6 **SPECIAL EQUIPMENT** Food processor, Vita-Mix, Champion or Green Power / Star juicer with a solid blank

INGREDIENTS

9 bananas

2 cups blueberries

1 1/2 to 2 cups strawberries, hulls removed

1 pineapple, peeled and sliced

4 to 6 fresh mint leaves, plus more for garnish

DIRECTIONS

Freeze 6 of the bananas, all of the blueberries, strawberries, and pineapple, for at least 8 to 12 hours.

Blend 2 of the frozen bananas, the blueberries, mint leaves, and 1 of the fresh bananas in a food processor fitted with an "S" blade. Divide among 4 to 6 parfait glasses, and place the glasses in the freezer.

To make the second layer, blend 2 more of the frozen bananas with the frozen strawberries, and 1 of the fresh bananas in the food processor. Spoon on top of the first layer, and return the glasses to the freezer.

To make the third layer, blend the 2 remaining frozen bananas, the frozen pineapple, and the remaining fresh banana in the food processor. Spoon on top of the second layer, garnish with additional fresh mint leaves, and serve immediately.

Smooth Coconut Ice Cream

BY SHAZZIE

ADVANCED PREP: 36 hours for freezing bananas   **IMMEDIATE PREP:** 15 min

SERVES 4   **SPECIAL EQUIPMENT** Blender; Champion juicer or food processor

INGREDIENTS

- meat of 2 to 4 young coconuts, depending on yield
- 1 vanilla bean
- 4 frozen bananas (whole if using a Champion juicer, finely chopped if using a food processor)

DIRECTIONS

Put the coconut meat in a blender. Scrape the seeds out of the vanilla bean, and add to the blender. Blend until smooth.

Combine the bananas and meat and process through a Champion juicer using the blank plate. The easiest way to do this is to add one banana and a little coconut meat at a time. You may need to mix the ice cream a little afterward to distribute the coconut evenly.

If you don't have a Champion, process the finely chopped frozen banana in a food processor. When the "ice cream" is white and fluffy, add the meat, and process for a little while longer. If you're not eating it immediately (a tough task!), put it into individual bowls and return to the freezer.

Variation 1: Add chopped fruit or nuts.

Variation 2: Make a fruit or carob sauce, and pour it over the top.

Contributor's note: When you drink a lot of young coconut water, you get a lot of meat left over. Here's an easy way to make use of it.

Tutti Frutti Ice Cream

BY KAREN KNOWLER

ADVANCED PREP: 36 hours for freezing bananas   **IMMEDIATE PREP:** 10 min

SERVES 1   **SPECIAL EQUIPMENT** Blender

INGREDIENTS

2 frozen bananas

chopped cherries

apple or pineapple, finely chopped

other fruit of your choice

DIRECTIONS

Blend 2 frozen bananas to make the ice cream. Mix in the chopped cherries, raisins, apple or pineapple, or any other fruit you like!

Whip the Mister

BY SHAZZIE

ADVANCED PREP: 36 hours for freezing bananas   **IMMEDIATE PREP:** 5 min

SPECIAL EQUIPMENT Champion juicer or food processor

INGREDIENTS

frozen bananas, peeled

DIRECTIONS

If you have a Champion juicer, put whole, peeled, frozen bananas through it using the blank plates.

Alternatively, if you have a food processor, thinly slice a couple of bananas and freeze them at least overnight. Thaw the bananas for five minutes and process them in the food processor. You may have to do this three or four times, stirring the bananas each time, but the mixture will soon turn white and fluffy like ice cream.

Hint: Cinnamon, carob powder, chopped nuts and soft fruit all go well with this ice cream.

Contributor's note: This recipe is from Shazzie's Detox Delights. It's a dream come true!

Puddings

Aloe Super Mousse

BY SHAZZIE

ADVANCED PREP: None   **IMMEDIATE PREP:** 10 min

SERVES 4   **SPECIAL EQUIPMENT** Blender

INGREDIENTS

1 avocado, peeled and pitted

2 bananas, peeled

1 mango, peeled and pitted

1 to 4 inches fresh aloe gel, depending on leaf width

1 dessertspoon (about 2 teaspoons)
Superfood

lemon peel for garnish

DIRECTIONS

Place the avocado, bananas, mango, aloe, and superfood in your blender and
process until smooth. Pour into individual bowls, and garnish with lemon peel.

Cacao Crème

BY JEREMY SAFRON

ADVANCED PREP: 30 min for soaking   **IMMEDIATE PREP:** 10 min

SERVES 2 to 4   **SPECIAL EQUIPMENT** Blender or mini food processor

INGREDIENTS

10 dates, pitted, soaked

1 cup almond butter

1/4 cup coconut butter or flax oil

10 cacao beans, peeled

DIRECTIONS

Blend all the ingredients in blender cup or mini food processor until smooth.

Carob Pudding

BY ROSE LEE CALABRO

ADVANCED PREP: 1 to 4 hours for soaking   **IMMEDIATE PREP:** 10 min

SERVES 2 to 4   **SPECIAL EQUIPMENT** Blender

INGREDIENTS

1/2 cup pecans, soaked 1 to 4 hours

2 cups coconut meat (reserve water)

1 teaspoon vanilla extract

1 to 2 tablespoons raw carob powder

1 tablespoon coconut oil (optional)

DIRECTIONS

Process all the ingredients in a blender until smooth. Add water or coconut to desired consistency.

Coconut Flan with Orange Glaze

BY MATT SAMUELSON

ADVANCED PREP: None   **IMMEDIATE PREP:** 15 min

SERVES 2   **SPECIAL EQUIPMENT** Blender

INGREDIENTS

For the flan:

2 cups young coconut meat, packed

1/4 cup dates, pitted and packed

2 1/2 teaspoons vanilla

1 1/2 teaspoons psyllium powder

pinch Celtic sea salt

1/4 to 1/3 cup coconut water

For the orange glaze:

2 cups orange juice

1 1/2 cups dates, pitted and packed

3/4 teaspoon cinnamon

pinch Celtic sea salt

2 teaspoons psyllium powder

DIRECTIONS

Put all the ingredients for the flan in the blender. Start with 1/4 cup coconut water, and add more if needed. The mixture should be a very thick consistency. Pour into a pie mold, 8-inch x 8-inch baking pan, or individual tart molds.

To make the glaze, blend 1 cup of the orange juice with the dates until creamy. Add the remaining ingredients and blend well. Spread over the flan and enjoy!

Dreamy Rice Pudding

BY ROSE LEE CALABRO
ADVANCED PREP: 3 to 5 days for soaking
SERVES 4 to 6 **SPECIAL EQUIPMENT** Blender

INGREDIENTS

1 cup wild rice, soaked 3 to 5 days
3 cups young coconut meat (reserve water)

1 cup coconut water
2 teaspoons cinnamon
2 teaspoons vanilla extract

DIRECTIONS

In a blender, process the coconut meat and water, cinnamon, and vanilla until smooth. Combine in a mixing bowl with the sprouted rice; mix well. Dust with cinnamon and enjoy.

Fruit Parfait

BY EDDIE D. ROBINSON
ADVANCED PREP: 4 hours for soaking + 30 min for refrigerating   **IMMEDIATE PREP:** 15 min
SERVES 2 **SPECIAL EQUIPMENT** Vita-Mix or food processor

INGREDIENTS

1 young coconut (reserve water)
1 small vanilla bean, chopped
4 tablespoons lime juice
1/4 cup coconut water
1/2 cup pecans, chopped and soaked

for 4 hours
2 cups mixed fruit (blueberries, pineapple, strawberries, etc.)
6 to 8 dates, pitted
1/2 cup raisins

Mexican Stuffed Peppers By Rose Lee Calabro

Vitality Soup and Salad By Cherie Soria

DIRECTIONS

Combine the coconut meat, vanilla beans, lime juice and coconut water in a Vita-Mix or food processor. Blend on high until creamy. Layer the cream, pecans, fruit, dates, and raisins in a serving cup or bowl. Chill and serve.

Fruity Flaxseed Pudding

By Rita Romano

Advanced prep: 32 hours for soaked + dried almonds (Almond Milk 8-12 hours)   **Immediate prep:** 10 min (Almond Milk 15 min)

Serves 4   **Special Equipment** Dehydrator, coffee grinder, Cuisinart

INGREDIENTS

- 1/2 cup flaxseed, dry
- 1 cup Almond Milk (page 182)
- 1/2 cup almonds, soaked 24 hours and dehydrated at 105°F for 8 hours
- 2 ripe bananas
- 2 tablespoons frozen orange juice concentrate
- 1 apple, cored and sliced
- 1 teaspoon psyllium husk powder

DIRECTIONS

Pulse flaxseed in a coffee grinder until very fine and whisk into the Almond Milk.

Grind almonds in a Cuisinart fitted with the "S" blade until fine. Add the bananas, frozen orange juice, apples and psyllium seed powder and pulse until well mixed, keeping the apples a bit chunky.

Add flaxseed mixture to processor and pulse for a few seconds.

Place the pudding in a bowl, chill, and let thicken.

Macadamia Pudding

By Paul Nison

Advanced prep: None   **Immediate prep:** 5 min

Serves 2   **Special Equipment** Blender

INGREDIENTS

1 cup macadamia nuts
1 cup Medjool dates, pitted

DIRECTIONS

Blend all the ingredients together with 1 cup of water and serve.

Mousse de Naranja

By Shazzie

Advanced prep: 4 hours for soaking + 2 to 4 hours for refrigeration

Immediate prep: 10 min

Serves 4   **Special Equipment** Food processor

INGREDIENTS

3 cups dried apricots, soaked at least 4 hours
4 oranges, juiced
pinch ground cinnamon
pinch ground cloves
lavender flowers or other delicate edible flowers for garnish

DIRECTIONS

Drain and squeeze any excess moisture from the apricots. Place the apricots in a food processor with orange juice, cinnamon, and cloves. Process until smooth. If it's too watery, add more dried apricots and process again until you have a thick pudding.

Spoon the mixture into individual serving dishes and sprinkle flowers on top. Place in the fridge to set for 2 to 4 hours or overnight.

Serve with a generous helping of Vanilla Crème (page 340).

Contributor's note: This is a lovely summer treat, and it's very light—so you can eat lots of it!

Papaya Banana Pudding

BY NOMI SHANNON

ADVANCED PREP: None   **IMMEDIATE PREP:** 5 min

SERVES 1   **SPECIAL EQUIPMENT** Blender

INGREDIENTS

1 cup papaya chunks (approximately 1/2 Hawaiian papaya, peeled and seeded)

1 banana

1 to 2 teaspoons raw tahini

DIRECTIONS

Blend all the ingredients until smooth. Serve immediately.

Contributor's note: This is one of my favorite breakfasts and also makes a great snack or dessert. It's wonderful topped with berries.

Pecan Pudding

BY JALISSA LETENDRE

ADVANCED PREP: 8 to 12 hours for soaking (Almond Milk 12 hours)
IMMEDIATE PREP: 15 min (Almond Milk 15 min)
SERVES 5   **SPECIAL EQUIPMENT** Blender

INGREDIENTS

1 cup pecans, soaked and drained

1/2 cup Brazil nuts, soaked and drained

1 cup grated dried coconut, soaked and drained

1 orange, peeled

2 teaspoons vanilla extract

1 1/4 cups Almond Milk (see recipe page 208)

1/4 cup honey

pinch sea salt

2 bananas, peeled and sliced

ground cinnamon, for garnish

DIRECTIONS

Blend the pecans, Brazil nuts, coconut, orange, vanilla extract, almond milk, honey, and sea salt to a creamy consistency.

Cover the bottom of 5 serving cups with sliced bananas. Spoon the pudding over the bananas. Garnish with cinnamon, and chill before serving.

Purple Brosia

BY JEREMY SAFRON

ADVANCED PREP: 12 hours for soaking **IMMEDIATE PREP:** 10 min

SERVES 2 to 4 **SPECIAL EQUIPMENT** Blender

INGREDIENTS

1 cup walnuts, soaked

1 cup dates, soaked (reserve water)

1/2 cup black raspberries

1/2 cup date soak water

DIRECTIONS

Blend all the ingredients together until smooth.

Raspberry and Physalis Dream

BY SHAZZIE

ADVANCED PREP: 4 hours for soaking   **IMMEDIATE PREP:** 10 min

SERVES 4   **SPECIAL EQUIPMENT** Coffee mill, hand blender

INGREDIENTS

20 Brazil nuts, soaked at least 4 hours

1/4 avocado

3 Medjool dates, pitted

1-inch piece vanilla pod

30 physalis (cape gooseberries)

60 raspberries

DIRECTIONS

In a coffee mill, blend 15 Brazil nuts with the avocado, dates and vanilla pod. Add a little water if needed; it should resemble a very thick cream. Set aside.

Remove the paper from 26 of the physalis. Using a hand blender, blend with the 5 remaining Brazil nuts and 20 of the raspberries.

Place equal amounts of the fruit mixture in the bottoms of 4 serving glasses.

Add equal amounts of the cream to each glass. Divide the whole raspberry mixture among the glasses. Top each with 1 physalis with the paper wings spread out.

Contributor's note: The pungent, musky flavor of physalis makes this a very sexy pudding.

Semolina Pudding with Figgy Jam

BY SHAZZIE

ADVANCED PREP: 12 to 24 hours for soaking   **IMMEDIATE PREP:** 10 min

SERVES 2   **SPECIAL EQUIPMENT** Hand blender, blender

INGREDIENTS

4 dried figs, soaked 12 to 24 hours or fresh figs, peeled

1 heaping tablespoon raisins, soaked 12 to 24 hours

2 bananas, peeled

1 sweet apple, peeled and cored

1 stalk celery, finely chopped

DIRECTIONS

Using a hand blender, blend the figs and raisins to a jam, and set aside.

Combine the bananas, apple, celery, and 1 cup water in the blender and process until smooth. This is your semolina.

Pour the semolina into a bowl, and pour the jam in the middle. Swirl the jam so it looks beautiful.

Toffee and Raspberry Fool

BY SHAZZIE

ADVANCED PREP: 36 hours for soaking   **IMMEDIATE PREP:** 15 min

SERVES 4   **SPECIAL EQUIPMENT** Hand blender, blender

INGREDIENTS

2 cups sunflower seeds, soaked for 24 hours (rinsed periodically)

20 dried apricots, soaked for 36 hours (rinsed periodically)

15 raspberries

1-inch piece vanilla bean

12 fresh dates, skins and pits removed, or dried dates, soaked for 24 hours

DIRECTIONS

Using a hand blender, blend drained sunflower seeds, 10 drained apricots and 11 raspberries to a smooth cream. Set aside and rinse the blender.

Scrape the seeds out of the vanilla bean into a bowl and add the remaining apricots and 10 of the dates. Blend to a smooth cream.

Spoon a layer of the date mixture into 4 stemmed glasses. Add a layer of the raspberry mixture on top of this, and repeat until you have about 6 layers in the glasses and all the mixture is used up.

Top each glass of pudding with a raspberry in the center. Cut the remaining 2 dates into thin strips and place them around the raspberry in a sun ray pattern. Serve as it is or chilled on a hot day.

PART III

APPENDIX & RESOURCES

Raw Food Glossary

AFA acidophilus One of more than 400 different kinds of bacteria that live in our gastrointestinal tract. Acidophilus supplements can reintroduce these beneficial bacteria into the system.

agar-agar Thickening agent made from seaweed. Also known as Japanese gelatin and kanten. A flavorless, dried seaweed that acts as a setting agent. Available in Asian markets, health food stores, or well-stocked grocery stores. Agar-agar comes in powder, strand or block form and can be substituted for gelatin, although because it is stronger, you can use less. It is freeze-dried, and therefore not raw.

agave (cactus) nectar The distilled juice of the agave cactus is a natural low-glycemic sweetener, but not all brands are raw.

airing cupboard (*chiefly British***)** a linen closet, usually gently warmed by hot water heater.

allspice Also known as Jamaica pepper, allspice is a seasoning made from allspice berries, the tiny fruit of the Pimiento Tree. You can purchase the dried berries whole and grind them yourself, or simply purchase ground allspice. Used in many Middle Eastern dishes, and in sweet as well as savory fare, allspice derives its name because it is reminiscent of so many other spices such as cinnamon, nutmeg and cloves.

almond milk Beverage made from almonds blended with water, and then strained. Used in place of dairy as a beverage, soup, or sauce base.

almond pulp The residue left after making almond milk. Can be used to make pâté, "almond cheese," or used in other recipes to add bulk.

aloe gel Gel from the aloe vera plant; thought to be soothing to inflamed tissues; great for stomach or intestinal problems, and for burns.

amaranth leaf (callaloo) Leafy green vegetable similar in flavor to spinach. The leaves, which have a slightly sweet flavor and high protein content, are used in salads and cooking. Amaranth seeds are used as cereal, or ground into flour for bread. You can find amaranth at health foods stores, well-stocked grocery stores, and Asian markets.

amazu shoga Shredded or sliced ginger, pickled in a sweet vinegar marinade. Most people encounter amazu shoga, which ranges from pink to beige in color, as an accompaniment to sushi. Amazu shoga is available in Asian markets or well-stocked grocery stores.

amchoor Also known as mango powder, amchoor is an East Indian seasoning made of pulverized sun-dried green mango. Sometimes used to tenderize meat; amchoor adds a tart yet fruity flavor to many dishes, including curries. Amchoor is available in Indian markets, and may also be found under the spellings amchor, amchur or aamchur.

Aphanizominon flos-aquae (AFA) An ancient strain of blue-green microalgae found in Klamath Lake, Oregon.

apple cider vinegar A raw vinegar produced through fermentation of apples.

aramé Sea vegetable that looks like slender, black threads. Like most sea vegetables, it is high in trace minerals; however, steaming is a traditional part of its processing.

arugula A leafy green with a distinct peppery taste and a common ingredient in Italian cuisine. Also known as rocket, roquette, arugula, and rucola.

Asian cut: thinly cut, sliced on a diagonal

Atlantic sea flakes Blend of sea vegetable flakes available from EDEN brand Sea Vegetables®. Sea vegetables are ancient life forms, and one of the richest sources of minerals and nutrients.

aubergine (*French*) Eggplant.

balsamic vinegar Intensely flavored, slightly sweet vinegar. Made from the unfermented juice of ripe grapes, usually aged for a long time. (not usually raw).

biryani Traditional Indian dish, usually rice-based with vegetables, nuts, and legumes added.

Batavia A type of loose-headed lettuce.

bean threads A spaghetti substitute. Also called cellophane noodles, Chinese vermicelli and glass noodles, these translucent threads are made from green mung bean starch. Available in Asian markets and many supermarkets (not raw).

bhajis Onion fritters, popular in Indian cuisine.

biscuit (*British*) Cookie.

black radish Similar in flavor to the red radish; believed to be healing for the gall bladder.

blue-green algae or **spirulina** Single-celled algae considered to be a *superfood*. High in protein (65 percent vs. 28 percent for beef), in B vitamins, and trace minerals.

bok choy Also known as Chinese cabbage, bok choy is a crunchy vegetable with white stalks and green leaves. Baby bok choy is also available.

Bragg Liquid Aminos® A non-enzymatic salty seasoning that contains natural MSG. Quite popular among some beginner raw foodists.

brewer's yeast Yeast powder or flakes. Brewer's yeast is a good source of B vitamins for raw fooders. Because live yeast cells have been destroyed, it is not considered raw.

Brown or Red Miso Miso made from fermented grains (usually rice or barley) and soybeans. Fermented for longer periods than white or yellow miso, which makes it saltier.

bulgur Cracked wheat (not raw).

candy floss (*British*) Cotton candy.

canistel An egg-shaped fruit with a thin, glossy skin. The flesh is pumpkin-colored and somewhat flaky. Canistels are rich in niacin and beta carotene (vitamin A) and a fair source of vitamin C. The flavor is similar to a cooked sweet potato mixed with heavy cream. Often eaten raw with salt, pepper, and lime or lemon juice or lightly baked.

cantaloupe Also known as muskmelon, the cantaloupe has a sweet refreshing taste and reddish-orange flesh.

carob Made from the sweet pulp inside the pods of the tropical carob tree. Carob is ground, and most often used as a healthy substitute for chocolate. It is available raw or toasted.

cardamom Spice with a distinctive earthy flavor and aroma. Both the small brown seeds and the white pods can be used.

carrot pulp Pulp left over from juicing carrots in Champion or other juicer. A component of carrot cake and other recipes.

cayenne A type of hot pepper. A very important spice used in raw food, as it is medicinal as well as culinary. Also comes in capsule form with rated "hotness."

Celtic sea salt, Celtic salt Sun-dried sea salt; a good source of minerals and friendly bacteria. Some sea salts are boiled, which removes minerals and trace elements. To ensure that it is raw buy it whole and grind it yourself. Celtic sea salt is from France, though other sea salts are harvested in many areas.

cheesecloth Fine-meshed 100% cotton cloth, traditionally used to press dairy cheese. Raw foodists use it as one of the choices for straining natural nut and seed cheeses or to separate juice from pulp when blending. (*Note:* be sure to purchase cheesecloth meant for culinary use-it is also sold in hardware stores to strain paint, not made for use with food.) Cheesecloth is also commonly used to cover sprout jars.

cherimoya Also known as custard apple, cherimoya is an unevenly shaped soft fruit with a light green peel and large pit. The flavor is similar to that of banana, pineapple, and papaya combined. When ripe, they will give to slight pressure. Store at room temperature to ripen, then refrigerate. Serve well chilled. Cherimoyas are rich in vitamin C, niacin, and iron.

chervil Aromatic herb of the carrot family used in soups and salads.

Chinese five-spice A blend of spices usually consisting of anise, cinnamon, cloves, fennel, and pepper.

Chinese leaves The edible leaves of a Chinese cabbage.

chip shop, Fish-and-chip shop (*British*) Store or restaurant where deep-fried fish and "french" fries are made for takeout.

Citrus zester A handy gadget that quickly and easily removes the zest from citrus fruit.

coconut butter or oil Thick, waxy butter from coconut.

compote Dessert made of a variety of fruits in their own juice (not usually raw).

confiture A candy or preserve usually consisting of fruits and nuts or roots preserved with sugar.

coulis A thick sauce of puréed vegetable or fruit.

courgette (*French*) Zucchini.

courgetti "Spaghetti" made from zucchinis or courgettes.

crudités Raw vegetables, usually served with a dipping sauce.

currants, red or black Native to Oregon, these bushes grow tiny, sweet-tart fruits, used in pies, jams, jellies, and syrups.

daikon Large, long white radish.

dehydrator see *Excalibur*.

detox Process in which the body eliminates toxins from its cells.

digestive enzymes A digestive aid derived from plants, usually containing the enzymes needed to digest protein, carbohydrates, fats, dairy, and starches.

dolmades Grape leaves stuffed with rice, meat, and seasonings (Greek dish).

dulse A reddish colored seaweed, usually dried. Found in northern latitudes; excellent source of minerals.

durian Large fruit from Malaysia. The semihard shell is brownish green and covered with thick spikes. The odor of the fruit can be off-putting, but the flesh is sweet, thick, and creamy.

E3Live® Brand name of edible algae. See *aphanizominon flos-aquae*.

endive Bitter lettuce-like plant used in salads.

Enoki Exotic mushroom with long, thin strands and tiny white caps; can often be bought dried.

enzyme inhibitors The chemicals that coat nuts and seeds to prevent them from germinating prematurely. Enzyme inhibitors are toxic in large quantities, but can be released by soaking nuts and seeds, then discarding the soak water. (see Chapter 4: Sprouting and Greening).

Essene bread See *manna bread*.

Excalibur® Brand name of the most popular dehydrator. Used to make crackers, bread, cookies, burgers, and the like without destroying enzymes with high heat. (see Chapter 2: Essential Tools).

extra virgin olive oil Comes from the first press of the olive harvest. Look for "cold-pressed organic extra virgin" to ensure that it is processed without heat.

falafel A spicy mixture of ground vegetables and chick peas usually formed into patties or balls.

five-spice See *Chinese five spice*.

fool A dessert, usually cooked, made of blended creamed fruits.

galangal (Thai ginger) Root.

galia An exotic, hybrid muskmelon from Israel; also grown in Florida.

garam masala A pungent, aromatic blend of spices used in Indian cuisine.

gem lettuce A compact crunchy lettuce, also known as Little Gem, with a dense heart and a single ring of outer leaves.

golden tomatoes Yellow tomatoes. Flavor similar to red tomatoes, they add visual appeal to certain recipes.

granulated kelp Dried powdered seaweed.

green or spring onions Scallions.

guava Sweet, tropical fruit, also known as guyava or kuawa.

habanero Very hot, lantern-shaped chili pepper. Do not touch eyes after use. If dehydrating, do not inhale when you check the oven.

hazelnuts Filberts.

Herbamare® Seasoning with sea salt and 20 different organic herbs produced by Bioforce Ltd, distributed by Rapunzel Pure Organics in New York.

hemp Hemp seeds have a nutty flavor akin to sunflower seeds. They are an excellent source of essential fatty acids and proteins.

hiziki Type of seaweed, usually dried.

jalapeño Smooth, dark green chili pepper. Very hot. Often used in Mexican cuisine. Do not touch your eyes after use. If dehydrating, do not inhale when you check the oven.

Jamaica pepper See *allspice*.

jicama White, crunchy, root vegetable shaped like a potato; flavor is somewhere between an apple and a turnip. Hard to find the organic variety.

Julienne Cut into fine sticks for finger food or plate decoration.

Kalamata olive (*Greek*) Purple-black raw olive. There are many types of raw olives; some varieties are cooked.

kale A member of the cabbage family that comes in many varieties, such as Dinosaur kale; high in Calcium; used in salads and for juicing.

kamut A high-protein wheat. Kamut can be sprouted and made into raw dough with excellent results.

kanten A pudding-gelatin creation usually thickened with *agar-agar* seaweed and commonly part of macrobiotic cuisine.

kefir Fermented soft yogurt-like cheese that contains probiotics. The milk used to make it may be pasteurized and therefore not raw. Also used to make commercial bottled smoothies.

kibble To grind food into small, rice-sized pieces.

kimchi, kimchee Traditional Korean dish of fermented cabbage; the bacteria that develop are very good for the intestinal tract.

kofta balls Meat balls popular in East Indian cuisine. Traditionally served in soup.

kumquat Oval orange-like fruit about 1 inch long.

ladies' fingers (*English*) Okra.

lamb's quarter A wild edible green.

lecithin A fatty substance made from egg yolks and legumes, lecithin belongs to the family of phospholipids, which are among the primary building blocks of all cellular membranes. Lecithin imparts a moist and creamy texture.

lychee, lichi, litchi Asian-Hawaiian fruit with a hard thin shell, sweet white flesh, and large pit.

Peruvian maca root A vegetable root, or tuber, distantly related to the Mexican Wild Yam. Maca grows naturally only in the Andean mountains of Peru. Contains significant amounts of amino acids, complex carbohydrates, vitamins B1, B2, B12, C, and E, and minerals, including calcium, iron, magnesium, phosphorus, and zinc.

macrobiotic A diet that consists largely of whole grains, vegetables, and seaweeds. An approach to health that views the self as a product of the foods we choose to eat, and the environment in which we live.

mandolin Vegetable slicer. (See Chapter 2: Essential Tools).

mangostine A tangerine-like fruit, with dark brown hard skin cultivated in Asia, flavor is sweet and tart.

Manitok wild rice Part of the traditional Chippewa Indian diet. Indigenous to Minnesota and parts of Canada. It is typically parched during processing and is not raw.

manna bread Bread made from sprouted grains and sometimes includes raw fruits and nuts. Manna bread is baked at 240°F and is therefore not raw.

marrow, vegetable marrow (*British*) Large zucchini-like squash.

Medjool Large, sweet date. The date palm (*Phoenix Dactylifera*) is known as the tree of life and is a holy symbol to Muslims. Originally from Morocco, the Medjool date was reserved for royal guests and other dignitaries.

melon baller A kitchen tool useful for scooping soft fruit into little balls for garnish.

mesclun Salad mixture comprised of several types of baby greens.

mesquite, mesquite flour, mesquite powder Raw sweetener made from bean and pod of mesquite tree; has a molasses-like flavor.

Meyer lemon A smooth skinned lemon with a very mild, slightly sweet lemon flavor; somewhere between a lemon and a mandarin.

milk bag A fine mesh bag, usually with drawstring and about a gallon in volume, used for filtering juices and nut milks.

miso A fermented paste made in Japan, usually made from soybeans and a grain, aged anywhere from several months to several years; has a salty taste. Although it is not raw, miso is an excellent source of live enzymes and friendly bacteria. The grain used determines the color; darker misos have been fermented longer and are therefore saltier.

muesli Recipe originally made with dried and fresh fruits mixed with juice or milk and rolled oats, usually soaked for a few hours. *Swiss.*

mung bean sprouts Type of bean sprouts, often used in Chinese cuisine. It is easy to grow your own by sprouting mung beans for a few days.

Nama® Shoyu A brand of raw soy sauce that contains wheat.

neatballs A name sometimes used for various meatball substitutes.

nori Green or purple-green square seaweed sheets used to wrap sushi. May be raw or toasted. (The word "toasted" may be written in Japanese.) Useful for wraps instead of bread.

nut butter Raw butters such as almond butter or cashew butter, can be purchased or made at home with a heavy-duty blender, juicer or in small quantities in an electric coffee grinder.

nutritional yeast flakes See *brewer's yeast.*

oat groats Whole oat grain that has been hulled.

prickly pear Fruit of several varieties of cactus. Also called cactus pear.

mullaca An herb found in the tropics. It bears small, cream-colored flowers and produces tiny, light yellowish-orange fruit sometimes called cape gooseberry.

persimmon, fuyu persimmon, hachiya persimmon Orange fruit with small brown seeds. The fuyu variety is shaped like a tomato and can be eaten as soon as it is ripe. The hachiya persimmon looks like an acorn; wait until it is very soft to eat, or it may taste bitter from the tannins.

piel de sapo Spanish melon with a mottled rind and sweet, yellow flesh; a favorite in Latin America.

pignoli, pignolia See *pine nut.*

pine nut Small white nut extracted from pinecones. Imported mostly from China and Portugal, although some grow in the western USA. Suitable for cake frosting and creamy sauces.

Pizza Seasoning Blend® A brand-name herb and spice mixture from Frontier Natural Products that includes dehydrated onion, bell pepper, fennel, oregano, dehydrated garlic, basil, chili peppers, parsley, thyme, marjoram and celery flakes.

portobello Large flat mushroom useful as individual serving container for pâtés and nutmeats. Crimini mushrooms are baby portobellos. They are smaller and brown and are sold in supermarkets. Along with the white button mushrooms, Criminis and portobellos have more flavor.

probiotic Supplement that provides "friendly bacteria" for the intestinal tract.

psyllium seed, psyllium husk powder Raw thickening agent; high in fiber. Both psyllium seed and psyllium husk can be ground to powder. Look for organic brands; the non-organic, often from India, may be heavily laced with pesticides.

quinoa Pronounced *kéen-wa*, quinoa is an ancient grain-like seed that has recently been "rediscovered." Quinoa has a light, delicate flavor, and is very high in protein and iron.

radicchio A type of red chicory with variegated leaves; used in salads.

ragoût A thick stew of meat and/or vegetables.

raita An East Indian condiment usually made with yogurt and cucumber.

rambutan An oval-shaped fruit similar to the lychee. Rambutan usually has a bright red/orange skin when ripe (depending on the variety).

Rapadura® Unrefined sugar made from the natural juice of sugar cane. See Sweeteners sidebar on page 10.

rejuvelac, rejuvilac A 2- to 3-day fermentation of cracked sprouted wheat or rye berries, which is enzymatically active. High in friendly bacteria and considered a digestive aid.

rocket Any of several plants of the mustard family, such as arugula.

Roma Tomato variety with a meaty flavor, often used for sauces.

saffron, saffron threads A deep orange dried herb or powder derived from the crocus plant and used to color and flavor foods.

spiralizer, spiral slicer Kitchen tool that cuts vegetables into paper-thin slices or spaghetti-like strands. Also called a Saladacco.

samosa An Indian turnover usually filled with meat and vegetables and fried.

sapodilla A rough-skinned, brownish fruit with yellowish, translucent, sweet flesh.

satay Indonesian dish of marinated meat, poultry, or vegetables cooked and served on a skewer, usually with peanut sauce.

S-blade The blade of a food processor designed to process hard products such as nuts or carrots, as well as soft foods.

sea lettuce A type of sea vegetable that is high in minerals.

serrano pepper A small, very hot chili pepper.

sharlyn melon Melon with orange-white flesh and delicate flavor of honeydew.

Shoyu See **Nama® Shoyu.**

shredding blade The non S-shaped blade of a food processor. Most food processors come with several blades that are used for different types of shredding and grating processes.

soak water The water remaining after soaking nuts, grains, seeds, or fruit. If a recipe calls for "soak water" it is often in reference to the water used to soak raisins, or other dried fruit. One should not consume the soak water from nuts and seeds; throw this out because of the enzyme inhibitors and tannins.

Spectrabiotics, Spectrabiotic® Cell Tech's brand-name friendly bacteria probiotic support formula.

Spike® Brand-name blend of vegetables and salt sold in health food stores.

spring onions *(English)* Green onions; scallions.

sprouting bag A linen, nylon or canvas bag with a drawstring. May be interchangeable with a milk bag, if the fabric is fine enough. Designed for containing and rinsing sprouting nuts or seeds.

star fruit, carambola A sweet-sour exotic fruit with a star-shaped cross-section, useful for decorations

stevia A raw natural sweetener 10 times sweeter than sugar. See Sweeteners sidebar on page 10.

Stoned *(English)* Pitted.

Sucanat® Brand name for an organic enzymatic dehydrated sugar cane juice. See Sweeteners sidebar on page 10.

superfood Any type of food or food-based supplement thought to be extremely nutritious or provide complete nutrition (e.g. spirulina, bee pollen, chlorella, wheatgrass juice).

tabouli, tabouleh A traditional Middle Eastern dish made with cracked wheat.

tahini Sesame seed butter. Because it is usually roasted, shop for raw tahini.

tamari Raw fermented soy; provides salty seasoning.

tamarind Fruit with an acidic pulp used to make a paste popular in Indian cuisine; if unavailable, substitute lemon juice.

tandoori, tandori Indian method of cooking using a clay-fire oven.

Teflex® Brand-name for the drip-proof liner sheets used with a dehydrator. Also sold by the roll.

Thai coconut Young coconut encased in white fibrous outer shell in which meat is soft and tender; also contains young coconut water.

toffee *(English)* Traditionally made by first blending sweet cream butter with sugar and boiling to create a rich, chewy, aromatic mixture.

tomatillo Small, round, pale green or yellow fruit, similar in appearance to a tomato, used in Mexican cuisine.

turmeric root An Indian seasoning of the ginger family; gives curry powder its traditional yellow color. Thought to be an anti-inflammatory.

tutti-frutti *(Italian)* "All fruits." A delicious ice cream containing many candied fruits.

udon Wheat noodle used in Asian cuisine.

UME vinegar Vinegar made from umeboshi plums (dried Japanese salt plums); has a salty, sour taste.

wakamé, wakami Sea vegetable, very mucilaginous after it's soaked.

Xoçai™ A patented raw healthy chocolate with high antioxidants (for more info, see Peggy Kenney's biography at end of book).

Yamaki Organic Soy Sauce® Brand-name organic soy sauce containing soybeans, whole wheat, minerals, and sea salt; twice fermented, aged 48 months. Unpasteurized, with 17 percent less salt than regular soy sauce.

yerba maté, maté A tea-like beverage, popular in South America. It is greenish in color, contains caffeine and tannin, and is less astringent than tea. Also called Paraguay or Brazilian tea.

za'atar A Middle Eastern spice blend of thyme, sesame, salt, sumac, and marjoram.

zest The colored part of the rind of citrus fruit (oranges, lemons, limes, grapefruit). Extracted with special tool or with the fine side of a grater.

Suggested Reading

The following books will provide the new raw food enthusiast with additional resources. The listing starts with books by our contributing chefs and then is arranged by subject matter. Please note that some of these titles are available only from the author.

CONTRIBUTORS' BOOKS

Adi, Michal. *Pleasure Palate: Your Favorite International Culinary Delights in the Raw.* Forthcoming.

Amsden, Matt; *RAWvolution: Gourmet Living Cuisine*. New York: HarperCollins, 2006)

Stephen Arlin

Arlin, Stephen (Editor), and Wolfe, David (Editor); Seaney, Ken (Illustrator); Mordecai, Dafna (Illustrator); McCabe, John (Editor), Arlin, Jolie (Editor). *The Sunfood Diet Success System: 36 Lessons in Health Transformation.* San Diego, CA: Maul Brothers Publishing, Revised edition, 2000.

Arlin, Stephen; Dini, Fouad; Wolfe, David; Dini, RC; Seaney, Ken and Wolfe, Marc. *Nature's First Law: The Raw-Food Diet.* San Diego, CA: Maul Brothers Publishing; 2nd edition, 1997.

Arlin, Stephen; Wolfe, David (Editor). *Raw Power! Building Strength and Muscle Naturally.* San Diego, CA: Maul Brothers Publishing, 2nd edition, 2000. Large print available.

Baker, Elizabeth

Baker, Elizabeth. *Does the Bible Teach Nutrition?* Mukilteo, WA: WinePress Publishing, 1997.

Baker, Elizabeth. *The Un-Diet Book: The All-Natural Lifestyle for Weight Loss and Eating, Good Health and Exercise*. San Diego, CA: ProMotion Publishing, 1992.

Baker, Elizabeth. *Unmedical Miracle—Oxygen*. Drelwood Communications, 1991.

Baker, Elizabeth. *Unsuspected Killers: Mercury and Mold*. Forthcoming.

Baker, Elizabeth: *The Gourmet Uncook Book: The Elegance of Raw Foods*. San Diego, CA: ProMotion Publishing, 1996.

Baker, Elizabeth; Baker, Elton. *The Uncook Book: Raw Food Adventures to a New Health High*. Drelwood Communications, 1980.

Baker, Elizabeth; Baker, Elton. *Unmedical Book*. San Diego, CA: ProMotion Publishing, 1987.

The Boutenko Family

Boutenko, Sergei and Boutenko, Valya. *Eating Without Heating*. Ashland, OR: Raw Family Publishing, 2002.

Boutenko, Victoria. *12 Steps to Raw Foods: How to Overcome Your Addiction to Cooked Foods*. Ashland, OR: Raw Family Publishing, 2001.

Boutenko, Victoria; Boutenko, Igor; Boutenko, Sergei and Boutenko, Valya. *Raw Family: A True Story of Awakening*. Ashland, OR: Raw Family Publishing, 2000.

Brotman, Juliano: *The UnCook Book: New Vegetarian Food for Life*. New York: ReganBooks, 1999.

Calabro, Rose Lee: *Living in the Raw: Recipes for a Healthy Lifestyle*. Santa Cruz, CA: Rose Publishing, 1998, 2003.

Clingo, Karie: *The Spin of Life Journal: A Kid's Life Journal*. Web publication, columnist as the "Laughing Mother."

Gabriel Cousens

Cousens, Gabriel: *Conscious Eating.* Berkeley, CA: North Atlantic Books, 2000.

Cousens, Gabriel; Parker, Karen, et al. *Rainbow Green Live Food Cuisine.* Berkeley, CA: North Atlantic Books, 2003.

Fielder, John: *The Farm Recipe Book.* Queensland, Australia: Clohesy River Health Farm, 1990.

Graff, Jackie and Gideon

13 themed recipe books, each with 12 to 15 recipes: Caribbean, Valentine, Brunch, Thanksgiving, Country Barbeque, Holiday, Indian, Italian, Tex Mex, Middle Eastern, Oriental, Passover, Pizza.

Raw food recipe book featuring delicious creations served at the Sprout Café. Available in mid 2003 through the Shinui Learning Center Web site: http://www.livefoodsunchild.com/jackie.htm

David Klein

Klein, David; Fry, T. C; Shelton, Dr. Herbert M. *Self Healing Power! How to Tap into The Great Power Within You.* #1140.

Klein, David; Fry, T. C; Shelton, Dr. Herbert M. *Your Natural Diet: Alive Raw Foods,* 3rd. Edition by T. C. Fry and David Klein.

Karen Knowler

Knowler, Karen and Miller, Susie. *Feel-Good Food.* London, UK: Trafalgar Square Publishing, 2000.

Knowler, Karen. *Diary of a Raw Pregnancy.* London, UK: The Fresh Network, 2003.

Knowler, Karen. *Pure & Simple: Raw Food Prep & Menu Planning.* London, UK: The Fresh Network, 2003.

Viktoras Kulvinskas

Kulvinskas, Viktoras (Editor), White, Jean (Illustrator). *Life in the Twenty-First Century.* Mount Ida, AR: Twenty-First Century Publications, 1981

Kulvinskas, Viktoras. *Love Your Body.* Mount Ida, AR: Twenty-First Century Publications, 1972.

Kulvinskas, Viktoras. *New Age Directory Holistic Health Guide.* Mount Ida, AR: Twenty-First Century Publications, 1981 (revised and updated).

Kulvinskas, Viktoras: *Sprouts for the Love of Everybody.* Mount Ida, AR: Twenty-First Century Publications, 1988.

Kulvinskas, Viktoras. *Survival in the Twenty-First Century.* Millennium limited edition. Mount Ida, AR: Twenty-First Century Publications, 2002

Kulvinskas, Viktoras. *The Lover's Diet.* Mount Ida, AR: Twenty-First Century Publications, 2002.

Kulvinskas, Viktoras. *Youthing With Enzyme Systems.* Mount Ida, AR: Twenty-First Century Publications, 1975.

Jalissa Letendre

French version: *Les Délices de L'alimentation Vivante.* Montreal, Quebec: 2003.

English version: *Delights of Live Food.*

Elaina Love

Love, Elaina. *Elaina's Pure Joy Kitchen Recipe Binder: 115 Healthy, Simple Recipes The Whole Family Will Enjoy.*

Love, Elaina. *Elaina's Pure Joy Kitchen.*

Love, Elaina. Recipe Booklets: *Winter Warming Foods, Easy Thai Foods, Healthy Heart-Warming Foods, Southeast Asian Feast, Mexican Feast.*

Rhonda Malkmus

Malkmus, Rhonda J., et al. *Recipes for Life: From God's Garden.* Shelby, NC: Hallelujah Acres Publishing. 1998.

Malkmus, Rhonda J., *Salad Dressings for Life.* Shelby, NC: Hallelujah Acres Publishing, 2002.

Elysa Markowitz

Markowitz, Elysa and Brainen, Howard. *Baby Dance: A Comprehensive Guide to Prenatal and Postpartum Exercise.* Englewood Cliffs, NJ: Prentice Hall, 1980.

Markowitz, Elysa. *Living With Green Power: A Gourmet Collection of Living Food Recipes.* Burnaby, BC, Canada: Alive Books, 1998.

Markowitz, Elysa. *Warming Up to Living Foods.* Summertown, TN: Book Publishing Company, 1998.

Paul Nison

Nison, Paul. *The Raw Life: Becoming Natural in an Unnatural World.* New York: 343 Publishing Co., 2001.

Nison, Paul. *Raw Knowledge: Enhance the Powers of the Mind, Body and Soul.* New York: 343 Publishing Company, 2002.

Karen Parker

Cousens, Gabriel; Parker, Karen, et al. *Rainbow Green Live Food Cuisine.* Berkeley, CA: North Atlantic Books, 2003.

Romano, Rita. *Dining in the Raw.* New York: Kensington Books, 1992, 2003.

Rhio. *Hooked on Raw.* New York: Beso Entertainment, 2000.

Jeremy Safron

Safron, Jeremy. *Dining from an Empty Bowl: A Fasting Handbook.*

Safron, Jeremy. *Raw Truth: Art of Preparing Living Foods.* Forthcoming.

Sarno, Chad. *The Raw Chef; A Journey Through the Senses.* Forthcoming.

Nomi Shannon

Shannon, Nomi. *Simply Raw.* Forthcoming.

Shannon, Nomi. A booklet: *The Little Book of Raw Soups.* Burnaby, BC, Canada: Alive Books; 1999.

Shannon, Nomi. A booklet: *Raw But Not Naked: A Little Book Of Salad Dressing.* 2000.

Shannon, Nomi and Duruz, Cheryl. *Raw Food Celebrations.* Summertown TN, Book Publishing Co. Due Sept 2008

Shannon, Nomi. *The Raw Gourmet.* Summertown TN, Book Publishing Co, 1999

Shazzie. *Detox Your World.*

Sheridan, Dr. Jameth, N.D. *Uncooking with Jameth and Kim.* HealthForce Publishing, 1991 & 2003 (updated).

Soria, Cherie. Angel Foods: *Healthy Recipes for Heavenly Bodies.* Santa Barbara, CA: Heartstar Productions 1997.

Talifero, Jinjee and Talifero, Storm. *The Garden Diet. The Definitive Guide to The Raw-Vegan Diet.* Ebook: http://www.thegardendiet.com.

David Wolfe

Arlin, Stephen (Editor), and Wolfe, David (Editor); Seaney, Ken (Illustrator); Mordecai, Dafna (Illustrator); McCabe, John (Editor), Arlin, Jolie (Editor). *The Sunfood Diet Success System: 36 Lessons in Health Transformation.* San Diego, CA: Maul Brothers Publishing; Revised edition, 2000.

Arlin, Stephen; Dini, Fouad; Wolfe, David; Dini, RC; Seaney, Ken and Wolfe, Marc. *Nature's First Law: The Raw-Food Diet.* San Diego, CA: Maul Brothers Publishing; 2nd edition, 1997.

Arlin, Stephen; Wolfe, David, Ed. *Raw Power! Building Strength and Muscle Naturally.*

San Diego, CA: Maul Brothers Publishing; 2nd edition, 2000. Large print available.

Wolfe, David. *Eating for Beauty: For Women & Men.* San Diego, CA: Maul Brothers Publishing, 2002.

Wright, Abeba. *Absolutely Abeba's Krazy Krackers.* Abeba Wright Publishing, 2003.

CLASSICS OF RAW FOOD

McDermott, Stella. *Metaphysics of Raw Foods.* Kessinger Publishing Company, 1997.

Wigmore, Ann and Kimball, Betsy (Editor). *Ann Wigmore's Recipes for Longer Life.* New York: Avery Penguin Putnam, 1982.

Wigmore, Ann. *The Wheatgrass Book.* New York: Avery Penguin Putnam, 1985.

Wigmore, Ann and Pattinson, Lee (Contributor). *The Blending Book: Maximizing Natures Nutrients: How to Blend Fruits and Vegetables for Better Health.* New York: Avery Penguin Putnam, 1997

Wigmore, Ann. *The Hippocrates Diet and Health Program.* New York: Avery Penguin Putnam, 1984.

Wigmore, Ann. *The Sprouting Book.* New York: Avery Penguin Putnam, 1986.

ENZYMES

Howell, Dr. Edward. *Enzyme Nutrition: The Food Enzyme Concept.* Wayne, NJ: Avery Publishing Group, Inc., 1985.

Santillo, Humbart, M.H., N.D. *Food Enzymes: The Missing Link to Radiant Health.* Prescott, AZ: Hohm Press, 1993.

CLEANSING AND FASTING

Anderson, Dr. Richard, N.D.; N.M.D. *Cleanse and Purify Thyself: The Clean-Me-Out Program.* 1988.

Cott, Alan, M.D. *Fasting: The Ultimate Diet.* New York: Bantam Books, 1975.

Walker, Dr. Norman W.; O' Sullivan, Woodside. *Colon Health: Key to Vibrant Life.* Prescott, AZ: Norwalk Press, 1979.

HEALING & HEALTH

Burton Goldberg Group, The. *Alternative Medicine—The Definitive Guide*. Fife, WA: Future Medicine Publishing, Inc., 1994.

Carper, Jean. *Food—Your Miracle Medicine*. New York: HarperTorch; Reissue edition, 1998.

Carper, Jean. *The Food Pharmacy: Dramatic New Evidence That Food Is Your Best Medicine*. New York: Bantam Books, 1988.

Chopra, Deepak, M.D. *Perfect Health: The Complete Body-Mind Guide*. New York: Harmony Books, 1991.

Clark, Hulda Regehr, PhD, N.D. *The Cure for All Cancers? With 100 Case Histories*. San Diego, CA: ProMotion Publishing, 1993.

Diamond, Harvey. *Fit for Life, Not Fat for Life*. Health Communications. Forthcoming.

Douglas, William Campbell, M.D. *Into the Light—Tomorrow's Medicine Today: The Exciting Story of the Life-Saving Therapy of the Age*. Dunwoody, GA: 2nd Opinion Publishing, 1995.

Hoffman, Debbie L. *The Raw Food Program: Why, When, How, Length of Time of The Blood Cleansing Regime*. Professional Press Publishing Company,

Karas, Jim and Griesse, Carolyn. *The Raw Foods Diet: The Vital Gift of Enzymes*. New Century Publishers, 1981.

Kelder, Peter. *Ancient Secret of the "Fountain of Youth."* Gig Harbor, WA. Harbor Press, 1985.

Murray, Michael, ND & Pizzorno, Joseph, ND. *Encyclopedia of Natural Medicine*. Rocklin, CA: Prime Health, 1998.

Nolfi, Kristine K. *Raw Food Treatment of Cancer and other Disease*. Cancer Book House, 1980.

Rubin, Jordan S., N.M.D., C.N.C. *Patient, Heal Thyself—A Remarkable Health Program Combining Ancient Wisdom with Groundbreaking Clinical Research*. Topanga, CA: Freedom Press, 2003.

Vonderplanitz, Aajonus. *The Recipe for Living Without Disease*. Los Angeles: Carnelian Bay Castle Press, 2002.

Vonderplanitz, Aajonus. *We Want to Live.* Los Angeles: Carnelian Bay Castle Press, 1997.

Wade, Carlson. *The New Enzyme-Catalyst Diet: Amazing Way to Quick Permanent Weight Loss.* New York: Prentice Hall Trade, 1976.

Walker , Dr. Norman W. *Pure and Simple Natural Weight Control.* Prescott, AZ: Norwalk Press, 1981.

Walker, Dr. Norman W. *Water Can Undermine Your Health.* Prescott, AZ: Norwalk Press, 1996.

Walker, Dr. Norman W. *Become Younger.* Prescott, AZ: Norwalk Press; 2nd edition, 1995.

JUICING

Calbom, Cherie, M.S. et al. *Juicing for Life.* New York: Avery Penguin Putnam, 1992.

Calbom, Cherie, M.S. *The Juice Lady's Guide to Juicing for Health: Unleashing the Healing Power of Whole Fruits and Vegetables.* New York: Avery, 1999.

Calbom, Cherie, M.S. *The Juice Lady's Juicing for High-Level Wellness and Vibrant Good Looks.* New York: Three Rivers Press, 1999.

Charmine, Susan E. *The Complete Raw Juice Therapy.* Wellingborough, Northhamptonshire, UK: Thorsons Publishers, 1982.

Kordich, Jay William. *The Juiceman's Power of Juicing.* New York: Morrow, 1992.

Kordich, Jay; Murray, Michael T. *Complete Book of Juicing.* Prima Publishing, 1997.

LaLanne, Elaine with Richard Benyo. *Total Juicing.* New York: Plume, 1992.

Lee, William H. *The Book of Raw Fruit, Vegetable Juices and Drinks.* New York: McGraw-Hill Trade, 1991.

Meyerowitz, Steve et al. *Juice Fasting and Detoxification: Use the Healing Power of Fresh Juice to Feel Young and Look Great: The Fastest Way to Restore Your Health.* Great Barrington, MA: Sproutman Publications, 1966

Meyerowitz, Steve et al. *Wheatgrass Nature's Finest Medicine: The Complete Guide to Using Grass Foods & Juices to Revitalize Your Health.* Great Barrington, MA: Sproutman Publications, 1999.

Meyerowitz, Steve. *Power Juices Super Drinks*. New York: Kensington Publishing Corporation, 2000.

Tobe, John H. *The Miracles Of Live Juices And Raw Foods*. St. Catharines, Ont., Canada: Provoker Press, 1977.

Vale, Jason. *The Juice Master's Ultimate Fast Food: Discover the Power of Raw Juice*. New York: HarperCollins Publishers, 2003.

Walker, Norman.W., D.Sci. *Raw Vegetable Juices*. New York: Pyramid Communications, 1971.

KIDS

Halfmoon, Hygeia. *Primal Mothering in a Modern World*. San Diego, CA: Maul Brothers Publishing; 2nd edition, 1998.

Hilmar-Jezek, Kytka. *Reiki for Children: Using Healing Touch and Raw Foods to Tap into the Power of the Universe*. Bloomington, IN: 1stBooks Library, 2003.

Stoycoff, Cheryl L. and Sananda, Solomae. *Raw Kids: Transitioning Children to a Raw Food Diet*. Stockton, CA: Living Spirit Press, 2000

RECIPES

Anderson, Henry. *Helping Hand: 8-Day Diet Programs for People Who Care About Wellness*. Tucson, AZ: Publius Press, 1986.

Brooks, Clara W. (Editor). *Why People Eat in the Raw: A Guide to Raw Food*. Womancare Publications, 1991.

Brown, Sarah. *Raw Food (Sarah Brown's Healthy Eating Cookbooks.)* London: Penguin Books Ltd., 1986.

Buckley, Peter. *Eat It Raw*. New York: Dodd Mead, 1978.

Estes. E. L. *Raw Food Menus & Recipe Book*. Health Research. 1992.

Ewald, Ellen Buchman. *Recipes for a Small Planet*. New York, NY: Ballantine, 1973. Ballantine Books; reissue edition, 1985.

Ferrara, Suzanne Alexander et al. *The Raw Food Primer*. Tulsa, OK: Council Oak Books, 2003.

Harrelson, Woody and Underkoffler, Renée Loux. *Living Cuisine: The Art and Spirit of Raw Food.* New York: Avery Penguin Putnam, 2003

Hutchins, Imar. *Delights of the Garden: Vegetarian Cuisine Prepared Without Heat.* Delights of the Garden Restaurants Main Street Books, 1996.

Klein, Roxanne and Trotter, Charlie. *Raw.* Berkeley, CA:

Lappé, Frances Moore. *Diet for a Small Planet: How to Enjoy a Rich Protein Harvest by Getting off the Top of the Food Chain.* New York, NY: Ballantine, 1969.

Lau, Mary Louise. *The Delicious World of Raw Foods: A Culinary Guide to Preparing Appetizers, Soups, Salads, Vegetables, Main Dishes, and Desserts with Little or No Cooking.* New York: Scribner, 1977.

Mavilya, Marya. *Natural Food Cookery.* Dover Publications, 1997.

Meyerowitz, Steve. *Sproutman's Kitchen Garden Cookbook.* Great Barrington, MA: Sproutman Publications, 1994.

Patenaude, Frederic. *Sunfood Cuisine: A Practical Guide to Raw Vegetarian Cuisine.* San Diego, CA: Maul Brothers Publishing, 2002.

Reekie, Jennie. *Everything Raw: The No-Cooking Cookbook.* New York: Viking Press, 1977.

Rosenast, Eleanor S. *Soup Alive!* Santa Barbara, CA: Woodbridge Press Publishing, 1993.

Thornton , Millie I. *Raw Food Ideas: For Your Creative Dishes.* Thornton Associates, 1997.

Voltz , Jeanne. *The Los Angeles Times Natural Foods Cookbook.* New York: New American Library, 1980

Walker, N. W. *The Vegetarian Guide to Diet and Salad.* Longman Trade/Caroline House; Revised edition, 1995.

Wigmore, Ann. *Ann Wigmore's Recipes for Longer Life.* Wayne, NJ: Avery Publishing Group, Inc., 1978.

SPROUTING

Cairney, Edward; Bellamy, David. *The Sprouters Handbook.* Argyll, UK: Argyll Publishing, 1997.

Wigmore, Ann. *The Sprouting Book: How to Grow and Use Sprouts to Maximize Your Health and Vitality.* Wayne, NJ: Avery Publishing Group, 1986.

SUPPLIES

Zipern, Elizabeth and Williams, Dar, with help from Heather Hork and friends. *The Tofu Tollbooth: A Guide to Natural Stores and Eating Spots (With Lots of other Cool Stops Along the Way).* Woodstock, NY: Ceres Press in collaboration with Adwork Press. 2nd edition, 1998.

Meet Our Chefs

MICHAL ADI

Michal had been aware of raw foods for many years but did not take the steps to become a 100-percent Lifefoodarian until October 2001. Her diet, Michal thought, was great. She was vegan and eating a lot of salads, whole grains and steamed vegetables and drinking plenty of fresh pressed juices. Her sugar/starch habit, however, was starting to get the best of her. Michal would feel tired after eating almost all of the time, sometimes to the point of passing out! She soon discovered she was exhibiting all the symptoms of candida.

Michal knew she had to improve her diet and that, until she did, she would not feel good regardless of how much yoga she was practicing. Michal had gone through periods of fasting and eating 80- to 90-percent raw food. She longed for the same clarity of mind and the amazing feeling of boundless energy that she had felt then. It was clear to her that she wanted to go completely raw, but she wanted to learn more about it. Michal decided to participate in a work exchange program at the Ann Wigmore foundation in New Mexico, where she learned almost everything she needed to learn to go 100-percent raw.

Michal began feeling better almost immediately but still had a few candida symptoms. It was only after reading David Wolfe's *The Sunfood Diet Success System* that Michal understood exactly how raw and living foods would help her overcome candida. David's book presented and organized all the information she needed in an effective and inspiring way. She understood now exactly what her body required and the specific effects of cooked and Raw/Live foods on the body. She was able to go 100-percent raw, and has been so to this day.

Raw food has enhanced every aspect of Michal's life. Her first raw catering business, "Healing Meals on Wheels," in Key West, Florida, was a huge success. She was able to experience the powerful effect of healing others through food. Being a Raw/Livefood Chef is one of her greatest pleasures. Michal loves turning people on to raw/live foods and watching their faces light up as they enjoy a delicious uncooked meal. Since relocating to New York, she has been catering raw/live food events and offering raw and life food preparation classes, seminars, and retreats. She has guided many to better health and continues to do so through her private Nutritional Advising practice where she helps people make the transition to a diet of Raw/Live foods.

Since going completely raw, Michal's yoga/spiritual practice is deeper, she does not need as much sleep and she feels able to attain all of her personal goals. As a teacher of both Vinyasa and Kundalini yoga, Michal finds the philosophies of Raw/Life foods and yoga to be complementary. Michal believes that when we increase the life-force in our bodies—from within, through yoga practice, and from without, through the food that we eat—we become more flexible in body and mind and can experience a state of heightened awareness and expanded consciousness. Michal feels that her body is a tool through which she is able to connect with the universe and experience joy, peace and bliss.

E-mail: rawpeach25@yahoo.com
Phone: 917-514-3886

MAYA ADJANI

Maya Deva Adjani was born in Togo, West Africa and raised in California. Maya is a raw food chef and educator, dancer, yogini, author, world traveler and lover of life! She began focused study on living foods eight years ago, and has since given presentations on the benefits of living food, taught hands-on live food preparation around the country, led intensive retreats and worked at several of the world's leading raw food restaurants including Roxanne's, and Café Gratitude. A second generation yogini, Maya received certification in Kundalini yoga from her father, Dr. Siri Gian Singh Khalsa, PhD (www.reichianinstitute.com) and completed further study in Hatha (Iyengar) and Ashtanga yoga styles. For seven years, Maya apprenticed with Don Miguel Ruiz, author of *The Four Agreements* (www.miguelruiz.com). *Breathe, Eat, Dance-Evolve!,* the dynamic process Adjani offers internationally and abroad, incorporates the wisdom of breath work, raw food nutrition and ecstatic dance. This unique combination of tools empowers people to open their breath, bodies and lives to a new way of being in the world. It is potent planetary medicine, drawing upon ancient wisdom, applied in a format that is universal and beneficial to all.

Maya Adjani is a dancer, certified Transformational Breath Facilitator and co-author of *The Yantra Deck: The Art of Being Present* (www.yantradeck.com), a tool for self-inquiry and awakening. When not traveling, Maya volunteers her time teaching classes on a variety of topics from yoga and dance to developing healthy eating habits to underprivileged communities and offers mindfulness meditation classes to women in prison. Maya is available for workshops, retreats and consultations and is committed to bringing the transformational, healing power of conscious breathing, dance, and vibrant living foods to the world.

Email: maya@yantramountainretreat.org
Phone: 360–556–5602
Website: www.yantramountainretreat.org;
www.yantradeck.com

MATT AMSDEN

Author of *RAWvolution: Gourmet Living Cuisine* (Harper Collins 2006), Matt Amsden has established himself as one of the world's premier raw chefs. Matt's company RAWvolution was the first of its kind, delivering prepared raw meals throughout Los Angeles and eventually throughout the entire United States. Matt began eating a diet of exclusively raw foods virtually overnight after hearing an interview with author David Wolfe on the Howard Stern show in 1998. Matt has since opened a raw cafe with his wife in Santa Monica, California, expanded the RAWvolution delivery service to New York City and has shared his talent with thousands including Alicia Silverstone, Cher and Susan Sarandon.

E-mail: rawvolution@yahoo.com
Phone: 1.800.9976.RAW
Web site: www.rawvolution.com

STEPHEN ARLIN

Stephen Arlin became a Raw-Foodist over eight years ago.

"It was hard at first because cooked food is addictive and getting over any addiction is tough," Stephen says. "But it was well worth the effort...I see the world much more clearly now. Every day is a great day."

Since going 100-percent raw, Stephen has shed 51 unwanted, unhealthy pounds and has since then gained back 45 pounds of healthy, solid muscle. Stephen is an expert on natural body-building, and his unique training work-outs and fitness philosophies are outlined in his latest book, *Raw Power!*

"All living organisms on planet Earth are designed to nourish themselves with raw nutrition," Stephen says. "Humans are certainly no exception. A raw-foodist is not something you become; it is something that you already are. Every single natural organism on the planet is born to eat exclusively raw foods. It transcends all diets; it is simply the natural way to nourish your body."

In 1996, Stephen co-founded Nature's First Law along with his partners, David Wolfe and R.C. Dini. As the world's largest distributor of raw food products, books, equipment, and organic foods, Nature's First Law continues to help hundreds of people each year adopt and maintain the living foods diet (www.rawfood.com).

Stephen is co-author of several innovative and controversial books on the raw food lifestyle, including *Nature's First Law: The Raw-Food Diet*, which offers a complete philosophy of natural nutrition.

E-mail: stephen@rawfood.com
Phone: 619-596-7979, 800-205-2350, 888-RAW-FOOD
Web site: http://www.rawfood.com

JACKIE AYALA AND DAVID STEINBERG

David is a gourmet raw food chef with 18-plus years of professional food preparation experience. After studying with professional chefs of Italian, Chinese, Mexican, and American cuisine for over 15 years, and being employed as a pastry chef, sous-chef, bread baker, and chef all over the world, he switched his talents and energies to the field of living food art. He's been living the raw life for 5 years. David feels that it is possible to plug directly into the source and channel the "Living Foods Diva" to achieve easy recipe-free gourmet cuisine.

Jackie has been an avid student of health, nutrition, and cuisine for 15 years. A life of traveling, taking antibiotics, and working as a flight attendant for 10 years compromised her immune system and weakened her kidneys. Knowing it was possible to heal all illness naturally, she came upon the raw food diet and felt better than ever. She has been 100 percent raw for two years. She has spent time with Gabriel Cousens at the Tree of Life Rejuvenation Center kitchen, and learned about raw food preparation under the experienced instruction of Renee Underkoffler (author of *The Raw Truth*).

Together, Jackie and David have created Cosmic Pepper Productions, a unique cutting-edge company dedicated to bringing light into a dark (cooked) world. They are David Wolfe's personal chefs, and have catered many raw events, including the raw party of the century on March 30, 2002. Some of their recipes are featured in David Wolfe's new book, *Eating For Beauty*. Their mission is to bring the finest dimensions of health, passion, excitement, rejuvenation, flavor, stimulation, creativity, originality, and, of course, beauty, to the widest variety of delectable "goodies and treats" ever conceived of on this planet.

Phone: 619-596-7979

ELIZABETH BAKER

Elizabeth Baker, M.A., university professor, novelist, and travel writer, turned to nutrition and alternate therapy when faced with terminal illnesses. Since taking responsibility for her own survival, she has battled the long road back to complete recovery and vibrant health.

Elizabeth attributes her remarkable recovery from four terminal illnesses and many lesser ones to faith and a raw diet, which includes wheat grass juice. In addition to spreading the word about the efficacy of raw foods, she is dedicated to teaching others how they can survive and conquer by adopting a lifestyle that includes all-natural foods and supplements, a positive attitude, regular exercise, sufficient rest and relaxation, and faith.

In addition to years of research, travel, lecturing (with her scientist husband), holding seminars, counseling, and appearing on TV and radio, Elizabeth has authored seven books: *The Gourmet Uncook Book; The Uncook Book, The Un-Diet Book; The UnMedical Book*; the best-selling *UnMedical Miracle—Oxygen* (In an oxygen poor world, it is the book every adult should read); and *Does The Bible Teach Nutrition?* Recently released is her new book *Unbelievably Easy Sprouting*.

Due out in the autumn of 2003 is *Unsuspected Killers: Mercury and Mold.*

Elizabeth Baker is 90 years old. Her hair is its original auburn color, her teeth are her own and she wears glasses only to read fine print. She walks and exercises everyday. She entertains, drives her car, and travels out of country. She credits all the above to her lifestyle. And the most important of that is eating raw foods and smiling instead of frowning.

Email: deana.m.healy@worldnet.att.net

THE BOUTENKO FAMILY

Victoria, Igor, Sergei and Valya Boutenko are 100-percent raw food eaters, chefs, writers, and world-renowned raw food teachers. They are often referred to as the "Raw Family." They have thousands of followers. As a result of their teachings, many raw food communities have been formed throughout the world.

Nine years ago, the Boutenkos were desperately ill with serious diseases, including juvenile diabetes, arrhythmia, asthma, obesity, hyperthyroid, depression, chronic fatigue and arthritis. Conventional medicine did not help them. The family went on a raw food diet on January 21, 1994. By radically changing their diet to 100-percent raw food, they managed to completely heal their bodies and learned to live in happiness. The Boutenkos became famous among those who eat raw food not only because they went on raw diet as a family, but mainly because of their sincerity in communication, compassion and dedication to helping people.

The Boutenkos believe that knowing how to prepare delicious raw food is very important. Complicated and time-consuming recipes simply don't survive. Raw Family recipes have proven to be tasty, quick and inexpensive.

Victoria Boutenko

Victoria Boutenko lives in Ashland, Oregon. She is the award-winning author of *Green For Life, Raw Family, 12 Steps to Raw Foods* and several raw recipe books. She teaches classes on raw food all over the world. As a result of her teachings, many raw food communities have formed in numerous countries. She continues traveling worldwide sharing her gourmet raw cuisine and her inspiring story of change, faith and determination.

Igor Boutenko

Igor doesn't speak much but the few words he shares have a big impact on every audience. Most people know Igor as a silent, hard-working man who single-handedly prepares delicious raw meals for hundreds of people. Igor's flax crackers are everyone's favorite. His live gardenburger on a cracker makes a sandwich "to live for."

Sergei Boutenko

Sergei Boutenko, a raw foodist for 15 years, graduated from Southern Oregon University with a Bachelor of Science in Human Communication. He is the co-author of the books, "Raw Family," "Eating Without Heating," and "Fresh." Sergei holds numerous certificates from different culinary schools. He is a raw food chef, has taught classes all over the world, and has co-produced an award winning movie, "Interview With Sergei Boutenko." Sergei resides in Ashland, Ore., is an avid hiker, biker, runner, and a student of capoeira, a south American dance-fight-game.

Valya Boutenko

A raw foodist for 15 years, graduated from Southern Oregon University with a Bachelor of Arts in Fine Art. Valya is a certified raw food chef who specializes in desserts. She is the co-author of the books, "Raw Family," "Eating Without Heating," and "Fresh." as well as the co-producer of the award winning movie, "Interview With Sergei." She has been researching the ways to inspire children to eat healthier. She practices nonviolent communication and is a student of Byron Katie. Valya enjoys gardening, dancing, sewing, and painting.

LILLIAN BUTLER

Lillian Butler has a knack for creating delicious live meals from traditional recipes. Her Down Home Greens is a classic example of her ability to take a favorite family recipe and turn it into a healthy raw offering, while maintaining its cooked flavor and texture. Her goal is to recreate many of the southern dishes that she grew up with and that hold such fond memories, into tasty raw/living specialties. By instinctively marrying the freshest ingredients from organic farmers with the indigenous flavors of the south, Lillian has created the culinary magic that is Raw Soul. Lillian continues to expand her knowledge in living foods preparation by bringing together many master chefs through workshops, food demonstrations and educational lectures.

Lillian's indoctrination into the Living Foods Lifestyle began in 1999 when she accompanied a friend to the Ann Wigmore Institute in Puerto Rico. Upon returning home, Lillian shared what she learned with her husband, Eddie, and they began slowly incorporating living foods into their lifestyle. After two years, Lillian visited the Optimum Health Institute in California for a "tune up" where she increased her knowledge, understanding, experience and level of commitment.

One day on the way to work at the law firm, Lillian realized it was time to leave that job. She could no longer stomach the "corporate" environment. She didn't know exactly what she was going to do, but knew instinctively that something great was on the horizon. Soon afterward, she visited the Optimum Health Institute in Austin, Texas. It was during this visit that it became evident to Lillian that she must teach others about living foods. She recalls asking herself, "what about all the people who cannot get to the institutions, how do they gain firsthand knowledge about live foods?" Upon her return home, Lillian created The Living Foods Workshop. In June of 2002, with Eddie by her side as chef, Lillian conducted the first Living Foods Workshop, a one-day workshop in which participants learn all about living foods, including sprouting, wheat grass and food preparation, and are served a delicious four course lunch. But Lillian's pride and joy is the workbook that she developed, containing the information discussed in the workshop, recipes, a local resource directory and additional reading on topics not covered in her workshop.

The workshop has grown quickly and has expanded its programming to include a monthly support group, a quarterly open house, food preparation courses and demonstrations, lectures and participation in health fairs and expos. Additionally, Ms. Lillian's Organic Treats can be purchased at many health food stores through New York City.

Phone: 212-875-7112
Website: www.rawsoul.com

KARYN CALABRESE

Karyn Calabrese is one of the most popular and innovative leaders in the holistic health industry, and the owner and founder of KARYN's in Chicago, IL. KARYN's includes a vegan raw-food restaurant where one can find delicious, organic raw food entrees, and a holistic center where clients receive nutritional counseling and other holistic therapies.

Karyn strives to create an all-encompassing environment of food, health, guidance and care where we can all participate in our own well-being. "If you don't take care of your body," Karyn asks, "where are you going to live?"

Karyn has been a guest on numerous radio shows such as "For Your Health Matters." She has been featured on local television news programs as an expert in the holistic health field, and has spoken at the Black Women's Expo. Karyn has made numerous appearances on local and national television broadcasts, including "The Oprah Winfrey Show" and "Bill Campbell's CBS Show."

Karyn has done extensive counseling with clients on a fee basis and for those who could not afford her services, on a charitable basis. Her ageless physical appearance and boundless energy at age 56 directly demonstrate her message of good health. She is a glowing model for men and women who feel the need to change their lifestyles.

Karyn's philosophy is that we can heal ourselves naturally to correct damage done to our bodies from unhealthy environments and poor food choices. Her restaurant and her philosophy have been featured in numerous magazines and newspaper articles.

Karyn is an often sought after guest speaker at events with community clubs, churches, service groups and youth groups. She also enjoys providing delicious raw food samples and events at her restaurant.

Karyn has a son, a daughter and two grandchildren. She has been a student of classical piano for 17 years and studied acting at the Ted Liss School of

Acting and at the Jane Brody School. She currently lives at home with her entrepreneur husband and Bengal tiger cat.

E-mail: karynraw@aol.com
Phone: (312) 255-1590
Website: www.karynraw.com

ROSE LEE CALABRO

Over six years ago, Rose Lee Calabro began a journey that would enable her to achieve things she never thought possible. It started on July 1, 1992, when Rose went to see a nutritionist for a host of health issues that included high cholesterol (239), high blood pressure (154/95), allergies, chronic fatigue, depression, hypoglycemia, hypothyroidism, early signs of cancer in her breasts and lungs, and a severe case of gout.

Rose had endured these health issues for over 20 years, but was not motivated to address them until her father passed away at age 59 from lung cancer and her mother, age 69, died of heart failure. Her mother had also had high blood pressure, high cholesterol, diabetes, and gout.

Rose began seeing a nutritionist every week to learn about vitamins, minerals, healthy food, and the role they play in better health. She began eating a low fat diet and stopped eating red meat. The first thing she noticed was that she began to lose weight, although that had not been her original intention. As the weight came off, she began to feel better about herself and eventually made the commitment to lose all her excess weight. She made two promises to herself at this point: First, that she would never give up; and, second, that she would never regain the weight. Covert Bailey and Rhonda Gates were a big inspiration in Rose's life and furthered her knowledge of weight loss, exercise, and nutrition. The first year of her diet, Rose lost 60 pounds, her blood pressure dropped to normal, and her cholesterol dropped from 239 to 219. Rose struggled for the next few years, sometimes gaining and sometimes losing weight, but she never gave up and continued her search for answers.

Rose eventually became a vegan. Her health continued to improve and her cholesterol dropped to 198. In April 1996, she attended Pam Master's introductory raw food class and then signed up for an eight-week course. Within three weeks her diet consisted of 80-percent raw living foods. She was delighted to find herself once again losing weight—up to three, four and five pounds a week. Rose had finally found an answer to controlling her weight: raw living foods. And the longer she ate living food, the better she felt.

Rose began to change—mind, body and soul. After six months of living food her chronic fatigue was gone, and she lost an additional 55 pounds—a total of 150 pounds of fat.

Rose has been on raw living foods since April 1996, and her body has gone through some dramatic changes. Her cholesterol has dropped to 151, and she no longer has chronic fatigue, allergies, depression, hypoglycemia, hypothyroidism, gout, or cancer.

Raw living foods have given Rose joy and a new purpose for being on the planet. She has experienced a spiritual awakening and closeness to God. Rose lives in Santa Cruz where she publishes and promotes books on living food. She is the author of *Living in the Raw*, and hopes to one day start a retreat facility to teach people how they can heal their bodies and have radiant health.

E-mail: roselee@rawlivingfoods.com
Phone: (877) 557-4711
Web site: www.rawlivingfoods.com

KARIE CLINGO

Karie learned to love the kitchen from her Nana, yet she never really enjoyed preparing foods until she found the Raw Food Diet. Starting in the late 1990's she found like-minded friends at the local Health Food stores around San Diego and when she "found Wolfe, Dini and Arlin in a tree," on the cover of their first book, *Nature's First Law*, she knew she had to meet them, and . . ."the rest is history!" Karie watched, and participated in, the beginnings of the raw food movement and was swept along with it; to retreats at Harbin Hot Springs, Arizona; Maui for *Nature's First Law* second retreat, "where almost everything was simply blended and tasted pretty bland, but we were 'raw!.' . . . We really didn't know how to do a tasty raw food diet yet." But it wasn't until Karie's went to a Chef training in Northern California at Living Light International that her actual raw food preparation greatly improved. When her family moved to Utah she "starved at first," due to the lack of organics and fresh foods in her local grocery stores at the time, but she started training and teaching and meeting wonderful support all around town and "we changed all that!" They got together often for "kitchen fun" at her home where each in attendance would bring a recipe with the ingredients and they would, "Figure out how to make these mysterious raw food recipes in our own kitchens," said Karie. "However, the best part, beyond the delicious meals we created were the lasting friendships we forged." Now Karie, her family, and her community truly benefit with more awareness of living foods in a daily diet. "At any time, we can drop into Agi's Raw Food in Provo and grab a healthy snack, or attend a weekly food lecture somewhere in Utah, buy organics in every grocery store and drive up to Salt Lake City and enjoy a leisurely raw food meal at Sage's Café." Karie suggests for those just starting out, "Start slow, one meal at a time and bring your friends and family along with you, respecting their diet decisions always! If your friends won't come along, make new ones, but keep the old friends and definitely, keep your family! After all, love is what matters in the end."

E-mail: eveskitchen@yahoo.com
Phone: (801) 234-0315
Web site: www.EvesKitchen.com

VERN CURTIS

Vern Curtis has eaten almost 100% raw since 1999 and before that, he was an oval lacto vegetarian for 20 years after being a two-hamburger a day man. Vern's interest in raw foods arose when he wanted to go vegan, but saw too many vegans who looked sickly or undernourished. The answer came when he read *The Essene Gospel of Peace*, in which Jesus said "eat not anything which fire, or frost, or water has destroyed." also, "your bodies become what your foods are, -your spirits become what your thoughts are." Soon after learning about the Essene way, Vern met the Boutenko family and began to collaborate and train with them.

Today's he's particularly enthusiastic about Victoria Boutenko's green smoothies, as described in *Green for Life*. He says: "I had health problems that cleared up with the help of herbs, fasting, cleansing and living the Raw Food lifestyle. When I occasionally eat a burrito or other cooked food nowadays, I almost always regret it. My system is just happier and healthier on 100% raw nutrition." A typical day's menu for Vern will be green smoothies and nibbling from a nut tray during the day, along with snacks of about 4–5 bananas and Vern's raw cookies. At night he will eat a huge bowl of salad with homemade dressing with nuts, flax oil, hemp oil, avocados and whatever else is handy.

Vern has been active in raw food potluck groups wherever he lives, which is currently Salem, Oregon. He's also very interested in the science behind raw food diet and the responsibility of mind.

ELLEN W. CUTLER

Ellen W. Cutler, DC, is a chiropractor who also holds a medical degree and has over 25 years of clinical experience. Dr. Cutler is one of the pioneers of contemporary natural medicine. She is the developer of BioSET®, a method of energy medicine that eliminates allergies and resolves chronic health conditions. She is also an expert in the use of enzyme therapy and has successfully used this approach to treat thousands of patients with chronic illness. Her expertise and clinical successes have established Dr. Cutler's reputation for excellence. Her peers in this emerging field consider her an innovative leader.

Through her books, workshops and presentations, and media appearances, she has become a recognized authority on enzyme therapy and allergy treatment and teaches about these topics worldwide. Dr. Cutler travels extensively, giving professional seminars at least twice a month at conferences and universities across the United States and in Europe.

Dr. Cutler is the author of three books on natural medicine. *The Food Allergy Cure* (Harmony Books, 2001); *MicroMiracles, Discover the Healing Power of Enzymes* (Rodale, 2005); and *Live Free from Asthma and Allergies* (Celestial Arts, 2007).

Dr. Cutler has been featured on CNN, The Discovery Channel, Fox News, Lifetime, Alternative Medicine, QVC, KRON-TV (San Francisco), and MSNBC. She is also a favorite guest on radio shows nationwide. Dr. Cutler appears regularly in publications and many newspapers throughout the US in which there are BioSET® practitioners. There are also dozens of papers, articles, and website references to her work and the BioSET® system on the Web.

Dr. Cutler is the developer and founder of BioSET®, a highly effective system of healing and natural health. BioSET® emphasizes enzyme therapy and acupressure treatment for a wide range of allergy-related conditions, digestive disorders, immune dysfunctions, and many other types of chronic illness. Dr. Cutler is founder of the BioSET® Institute, which supports practitioner training, publishes a newsletter for healthcare professionals, and hosts a premier web site (www.bioset.net.) The BioSET®, system is taught through a series of seminars for healthcare professionals and workshops for consumers.

Web site: www.bioset.net

SHARON ELAM

Sharon was introduced to the raw foods diet four years ago. She had come to feel unbalanced and lethargic, and decided to take steps to improve her health and well-being. Sharon was already an avid reader of health literature, and she set out to educate herself and explore alternative treatments.

One of the first books Sharon read was *Fresh Fruits and Vegetables* by Norman Walker. Next, she read all of the rest of his books, and also picked up *Conscious Eating* by Gabriel Cousens, and *The Kitchen Garden* by Steve Merkowitz. Shortly thereafter, Sharon signed up for a 10-week course on preparing raw foods. She was eager to learn everything she could about the living foods diet.

Sharon has since had a lot of fun in her kitchen creating new recipes and experiencing a new way to preserve and enjoy a continuously healthy lifestyle. She has shown many how gratifying raw foods can be and she regularly prepares complete raw spreads for her close-knit group of friends.

E-mail: Heartspace7@yahoo.com
Phone: 541-482-6097

JOHN FIELDER

John Fielder operates Clohesy River Farm in Australia as a health retreat cum Hygienic Centre. He is the founder of the organic farm, the Academy of Natural Living, and the Natural Health Society of South Australia. He is also a member of the British Register of Naturopaths, the Incorporated Society of Registered Naturopaths in the UK, and the International Association of Hygienic Physicians.

"I have this childhood memory of always wanting to eat the food before it was cooked and being told that I couldn't do so as it would make me ill." John says. Yet, despite the cooked "three veg and meat" diet he was raised on, John suffered constantly from bronchitis and migraine for the first 28 years of his life. He spent more time at home than at school, developed arthritis at 18 and asthma at 28.

As a result of an accident that hurt his back, John came into contact with Chiropractic, and through Chiropractic, Nature Cure, and through Nature Cure, Natural Hygiene. He tried all the other alternatives, supplements, vitamins, and homeopathic remedies, and felt they were not the answer he was looking for.

After working through his twenties as a tour guide, John enrolled at the Naturopathic College of South Australia, studying Naturopathy, Chiropractic, and Osteopathy. Kenneth S. Jaffrey became his first mentor, and introduced John to the teachings of Dr. Shelton of the Edinburgh School of Natural Therapeutics and to Dr. E.B. Szekely of the Rancho La Puerta in Mexico.

John remembers an incident that could have meant his death. When helping a friend to build with timber which had been treated for termites, John became seriously ill from handling the toxic chemicals, and was incapacitated for the next eight months. He used only hygienic methods to nurse himself back to health, and he found them very successful. He treated himself by periodic fasting, eating only raw foods, sunbathing, being outside in the fresh air, bathing in the river, and exercising, as he was able. At one stage, John spent 13 weeks on grapes and when they ran out, four weeks on pears. He was restored to full health.

John has found it easy to maintain a 100-percent raw food diet. He strongly believes that food is best consumed in its whole raw state to achieve fullness of life, health and healing. He is a raw food ovo-lacto-vegetarian--he eat eggs when he feels that he needs to (raw) and raw goats' yogurt twice a week.

E-mail: academy.natural.living@iig.com.au
Phone: +61 07 4053 7786 (Tu Fri, Sat), +61 07 4093 7989 (Mon, Wed, Thu, Sun)
Web site: www.iig.com.au/anl

JACKIE AND GIDEON GRAFF

Jackie and Gideon Graff have been teaching raw food preparation and food science for the last eight years. They owned and operated The Sprout Café, known world over for its varied and delicious raw food. Jackie is a graduate of the University of South Carolina with a B.S. degree in Nursing. She has forty years experience in various areas of patient care and education. Jackie Graff is the author of seventeen theme recipe books, and is a gifted raw chef, considered by many in the raw food movement to be the best in the country. Gideon is a graduate of Haifa Institute of Technology, Israel, in Hospitality Management, and has years of experience in managing resorts and luxury hotels. They work great together as a team in the kitchen and demonstrate how easy, fun and satisfying raw food preparation can be for the whole family. Their DVDs *Nuts About Coconuts* and "*Country Barbecue* each contain about 12 delicious recipes, demonstrated and explained. The DVD-rom feature lets you view and print recipes from your computer. The DVDs are professionally produced with 6 high resolution cameras, studio light, sound, and original music. Scene selection feature lets you jump to the recipes you want to watch.

E-mail: jackie@sproutrawfood.org
Phone: 770 992-9218
Web site: www.sproutrawfood.org

JULIAN HUERTA

Chef Julian has been actively involved in gourmet Living food preparation for three years. He greatly enjoys lifestyles that allow for learning and well being in fun and easy ways. He shares this with people by offering brightness in people's lives, spontaneous classes, theme based gourmet dinners, and a living foods service he started in 2007 called "Green Life." Julian studied music at Bowling Green State University and is a lifelong violinist. Bicycling is his favorite method of local transportation as he likes the physical activity along with the journey it brings. Also, he is very passionate about creating sustainable relationships. Being part of a society that values all peoples needs equally is something he works for daily. He finds hope in realizing this vision, when he does activities that contribute to his well being, as well as the well being of others. "A long journey becomes joyful when each step enables joy, or . . . is enjoyable." That is, he likes to focus on an enjoying every step of the way, while letting the goal change as new information comes to light. Following this, currently Julian finds his self balancing preparing living foods, with designing organizations to sustainably provide need based services.

> Email: Julian@greenlifecafe.net
> Address: 135 Liberty St. SE Salem, OR 97302
> Website: www.greenlifecafe.net

JULIANO

Juliano was raised in Las Vegas in the restaurant world. At a mere eight years of age, he quit school and his training began. Juliano Sr., a third generation master chef to celebrities and Arab royalty, was his teacher, passing down all of his ancestral secrets and international culinary wisdom.

When Juliano turned 15 he was already burnt-out on rich, gourmet foods and became a vegetarian, turning to books to formulate some sort of diet. As the years passed, and the more he read, the smarter and the more raw he became.

On August 27, 1995, Juliano opened Juliano's Living Cuisine, a restaurant in San Francisco. Instantly patrons and press took notice and began to fill the restaurant. Newspapers and magazines exploded in awe, with Juliano on their front covers, and stories about the amazing, new cuisine he conceived. HarperCollins Publishing was next to the feeding frenzy and published *RAW: The UnCook Book*. The hardback, full-color book took roots in a smashing wave, expanding people's minds as they scanned over the perfectly healthy raw, organic, vegan versions modeled after junk food. Never before have pizza, cheese burgers, enchiladas, falafel, breads, cakes, cookies and pies been replicated in such a manner. As Juliano says, "It's the way everyone wants to eat but doesn't realize exists!"

Juliano compares his food to the pyramids of Egypt, indicating that their production created no trash and nothing detrimental to the environment. His RAW cuisine is made from all non-packaged and unprocessed foods that come, not from a factory, but directly from the ground, a tree or a bush.

In the year 2000, Juliano ventured to Hollywood with his unique cuisine in pursuit of educating, entertaining and nourishing everyone through a TV show and new restaurant Juliano's Raw, in Santa Monica.

PEGGY KENNEY

Peggy Kenney a Premier Tropical Fruit Horticulturist and Agricultural consultant. International Plant collection explorations to Honduras, Costa Rica, Ecuador, and Colombia. Developed and managed South Florida's showcase seventy-five acre tropical fruit grove. Peggy conceived, developed and implemented all phases of a seventy-five acre grove from start-up to production to marketing throughout the United States. This tropical fruit grove produced eighteen varieties of Mangos on five acres, six varieties of Lychee on ten acres, four varieties of Longan on ten acres, four varieties of Carambola on fifteen acres, Atemoya, Passion Fruit, Black Sapote, Sapodilla, Jakfruit, Canistel, Loquat, Kumquat, Pomelo, and smaller commercial quantities of Mammae Americana, Wax Jambu, Jaboticaba, Green Sapote, Bilimbi, Spondias, Allspice, Rheedia, Cherry of the Rio Grande, Santol, Tamarind, Persimmon, Illama and others.

After years of globe trotting Peggy decided to settle down. Peggy has always enjoyed cooking and baking. Her mother, Mary Christie Kenney participated in the competitive cooking circuit and won many awards for her original recipes.

With her years in the agricultural field a vegan diet was a natural for Peggy. She has always had her own garden to feast from and plenty of trees to pick the fruits of her labor. One of her most favorite fruits has always been the cacao plant. She has grown the tree and processed the fruit. The tree is beautiful and the fruit is spectacular, its shape and color are amazing. Another favorite tropical fruit is the Chocolate Sapote, a hardy tropical tree of the persimmon family.

A note from Peggy: "The benefits of a healthy chocolate solid nugget or beverage, high in natural antioxidants with blueberries the Açai berry are multifold. As scientific research has discovered, cooking foods takes away most of the nutrients. This is also true for processing cocoa. During the typical processing of the cacao bean the heat will destroy most of its natural nutrients. It was not until Xocai(tm) developed the cold process of cocoa that the complete set of cacao nutrients have been made available to benefit a healthy lifestyle."

Email: Peggy@MakeItBigWithChocolate.com
Phone: 360–446–3060
Website: www.MakeItBigWithChocolate.com

DAVID KLEIN

From the age of 17, Dave Klein's robust health began to gradually decline. A heavy eater of meat and junk food, his physical and mental energies quickly deteriorated over a period of six months, and he was diagnosed with ulcerative colitis. Dave was hospitalized and given medicines. The symptoms subsided, temporarily, but the drugs further ruined his health.

Eight tortuous years ensued with colitis flare-ups and off-and-on drug therapy. At age 26, Dave was reduced to a weak, sickly shadow of his former self, and his nervous system was shattered. Each of the seven gastroenterologists he saw said that diet had nothing to do with the cause of his disease and there was no diet or natural approach that could help anyone overcome ulcerative colitis. Dave was not satisfied with their position.

After an exam confirmed that Dave had advanced ulcerations throughout his colon, his gastroenterologist recommended that he either try an experimental drug that knocks out the immune system, or have his colon surgically removed. Upon hearing this, Dave realized he'd be dead soon if he didn't find an answer himself.

In 1984, Dave found a Doctor of Natural Hygiene, Laurence Galant, who introduced him to the Natural Hygiene concepts of self-healing and eating a raw fruit-based diet. Dave threw away his medicines, divorced himself from all medical intervention for good, and gave up all meat and dairy forever. He adopted a fruit-based diet with which he quickly healed and his energies continuously increased. Soon, he was able to enjoy eating and life again as he began a new healthful lifestyle. He had set himself free of illness, doctors and medicines for good, and eventually attained vibrant robust health.

Dave is now a certified Nutrition Educator and has helped over 1,000 colitis and Crohn's sufferers recover their health. He is the author of *Self Healing Colitis & Crohn's*, and co-author of *Your Natural Diet: Alive Raw Foods* and *Self Healing Power!* He has published *Living Nutrition Magazine* since 1996, and is cofounder of Healthful Living International, a health organization that teaches Natural

Hygiene. He is also a partner in Raw Passion Productions, which holds seminars and Rawstock festivals. Today, at age 45, Dave enjoys excellent youthful health.

E-mail: dave@livingnutrition.com
Phone: (707) 827-3469
Web sites: www.livingnutrition.com; www.colitis-crohns.com; www.healthfullivingintl.org; www.raw-passion.com; www.rawstock.us; www.rawndelish.us

KAREN KNOWLER

Karen Knowler is the Managing Director of The Fresh Network, one of the world's most extensive and comprehensive raw and living foods organization, based in the UK, and author of several publications, including Feel-Good Food: A Guide to Intuitive Eating, Pure & Simple: Raw Food Prep & Menu Planning, and Diary of a Raw Pregnancy. Karen divides her time between running the Network, writing, speaking, networking and consulting, both nationally and internationally, and spending time with her friends and family.

Karen discovered raw food in the spring of 1993, at age 20. Inspired by the powerful changes she felt and saw in herself as she added more fresh foods to her diet, she went looking for as much information on the subject as she could find. Very soon into her search she spotted a tiny ad in *The Vegetarian* magazine for The Fresh Network, which read: Raw Food for Vibrant Health! She joined the network shortly after, and soon became one of its most pro-active members—little did she know that only five years later she'd be running the organization herself!

In the years that followed, Karen was to face many challenges. In April 1984, just a year after adopting a more raw diet, Karen was diagnosed with "severe cervical cell abnormalities" after a routine smear test. She was advised by her doctor to have laser treatment as soon as possible. Knowing that she had to take her condition seriously, yet in the back of her mind aware that there was another way, she decided to take responsibility for her own health and adopted an all raw diet, took wheatgrass juice, and also practiced visualization techniques to see her cells healthy and well again. When she was re-tested some months later her test came back negative—she was completely clear.

Further inspired to teach and spread the word about the benefits of eating naturally, Karen spent every spare moment reading and researching her chosen subject for the next 4 years, until she finally came to maintain a 100-percent raw diet on a permanent basis. At this point she took on the role as co-coordinator for The Fresh Network, and the rest is history.

In the years since, Karen has expanded the Network to offer a higher level of help and support. It provides a massive array of raw resources and events, publishes its own magazine (Get Fresh!) and has a unique membership package, plus Fresh Groups around the UK. "And this is just the start!" says Karen, who clearly is on a mission!

Now in her thirties, Karen is a mother and is looking forward to developing delicious raw meals for her new family as much as she is to introducing the UK to gourmet raw cuisine through all the events and promotion she has planned. She maintains that her philosophy is simple: "If you feed yourself right, you feel much more able to take life on and make the most of it in every way. When people begin to experience raw energy for the first time it can be truly life-changing, like finally someone switched the light back on."

Email: karen@fresh-network.com
Phone: +44 (0) 870 800 7070
Web site: www.fresh-network.com

VIKTORAS KULVINSKAS

Viktoras was born in Lithuania, at the beginning of World War II, and came to the United States in 1950. He received an M.S. Degree in Pure Mathematics from the University of Connecticut, and was a computer consultant for four years for Harvard University, the Massachusetts Institute of Technology, the Smithsonian Astrophysical Observatory, and the Apollo Project.

Just like everyone else, Viktoras consumed large amounts of fast food in his youth—sometimes as many as three McDonalds hamburgers in a day. He ate mostly cooked food, drank, used medication, and consumed up to 20 cups of coffee and 3 packs of cigarettes per day. He ate more than most, did not rest, and was overworked. He did not drink water. He did not exercise.

The combination of all of these factors did extensive damage to his health. By his mid-twenties, Viktoras was suffering from advanced arthritis, edema, insomnia, tumors, hardening of the arteries, hair loss and graying, migraines, systemic pain, hypoglycemia, depression, chronic fatigue, environmental sensitivity, allergies, ulcers, skin disorders, sinus problems and at least 5 colds per year. Viktoras says he feels fortunate to have been this ill, because it forced him to make serious lifestyle changes to improve his health. "I would have been dead long ago," he says "if I did not upgrade my lifestyle choices." His books capture this physical, mental, emotional, and spiritual transformation.

For help, after working with several naturopathic doctors, Viktoras joined Rev. Ann Wigmore of the Rising Sun Christianity, where she was pioneering wheatgrass therapy for individuals with incurable diseases. After several years together, working and conducting research, they decided to join forces and co-founded the Hippocrates Health Institute (www.hippocratesinst.com).

As a self-taught live food nutritionist, Viktoras was the personal health consultant to comedian/activist Dick Gregory during his 900-mile run for peace.

While doing research for his own book at Harvard Medical Library, Viktoras discovered the manuscript of Dr. Edward Howell, MD, *The Status of Food Enzymes in Digestion and Metabolism*. He was granted permission to publish 10,000 copies under the new title, *Food Enzymes for Health and Longevity*, and wrote the new introduction himself. This was the first book to go into print in Enzymology and it laid the foundation for all future popularization of food enzymes and live/raw foods.

Viktoras is the author of five books and has contributed articles to many New Age journals, among them, *Vegetarian Voice*, *Vegetarian Times*, *Vegetarian World*, *Health Street Journal*, *New Life*, *Magical Blend*, *Alternatives* and many others.

He has given seminars for the World Symposium on Humanity in Canada, Australia, the Philippines and Germany, and has lectured well over 10,000 hours at such events as the New Earth Exposition, the Whole Earth Festival, the World Vegetarian Congress, the Cancer Victims and Friends Convention, the National Health Federation Convention, and others.

E-mail: youthing@alltel.net
Phone: 1-870-867-4521
Web sites: www.naturalusa.com/viktor/; www.bluegreenorganics.com/viktoras/
www.youkta.org; www.youthing101.com

JOHN LARSEN

For Master Raw Food Chef John Larsen, the joy of creative food invention began many years ago. At a very young age, John would concoct different combinations of lotions and shampoos in his family's bathroom. Soon, his mother recognized his innate need to prepare and mix, and gave him real food ingredients to experiment with. John began with traditional fare—creative egg dishes, unusual sandwich combinations, and different blends of fruit smoothies.

At the age of six, John tragically lost his father in a car accident. For several years afterwards, he sought to soothe the pain of this loss with sugary and fatty "comfort foods." Both John and his mother gained a lot of weight during this period, which was compounded by the ill feeling that results from consuming large quantities of unwholesome denatured foods.

John changed his pattern of eating at just ten years old, awaking one morning to announce that he was no longer going to eat this way. He wanted to lose weight and be healthier—he was swearing off sugar!

No one thought that this whim would last very long, for how much will power does a ten-year-old have to avoid sugar and fat? A lot, in John's case. Halloween came around, along with holidays and birthdays. John stayed true to his goal, to the astonishment of his family and friends. He went on to become a vegetarian in high school and has remained very health conscious throughout his life. Not surprisingly, John gravitated towards work as a chef after high school.

During his 12-year career as a professional chef, John has cooked in four-star restaurants, catered for private events, and prepared different styles of cuisine up and down the West Coast. The journey to raw foods began while traveling five years ago; John's seat companion turned out to be a raw food enthusiast and chef. After talking for hours about this exciting new style of cuisine, John changed his approach to food, met and became a student of Victoria Boutenko, and later that year, ran the first raw food café in Ashland, Oregon.

John enjoys ethnic foods, especially Mexican cuisine, and has invested a great deal of his energy in creating raw recipes that replicate the cooked ethnic dishes that he and his wife Hamsa love. John is currently a living foods chef for a private household in the Ashland area and continues to cater raw food for festivals and individual customers. Friends and clients are constantly begging John to share his delicious recipes, relished by so many in Ashland's expanding raw food community. This is the first time that a sample of his recipes has been committed to print. John plans to publish an extensive collection of his own in the near future and will be opening a raw food restaurant, Luminescence.

E-mail: threelarsens@charter.net
Phone: 541-488-0931
Web site: www.NewParadigmNutrition.com

JALISSA LETENDRE

Jalissa was born in Puerto Rico, where delicious exotic fruits abound all year long. The traditional Puerto Rican diet consists mainly of rice, beans and chicken with a lot of fried foods and very few raw vegetables. The only raw veggie Jalissa remembers eating as a child is lettuce.

Jalissa had chronic tonsillitis growing up, and received many shots of antibiotics. She became overweight and was often sick. At the age of 18, she moved to Tulsa, Oklahoma, where she learned to eat salads and discovered new vegetables. She also discovered barbecued beef, and ate it even though it made her sick. Her favorite hobby was looking at magazines and books to find and try new recipes.

Jalissa was married in 1999, and moved to Montreal, Canada. Before the wedding, some of her friends asked her, "Are you really going to marry a vegetarian?" She laughed and told them she would try to bring him back to a "normal" diet. Little did she know that she was the one who was going to change.

Jalissa's husband convinced her to start reading books and watching videos about nutrition. She attended a 3 day training workshop with George Malkmus, the founder of Hallelujah Acres, on achieving optimum health through the living foods diet. Jalissa began to realize the importance of nutrition. She stopped eating animal products, and noticed an improvement in her health. Her chronically inflamed tonsils shrunk and she did not get a single cold or flu during her entire first winter in Canada.

Jalissa became interested in vegan cooking. She met the Boutenkos, and, after tasting their dishes, learned how delicious raw food could be. Jalissa started to experiment on her own, preparing raw foods in tasty new ways. Together with her husband, she organized conferences in which he talked about healthy nutrition and she prepared raw meals for each guest to eat. The many positive comments from those who attended these dinners led Jalissa to write her first recipe book, *The Delights of Living Food*, available now in English, French and Spanish. Jalissa continues to encourage people to add living foods to their diet. She hopes we will enjoy her recipes and have a good time around the table.

E-mail: info@jalinis.com
Phone: (514) 898-8273
Web site: www.Jalinis.com

ELAINA LOVE

Elaina Love is a professional raw food chef, instructor, author, and founder and operator of Pure Joy Living Foods.

Elaina has been a presenter at events such as The South Bay Vegetarian Faire, The Portland Raw Foods Festival, Raw World, Nature's First Law's Eden retreats, and many more. She also conducts monthly classes in California and travels nationwide to personally train people in their own kitchens. She has catered raw food retreats, events, and weddings for many recognized leaders in the living food community. She spoke and taught culinary classes at the 2001, 2002, and 2003 Portland Raw Foods Festival.

Elaina and Matt Samuelson co-created the menu at David Wolfe's 2002 book release party and headed the team of chefs to serve the largest raw food fine dining event yet presented. With a total of 300 plates served, the party was regarded as a true accomplishment in the raw culinary arts.

Elaina's recipes have been published internationally. She is a faculty member for the Living Light Culinary Arts Institute where she helps to conduct weeklong raw food trainings for professional chefs and instructors. She is also a mom to Dominic, age 7, and she understands how to teach kids to enjoy healthy, delicious foods.

E-mail: elaina@purejoylivingfoods.com; raw4life@yahoo.com
Phone: (831) 338-1104, (831) 477-0129
Web site: www.purejoylivingfoods.com

RHONDA J. MALKMUS

Rhonda J. Malkmus was born and raised in north central Iowa. During her junior high years she became a Christian and dedicated her life to the Lord. After graduation, she left the farm and lived in various cities in the Mid-West, finally settling in Prairie du Chien, Wisconsin, nestled along the Mississippi River.

In 1981 an event occurred that would change Rhonda's life forever. She was involved in a car/train collision that could have been fatal, and credits God for intervening to protect her and her passenger. Both walked away with no broken bones. The accident left Rhonda with arthritis in every joint in her body, however.

When she met Dr. Malkmus in 1990 she was in constant pain. When he shared the "Hallelujah Diet" with her she decided to try it. After being on the "Hallelujah Diet" a short time, she realized that the pain was beginning to lessen. Within a year she could not only walk a block but a 15-minute mile. She has been on the diet for years now and all her pain from the car accident is a thing of the past.

Dr. George and Rhonda Malkmus initiated Hallelujah Acres in 1992 as a Christian health ministry to help alleviate the suffering they were seeing in the lives of so many people. Their goal is to help lead people back to what they see as God's original diet for mankind. They have brought new hope and health to multitudes with the message, "You do not have to be sick." They have taken this ministry to the world with newsletters, books, and Dr. Malkmus' seminars and radio and television appearances, including the 700 Club. Since 1993, Dr. Malkmus has published *Back to the Garden*, a free newsletter that goes out to more than 100,000 households. His two previous books—*Why Christians Get Sick* and *God's Way to Ultimate Health*—have had an incredible impact. Every day, hundreds of people write or call Hallelujah Acres to say how these books have changed their lives. Now, with *Recipes for Life...from God's Garden*, Rhonda Malkmus has provided the most detailed information yet on how to return to the "God's original diet."

Presently George and Rhonda Malkmus are fulfilling the dream of "Hallelujah Acres" (p. 413) by proclaiming the message "YOU DON'T HAVE TO BE SICK!" to the world. Their books and newsletters are sent around the world. Rhonda Malkmus is also the founder and host of the Annual Women's Retreat held at Hallelujah Acres in Shelby, North Carolina, for women who want to experience a deeper commitment to their diet and their religion.

Email: ministry@hacres.com
Phone: 704-481-1700
Web site: www.hacres.com

ELYSA MARKOWITZ

As an author, gourmet raw food chef, radio and TV hostess, Elysa has a wide spectrum of interests in the health and personal growth arenas. Most recently, Elysa produces and hosts Opening New Doors, an Internet radio program on www.HealthyLife.Net. The spotlight is on authors and other "famous folks" who open the doors of health, healing, and hope. Her vivacious and enthusiastic style is contagious. Her food is divine. Her interviews are perceptive and insightful.

In 1991, Elysa began taping the first West Coast TV program about raw and living food preparation. Episodes of *Elysa's Raw & Wild Food Show* are available in DVD format. On each episode, Elysa and her talented guest chefs teach viewers to prepare a wide variety of raw and living food menus. Elysa's show strives to demystify gourmet raw food preparation, and simplify your kitchen experience. Her goal is to show you how to create live food culinary masterpieces in your own home.

Elysa's experience with raw food began when her mother died of cancer. "I realized that I needed to adapt to a healthier lifestyle in order to avoid the same fate," Elysa says. Elysa's interest and introduction to raw and living foods is detailed in a chapter of her second recipe book, *Warming Up to Living Foods*. She is also the author of *Living With Green Power: A Gourmet Collection of Living Foods* and *Smoothies and More—For the Health of It !*

E-mail: elysatv@earthlink.net
Phone: 760-251-7488
Web site: www.galaxymall.com/health/livingfoods/aboutmarketplace.html

PAUL NISON

Until he was 19 years old, Paul Nison ate the Standard American Diet (SAD). Then he received a wake-up call, and was diagnosed with ulcerative colitis.

For years, Paul endured a long list of painful symptoms. Every time he went to the doctor, he was told to stay away from certain foods temporarily. After a while he would feel better and resume his normal diet. Soon after, he would get sick again.

Paul started to see a pattern. He stopped eating dairy altogether, then eggs, meat and sugar, and told his doctor he felt better without these foods. She told him that food had nothing to do with his condition.

At 23, Paul left his stressful job in the financial district in New York as an office manager for a big Wall Street company, and moved to West Palm Beach, Florida. He was still having colitis flare-ups, but not as often or severe. By seemingly sheer coincidence, he moved near a place called The Hippocrates Health Institute. Paul would visit the institute often during his daily walks around the neighborhood.

At the institute, Paul learned about the raw-food lifestyle and about live foods. He immediately put himself on an 80-percent raw-food diet. It made enormous difference to Paul's health, and he stuck with it—even though his doctor said that raw foods were no good for his condition.

At 25, Paul moved back to New York and resumed working the stressful job he had left. In New York, he met many people who adopted a raw-food diet, and began reading more books on the raw diet and lifestyle. In a bookstore in Manhattan Paul found a book by David Klein called *The Fruits of Healing-A story about a Natural Healing of Ulcerative Colitis*. It was exactly what he needed to read. He then heard David Wolfe of Nature's First Law speaking on a local radio show about the raw-food diet. Soon after, he decided to switch to a 100-percent raw-food diet, and joined a raw-food support group.

The more Paul got involved with the raw-food lifestyle, the more positive his outlook became on life, and his health consistently improved.

Since going 100-percent raw, Paul has completely overcome ulcerative colitis. He feels better than ever and has become increasingly inspired about life. He quit his stressful job and began working as a raw-food chef in a vegetarian restaurant. He organizes raw-food potlucks every month.

Paul is author of *Raw Knowledge, Raw Knowledge II*, and *The Raw Life*. He has been featured on The Food Network and in several magazines and newspapers around the world. He leads a raw food support group in New York City and is featured on a raw food television show every week in New York City. He travels the world giving lectures on the raw life and teaches food prep classes to show people how easy and fun the raw life can be.

E-mail: paul@rawlife.com
Phone: 917 407 2270
website: www.Rawlife.com

PHILIP McCLUSKEY

Philip McCluskey is a 31-year-old entrepreneur, motivational speaker, and author, and is passionate about raw foods! Being overweight his entire life, and after 30 failed diet attempts, he surpassed morbid obesity and skyrocketed to a max weight of 400 lbs. He thought gastric bypass surgery was the only option, and after a month of tests he was ready to have it done when he discovered raw foods. He switched to eating 100% raw vegan overnight and has never been off a day since.

To date he has lost over 200 lbs and is on the fast track to rediscovering his life in a way he never thought was imaginable. Everything in his life has changed including his health, mental clarity, spiritually, job, and a newfound passion for raw food. He decided to share his message through inspirational blogs, videos, pictures, and advice through his website Lovingraw.com. He tours the country speaking about his experiences with overcoming obesity, healthy weight loss, his 100 day juice fast, and breaking patterns of emotional eating. He has also embarked upon writing his first book, which should be available in stores next year.

E-mail: lectures@lovingraw.com
website: www.lovingraw.com

KAREN PARKER

Karen Parker is Master Chef and Culinary Consultant for the Tree of Life Rejuvenation Center in Patagonia, Arizona. Her culinary expertise combines the concepts of elegant and gourmet cuisine with raw and living foods. Because flavor is the true ambassador of any dietary culture, her approach fuses sumptuous flavors and textures with the artistry of nature, stimulating the senses and satisfying the diner's physical and emotional faculties.

Karen's role at Dr. Gabriel Cousens' Tree of Life Rejuvenation Center is to counsel clients one-on-one in regard to live food preparation and the individual's goals. Those goals range from lifestyle implementation issues, including nutritional and healing-related concerns, as well as the demands of one's family, time, and work. Karen's particular focus is to provide personalized instruction so that clients can easily create truly delicious meals that taste even better than their cooked counterparts. She provides this service at the Tree of Life and also travels to clients' homes around the country. She is also available for restaurant and spa menu consultations.

Karen is also the Lead Instructor for the culinary component of the Masters Program in Live Vegan Nutrition, offered through the University of Integrated Learning. Karen is thrilled to be a part of the first Masters program in the world focusing on the live food lifestyle. She facilitates gourmet food preparation classes in the Live Food Chef Apprenticeship Program and in specialty workshops at the Tree of Life.

Before relocating to Arizona and the Tree of Life, Karen offered workshops in live-food nutrition and its preparation in the state of Washington, often in conjunction with yoga retreats. She holds a Bachelor's degree from the University of Nevada, and did her coursework in Environmental Management and in Nutrition and fieldwork in Costa Rica, Panama, and Guatemala.

E-mail: gnoSister@yahoo.com
Web sites: www.sunraw.com; www.quantumraw.com

RHIO

Rhio is a singer, actress and author, as well as an investigative reporter in the area of health. As a performer, she has appeared on over 50 TV shows. Currently she is completing a CD album called *Time to Start Believing Again*, 10 original songs which cover environmental and raw food related themes. Rhio is of Hungarian-Cuban descent and completely fluent in Spanish. CNN and American Journal aired stories on the raw food lifestyle featuring Rhio. She is considered an expert in the area of raw and living foods.

A series of videos is in the works, entitled *What's Not Cookin' in Rhio's Kitchen*, which will demonstrate how to prepare some of the easy, but lesser known raw foods, like yogurts, seed cheeses and ice creams. This series will also include all categories of foods with a special focus on delicious and satisfying main course dishes. The first DVD in the series is set for release in May 2008.

Rhio is a passionate activist against the genetic engineering of seeds/plants, animals and people. She believes that the multinational corporations, and their political allies in the government, that are promoting GE demonstrate a flagrant disregard and disrespect for the integrity of the Natural World. With an estimated 60–70% of foods in the supermarkets contaminated with GMOs that remain untested and unlabeled, the public is being forced to be the guinea pigs in this colossal experiment. Rhio lectures across the country periodically, encouraging people to take grassroots action to get GE food production banned from their communities and at the very least labeled and tested.

As an avid organic gardener, Rhio is currently developing an organic farm in upstate New York. She has incorporated permaculture principles and created a diverse variety of heirloom fruits, berries, nuts, vegetables, herbs, and wild edibles on the property.

Rhio hosts an internet radio show that can be heard all over the world at: www.tribecaradio.net. Rhio also covers national and international information about the raw/live food lifestyle on her extensive website: www.rawfoodinfo.com. She offers a monthly newsletter to people who join her free e-zyne.

Periodically, Rhio hosts living food potluck dinners at her spectacular Tribeca loft in downtown Manhattan. She also offers classes on how to prepare raw and living foods for students in both English and Spanish. Medical doctors, who believe in the benefits of the raw lifestyle, regularly send her their patients to be trained in raw food preparation.

E-mail: Rhotline@aol.com
Phone: (212) 343-1152 (hotline)
Web site: www.rawfoodinfo.com

EDDIE D. ROBINSON

Eddie Robinson was born with the desire to be a chef in his blood. His mom, grandmother, aunt, sisters, brother, and everybody else in his family have had their hands in the food service pot. As the eldest son, Eddie remembers preparing meals for his siblings at the age of 11. For several years Eddie prepared and served evocative vegetarian meals for the Sivananda Yoga Center in New York City that had aspirants waiting in line for seconds. So when his wife, Lillian, needed a chef to prepare meals for her living foods workshops, Eddie was the natural choice. Having been on the living foods path for several years, Eddie had already created many tasty dishes as the family chef. His artistic eye, creativity and natural ability have led him to come into his own as a master raw/living foods chef, turning out sumptuous creations such as "De Lime Pie," and "Spicy Spring Rolls." Living the living foods lifestyle continues to broaden his experience as a living/raw foods chef and teacher.

Phone: 212-875-7112
Website: www.rawsoul.com

JULIE F. RODWELL

Rodwell was born in the UK and raised on a small farm in northern Yorkshire, so she grew up eating healthy home-grown bacon, eggs, cream, potatoes, rabbits and vegetables, including nettles and whole-wheat bread made from local flour purchased by the sack. Sweet foods were a rare treat.

She has lived and worked in North America her entire adult life, carving out a technical analysis and writing career in transportation and public policy. Her expertise includes aviation, commuter and freight rail, bus transit, pipelines and highways. Since 1983 she's been the author of a nationally published college text-book, *Essentials of Aviation Management.* She was the coordinator of the first Environmental Impact Statement for Boston's "Big Dig" in the early 1970s (and disavows all leaks!). Julie is also a founding member of North America's first owner-built "cohousing" community, Winslow Cohousing on Bainbridge Island, Washington where she lived for 7 years. She currently serves as the Washington State Department of Transportation's Coordination Branch Manager, leading a team which assists 24 regional transportation planning organizations around the state to address the many issues which face them.

In her free time, Julie designs one-of-a-kind beaded stone and glass jewelry, partly as a fund-raiser for women in prison. For the past couple of years, she has been assisting Toastmasters International to operate a club inside a women's prison, and the fundraising helps pay their club dues. She believes that helping women prisoners speak well on their own behalf is a lifetime skill that will aid them immeasurably when they re-enter the outside world (as 99 % of them will).

She first got involved in the raw food movement on a whim in 2001 and discovered that a raw diet not only brought about many health improvements but increased her mental and spiritual clarity. She was the lead contributing editor to the first edition of *The Complete Book of Raw Food,* published in 2003 and is the contributing editor of its second, 2008 edition. "Being creative, herding cats and hammering order out of chaos are what I love best," she says. While not a 100%

raw-fooder, Julie says that the farther she gets toward 100%, the more energized and empowered she feels.

She's the proud mother of a beautiful 27-year old daughter, Virginia.

E-mail: Julie.cfd@ccountry.net
Phone: 360-402-8454

RITA ROMANO

Rita Romano has had a unique interest in food as medicine for many years. What started as a hobby has become her life's work. Her creative ability and desire to nurture has resulted in an exciting new genre of life-giving recipes, making her a pioneer in the industry.

Rita's educational background includes a Bachelor of Arts degree from the State University of New York in Stonybrook and post-graduate nutritional studies at Hofstra University in New York. She is also a graduate of Kushi Institute in Massachusetts where she studied nutritional food preparation, oriental medicine, shiatsu massage and visual diagnostic techniques. After co-owning and operating New Horizon Natural Foods Restaurant in Key West, Florida, she went on to serve as the Executive Chef and Food Director at Hippocrates Health Institute in West Palm Beach, Florida.

After West Palm Beach, Rita returned to Key West. She opened Dining in the Raw Creative Kitchen and provided wonderful raw food cuisine for the local community and incoming tourists. A series of classes were presented mornings and the students creations were later marketed to those committed to a raw food lifestyle.

For the past twenty years she has been providing specially prepared meals as well as teaching theory and technique to a wide array of people ranging from those interested in maintaining health to the seriously ill. Her vast knowledge of different vegetarian styles and philosophies has helped her to satisfy just about anyone's palate.

After many years of observing the transformational effect of a healthy diet, Rita has compiled her favorite recipes to share with others that are interested in optimum well-being. She also has an online store at www.rawkitchen.com, which offers raw food cakes to go. As well as providing a complete knowledge of raw food cuisine, Rita also teaches macrobiotic techniques that are easily implemented and provide a variety of choices to fit every lifestyle.

E-mail: realitychef@rawkitchen.com
Phone: 305 294-6644
Web site: www.rawkitchen.com

MARY RYDMAN

Mary Rydman is the author of *Raw and Radiant: Simple Raw Recipes for the Busy Lifestyle* and has been offering raw-food based nutritional consultations since 1995. She is also a certified EBE (Emotional Body Enlightenment) facilitator with a great desire to help individuals and couples live to their potential through emotional as well as physical health. She left her former career as a commuter airline pilot in 1993 to study health and nutrition, and is the co-founder of Original Radiance, which offers a new paradigm for physical health and nutritional healing. She began her own EBE journey in 2001 and discovered the importance of emotional health in reaching a state of vibrant aliveness and passion for life. She offers individual and group EBE facilitation in addition to consultations on live-food based nutrition, and Radiant Life Chi gong classes for those interested in all aspects of well-being and ready for a new level of health and vitality.

For more information please see www.originalradiance.com. She can be reached through e-mail at rydman@gmx.net *Raw and Radiant: Simple Raw Recipes for the Busy Lifestyle* is self-published through Outskirts Press and is available through Amazon.com and Barnesandnoble.com.

JEREMY SAFRON

At the age of 9 Jeremy Safron began his explorations into the world of natural medicine and health beginning with his studies of Chinese kung fu and natural magic. Inspired by his vegetarian mother's work on the gifted and talented program for US school systems Jeremy used his 188 IQ to acquire as much knowledge as possible. His voracious appetite for arcane wisdom led him to study a diverse variety of martial arts, mysticism, alchemy, alternative science, herbology, yoga, and eventually living foods. In 1994 Jeremy lived with Dr. Ann Wigmore at her Puerto Rico institute and immersed himself in his studied of dietary health and the use of food as medicine. He then continued on seeking out raw food educators and martial art masters and apprenticed himself to gain greater experience and knowledge. Jeremy also studied varied forms of diagnosis including Chinese medicine techniques such as pulse analysis and the ancient Egyptian art of Iridology. In 1996, on the Isle of Maui, Jeremy opened the doors of his Raw Experience Restaurant. It was one of the first of its kind and pioneered many of the concepts and dishes that are common in all raw eateries today. Jeremy began teaching classes and published his first book "The Raw Truth" as the world livened up to raw foods. Traveling the globe, spreading the message Jeremy continued to teach living foods lifestyle and consulted for many raw food eateries and businesses. The huge response brought forth the creation of a newsletter "The Living Planet" and 2 more books "Raw Resources" and "The Fasting Handbook." In 1998 Jeremy gathered the top living food educators around for a raw food educational workshop in Maui and helped inspire and influence many of the key people in today's raw food movement. Jeremy has continually teamed up with like-minded individuals for the purpose of elevating consciousness and promoting a sustainable way of healthy living. Jeremy's contributions and inventions, such as: Monkeynut a non violent video game, Powerwraps, Rawmesean and Buckybars living food products, his revolutionary Dragon Yoga DVD which unifies yoga and martial arts, and his fabulous music continue to uplift and influence the world. Currently Jeremy offers custom designed private educational workshops and classes on his farm in Hawaii and consults with corporations and individuals regarding sustainability and eco friendly options for improving health and fitness while maximizing brainpower and productivity.

E-mail: dragon@lovingfoods.com
Phone: 808 878 8091, 310 RAW FOOD (729 3663)
Web site: www.jeremysafron.com

MATT SAMUELSON

Matt Samuelson is one of the leading raw food chefs in the industry. He currently holds the esteemed position of Head Chef and Instructor for Living Light Culinary Arts Institute where he is part of the team that conducts month-long chef and instructor training courses. Matt is also the chef for all Living Light retreats, including Raw World. He has catered retreats and events in Bali, Costa Rica, and Hawaii, as well as in numerous locations throughout the U.S. Matt recently trained the culinary staff at The Farm, the Hippocrates resort in the Philippines.

Matt and Elaina Love co-created the menu for David Wolfe's book release party in 2002. The party was the largest raw food fine dining event yet presented, with a total of 300 plates served. It was regarded as a true accomplishment in the raw culinary arts.

Matt offers services including personalized raw food lifestyle training, gourmet personal chef services, menu development and help with setting up kitchens for major spas and retreat centers. His simple approach makes learning easy and food preparation fun.

E-mail: MattSamuelson@yahoo.com
Phone: (831) 661-2611

CHAD SARNO

Called "the king of uncooked and vegan cuisine, and chef to the stars" by GQ magazine, and "the Michael Jordan of living foods" by actor Woody Harrelson, Chad has been bringing his approach to healthy cuisine to some of the world's premier organic vegan restaurants, spa resorts, film sets, healing centers and individuals for over a decade.

His chef training programs and seminars have attracted an extensive world-wide audience of professional chefs, culinary school students and food connoisseurs. Director and Founder of Vital Creations, LLC, he specializes in restaurant and spa consultation, along with guest chef / presenter at health conferences globally, working with chefs and restaurateurs to increase their creativity and develop delicious and healthy vegan menus. Throughout the years of training, V.I.P catering and consulting, celebs and musicians have enjoyed Chad's culinary services,

Chad grew up in restaurants and with gastronomy being a family passion and was highly influenced by the delicious and comforting home-cooked meals and love for cooking of his mother and paternal Italian grandmother. Being raised in New England with vibrant flavors and abundance of fresh produce from his mother's gardens has made him aware of the 'garden to table' philosophy that he believes strongly in today.

Chad partnered with The LifeCo in mid-2006, an international Lifestyle company based in central Europe, to develop the SAF Cuisine pure vegetarian restaurant concept (Simple Authentic Food); an exciting green gastronomy concept highlighting raw, vegan cuisine and organic wine bars. Currently overseeing his restaurants in Istanbul, Munich, London and soon in Geneva and Dubai, Chad is now based in London.

E-mail: info@rawchef.org
Phone: 1-888-276-7170
Web site: www.rawchef.org

SHANNON ISLEY SCHNIBBE

Shannon first learned about what is now the raw food movement while on her path to lessen her severe sensitivities and asthma. In 1990, she went to a health practitioner who studied with Ann Wigmore, and learned about juicing, organic food, food combining, colonics, etc. She slowly incorporated the ideas into her life. She also started practicing yoga at that time to work on the mind body connection; becoming a certified Integral yoga teacher in 1998.

In 2000, while living in Chicago, she was eating at Karyns' (Fresh Corner) and decided to go all raw. (Karyn's is a fabulous raw restaurant.) After being raw for a while, she stopped taking all her medications and did a green juice fast for four weeks. She doesn't recommend this path to anyone because of the intense detox she experienced. After that she didn't need her inhaler. That was a miracle to her and she realized she was onto something.

A few years later, and inhaler free, she and her husband, Warren, founded Eat in the Raw, had their first baby, and started bottling her creation, Parma! Vegan Parmesan. Parma! is now available all over the country and in Canada. Parma! is Good Karma!

E-mail: shannon@eatintheraw.com
Web site: www.soulsandals.com; www.eatintheraw.com
Phone: 541-665-0348

NOMI SHANNON

Nomi Shannon is the author *The Raw Gourmet* (Book Publishing Co). Published in 1999 and now in its 15th printing, *The Raw Gourmet* has become a raw food classic and a best-seller. With over 250 recipes and filled with full-color food photographs, *The Raw Gourmet* is a complete resource guide to one of the world's fastest growing nutrition and health movements, the raw food lifestyle. Inside you will learn how fresh non-cooked fruits, vegetables, nuts and seeds can boost your vitality without sacrificing flavor.

In *The Raw Gourmet* Nomi tells you everything you need to know about equipment, soaking and sprouting, seasonal buying, food storage, where to find ingredients as well as providing a food glossary and much more. Nomi says, once you have read *The Raw Gourmet* from cover to cover, you will know everything you need to know to have a raw food kitchen! Entering its ninth year, *The Raw Gourmet* is still a top raw food best-seller!

Nomi graduated cum laude from Framingham State College in Massachusetts in 1983 with a degree in psychology and attended the Masters Degree program at Boston University's school of Social work. During those years Nomi realized that the effects of food from a holistic point of view-body and mind-were more of a passion for her than psychological counseling. In 1987 Nomi began her own raw food journey by starting at 50% raw and becoming 100% raw the following year. Now, Nomi maintains a 100% raw regime most of the time, with some cooked food some of the time.

During her years working as Director of the Health Education Program and as a Program Counselor at Hippocrates Health Institute in Florida, Nomi saw profound improvements in people's health when they adopted a raw foods lifestyle. Nomi feels so honored that she has been able to observe first hand many times over the miracles of healing that can occur when a sick person utilizes a 100% raw food cleansing and detoxifying program. She feels that it only stands to reason that a high raw food program in a healthy person will help to avoid illness. Over the years Nomi has proven to herself both personally and by observation of others that the delights of looking and feeling years younger than their actual age, along with being vibrantly healthy, far outweigh any small inconvenience in time and effort to learn how to eat well.

A Certified Hippocrates Health Educator since 1995, Nomi is also Certified as an iridologist by Dr. Bernard Jensen, is a reiki master (non-practicing), and has training and experience in many alternative health modalities including herbal and homeopathic remedies. But the dominant subject that Nomi writes and teaches about is raw food- from therapeutic to gourmet.

Nomi currently resides in Wilmington North Carolina with Rocky the Dog. Nomi has two children and one grandchild.

To learn more about Nomi Shannon, go to rawgourmet.com.

E-mail: nomi@rawgourmet.com
Phone: 888-316-4611
Web site: www.rawgourmet.com

SHAZZIE

Shazzie was born in East Yorkshire, England, on the 23rd of January, 1969. She became a vegetarian at the age of 16, and a vegan two years later. Though Shazzie was the only vegan she knew at the time, she never regretted sticking with this decision. It suited her feelings towards compassionate living, which was well worth the inconvenience.

By the time she was a vegan, Shazzie had already suffered a lifetime of feeling isolated, tired and unhappy, and as an adult this had blossomed into depression, lethargy and brain fog. The physical aches and pains were constant, as was the knowledge that she wasn't living the life she was born to live.

Becoming a raw fooder at the age of 30 was an intrinsic part of Shazzie's journey toward mental, spiritual and physical freedom. For the first time ever, she was loving life and she felt rebuilt in every way. No more crippling period pains, no more bad skin, or backaches, and finally, no more depression. Deciding to allow only positive energy into her body helped her to fulfil her lifelong dream— happiness!

When Shazzie went raw, she documented her journey in great detail at www.shazzie.com/raw/journal/. Then something amazing occurred...Her Web site started getting thousands of hits per week, and she was receiving letters from strangers saying that the information she had shared had changed their lives.

Shazzie.com currently gets over 2,000 hits per day, and is home to a unique set of step-by-step raw food preparation videos, covering a week's worth of breakfast, lunch and dinner meals. You can also check out her detox workshop on video, for anyone who can't get to see her in person.

Shazzie's new book, *Detox Your World* is a unique and holistic guide to living a lighter life. Just like her previous publication, it doesn't say "raw" on the cover, so it continues to secretly bring the raw message to the unsuspecting mainstream!

You can catch Shazzie at the workshops and talks she gives on food preparation, holistic detoxing, and love, life and liberty.

E-mail: shaz@shazzie.com
Phone: +44 (0)8700 113 119
Websites: www.shazzie.com; www.detoxyourworld.com;
www.wholisticraw.com; www.rawcreation.com

DR. JAMETH SHERIDAN

Dr. Jameth Sheridan became interested in health at a very young age. He grew up an avid athlete, and became involved in nutrition's effects on physical performance. He eventually became a whole food Vegan (NOT a junk food Vegan— BIG difference) and watched his health and performance soar. When he discovered raw foods, his health reached a whole new level. Dr. Sheridan approaches raw foods very scientifically, and has done perhaps the only modern research on of its kind on raw foods including leukocytosis and enzyme temperatures. He and his wife Kim wrote the book *Uncooking With Jameth and Kim* in 1991. It introduced many new raw food recipes and recipe concepts that have been widely adopted since. Today he writes, researches and produces healing programs and products through HealthForce Nutritionals (www.healthforce.com) and also conducts on-going research into health excellence, Veganism, raw foods (www.rawfoodresearch.com) and overcoming serious diseases.

Dr. Sheridan has always sought a higher level of health and excellence, and in 1984 his passion for nutrition and health was ignited while participating in competitive athletics. He delved into nutrition and sports nutrition, gave up red meat, hydrogenated oil, white sugar and white flour and moved towards a whole food and plant-based lifestyle. He also started taking many supplements.

He got excellent results, and, after a few years, became a full-fledged Vegan, eating mostly whole foods. He has remained Vegan ever since.

Dr. Sheridan discovered raw foods in 1986 through Natural Hygiene, T.C. Fry, the works of Herbert Shelton and others. He gave up all of his supplements and herbs, as they were merely "toxic suppressive potions and elixirs" according to this philosophy. He began to water-fast, and became as hard core a raw foodist as anyone could imagine. A whole new world of cleansing and healing opened up to him.

Eventually, Dr. Sheridan discovered the works of Viktoras Kulvinskas, began growing and juicing wheat grass and sprouts, and started exploring "supplements" like algaes, superfoods and herbs (all taboo in Natural Hygiene). He also started dehydrating and making recipes. With this new approach to raw food Veganism, his health reached another level.

He and his wife Kim presented "Uncooking With Jameth & Kim" workshops all over the country (including being guest chefs at Hippocrates Health Institute) and eventually co-authored a book of the same name which includes the original Flax Seed Cracker recipes. They then went on to found HealthForce Nutritionals, which provides unique cleansing and healing products and programs.

Since he discovered raw foods in 1986, Dr. Sheridan has conducted extensive research on raw vegan foods and healing. He makes use of Kirlian photography, live blood cell analysis, traditional blood testing, iridology, and energetic measurements. Dr. Sheridan has established www.rawfoodresearch.com to further this on-going research. From his research, Dr. Sheridan has learned new reasons why raw vegan foods are so beneficial, and that many long held notions about raw foods were incorrect. Some of his findings include the following:

There is an immense difference between isolated or synthetic vitamins and minerals and what Dr. Sheridan has termed "Bio-Compatible Nutritional Superfoods™" This realization led him to create many natural superfood and herbal formulas to greatly enhance cleansing, healing, and regeneration.

Superfood/juice/herbal healing programs are far more effective at cleansing and healing and much easier on the body than water fasting.

Animal products are even more harmful than Dr. Sheridan had previously thought.

Dr. Sheridan's research has also proven to him, over and over again, that if you want to achieve the highest level of health possible (in addition to being a whole foods Vegan), you simply must include a large percentage of high water content raw foods in your diet.

Phone: 800-357-2717
Web sites: www.HealthForce.com; www.RawFoodResearch.com;
www.JamethSheridanND.com

KIM SHERIDAN, N.D

Kim's interest in nutrition was originally spurred by some health and nutrition courses she took during her first year in college. Initially, she took these courses out of personal interest and never intended to turn health into a career, but the more she learned, the more passionate she became about all things health-related. So she majored in both Health Education and Nutrition.

In the mid-1980s, Kim received some literature in the mail from the late T.C. Fry. Although she already instinctively felt drawn to fresh fruits and vegetables (and had decided to go vegan for ethical reasons), the Natural Hygiene literature from T.C. was her official introduction to raw foods. Kim was instantly hooked. She went on to study extensively under T.C. Fry at his retreat in Texas. She read everything she could get her hands on about raw foods and joined the original raw food support group in San Diego.

In 1990, Kim met her future husband, Jameth, at a Natural Hygiene conference on the east coast. She flew cross-country to attend that conference because she somehow knew that the man she would marry would be there. And he was.

The very first thing Kim and Jameth learned about each other was that they had both gone 100-percent raw the same day, long before they met. Kim and Jameth soon discovered that their life paths had been amazingly similar. Their connection was immediate, and they've been together ever since.

Kim and Jameth's very first date was spent experimenting with different dehydrator recipes, and their very first creation was the original Flax Cracker recipe (page 166). Kim and Jameth both went on to earn degrees in Naturopathy as well as certification in myriad health and healing modalities. They gave regular raw food classes, lectures, dinners, and workshops; catered their own 100-percent raw wedding; jointly authored a recipe/nutrition book (*Uncooking with Jameth and Kim*); started a private practice; conducted and compiled research on multiple aspects of health and nutrition; and founded HealthForce Nutritionals to help people lead happier, healthier lives.

After many years, Kim has changed career paths and is still happily married to Jameth. Her time is now dedicated to many other projects, including her new book, *Animals and the Afterlife*. (Visit www.animalsandtheafterlife.com or www.animalove.com for more information.) Kim is also heavily involved in animal rescue, and maintains a wealth of resources and information on healthy diets and longevity for animals at www.veganpets.com.

Web sites: www.Animalove.com; www.AnimalsAndTheAfterlife.com; www.HealthForce.com; www.VeganPets.com

CHERIE SORIA

Raw food revolutionary Cherie Soria is the founder and director of Living Light Culinary Arts Institute. She has been teaching gourmet raw vegan cuisine to individuals, chefs, and instructors for well over 15 years and vegetarian culinary arts for more than 35 years. Cherie is also the author of several books, including *Angel Foods: Healthy* Recipes for Heavenly Bodies, and the soon-to-be-released *Raw Food Diet Revolution: Feast, Lose Weight, Gain* Energy, Feel Younger!

Cherie began her love affair with food at the age of 12, when she won her first cooking contest, and went on to become one of the world's leading gourmet vegetarian chefs. She is highly regarded in the international vegetarian community.

In 1992, while studying with Dr. Ann Wigmore in Puerto Rico, Cherie learned the principles of using whole live foods to aid in healing and rejuvenation. She recognized the need to make these simple foods as nurturing to the soul as they are nourishing to the body, so she began creating a gourmet cuisine that would rival the most delicious traditional cooked foods. Since then, Cherie has personally trained many of the world's top raw food chefs and instructors and is often referred to as the mother of gourmet raw vegan cuisine.

At the age of 60, Cherie was awarded her third black belt in the art of karate, one of her many interests. She is as trim as she was in high school, and is a beautiful example of the health benefits of a raw vegan diet.

Cherie is available for speaking engagements and culinary presentations and is a veteran of radio and television.

E-mail: cherie@rawfoodchef.com
Phone: (707) 964-2420, (800) 816-2319
Web sites: www.RawFoodChef.com; www.RawWorld.org

ROBERT YAROSH AND LISA SOTO

Robert has apprenticed for over ten years on Optimal Health and Nutrition with world renowned scientists Dr. Dan West and David Jubb, PhD. He has lectured and performed classes in cities from coast to coast.

Lisa has been Top Chef at the Grange Gourmet Catering Service and Cafe for 7 years. She has performed jobs at such highly prestigious venues as the State House in Boston, the Cranes Castle, Hammond Castle, and the Annisquam Yacht Club on the North shore.

Robert and Lisa helped to open the Organic Garden Restaurant in Beverly, Massachusetts, as well as the Cilantro restaurant on 3rd Avenue in Chula Vista,

California, and offer a training package recognized and implemented by the most progressive and advanced Healing Retreats.

Conscious Cuisine is dedicated to providing a completely healthy and totally delicious dining experience. Robert and Lisa use only organic living foods to prepare their cuisine, and serve those who know and appreciate the best. Their Life Force Cuisine continues to enhance the healing and enjoyment of those on retreats and strives to promote a healthier lifestyle for people and the environment, via that which we consume with our mouths.

Robert and Lisa are currently living in San Diego and have just started a new company, Exotica Gourmet (www.exoticagourmet.com). They offer a complete operation manual for living foods restaurants and are looking to open many more.

E-mail: lifeforcefoods@yahoo.com; robert@lifeforcefoods.com; lisa@lifeforcefoods.com
Phone: 1-800-384-6076
Web site: www.lifeforcefoods.com; www.exoticagourmet.com

JINJEE AND STORM TALIFERO AND FAMILY

Storm has been eating a raw-vegan diet of fruits, vegetables, nuts and seeds in their natural unheated state for over 30 years and has become known amongst raw-vegans for his body builder's physique. At 58 he appears decades younger. Jinjee first started eating a raw food diet 13 years ago. Her before and after pictures show her radical weight loss transformation. Now, their whole family is 100% raw-vegan (with no supplements or dehydrated foods) and thriving! Visit their website to see family photos and stories of how we found the raw diet, photo journals of the children growing up as raw vegans over the years, articles about raw vegan nutrition from a scientific standpoint, and video clips of raw vegan cuisine being prepared. The Talifero's also sell their 12 raw vegan ebooks, which share their simple and nutritious recipes and raw lifestyle tips, on their website. In addition, they have created a movie about our family and the raw food diet on DVD!

E-mail: info@thegardendiet.com
Phone: 804-458-4442
Web sites: www.TheGardenDiet.com; www.TakeAFruitBreak.com

JONATHAN WEBER

Several years ago, Jonathan Weber realized that his life was out of balance. He lacked passion and felt like he was keeping the brakes on in many areas of his life. He was afraid to live as he should—with vitality and courage.

Jonathan knew what he was looking for. He wanted to discover his passions and live with authenticity and integrity. He needed to feel vital and strong and conscious that he was living as he was born to live.

Two months later, Jonathan found himself in a class on raw foods with Victoria Boutenko and her family. He was curious and intrigued, but it was not until the third class that light bulb of awareness went on within him. This was what he had been seeking. Jonathan resolved to go raw and discontinued eating all cooked foods that evening.

Living in a country studio home in southern Oregon, Jonathan has been thriving on a fully raw/living foods diet for four years. He now feels fully connected to his life, and he shares his knowledge, skills, and inspiration with others on a regular basis. Jonathan is a loving father, and an avid hiker and backpacker. He also enjoys bicycle riding, swimming, running and sleeping outdoors under the stars. He is a residential remodeling contractor and finish carpenter and enjoys creating rugs, clothing and wall art as a skilled handloom weaver. At 51, Jonathan feels himself to be getting younger rather than older, living life with more passion, vitality and clarity than he has known before.

Email: jw@mind.net

DAVID WOLFE

Considered by peers to be the world's leading authority on raw food nutrition, David Wolfe is one of the most sought-after success and health speakers in the world today. In his books, seminars, and at his retreats, David shows you how to successfully use raw plant foods, right lifestyle, and positive thinking to become healthy and to achieve your full potential.

Whether you choose to be a vegetarian or a vegan or simply wish to succeed with another organic diet, David's message will help you to live with more abundance and enjoyment.

David is the middle son of two medical doctors. His father has over 35 years experience as an osteopath and MD. His mother is an anesthesiologist.

At age 14, David became inspired by motivational and inspirational literature. At age 18, he read the book *Fit For Life* and adopted its plant-based diet lifestyle. In 1995, David adopted a 100-percent raw-food vegetarian diet.

Through years of experimentation, research, nutritional counseling, seminar speaking, and communicating with thousands of individuals experimenting with raw-food vegetarian lifestyles, he eventually developed "The Sunfood Diet Success System."

In 1995, along with Stephen Arlin and R.C. Dini, David founded Nature's First Law Inc., the world's largest distributor of books, booklets, juicers, audio/videotapes, and bulk organic foods to assist people in adopting, maintaining, and enjoying raw plant-food-based lifestyles. Along with his partners in health, Mr. Wolfe co-authored the book: *Nature's First Law: The Raw-Food Diet* in 1996, which attracted world-wide notoriety, as has its follow-up volume, *The Sunfood Diet Success System.*

David has degrees in Mechanical and Environmental Engineering and Political Science. He has studied at many institutions including Oxford University. He concluded his formal education with a law degree from the University of San Diego.

David also operates healing and detoxification retreats in various locations around the world, including the historic Eden Hot Springs Ranch in Arizona.

Currently, David travels and conducts success seminars and lectures world-wide. He appears regularly on radio and television shows around the world, including Howard Stern (twice) and Roseanne, and is a favorite guest on the Big Boy program on POWER 106 FM, Los Angeles' #1 morning show. He is also the author of *Eating for Beauty* and has been interviewed or mentioned in *Cosmopolitan, Vogue, Jane, Vegetarian Times, USA Today, Men's Health*, and *Woman's Day.*

ABEBA WRIGHT

Abeba Wright has been a Raw Foodist since January, 2000. It hasn't always been easy, but she is committed to this lifestyle.

Abeba became a Raw Foodist on an accidental, half-planned trip to the Optimum Health Institute. She had been told about Optimum three years prior, but didn't want to be around sick, lethargic people. That was what she had envisioned Optimum to be about, so she was surprised when the people there looked just like her and were all on a quest for good health.

Abeba was looking for a much-needed rest and a good detox program. Her blood pressure was beginning to elevate and she did not want to take medication. After being at Optimum for two weeks, Abeba's blood pressure stabilized and is still around 120 over 80, sometimes 85. She lost weight, gained energy, and felt just great.

Abeba continued eating raw food. She took classes from Victoria Boutenko to learn how to prepare gourmet raw dishes, and was hooked after Victoria shared her experience with this lifestyle. Abeba felt inspired to experiment more with living food, and started conducting classes for anyone who wanted to incorporate raw foods into their diet. She does not advocate that everyone become a raw foodist, because the lifestyle has its challenges. But she does advocate having at least one raw food meal a day.

One of Abeba's favorite foods is crackers. Raw foodists as well as cooked foodists rave about her crackers. So many people asked about her cracker recipes that she ultimately decided to write a booklet about the secret to a good cracker. The book is entitled *Absolutely Abeba's Krazy Krackers.*

"I consider it to be a privilege to be part of this book to share some of my favorite recipes with you," Abeba says. "May God bless you and keep you in good health."

E-mail: AbsolutelyAbeba@aol.com
Phone: (510) 351-3157, (510) 632-3591

AMY YOCKEL

Amy first got into raw foods three years ago, when she was training for a triathlon and wanted to improve her stamina. At the time, she was on a protein based diet and eating a lot of SAD food.

One day, Amy met a Natural Hygienist named Arthur Andrews and asked him what he thought was a good diet for athletes. He told her to eat only fresh, whole fruits and vegetables, nuts and seeds. "I thought he was crazy!" Amy says. "How would I get my protein? How was I going to run triathlon on just that?" she thought.

Arthur gave Amy two books to read, *Superior Nutrition* and *Fasting Can Save Your Life* by Herbert Shelton and her life has never been the same since. Amy was very skeptical in the beginning, but as she began reading and educating herself, her fear and skepticism went away. She went from eating a SAD American diet to a 100-percent raw food diet overnight—something she does not recommend to people. "Be gentle with yourself," Amy says. "Going raw should be taken in steps, because when you initially start incorporating raw foods into your diet, lots of changes start to occur. Raw food is very healing, and it will bring out the stored toxins in your body whether you like it or not."

Once Amy understood what detox was, she was prepared to handle the weird feelings she was having. She kept eating raw foods and began to feel great. She ate only raw, fresh, whole, ripe vegetables, nuts and seeds.

Today she feels stronger and healthier than ever. She follows a raw food lifestyle, which is more than simply food.

E-mail: amyockel@earthlink.net
Phone: 1-877-RAW-CHOC
Web site: www.rawgoddesschocolate.com

SERVICES & SUPPLIES

Below is a listing of raw food distributors, equipment and supply manufacturers, growers, magazines, restaurants, workshops, classes and retreats being offered in your area.

These listings were current at press time, but you may want to check to make sure that a company is still in business and in the same location before heading there.

Please also remember to check out the various ads from our chefs and corporate contributors in the Resources section. Many of them offer products and services to help you make the most of your experience with living foods.

DISTRIBUTORS

Arizona

Livingright.com
Open Chute, Inc.
5221 W. Montebello Dr.
Suite B-15
Glendale, AZ 85301
(800) 259-3015
www.livingright.com
Blenders, juicers, dehydrators, grain mills, and sprouters.

New Harvest Organics
P.O. Box 148
Patagonia, AZ 85624
www.newharvestorganics.com
philip@newharvestorganics.com
Organic produce.

California

A listing here does not reflect any partiality on the part of the raw food community, nor does it constitute an endorsement by Healthy Living Books or Hatherleigh Press.

Bariani Olive Oil
301 11th St.
Suite 3A
San Francisco, CA 94103
www.barianioliveoil.com
emanuele@barianioliveoil.com
Cold-pressed olive oil.

Deer Garden/Rejuvenative Foods
P.O. Box 8464
Santa Cruz, CA 95060
www.rejuvenative.com
Raw cultured vegetables and nut and
seed butters.
www.rejuvenative.com

Diamond Organics
P.O. Box 2159
Freedom, CA 95019
www.diamondorganics.com
info@diamondorganics.com
Organic produce.

Gold Mine Natural Food Co.
7805 Arjons Drive
San Diego, CA 92126
www.goldminenaturalfood.com
sales@goldminenaturalfood.com
Source for nama shoyu and other macrobiotic products.

Govinda's
2651 Ariane Drive
San Diego, CA 92117
www.govinda-foods.com
info@govindabars.com
Raw snack foods.

Guayaki Sustainable Rainforest
Products
P.O. Box 14730
San Luis Obispo, CA 93406
www.guayaki.com
info@guayaki.com
Yerba mate, energizing tea.

HealthForce Nutritionals
1835A S. Centre City
Pkwy. #411
Escondido, CA 92025
(760) 747-8822
www.healthforce.com
Juicers and dehydrators.

Jaffe Brothers, Inc.
28560 Lilac Rd.
Valley Center, CA 92082
www.organicfruitsandnuts.com
JB54@worldnet.att.net
Dried fruits and vegetables, nuts,
seeds, and grains.

The Living and Raw Foods
Marketplace
6366 Commerce Blvd. #200
Rohnert Park, CA 94928
www.discountjuicers.com
sales@discountjuicers.com
Juicers, sprouters, dehydrators, and
blenders.

Living Tree Community
P.O. Box 10082
Berkeley, CA 94709
www.livingtreecommunity.com
info@livingtreecommunity.com
Raw nut butters and dried fruits.

Nature's First Law
P.O. Box 900202
San Diego, CA 92190
(619) 596-7979
www.rawfood.com
nature@rawfood.com
Equipment and ingredients.

Nutiva
P.O. Box 1716
Sebastopol, CA 95473
www.nutiva.com
info@nutiva.com
Hemp seeds and oil.

The Raw World
11862 Balboa Rd.
PMB #143
Granada Hills, CA 91344
www.therawworld.com
Equipment and ingredients.

Colorado
Nature's High Unique Foods
P.O. Box 19495
Boulder, CO 80308
www.natureshighuniquefoods.com
Prepared food made from raw ingredients.

Florida
Yahweh's Alive and Well
2127 Oak St.
Bunnell, FL 32110
www.yahwehsaliveandwell.com
info@yahwehsaliveandwell.com
Seeds, grains, dried fruits, sea vegetables, and nuts.

Hawaii
Island Organics
P.O. Box 1100
Honoka'a, HI 96727
www.islandorganics.com
info@islandorganics.com
Dried fruits, nuts, and nut butters.

Iowa
Frontier Natural Brands
3021 78th St.
Norway, IA 52318
www.frontiercoop.com
customercare@frontiercoop.com
Herbs, spices, essences, and sprouting seeds.

Massachusetts
Blessed Herbs
109 Barre Plains Rd.
Oakham, MA 01068
www.blessedherbs.com
blessedherbs@blessedherbs.com
High quality dried organic herbs.

South River Miso
888 Shelburne Falls Rd.
Conway, MA 01341
www.southrivemiso.com
mail@southrivermiso.com
Miso and miso products.

Maine
Pinetree Garden Seeds
P.O. Box 300
New Gloucester, ME 04260
www.superseeds.com
supersedes@superseeds.com
Sprouting and other seeds.

Michigan

Earthy Delights
1161 E. Clark Rd.
Suite 260
DeWitt, MI 48820
www.earthy.com
info@earthy.com
Truffle and other oils, whole truffles, and dried mushrooms.

Eden Foods
701 Tecumseh Rd.
Clinton, MI 49236
www.edenfoods.com
Organic foods.

North Carolina

The Grain & Salt Society
273 Fairway Drive
Asheville, NC 28805
www.celtic-seasalt.com
topsalt@aol.com
Salt, oils, nut and fruit butters, sea vegetables, fermented foods.

New Mexico

Seeds of Change
P.O. Box 15700
Santa Fe, NM 87506
www.seedsofchange.com
Organic seeds and foods.

New York

Didi's Baking For Health
511 E. 80th St.
New York, NY 10021
www.bakingforhealth.com
snacks@bakingforheath.com
Raw snack foods.

High Vibe Health and Healing

85 E. 3rd St.
Back courtyard
New York, NY 10003
www.highvibe.com
info@highvibe.com
Raw food ingredients.

Jubb's Longevity Live Food Store, Organic Juice Bar and Patisserie
508 E. 12th St.
New York, NY 10009
(212) 353-5000
Raw food ingredients.

Live Live
261 E. 10th St.
New York, NY 10009
(212) 505-5504
live.live@verizon.net
Raw friendly products and supplements.

Oregon

Rawganique
4715 SW Nash Ave.
Corvallis, OR 97333
www.rawganique.com
info@rawganique.com
Hemp products and maca, some equipment.

The Essential Oil Company
8225 SE 7th Ave.
Portland, OR 97202
www.essentialoils.com
office@essentialoils.com
Lots of oils, including hand pressed coconut oil.

Pennsylvania
Organic Provisions
P.O. Box 756
Richboro, PA 18954
www.orgfood.com
info@orgfood.com
Beans, seeds, and dried fruits.

Utah
True Foods Market
189 W. 635 South
Orem, UT 84058
www.truefoodsmarket.com
support@truefoodsmarket.com
Dried fruits, nuts, seeds and grains,
sprouting supplies, and juicers.

Washington
Barlean's Organic Oils, L.L.C.
4936 Lake Terrell Rd.
Ferndale, WA 98248
www.barleans.com
allen@barleans.com
Ground flax seeds and flax oil.

Flora, Inc.
P.O. Box 73
805 E. Badger Rd.
Lynden, WA 98264
www.florahealth.com
Fresh pressed oils.

Canada
Evergreen Juices, Inc.
P.O. Box 1
Don Mills, Ontario M3C 2RB
www.evergreenjuices.com
info@evergreenjuices.com
Wheatgrass juice.

Omega Nutrition
1695 Franklin St.
Vancouver, BC V5L 1P5
www.omegaflo.com
info@omeganutrition.com
High quality specialty oils.

MANUFACTURERS

California
Excalibur Dehydrators
6083 Power Inn Rd.
Sacramento, CA 95824
(800) 875-4254
www.excaliburdehydrator.com
Food dehydrators of all sizes, Teflex
sheets.

Green Star
14109 Pontlavoy Ave.
Santa Fe Springs, CA 90670
(888) 254-7336
www.greenpower.com
service@greenpower.com
Green Power twin gear juicers.

Plastaket Manufacturing Company, Inc.
6220 East Highway 12
Lodi, CA 95240
(209) 369-2154
www.championjuicer.com
sales@championjuicer.com
Makers of Champion juicers.

Tribest Corporation
P.O. Box 4089
Cerritos, CA 90703
(888) 618-2078
www.freshlifesprouter.com
service@freshlifesprouter.com
Makers of Freshlife automatic
sprouters.

New Jersey
Cuisinart
150 Milford Rd.
East Windsor, NJ 08520
(800) 726-0190
www.cuisinart.com
Cuisinart food processors.

Ohio
Vita-Mix
Household Division
3615 Usher Rd.
Cleveland, OH 44138
(800) 848-2649
www.vitamix.com
household@vitaxmix.com
High speed, heavy duty blenders.

Utah
Blendtec
1206 S. 1680 West
Orem, UT 84058
(800) 253-6383
www.blendtec.com
High-speed digital blenders.

GROWERS
UNITED STATES

Arizona
The San Pedro Mesquite Company
5840 N. Cascabel Rd.
Benson, AZ 85602
www.spmesquite.com
info@spmesquite.com
Mesquite flour from the southwest.

California
Adams Olive Ranch
19401 Road 220
Strathmore, CA 93267
adamsolives@ocs.net
Olives, olive oil, and pickled vegetables.

Anderson Almonds
6401 Hultberg Rd.
Hilmar, CA 95234
www.andersonalmonds.com
info@andersonalmonds.com
Almonds.

Big Tree Organic Farms
PMB 102
Turlock, CA 95324
www.bigtreeorganic.com
info@bigtreeorganic.com
Organic almonds.

The Date People
P.O. Box 808
Niland, CA 92257
(760) 359-3211
Organic dates. Exotic varieties are
available.

Dave's Organic Produce
35151 Marks Rd.
Barstow, CA 92311
www.davesorganics.com
davesorganics@bigfoot.com
Organic produce.

Exotica Rare Fruit Nursery
Nursery Location:
2508-B East Vista Way
Vista, CA 92085
Mailing Address:
P.O. Box 160
Vista, CA 92085
(760) 724-9093
Exotic fruit trees and unique edible
plants.

New Natives Farm
P.O. Box 1413
Freedom, CA 95019
(831) 728-4136
www.newnatives.com
Sprout seeds.

Mendocino Sea Vegetable Company
P.O. Box 1265
Mendocino, CA 95460
www.seaweed.net
info@seaweed.net
Huge variety of sea vegetables.

Sun Organic Farms
P.O. Box 2429
Valley Center, CA 92082
www.sunorganic.com
customerservice@sunorganic.com
Raw nuts and seeds and other bulk
products.

Florida
Starr Organic Produce, Inc.
P.O. Box 441745
Ft. Lauderdale, FL 33355
www.starrorganic.com
starrorg@bellsouth.net
Organic citrus and tropical fruits.

Georgia
Green Pastures Wheatgrass
1035 Ind Park Dr. #104
Buford, GA 30518
www.greenpastureswheatgrass.com
Wheatgrass, sunflower greens, and
seeds.

Maine
Maine Coast Sea Vegetables
3 Georges Pond Rd.
Franklin, ME 04634
www.seaveg.com
info@seaveg.com
Sea vegetables.

Maine Seaweed Company
P.O. Box 57
Steuben, ME 04680
(207) 546-2875
Sun and wind dried sea vegetables.

Massachusetts
Sproutman
P.O. Box 1100
Great Barrington, MA 01230
www.sproutman.com
sproutman@sproutman.com
Sprouts and sprouting seeds.

Vermont

Gourmet Greens
198 Dodge Rd.
Chester, VT 05143
www.gourmetgreens.com
greens@gourmetgreens.com
Wheatgrass and soil grown greens.

Wisconsin

The Sproutpeople
311 S. Main St.
Viroqua, WI 54665
www.sproutpeople.com
help@sproutpeople.com
Sprouts and seeds for sprouts, grasses,
and greens.

CANADA

Manitoba Harvest Hemp Foods & Oils
c/o Fresh Hemp Foods Ltd.
#15-2166 Notre Dame Ave.
Winnipeg, Manitoba R3H 0K2
www.manitobaharvest.com
Hemp seeds and oils.

Super Sprouts, Inc.
720 Bathurst St.
Toronto, Ontario M5S 2R4
www.supersprouts.com
store@supersprouts.com
Sprouts and sprouting seeds.

WORKSHOPS/CLASSES/RETREATS

Arizona

Tree of Life Rejuvenation Center
P.O. Box 1080
Patagonia, AZ 85624
www.treeoflife.nu
healing@treeoflife.nu
Retreat and raw food chef certification
program.

Arkansas

L.O.V.I.N.G. (Longevity from Organic
Vegetarian Enzymatic
Indigenous/Indoor Nutraceutical
Garden)
P.O. Box 2853
Hot Springs, AR 71913
(800) WHEAT-GRASS
A resort and school that promotes
micro-agriculture and live food prepa-
ration.

California

Healing for Bliss
P.O. Box 417
Ojai, CA 93024
www.healingforbliss.com
info@healingforbliss.com
Raw food lifestyle coaching and food
preparation classes.

Living Light Culinary Arts Institute
704 N. Harrison
Fort Bragg, CA 95437
www.rawfoodchef.com
info@rawfoodchef.com
Retreat and raw food chef training
program.

Optimum Health Institute of San Diego
6970 Central Ave.
Lemon Grove, CA 91945
www.optimumhealth.org
(619) 464-3346
Offers a comprehensive program covering many aspects of health maintenance and recovery, including raw food preparation classes.

Florida
Hippocrates Health Institute
1443 Palmdale Court
West Palm Beach, FL
(561) 471-8876
Spa and alternative health education institute that teaches the entire raw foods lifestyle.

Kwantamani Private Organic Gardens and Spiritual Retreat
P.O. Box 706
Chipley, FL 32428
www.livefoodsunchild.com
kwantamani@hotmail.com
Retreat that promotes consumption of raw foods as the first step to a holistic way of life.

Georgia
The Living Foods Institute
1530 Dekalb Ave., NE, Suite E
Atlanta, GA 30307
(404) 524-4488
Living foods center that teaches the essentials of a raw food lifestyle.

Shinui Living-Foods Retreat & Learning Center
1085 Lake Charles Dr.
Roswell, GA 30075
(770) 992-9218
Offers living-foods lifestyle training and classes, food demos, and catering.

Michigan
The Assembly of Yahweh Wellness Center
7881 Columbia Highway
Easton Rapids, MI 48827
(517) 663-1637
Raw and living foods retreat located on 20 acres of lush farmland just south of Lansing, MI.

Creative Health Institute
918 Union City Rd.
Union City, MI 49094
(517) 278-6260
A healing center that offers 1-3 week cleansing and detoxification programs using wheatgrass and raw foods.

New Mexico
Ann Wigmore Foundation
P.O. Box 399
San Sidel, NM 87049
(505) 552-0595
A retreat that follows the teachings of the late Ann Wigmore, a founder of the raw food movement.

New York

Didi's Baking For Health
511 E. 80th St.
New York, NY 10021
www.bakingforhealth.com
snacks@bakingforheath.com
Raw food preparation classes.

Felicia's Heart: Light, Live Soul Food
Brooklyn, NY
(718) 469-7262
Live food workshops and seminars for
children and adults, raw food catering.

High Vibe Health and Healing
85 E. 3rd St.
Back Courtyard
New York, NY 10003
www.highvibe.com
info@highvibe.com
Seminars, workshops, and raw food
preparation classes.

Labor of Love Productions
P.O. Box 7135
New York, NY 10150
www.rawsoul.com
(212) 875-7112
Living foods workshops and food
preparation classes.

Living Foods Gourmet Cuisine
New York, NY
(212) 505-5590
Raw food preparation classes.

Nadine's Kitchen
New York, NY
(212) 595-9599
Raw food preparation classes.

Oregon

International Essene Gathering
45 N. Third St.
Creswell, OR 97426
(541) 895-2190

Puerto Rico

Ann Wigmore Institute
Ruta 115, Km 20
Barrio Guayabo
Aguada, PR 00743
(787) 868-6307
A retreat that follows the teachings of
the late Ann Wigmore, founder of the
raw foods movement.

Texas

Optimum Health Institute of Austin
264 Cedar Lane
Cedar Creek, TX 78612
(512) 303-4817
Offers a comprehensive program covering many aspects of health maintenance and recovery, including raw
food preparation classes.

Canada

New Life Retreat
RR4, 453 Dobbie Rd.
Lanark, Ontario K0G 1K0
(613) 259-3337
www.newliferetreat.com
healing@newliferetreat.com
Retreat center that offers practical
hands-on education for implementing
and maintaining the living foods
lifestyle.

MAGAZINES

Fresh Network News
P.O. Box 71
Ely, Cambs CB7 4GU
UK
www.fresh-network.com
info@fresh-network.com
+44-0-8708-00-7070

Just Eat An Apple
6595 St-Hubert
CP 59053, Montreal (QC)
H2S 3P5, Canada
www.justeatanapple.com
info@justeatanapple.com

Living Nutrition
P.O. Box 256
Sebastopol, CA 95473
www.livingnutrition.com

RESTAURANTS

Because restaurants can open, move, and close, we've chosen to list only the city and phone number for each one. So be sure to call ahead.

Also, we've tried our best to be comprehensive, but if your favorite restaurant was left off the list, please let us know and we'll do our best to include it in an upcoming editon of *The Complete Book of Raw Food.*

Alaska
Enzyme Express
Anchorage, AK
(907) 345-1330

Arizona
Living Community Center
Tucson, AZ
(520) 623-0913

Tree of Life
Patagonia, AZ
(520) 394-2589

California
Roxanne's
Larkspur
(415) 924-5004

Georgia
Eternal Life
Atlanta, GA
(404) 942-9501

Here to Heal
Covington, GA
(770) 385-5273
Mutana
Atlanta, GA
(404) 756-9195

Illinois
Karyn's Fresh Corner
Chicago, IL
(773) 296-6990

Massachusetts
Organic Garden Restaurant & Juice Bar
Beverly, MA
www.organicgardencafe.com
(978) 922-0004

Minnesota
Eco-politan Organic Bar & Eatery
Minneapolis, MN
www.ecopolitan.net
info@ecopolitan.net
(617) 874-7336

Nevada
The Raw Truth Café, Healing Center,
and Eco-Shop
Las Vegas, NV
(702) 450-9007

New York
Caravan of Dreams
New York, NY
www.caravanofdreams.net
(212) 254-1613

Jubb's Longevity Live Food Store,
Organic Juice Bar and Patisserie
New York, NY
(212) 353-5000
Juice bar and raw food take-out.
Quintessence
Several locations throughout
Manhattan:
(646) 654-1823
(212) 501-9700
(212) 734-0888
www.quintessencerestaurant.com
Raw foods, organic.

Pennsylvania
Arnold's Way
Lansdale, PA
www.arnoldsway.com
(215) 483-2266
Raw vegetarian café and education
center.

Washington, D.C.
Delights of the Garden
Washington, DC
(202) 319-8747

Source of Life Juice Bar
At Everlasting Life Health Food
Supermarket
Washington, DC
(202) 232-1700

Canada
Super Sprouts
Toronto, Ontario
www.supersprouts.com
(416) 977-7796

Resources

Absolutely Abeba

Email: **AbsolutelyAbeba@aol.com**
Address: **163 Pelton Center Way**
San Leandro, CA 94577
Phone: **510-351-3157, 510-632-3591**

My part in the Living Foods Lifestyle is my Krazy Krackers. Order my books *Absolutely Abeba's Krazy Krackers* and *Absolutely Abeba's Krazy Krackers, Part 2*, and *Kookies Without Nuts*, and you will taste why. They're absolutely delicious.

The Mail Order Catalog

Web site: **askus@healthy-eating.com**
Phone: **800-695-2241**
Address: **PO Box 180**
Summertown, TN 38483
Web site: **www.healthy-eating.com**

Books on cooking and nutrition for vegetarian/ vegan/ raw foods, vegetarian products, and seeds and equipment for sprouting.

Cuisinart

Web site: **www.cuisinart.com**
Email: **Mary_Rodgers@conair.com**
Address: **1 Cummings Point Road**
Stamford, CT 06904
Phone: **800-726-0190**

Cuisinart designs and manufactures innovative products for consumers who love to cook and savor the good life.

Detox Your World

Web site: **www.detoxyourworld.com**
Email: **sales@detoxyourworld.com**
Address: **Rawcreation Ltd, PO Box 229**
Cottenham, Cambridge, CB4 8ZG, UK
Phone: **+44 (0)8700 113 119**

Online shop: Shazzie's products * books * videos * ionisers * InnerTalk CDs * juicers * superfoods * herbs * personal care. Based in the UK, serving the Universe.

Dining in the Raw Culinary Arts

Web site: **rawkitchen.com**
Email: **realitychef@rawkitchen.com**
Address: **Rita Romano, POB 5893**
Key West, Florida 33045
Phone: **305-294-6644**

This private school offers individualized instruction for career chefs and newcomers. Our Key West retreat lets you learn theory, technique, equipment use, and meal planning.

Elizabeth Baker

Web site: **http://www.rawfoodinfo.com/ catalog/books_gourmetuncookbook.html**
Address **1754 NE Mesford Rd. #63**
Poulsbo, WA 98370
Phone: **360-697-9381**

Author and distributor of Uncook Books, Videos and personal consultation tapes for your good health.

Elysa's Raw & Wild Marketplace

Email: elysatv@earthlink.net
Phone: **760-251-7488**
Address: **17551 Mountain View Road, Suite 47 Desert Hot Spring, CA 92240**
Selling food machines, recipe books, CD's of radio interviews, plus DVD's and videos of Elysa's Raw TV episodes.

Exotica Gourmet

Address: **3547 Bear Drive San Diego, C.A. 92103**
Phone: **800-384-6076**

The Fresh Network

Web site: **www.fresh-network.com**
Email: **info@fresh-network.com**
Address: **The Fresh Network Ltd. Chequers House, 9 Stratton Road, Hainford, Norwich, NR10 3AZ**
Phone: **+44 (0)870 800 7017**

The world's most comprehensive raw and living foods organization and publishers of Get Fresh! magazine. Mail order, events and more.

Hallelujah Acres

Web site: **www.hacres.com**
Address: **PO Box 2388 Shelby, NC 28151**
Phone: **704-481-1700**

Hallelujah Acres is a health and nutrition ministry sharing the message that "You Don't Have to be Sick!" For a free magazine call 1-800-915-9355.

Jalinis Publishing (a Division of D.O.S.)

Web site: **www.Jalinis.com**
Email: **info@jalinis.com**
Address: **Montreal, QC, Canada**
Phone: **514-898-8273**

We offer books, kitchen appliances, supplements, water filters etc. Visit our Web site to consult the list of courses and activities.

LIVEYOGA

Web site: **www.shantidevi.com**
Email: **devi@shantidevi.org**
Address: **Center Point Studios 324 Lafayette St. 7th Floor New York, NY 10012**
Phone: **917-514-3886**

LIVEYOGA is a synergistic system of healing that combines Yogic healing modalities with Raw and Lifefood Nutrition Science in conjunction with bodywork and creative sound therapy.

The Living Foods Workshop

Web site: **www.rawsoul.com**
Email: **rawsoul@rawsoul.com**
Address: **348 W145th Street New York, NY 10031**
Phone: **212-491-5859**

Lillian and Eddie Robinson conduct on-going monthly educational and food preparation courses, a support group/potluck, lectures, demonstrations and offer catering services.

Living Lifestyles

Web site: **www.chiDiet.net**
Email: **jcarey.jcarey.com**

Living Foods Lifestyle Transitioning. Live with elegant simplicity - Recreate your life. Recipe Creation, Spiritual/Emotional Components, Organic Vegetable Gardening, Exercise, More!

Living Light Culinary Arts Institute

Web site: www.RawFoodChef.com
Email: info@RawFoodChef.com
Address: Living Light Culinary Arts Institute
301-B North Main St.
Ft. Bragg, CA 95437
Phone number: 707-964-2420

LLCAI is the premier raw vegan chef school in the world, offering culinary training for novices and professional chefs, alike.

Living Nutrition

Web site: www.livingnutrition.com
Email: customers@livingnutrition.com
Address: P.O. Box 256
Sebastopol, CA 95473
Phone: 707-829-0362

Owner David Klein publishes the biannual Living Nutrition magazine and books on raw food eating, self-healing and Natural Hygiene.

Loving Foods

Web site: lovingfoods.com
Email: allraw@lovingfoods.com
Address: P.O. Box 790358
Paia HI 96779
Phone: 808-878-3729

Classes, Custom Workshops, Fasts, Raw/Living Food Education, Books, Living Cuisine, Raw Restaurant Consulting, Health Consulting, Raw Product Certification

Meet the Raw Family!

Web site: www.rawfamily.com
Email: victoria@rawfamily.com
Address: Raw Family
P.O. Box 172
Ashland, OR 97520 USA
Phone: 541-488-8865

Our books and classes promote the 12 Steps to Raw Foods approach that helps to maintain a raw lifestyle.

The Natural Chef, Matt Samuelson

Email: Mattsamuelson@yahoo.com
Address: 503 Hawk Ridge Lane
Watsonville, CA 95076
Phone: 831-661-2611

Private and Restaurant Consulting, Catering, Personal Training, Recipe and Product Development

Nature's First Law, Inc.

Web site: www.sunfood.com
Email: nature@rawfood.com
Address: 11653 Riverside Drive
Lakeside, CA 92040
Phone: 800-205-2350

Rawfood.com is the world's premier source of raw & living foods lifestyle products. Serving the world efficiently since 1996.

New Natives

Web site: www.newnatives.com
Email: info@newnatives.com
Address: PO Box 1413
Freedom, CA 95019
Phone: 831-728-4136

Certified Organic growers of wheatgrass, sunflower greens, buckwheat lettuce, pea shoots, microgreens, and a variety of young salad greens. Shipping available.

Plastaket Manufacturing Company, Inc.

Web site: championjuicer.com
Email: sales@championjuicer.com
Address: 6220 E. Hwy. 12, Lodi, CA
Phone: 209-369-2154

Plastaket has manufactured the Champion Juicer since 1955. The Champion Juicer has the reputation of being the best masticating juicer available today.

Pure Joy Living Foods

Web site: **www.PureJoyLivingFoods.com**
Email: **info@purejoyplanet.com**
Address: **Pure Joy Living Foods904 Evelyn AvenueAlbany CA 94706**
Phone number: **510-647-9474**

In Home Chef Trainings, Classes, Catering and a variety of recipe books and products for your raw food adventures!

The Raw Gourmet

Nomi Shannon, Health Educator, writer, lifestyle coach
Web site: **www.rawgourmet.com**
Email: **nomi@rawgourmet.com**
Phone: **888-316-4611**

All your raw food kitchen needs: juicers, blenders, dehydrators, saladacco slicer, mandoline, the Raw Gourmet book and videos, other Raw Food Books, gadgets and food items. Retail and wholesale. Plus personal consultations, raw food certification workshops, restaurant consultations, raw food related business support.

The Raw Vegan Network

Web site: **www.TheGardenDiet.com**
Email: **info@thegardendiet.com**
Address: **402 W. Ojai Ave. Suite 101-156 Ojai CA 93023**
Phone: **661-242-1479**

5-week Online Course for Raw Chef, Raw Nutritionist, Personal Trainer, and Raw Lifestyle Coach Certifications. Client referrals and personal support.

RAWvolution

gourmet living cuisine
Web site: **www.rawvolution.com**
Address: **Santa Monica, CA**
Phone: **310-721-4222**

Chef Matt Amsden of RAWvolution offers weekly raw food delivery, raw preparation classes, special events catering & personalized instruction.

Rhio's Raw Energy

Web site: **www.rawfoodinfo.com**
Email: **Rhotline@aol.com**
Address: **PO Box 2040, Canal Street Station New York, NY 10013**
Phone Number: **212-343-1152**

Rhio provides information and assistance in successfully adapting to a raw food lifestyle. Consultations, food preparation classes and lectures available.

Sprout Raw Food

Web site: **www.sproutrawfood.org**
Email: **info@sproutrawfood.org**
Address: **1085 Lake Charles Drive Roswell, GA 30075**
Phone: **770-992-9218**

Let us help you reach your perfect weight and peak performance, reverse aging, eliminate pain, overcome chronic disease, and obtain superior health. Recipes, consulting, classes and seminars.

Tree of Life Rejuvenation Center

Web site: www.treeoflife.nu
Email: info@treeoflife.nu
Address: P.O. Box 1080
Patagonia, AZ 85624
Phone: 520-394-2520 ext. 206

Tree of Life is a cross-cultural, spiritual, live-food, eco-retreat, educational facility and holistic medical spa located in the sacred high desert.

Tribest Corp, Green Power Int'l

Web site: service@greenpower.com
Email: service@tribest.com
Address: Tribest Corporation1143 N. Patt Street
Anaheim, CA 92801, U.S.A.
Phone: 888-254-7336

Since 1988, Tribest Corp. has offered the world's-finest, unique kitchen equipment, and the latest advancements and innovations in health appliances.

Vital Creations, LLC Chef Services

Chad Sarno, Chef/Director
Web site: www.rawchef.org
Email: info@rawchef.org
Phone: 1-888-276-7170
Fax: 1-360-287-8048

Your home of Raw Culinary Artistry, offering services in Restaurant and Medical Spa Consultation, Chef Trainings, Group and Personal Training, Apprenticeships and Elegant Catering.

Vita-Mix Corporation

Web site: www.vitamix.com
Email: household@vitamix.com
Address: 8615 Usher Road,
Olmsted Falls, OH 44138-2199
Phone: 800-848-2649

Vita-Mix Corporation designs and manufactures durable, versatile, high-performance kitchen appliances that are "more than a blender."

Kitchen Alive

Web site: www.laughingmother.com
Email: seekariego@aol.com
Address: P.O.Box 180
Springville, UT 84663-0180
Phone: 801-489-5514

www.kitchenalive.com is a place to find delicious raw food recipes, diet suggestions, support and networking on this beautiful living planet.

Please understand that by the time this book is published, information on the internet may be changed or updated. If you need the most recent information regarding any of the above resources, please contact the publisher (contact information on copyright page).

Index